D1496453

*Vocation across the Academy*

# Vocation across the Academy

*A New Vocabulary for Higher Education*

Edited by

DAVID S. CUNNINGHAM

OXFORD
UNIVERSITY PRESS

# OXFORD
UNIVERSITY PRESS

Oxford University Press is a department of the University of Oxford. It furthers
the University's objective of excellence in research, scholarship, and education
by publishing worldwide. Oxford is a registered trade mark of Oxford University
Press in the UK and certain other countries.

Published in the United States of America by Oxford University Press
198 Madison Avenue, New York, NY 10016, United States of America.

© Oxford University Press 2017

CIP data is on file at the Library of Congress
ISBN 978-0-19-060710-4

*Dedicated, with gratitude,*
*to the memory of*

*Bobby Fong*

*who worked tirelessly to create space*
*for the language of vocation across the academy*
*and whose faithful response to his own calling*
*continues to serve as a model for us all*

# *Contents*

PART THREE: *Called into the Future:*
*Professional Fields and Preparation for Life*

PART FOUR: *Vocation at Full Stretch:*
*Overcoming Institutional Obstacles to the Language of Call*

# *Foreword*

AMONG THE DISTINCTIVE features of American higher education, it seeks to prepare students not only to be specialists in a particular profession, but also to be well informed citizens who participate in civic life. An education rooted in the liberal arts provides students with exposure to a wide range of fields of study, each offering a way of exploring life's big questions: Who am I? Why am I here? What am I to do with my life? Today these assumptions about the purpose of higher education are themselves being questioned. Economic pressures prompt students—and, even more so, their parents—to wonder about their job prospects after graduation. Politicians and other opinion leaders have questioned the utility of a broad liberal arts education in favor of more narrow technical fields, some even proposing penalties on educating students in so-called "dead-end" fields such as philosophy and anthropology.

Yet the preponderance of evidence continues to suggest that the best preparation, both for a meaningful life and for a successful career, is a broad-based undergraduate education that engages students in the examination of deep questions about the circumstances they face today. When employers lament that college graduates are not well prepared for employment, the most desired skills they cite include critical reasoning, problem solving, creativity, and the abilities to communicate and work in teams—aptitudes that are best honed by engaging life's big questions. This edited volume consists of essays by a number of insightful thinkers into the question of how each of their professional fields reflects the choices made when pondering bigger questions. Through their work, these contributors provide answers to the question of how colleges and universities can help students draw upon their knowledge, skills, and values as they seek to discover the vocational paths for which they are best suited. These are questions raised by students not just at the level of general education but also within the academic disciplines and applied fields that students elect as their major areas of study. A student's understanding of vocation and calling will depend, at least to some extent, on the differing intellectual axioms, sources, and norms of that student's particular field of study. Mentors and advisors will find resources in this book to help students explore the congruence between the culture and practices of a given field and a student's vocational vision. In a rapidly changing world, higher education institutions need resources that use fresh vocabularies for the intellectual and theological exploration by students of their future work and lives.

This book is the second volume to be published as the result of the efforts of the Council of Independent College's (CIC) Network for Vocation in Undergraduate Education (NetVUE). NetVUE is a nationwide network of colleges and universities formed to enrich the intellectual and theological exploration of vocation among undergraduate students. NetVUE is built on almost two decades of prior endeavor by the Lilly Endowment, Inc. in support of eighty-eight independent colleges and universities through its Programs for the Theological Exploration of Vocation (PTEV). In 2009, CIC expanded and modified this legacy into NetVUE, which has grown to include a diverse group of some two hundred colleges and universities. CIC administers the programs of NetVUE with generous support from the Lilly Endowment and members' dues.

The NetVUE Scholarly Resources Project provides new materials to aid faculty members and campus leaders in their efforts to help students systematically explore their vocational choices, drawing upon diverse sources that facilitate a deeper understanding of vocation. Although a number of such resources were produced during the PTEV initiative, each new decade brings with it new questions related to faith and vocation. Under the direction of David S. Cunningham, professor of religion at Hope College, groups of scholars have recently collaborated on writing projects to address these emerging needs. The first book generated by the NetVUE Scholarly Resources Project was published in October 2015 as *At This Time and In This Place: Vocation and Higher Education*. Its goal was to support the understanding and cultivation of vocation at the undergraduate level, with a focus on questions of pedagogy. That volume is now complemented by this second in a projected series of three volumes. Produced by a second set of twelve scholars who collaborated over two years under Professor Cunningham's editorial leadership, this volume addresses themes and strategies through which colleges and universities can engage students and their professors in many fields of undergraduate concentration. The authors of these essays offer a fresh vocabulary through which faculty members and students with differing backgrounds, beliefs, and assumptions can approach questions of meaning and purpose.

The success of NetVUE and its Scholarly Resources Project is due in large measure to its leadership. I want to thank Shirley Roels, CIC senior advisor and director of NetVUE, who has worked closely with Professor Cunningham in this effort. I also want to thank Michael Cartwright, assistant director of NetVUE, who coordinates its grant initiatives, and Hal Hartley, CIC senior vice president, who oversees the entire NetVUE project. Finally, I want to express my gratitude to the Lilly Endowment for its generous support of the exploration of vocation on college and university campuses. I am grateful to Christopher L. Coble, vice president for religion of the Endowment, for his support and counsel. I also want to acknowledge the vision and support of Craig Dykstra, the former senior vice president for religion at Lilly, who along with Dr. Coble encouraged CIC to establish NetVUE and its Scholarly Resources Project.

In order for American higher education to continue to fulfill its distinctive purpose to prepare broadly educated citizens, fresh inroads into questions of purpose, meaning, and vocation will always be needed. Our hope is that this book will serve as a valuable resource to faculty members, advisors, and administrators for at least a generation as they engage their students in these explorations.

Richard Ekman
President
Council of Independent Colleges

# *Preface*

THIS BOOK IS the second in a projected series of three volumes on the increasingly important role of *vocation* and *calling* in higher education today. This language, which originally developed in a theological context (focusing on God's call of individuals into certain paths of life), has expanded to embrace a much wider range of concerns. It offers a more nuanced vocabulary for exploring, not only the many possible ways of earning a living, but all the contours of our lives: from the shape of our households to our engagement in community and religious organizations, from the patterns of our moral and intellectual development to the decisions we make about how to use our leisure time. The language of vocation encourages us to reflect on and to discern, not only our career choices, but also some of the deepest human questions of meaning and purpose. And although these questions often bear down particularly heavily on the shoulders of young people, they do not go away as we age. As the contributors to this volume will attest, we are likely to be engaged with the work of vocational reflection and discernment throughout our entire lives.

Given the wide-ranging significance of the language of vocation, it demands the broadest possible level of attention and examination. In the academic context, this means that it cannot be adequately addressed by a brief mention in a "welcome to college" course, nor can it be shouldered entirely by career counselors and the occasional advisor. Rather, the issue of vocation demands attention across the entire range of academic disciplines and fields of study; and in fact, it is already receiving that attention, as this volume's bibliographical citations will illustrate. Nevertheless, given the longstanding tendency of the disciplines to remain somewhat isolated from one another, they have not always been aware that they are already beginning to speak a common language. Hence, the goals of this book are, first, to draw these diverse fields into conversation with one another; second, to help them discover the many concerns that they already share;

and third, to give them a forum for contributing their own disciplinary insights to other fields of study—and to the larger enterprise of vocational reflection and discernment across the academy.

The authors whose work fills these pages have not only *written* about these matters; they also *exemplify* the diversity of scholarly reflection on vocation and calling. They bring backgrounds in a diverse range of academic disciplines and applied fields, and they have worked in a wide variety of professions; they are doctors and lawyers, college deans and presidents, research scientists and artists, health-care administrators and engineers. They gathered three times over the past two years—exploring common texts, engaging in spirited discussion, and reading one another's draft contributions. In the process, they began to discover just how much could be learned about vocation from someone whose calling was in another field or discipline.

Hence, these contributions range well beyond their authors' specific fields of expertise. Readers will not find, for example, a doctor speaking only to potential doctors and a lawyer only to lawyers. Instead, they will find a health-care professional exploring the importance of covenant; a law professor describing how lives can be redeemed; a computer-scientist-turned-historian explaining how to have productive conversations on religious topics; and an engineer extolling the virtues of the liberal arts (and even nudging us to use less technology!). These cross-disciplinary explorations were made possible not only by the broad backgrounds that our authors brought to the table, but also by their willingness to listen to one another and to think about how their own academic fields might contribute to—and learn from—those of others.

A volume such as this one is a communal undertaking. This reality is belied by the presence of one name on the title page; clearly, this book would have been impossible without the dedicated work of the other twelve contributors, along with a host of others. First among these is Shirley Roels, Director of the Network for Vocation in Undergraduate Education, the sponsoring organization of the NetVUE Scholarly Resources Project. In addition to finding the right balance between actively encouraging my editorial efforts and simply letting the work develop on its own schedule, Shirley has inspired all of us with her dedication to the cause of vocation in higher education and her sheer energy; indeed, she is a force of nature. I had already known (because Shirley had told me) that NetVUE's efficient operation and clear communications were largely the work of its fine program coordinator, Lynne Spoelhof; however, over the past year, as the project's first book was published and I began to work more closely with the NetVUE office, I have learned firsthand about her genuine resourcefulness, her sharp wit, and her commitment to providing hands-on support. Hope College continues to provide a home for the Scholarly Resources Project and to allow me to spend half my time on its various elements; my thanks especially to President John Knapp and to Steve Bouma-Prediger, Associate Dean for Teaching and Learning. The Project's administrative assistant is Shelly Arnold, who has provided outstanding service as the office manager for Hope's own vocation program since its inception and whose diligent work has provided me the necessary time and space for my own thinking on vocation to develop. Thanks also to the Council of Independent Colleges, and particularly to Rich Ekman and Hal Hartley, who have taken a personal interest in the Project from the outset, and to CIC's dedicated staff. As usual, the team at Oxford University Press has been attentive, helpful, and highly professional throughout the process; thanks especially to Cynthia Read, who advocated for this book, and to her assistants Glenn Ramirez and Marcela Maxfield, who have shepherded it to completion.

Finally, I owe a few personal words of thanks: to my dear wife Marlies, and to my fabulous children Nick and Lee, who surround me with their love on a daily basis and thereby support this project in more ways than they know; to my parents, Don and Patsy Cunningham, to whom my first book was dedicated and to whom every book is dedicated (at least in spirit), since they made it all possible; to the Writing Assistants at Hope College's Klooster Center for Excellence in Writing, who often double as personal assistants to me, chasing down bibliographical leads and helping me stay organized (and especially to Lauren Marchany who helped with indexing); and to my faculty and staff colleagues at Hope College, who fill in for me when I'm engaged in this project (and many others), and who help me maintain a sense of humor through it all.

In the end, however, the final word of thanks must be to the book's contributors. They made the production of this volume an absolute joy, and I am grateful to have been able to spend time in their company. They are professionals in their various fields, but during our time together, another aspect of their lives shone through: they are also dedicated teachers whose careers have been marked by an extraordinary degree of commitment to their students. Whatever else their various vocations may include (and readers are encouraged to get a glimpse of these, in the "Vocations of the Contributors" section that follows), they are all very clearly called to be educators of the highest order. I hope that the many teachers (and students) who read their contributions to this volume will recognize in their writing a true passion for the good work of higher education, and that many of them will be inspired to do some passionate teaching of their own.

This volume is dedicated to the memory of Bobby Fong, a scholar of English literature who served in a number of important administrative posts in higher education, including presidencies at Butler University (2001–2011) and at Ursinus College from 2011 until his untimely death in 2014. He was an avid supporter of vocational reflection and discernment as key components of undergraduate education; he advocated for these programs at the institutions that he served, and he faithfully promoted them as a charter member of the NetVUE Advisory Council. His broad vision for vocation and calling helped set the stage for our description of it, throughout this book, as "a new vocabulary for higher education" that spans the entire range of academic disciplines and applied fields. We miss Bobby quite profoundly, but we are grateful that his legacy continues through the work of the scholars he inspired.

David S. Cunningham
Professor of Religion and Director,
The CrossRoads Project
Hope College, Holland, Michigan

# *Vocations of the Contributors*

**JEFF R. BROWN** was a sophomore in a civil engineering program when he suddenly found himself in an anthropology class. It was intriguing enough that he considered changing his major, but he fought those urges and ended up with a degree in structural engineering. Fortunately, this was exactly what was required by math and science education programs in the Peace Corps, so he spent two years on the shores of Lake Victoria, teaching high school physics and learning to speak Swahili. After completing a Ph.D. in civil engineering, he moved to the shore of another large lake, teaching at Hope College and working with its student chapter of Engineers Without Borders to develop water projects in Cameroon. All of this helped him develop a deep appreciation for the liberal arts (known to him at one time as "subjects that do not require a calculator"). Apparently eager to gravitate toward an even larger body of water, he now lives in Daytona Beach, where he teaches engineering at Embry-Riddle Aeronautical University. He keeps hoping that some of his students will accidentally take an occasional anthropology class.

**MICHAEL E. CAFFERKY** served for many years as a church pastor, but he often found it easier to talk with people outside the church, and to talk about things that others thought weren't very theological. He found himself being called to work in health-care management, but this bothered him; he had always assumed that a "calling" was only for pastors and preachers. Those who left these roles to take up another line of work were, it seemed to him, *leaving* their calling (and perhaps even turning their backs on God). He took the plunge anyway, but he continued to wrestle with the idea of calling; slowly, he discovered that it needn't only be applied to pastors (though it can be), and that it isn't even necessarily found in one's job (though it can be). After twenty years in health-care administration, he has served for more than a dozen years in higher education—currently as the Ruth McKee Chair for Entrepreneurship and Business Ethics at Southern Adventist University. He has come to realize that, at a deeper level, our callings are deeply shaped by what is happening in the lives of the people around us.

DAVID S. CUNNINGHAM is an only child, which explains a lot. In his youth, he designed projects and imagined carrying them out by himself, but soon discovered that things like backyard carnivals, pretend towns, and musical theater productions actually required the involvement of other people. He thus learned a variety of techniques for roping his school-mates into putting his various schemes into action, and then basking in their success as though it were his alone. Comparisons to Tom Sawyer not-withstanding, this disposition has enabled him to run campus programs, organize academic conferences, and edit books of essays written by other people—all of which make him look more essential to these endeavors than he actually is. He did eventually do a few things mostly on his own (degrees from Northwestern, Cambridge, and Duke, followed by writing five books), and is increasingly drawn to academic journalism (reporting on conferences, dabbling in social media, and running a blog). It will be for his audiences to determine whether these endeavors represent a genu-ine service to the academy, or simply another attempt by an only child to remain the center of attention.

CELIA DEANE-DRUMMOND had a neighbor in her teenage years who was a scientist, and who told her about her research and her efforts to find a cure for cancer. This encounter solidified her plans to do the kind of science that made a difference. During her undergraduate training at Cambridge, she encountered deeply troubling ethical issues about using live animals in research; she sought to avoid these difficulties by becoming a plant physiologist. But here, too, she found herself surrounded by com-plex ethical questions, since new funding was being poured into research on genetically modified crops. After research and teaching appointments in Vancouver, Cambridge, and Durham, she decided that ethical issues were not going to go away (and that she did not want to wait until retire-ment to think about such things). So she retrained as a theologian and ethicist at Bristol and Manchester. She is still something of a scientist at heart; her work in theology and ethics remains actively engaged with the natural sciences. She was founding Director of the Center for Religion and the Biosciences at the University of Chester, where she served for ten years; in 2015, she helped to launch a new Center for Theology, Science, and Human Flourishing at the University of Notre Dame.

MARK U. EDWARDS Jr. has been unsure whether his calling—at least so far as his fashion choices are concerned—is drawing him more toward the "buttoned-down" look or to "geek casual." His professional computer programming career began in his undergraduate years with a 16-kilobyte computer that filled a room; his life as a professional historian began in graduate school where "cutting and pasting" was done with actual scissors and tape. At his first teaching position, he taught Western Civ in tweed coat and paisley tie; he then doffed both to teach introductory computer science in a shirt with rolled-up sleeves. At Purdue University, he did his own computer typesetting for his second monograph on Martin Luther; he bragged about this until a reviewer pointed out the many typos. (He decided to allow the publishers to typeset his subsequent books.) He became a professor at Harvard even as his software program *For Comment* appeared on the cover of *PC Magazine*. Even a college presidency (at St. Olaf College) and an academic deanship (at Harvard Divinity School) have done little to resolve his ambivalent fashion sense. Nor have they resolved two of his strongest tendencies: to try to trap every error condition, and to point out that to err is human. In the end, he is happy that Someone Else is not only doing the error trapping for us, but also has a broad appreciation for a wide range of fashion choices.

CHRISTINE M. FLETCHER had one vocational goal growing up: to get out of her small town in Pennsylvania so that she could see the world. Even though she attended college nearby, she was able to make good on her plans by spending her junior year in Vienna. This led to her to switch majors (from political science to philosophy), and to continue work in both these fields while pursuing additional degrees at Somerville College, Oxford. She worked as an investment analyst and a merchant banker (and, for a while, as a professional knitter), then temporarily left paid employment to become a wife and mother. After her children were grown, she completed a Ph.D. at Anglia Ruskin University, focusing on Dorothy L. Sayers's theology of work; this brought together two of her strongest interests, in theology and in work (both paid and unpaid). This eventually led to writing a book on Sayers, as well as another on the secular vocation of the laity (titled *24/7 Christian*). Since 2007 she has been teaching theology and business ethics at Benedictine University in Lisle, Illinois, where she still does some occasional knitting (but doesn't get paid for it).

**Catherine Fobes** graduated from Muhlenberg College with a major in psychology—the perfect choice for undergraduates who want to keep their options open as long as possible. Like many of today's students, she knew that she wanted to work with people, but she hadn't been encouraged to do much reflection and discernment about her vocation. She held several jobs throughout her twenties, from a one-week experience at the front desk of a rental car company to a four-year stint in a college development office. After going on a series of silent retreats, she discerned a call to attend Yale Divinity School, studying feminist theology and ethics. While there, a mentor encouraged her to continue graduate work; she soon found herself in Tallahassee, completing a Ph.D. in sociology at Florida State University and enjoying swimming outdoors throughout the entire year. Unfortunately, she has been unable to pursue this latter calling, as she now lives and works in central Michigan. But this has not lessened her appreciation for the meaningful and rewarding work that she has been able to do (despite the cold winters!) with students in her courses in sociology, gerontology, and women's and gender studies at Alma College.

**David Fuentes** was flung into music by his mother, who was trying to find him something productive to do. At a garage sale, on something of a whim, she bought him (of all things) an accordion. Needless to say, she quickly regretted her decision; still, it was clear that the boy had a knack for music, and that he liked making up his own songs. "How are you going to make a living at that?" she would ask repeatedly. When he got a generous scholarship to Roosevelt University, however, she changed her tune, deciding that if he had come this far (in spite of all her efforts to discourage him), he might just make it in the world of music. He wasn't sure whether plodding through graduate school at Iowa and Brandeis could count as "making it," but he has enjoyed composing music for theater, television, and the concert hall; most recently, he composed a rock opera in the style of the Beatles on the text of the last act of *A Midsummer Night's Dream*. He also likes to torture himself by trying to write down some cohesive thoughts about the place of music in human flourishing. All of this activity seems to assuage the concerns of the folks at Calvin College—who, like many people, aren't quite sure what "making it" would look like for a musician. Fortunately, they let him teach there anyway, even though he hasn't won a Grammy. [Yet. –ed.]

**Jason A. Mahn** financed his seminary education by slinging old shingles from the roofs of houses in St. Paul, Minnesota. An early mentor had told him that he could make a fine professor of theology; he considered that this might be a genuine call, and he took it to heart. Still, he was enjoying his life as a carpenter's assistant, and he often considered moving to Montana and learning that trade. Was that perhaps his true calling? Or was it just a backup plan? In an effort to discern the answer to these questions, he found himself driving not to Montana, but in the opposite direction; he ended up in graduate school at Emory University. Since then he has authored two books and has written about human choices, divine providence, Christian identity, fate, finitude, suffering, sin, and penance. His other vocations include teaching at Augustana College (in Rock Island, Illinois), editing *Intersections* (a journal about the vocation of Lutheran higher education), and fathering two sons. When his garage recently needed a new roof, Jason was somewhat disappointed to realize that he would have hire carpenters, rather than doing the work himself— as he might have done had he driven to Montana instead of to Georgia. Before the professional help arrived, however, he stepped momentarily into his previous calling by stripping off all the shingles, leaving an impeccably clean roof.

**Margaret E. Mohrmann** has spent much of her adult life in a recurring process of vocational reflection and discernment. At a young age, she felt an urge to become a physician, but she didn't examine that urge with much care; she simply moved straight through her studies at the College of Charleston, the Medical University of South Carolina, and Johns Hopkins. She then taught and practiced pediatrics, where her experiences with both patients and students encouraged her to think more deeply about what that earlier "call" to medicine was turning out to mean in her life. The ensuing discernment process soon led her to the University of Virginia for a Ph.D. in Religious Studies (Ethics) and to a second career teaching ethics to undergraduate and graduate students at UVA and supervising bioethics programs in the university's medical school. She has recently become Professor Emerita, eager to enter the next round of vocational discernment and content to let it unfold as it may. What has gone before has been rich and surprising; she thus has full confidence that whatever comes next will be equally so.

**JEROME M. ORGAN** was blessed with teachers at Catholic schools who reinforced his parents' reminder that "from those to whom much has been given, much is expected." His journey has been guided by a number of teachers, friends, and mentors, whose seeds of wisdom have sometimes fallen on good soil in his life (at least when he has been able to clear out the weeds and rocks). He went to law school because it seemed to maximize his options; he enjoyed the experience immensely, and was especially gratified by the retreats for graduate and professional students, some of which focused on questions of calling and vocation. After practicing law for several years, Jerry felt called to become a law professor, first at the University of Missouri, then as one of the founding faculty members at the University of St. Thomas School of Law in Minneapolis, where he also facilitates vocation retreats for students and alumni. A middle child, Jerry has become a natural consensus-builder and problem-solver, because—well, what other choice did he have? His multiple vocations include being a spouse and a parent of five children, a child and a sibling, a carpool driver and a soccer dad, an avid singer, and someone who likes to find patterns in numbers.

**MARK R. SCHWEHN** is a first-born son, as were his father and grandfather. Both of these forebears were parish pastors, so Mark always felt that he was, well, pre-ordained. His grandparents did everything they could to reinforce this sentiment. In high school, Mark began to flee this calling—rather like Jonah (though there were no whales involved). He decided that his grandparents might be willing to accept a compromise, so he decided to become a seminary professor. But when he arrived at Valparaiso University, he fled further still; after pausing to give thanks that the campus was not in the vicinity of any saltwater, he decided he would become a college professor in history or philosophy. But even in the absence of shipwrecks and large fish, the earlier call persisted; he soon found himself writing primarily about the academic vocation conceived as a Christian calling. Some reviewers observed that his writing sometimes seemed "preachy"; this probably would have pleased his grandmother. She would also have approved of the fact that two of Mark's three children have been ordained into the ministry of the Evangelical Lutheran Church in America, giving new meaning to the phrase "making up for lost time"—and reminding Mark once again that, fish or no fish, our callings have a way of catching up to us.

**SHIRLEY HERSHEY SHOWALTER** was given several dolls and stuffed animals as a child. She lined them up on the sofa and alternately preached or sang to them, delighting in their enthusiastic responses. Later, her siblings were drafted into service as her audience, proving to be a greater challenge. Brute force failed to keep them in their seats, but storytelling in imitation of her mother succeeded; thus a teacher was born. Though she grew up immersed in the Mennonite Church, she first understood her calling to teach in a school, knowing that she would need to leave Lancaster County, Pennsylvania—the land of nine generations of her ancestors. She attended college in Virginia, continued to graduate school in Texas, and then moved to Goshen College in Indiana. There, she and her husband Stuart combined academic and family life for twenty-eight years, the last eight of which she served as the Goshen College president. Whether her role was professor, mother, president, or foundation executive, she followed delight and asked for wisdom. She recently published a childhood memoir; her current project is "Jubilación: Vocation in the Third Act of Life."

# Introduction

## Language that Works

### VOCATION AND THE COMPLEXITY OF HIGHER EDUCATION

*David S. Cunningham*

OBSERVERS WOULD BE hard-pressed to find a more thoroughgoing success story than that of higher education in the United States. Its major
research universities are the envy of the world; students and faculty come
from every nation on earth to study and work here. Comprehensive universities and community colleges make postsecondary education available
to an enormous range of the population. The liberal arts college—that
peculiarly American invention—creates a community of learning that
has offered a broad general education to generations of students, many
of whom have gone on to populate the country's professions and its
intelligentsia. The diversity and depth of American higher education is
without peer; perhaps nowhere else in the world could a country's leader
announce, as Barack Obama recently did, that a college education should
be within reach of every citizen of the country.

But like all phenomenal success stories, this one has another side as
well. The very complexity and diversity of American higher education
has also been the source of some of its most enduring difficulties—difficulties that have led various commentators to declare "the end of the
university" or "the demise of American higher education."[1] Of course,

---

1. See, for example, Anthony T. Kronman, *Education's End: Why Our Colleges and Universities*

such jeremiads are a staple of every era; still, the tensions that inspire them are real. American higher education is supposed to be available to all, but its high cost and complicated financing mechanisms deter many people from even considering college as an option. Professors and social critics hail the significance of a broad general education as the foundation upon which a great society is built, while some economists and government officials attempt to measure the monetary value that a bachelor's degree adds to a student's future life. Many of these same officials see college primarily as a point of entry into the job market, whereas others describe it as a key stage in the development of young adults that cannot be limited to a particular economic outcome.

Alongside these headline-grabbing differences in perspective, however, lies a more basic complexity of the modern college or university—a complexity by no means unique to American institutions, but perhaps particularly noteworthy here. Institutions of higher education comprise various academic disciplines that often find themselves in conflict with one another; this is particularly evident between those subjects and fields that deal primarily with elements of the natural world and those that focus on human ideas and creations. Some academic departments have names that are deeply rooted in ancient scholarly tradition (philosophy, history, rhetoric, physics, biology, theology, theater, and music), while others were created in the nineteenth and twentieth centuries (psychology, sociology, and computer science, among many others). Still others are intentionally interdisciplinary programs that cut across the traditional disciplines (such as area studies based on race, gender, geography, or language, as well as emerging fields such as neuroscience or behavioral studies). To all these may be added the burgeoning interest in what are generally known as "applied fields": engineering, business, nursing, information technology, and other programs that employ the theoretical insights of traditional disciplines in order to address practical concerns. Each discipline or field has its own methods, sources, and

---

*Have Given Up on the Meaning of Life* (New Haven, CT, and London: Yale University Press, 2007); Frank Donoghue, *The Last Professors: The Corporate University and the Fate of the Humanities* (New York: Fordham University Press, 2008); Richard Arum and Josipa Roksa, *Academically Adrift: Limited Learning on College* Campuses (Chicago: University of Chicago Press, 2010); Jeff Selingo, *College (Un)bound: The Future of Higher Education and What it Means for Students* (Boston: New Harvest, 2013); Suzanne Mettler, *Degrees of Inequality: How the Politics of Higher Education Sabotaged the American Dream* (New York: Basic Books, 2014).

norms—some of which are likely to set it apart from, or even put it in conflict with, other disciplines and fields. The result is a broad panoply of subject areas that complicate the administration of colleges and universities, create strong differences of opinion among faculty members, and present a bewildering range of options to entering undergraduate students.

Needless to say, the various tensions and conflicts within higher education will never be eliminated; indeed, some of them arguably contribute to the university's success. Still, the authors of the chapters in the present volume are convinced that one particular concept can bring a measure of common purpose to this fragmented situation. This is the concept of *vocation* or *calling*, which we believe has the potential to provide higher education with a new vocabulary—one that can allow for better communication among the various elements and interests at work in American colleges and universities. Its relevance is not limited to one or another faction within the political, economic, and cultural divisions that currently trouble the higher educational landscape in this country. The language of *calling* and *vocation* has theological roots, but it has also been widely embraced in secular settings, since it is closely allied with concerns about meaning and purpose, about character development and moral formation. It therefore resonates with students, educators, and institutions that identify themselves with a great variety of faith traditions (or of none). It is attentive to questions of profession, work, and employment, but it also encompasses a much broader range of concerns that will arise during a college student's current and future life. The language of vocation and calling will certainly not eliminate the "conflict of the faculties" that can be traced back to the founding of the modern university (and before); but it does have the potential to bring the various academic disciplines and applied fields into a deeper, richer, and more lasting dialogue with one another.

This introduction intends, first, to trace a bit of the history and the philosophical forces that sustain the various tensions among the scholarly disciplines and applied fields; second, to describe the concept of vocation (as it is being used in the contemporary academic setting), and to show why it has the potential to bring academic departments and programs into more productive conversation with one another; and third, to introduce the four major parts of the book as offering four different pathways into this interdisciplinary conversation.

## The conflict of the faculties

Since at least the time of Aristotle, the various fields of study were grouped into methodological categories. Some of these focused on objects in the natural world that could be known by direct observation or deduction from first principles (reflected, for example, in such Aristotelian treatises as the *Physics*, the *Metaphysics*, and *On the Movement of Animals*). Others were matters that could only be known by a method of induction that moved from specific examples to a more general truth; these approaches are used in Aristotle's *Rhetoric, Politics*, and *Nicomachean Ethics*.[2] The division between these two methods was real, but not particularly stark; indeed, both for Aristotle and for the academic tradition that followed him for over 1,500 years, they were simply two sides of the same coin. They differed because their objects of study differed, but they overlapped in some respects, and they fit together in ways that seemed obvious to the thinkers who studied them. By the Middle Ages, they were well enshrined as "the seven liberal arts": the trivium (grammar, logic, and rhetoric) and the quadrivium (arithmetic, geometry, astronomy, and music).

We need not try to pinpoint some precise moment when all this changed. Some writers have focused on events as early as the development of medieval nominalism, which shifted the relationship between the philosophical concepts of essence and existence. Others believe that the Protestant Reformation played the largest role in shaking the foundations of the unified understanding of the disciplines. Still others would place the shift much later, among the concerns of the Enlightenment. In any case, sometime between the High Middle Ages and the late eighteenth century, many of the academic disciplines began to drift apart from one another. Differences in methodology, standards of evidence, authoritative sources, and teaching styles were increasingly prevalent; as noted above, these were especially marked in the division between those fields that studied objects in the natural world, on the one hand, and those that focused on human ideas and creations, on the other. This difference was enshrined in the division of the University of Berlin, founded in 1800, into the natural sciences and the human sciences (*Naturwissenschaften*

---

2. I have explored Aristotle's distinction between "analytic" and "dialectic" methods at greater length in *Faithful Persuasion: In Aid of a Rhetoric of Christian Theology* (Notre Dame, IN: University of Notre Dame Press, 1991), 15–17.

and *Geisteswissenschaften*)—a division that still marks German universities today. In the English-speaking world, the second of these divisions, the human sciences, was further divided in the late nineteenth century into divisions of social sciences and humanities; the latter of these was sometimes further divided, with fine and performing arts considered a separate division of the university.

These divisions have been the source of a great deal of discussion over the centuries. Kant wrote a treatise on *The Conflict of the Faculties*; he also labored to place philosophy, ethics, and aesthetics on a firmer foundation, comparable to that on which the natural sciences were thought to rest (even if that meant that that actual range of these humanistic disciplines would need to be severely circumscribed).[3] Leopold von Ranke sought to turn history into a form of natural science by emphasizing that its subject matter was limited to those things that had "actually happened."[4] In the 1950s, C. P. Snow gave a lecture on "The Two Cultures," suggesting that the natural and human sciences had moved so far away from one another in their assumptions and approaches that they could no longer exist side by side.[5] Today, of course, it is not only the traditional academic divisions (natural sciences, social sciences, humanities, and arts) that have largely parted ways from one another; individual academic departments, and programs within those departments, also tend to understand themselves as worlds unto themselves. If Snow were to give a similar lecture today, it might be called something like "The Fifty-Three Cultures."

Of special note in this history is the proliferation of programs in the applied fields. For a number of reasons, academic institutions have begun to put a great deal of energy into programs that employ the theoretical knowledge of the traditional disciplines as a means of helping students become adept in certain forms of practice, many of which seek to address important needs and to solve troublesome problems. Fields such as engineering, nursing, information technology, and business management are present in a great many colleges and universities, and they

3. Immanuel Kant, *The Conflict of the Faculties* (1798), trans. with an Introduction by Mary J. Gregor (New York: Albaris Books, 1979).

4. Leopold von Ranke, *Histories of the Latin and Germanic Nations from 1494–1514* (1824; 3rd ed. 1885), trans. Philip A. Ashwokth (London: Bell, 1887).

5. C. P. Snow, *The Two Cultures*, intro. by Stefan Collini (Cambridge: Cambridge University Press, 1964).

account for some of those institutions' most popular programs. They are often seen, by the students who enroll in them (and by their parents), as providing a fairly direct path from academic study into the job market. Because of their applied nature, these fields often face very different considerations from those that affect the traditional academic disciplines; in some institutions, they are separated off into their own schools or divisions. This creates stark structural divides, encouraging undergraduate education to develop a degree of specialization that was once reserved for graduate and professional schools. In addition, and especially in the applied fields, faculty and students often feel more closely connected to practitioners outside academia who work in their particular fields than they do to their counterparts in other academic departments and programs.

The historical, economic, and political forces that have created and reinforced the distinctions among academic fields have been the subject of hundreds of books and articles on higher education. Some authors lament the tendency of "academic silos" to isolate individual departments and programs; others argue that, without this system of division and separation, the university would be too large and diverse to accomplish anything. Some see the fracturing of systems of knowledge as tantamount to a war on truth, while others rejoice in the freedom of inquiry that results when one field comes to understand itself as not limited by the disciplinary restrictions of another. Whatever their perspectives, however, most commentators tend to agree that the "conflict of the faculties" has made it more difficult for the various disciplines and fields to develop meaningful conversations with one another about matters of common interest and concern. This difficulty manifests itself at every level: from administrative arguments about resource allocation, to faculty disagreements about curricula and graduation requirements, to students who find themselves sorted into residential and social groups according to their major field.

The differences among the disciplines and fields will not be going away any time soon, but it behooves us to consider ways in which deeper and more productive conversations might be fostered among them. The authors of this book are convinced that the language of *vocation* and *calling* holds a great deal of potential for bringing about this result. Providing the detailed warrants for this claim will be the business of the book as a whole; however, the next section of this introduction will offer some pointers as to why we find such enormous potential in what we are calling "a new vocabulary for higher education."

# Vocation: a once and future language

The word *vocation* derives from the Latin *vocare*, "to call." The English words *calling* and *vocation* can be traced to a single root, but in modern usage their nuances differ slightly. The word *vocation* is often thought to have a longer history (and one with more explicitly theological contours) than the word *calling*. In fact, both words came into English in the sixteenth century; still, the perceived difference between them has some historical justification, since the Latin noun *vocatio* was strongly associated with a specifically *theological* calling: God was clearly the "caller," the ultimate source of the call. In the medieval era, the word *vocatio* typically denoted what we would today call "religious vocations" (priesthood and the monastic life); this meaning still lingers in some environments, in which asking young people to "think about a possible vocation" is sometimes another way of saying that they should consider taking holy orders.

In cultural settings more strongly influenced by Protestantism, *vocation* tends to have a broader meaning, largely due to the Reformation tendency to employ the word *vocatio* well beyond its medieval range of reference. Martin Luther insisted that all people, in all walks of life, have a vocation; all are called by God into particular roles or "stations." He opposed the traditional claim that only priests, nuns, and monks had a divinely appointed path; he did not accept the notion that all other stations were merely inherited or accidental, nor that they somehow ranked "lower" than religious vocations. Nor did he restrict this language to whatever work one did to make a living; vocation included one's responsibilities in the domestic and civic realms, as well.

Obviously, this shift in meaning gave greater significance to a wide range of human activity, marginally offsetting the more hierarchical structure of medieval life. Over time, however, given that human beings spend so much of their waking lives working, this broader sense also functioned as a kind of narrowing: *vocation* and *calling* came to be associated primarily with a person's work or career. Luther himself would have objected to this account, given his broader emphasis on family and community life, as well as on one's paid employment; but particularly after the industrial revolution, one's occupation became increasingly identified with the shape of one's entire life. Today, we continue to experience these echoes: while *vocation* is usually taken to refer to more than just religious vocations, its primary range of meaning is still dominated by a person's paid employment—thus, the term "vocational education" is still sometimes used to designate training for a particular trade.[6]

In addition, the political and socioeconomic impacts of the shift in the meaning of *vocation* have often tended to ratify the status quo. After all, if one's life and work are seen as divinely ordained, then any attempt to change that life and work might well be understood as both politically revolutionary and disobedient to God. I have sometimes referred to this problem as the "core danger"[7] of using the language of *vocation* and *calling*: these words can be seen as cementing us into particular professions or stations in life, appointed by some powerful force outside ourselves. This can make it difficult to imagine that we might have actually been *mistaken* about our callings. As a number of contributors to this volume will emphasize, however, vocational discernment is a lifelong process; human beings change over the course of their lives, so they need to be aware that their callings, too, may change.

Similarly, our authors will regularly insist that, although we may associate vocation and calling primarily with a person's occupation or profession, its true range is considerably wider. Let us return to the Reformation-era language about the broad applicability of this language (not only to the world of work, but also to a wider range of questions about one's "stations in life"). It is easy to see how this led to a close association of vocation with work; as noted above, in that era and for centuries after, the great majority of one's waking hours had to be devoted to one's employment (either for subsistence or for wages). But today, particularly in the West, many people spend less time "working" than did their forebears; we have a great many more opportunities for leisure pursuits, secondary interests, volunteer activities, and "down time" than did our counterparts in the medieval and early-modern eras. Indeed, this fact is closely related to the creation and growth of the university itself. The concept of the "liberal arts"—which itself dates back to the Middle Ages and its "seven liberal arts"—is based on the notion that human beings are not merely beasts of burden; they have a certain degree of freedom, and they can use that freedom to pursue

---

6. As this introduction was being written, several government officials and political candidates have been reintroducing this use of the term. A number of comments are offered on this matter on the NetVUE Scholarly Resources Blog at www.vocationmatters.org.

7. "Time and Place: Why Vocation Is Crucial to Undergraduate Education Today," in *At This Time and In This Place: Vocation and Higher Education*, ed. David S. Cunningham (New York: Oxford University Press, 2016), 8.

something beyond paid employment. We call them *liberal* arts because they are available to people who have a certain degree of *liberty*. We live in a world in which human beings are—at least for a few hours a day—freed from the need to work merely in order to survive; they can thus turn their attention to other pursuits.[8]

Thus far, we have noted three important features of the language of *vocation* and *calling*: first, that it applies to all people (and not just to one particular profession or way of life); second, that it is rarely marked by a once-and-forever decision but, rather, involves an ongoing, lifelong process of discernment; and third, that although it is deeply concerned with one's profession or occupation (whether paid or unpaid), it also refers to the rest of one's life: in the household, among friends, in leisure pursuits, and in one's relationship with larger economic, cultural, and political structures. These factors help to explain why words like *vocation* and *calling* can serve as useful and effective terminology for carrying out conversations with today's undergraduates—and indeed why, as the title of a recent book on the subject claims, "colleges must talk to students about vocation."[9]

Most institutions of higher education are eager to help students think about their future careers; they already offer a number of programs and services that attend to these matters. Still, these institutions also recognize that their students' lives are already being shaped, and will continue to be shaped, by so much more than their chosen occupations. For this reason, most colleges and universities are sensing a need, not merely for additional programs and services, but for *an entirely new vocabulary* that can help them to speak with students in wide-ranging ways about their futures lives (and not just about that first job). This new language needs to *include* conversations about work and employment, but should not be exhausted by those topics; it must be expansive in its capacity to attend to the many other aspects of a student's future life. Ideally, this language would continue to be useful as these students' lives evolve, and as changes occur in the contexts in which they live. Finally, such language should apply broadly across the academy: not only in traditional disciplines but also in interdisciplinary programs and applied fields. It needs to be relevant

---

8. For an ongoing discussion of the importance of the liberal arts, see the website "Securing America's Future: The Power of Liberal Arts Education," sponsored by the Council of Independent Colleges; the public site is at www.liberalartspower.org (accessed July 25, 2016).

9. Tim Clydesdale, *The Purposeful Graduate: Why Colleges Must Talk to Students about Vocation* (Chicago: University of Chicago Press, 2015).

to *all* students, regardless of their majors, extracurricular interests, or future plans.

These are precisely the qualities that mark the language of vocation. It offers a vocabulary that can be retrieved from its complex historical origins, providing colleges and universities with a new way of addressing students across the entire academic spectrum. Its language has traditionally been connected to religious belief and to the world of work, but it also bears on all the other "worlds" in which students must live—both now and in the future. It can help students to make decisions in the present, but it also offers them a way of thinking that can adapt to new circumstances and provide them with resources throughout their lives. These features of vocation help to explain why we are willing to describe it as "the once and future language" of higher education.[10] To flesh out this claim, we want to introduce three specific elements that mark the language of calling and vocation, and that help to explain why programs for vocational reflection and discernment can have a particularly powerful impact on American higher education today.

## *Capacious, dynamic, elastic*

First, the language of vocation is *capacious*. As we have already observed, it includes, but is not limited to, questions about one's future work life; thus, although students sometimes enter the vocational discernment process with a focus on questions about their future careers, they often find that such matters are the least of their worries. Where and with whom they will live, how they will spend their leisure time, which religious and community organizations they will become involved with—these questions begin to loom large as students consider what it will mean to "emerge"

---

10. Over the past two decades, this language has made a considerable impact on American higher education, owing especially to various initiatives of the Indianapolis-based Lilly Endowment, Inc.; starting in 1999, this foundation provided grants to eighty-eight colleges and universities to establish programs in vocational discernment. After those grants came to an end, some of the participating institutions helped to establish a new consortium, the Network for Vocation in Undergraduate Education (NetVUE), which provides continued support for programs that focus on calling and vocation and invites additional institutions into the conversation (at latest count, over 200 of them). A more complete history of these developments can be found in Cunningham, "Time and Place." Further information on the original Lilly-funded programs is archived at www.ptev.org; NetVUE maintains a very active website at www.cic.edu/NetVUE/, as well as a community network site for member institutions at http://connect.cic.edu/NetVUE.

into adulthood.[11] The language of calling and vocation stretches across all these concerns, and many others as well.

Thus, even for those students whose career trajectories seem fairly straightforward, engaging in serious reflection on vocation can help them focus on larger questions about the direction and purpose of their lives. Along the way, of course, many of them may find themselves refining and redefining their career paths as well; the connections between work and "the rest of life" will be taken up by a number of authors in the chapters that follow. Discussions about vocation are likely to draw participants from across the spectrum of academic disciplines and programs—whether they are broad liberal arts disciplines that serve as a springboard to a great variety of career paths, or highly specialized applied fields in which students are sometimes placed in jobs a year or more before they graduate. No matter where they fall on this spectrum, all students are likely to have questions that can be more fruitfully addressed through the language of calling and vocation.

A second element: vocational thinking is *dynamic*. It recognizes the shifting contexts in which human beings live, and is therefore especially appropriate for the contemporary setting, in which the one unchanging fact is that *everything will change*. Students are often told that, across their future lives, they can expect to have not just a number of different jobs, but even a number of wholly different careers. Some of the fields they will enter will fade away during their lifetimes; later in life, they may well embark on careers that do not yet exist. Hence, vocational reflection and discernment is not just a single step in the process; it can never be classified among those things that some students "still need to get done" and that others have "already finished." It is an ongoing, lifelong endeavor.

This, in turn, has two important implications. First, the process of vocational exploration and discernment is something that all students need to undertake *throughout* their undergraduate careers (in ways that are appropriate to their particular age and stage of discernment), and in which they will continue to engage *throughout* their lives. Second, it is a process—we might, in fact, describe it as an *art*—that students need to learn and to practice while still in college (with plenty of advisors and mentors to help

---

11. Jeffrey Jensen Arnett, *Emerging Adulthood: The Winding Road from the Late Teens Through the Twenties* (New York and Oxford: Oxford University Press, 2004); see also Jeffrey Arnett and Nancy L. Galambos, eds., *Exploring Cultural Conceptions of the Transition to Adulthood* (San Francisco: Jossey–Bass, 2003), as well as Jeffrey Arnett and Jennifer Lynn Tanner, eds., *Emerging Adults in America: Coming of Age in the 21st Century* (Washington, DC: American Psychological Association, 2006).

them), so that they can continue to engage in that process in later years (when they may be, or at least may feel, very much on their own).

The dynamic nature of vocation means, again, that every academic department and program—whether traditional or interdisciplinary, theoretical or applied, broadly esoteric or highly practical—has a genuine stake in helping its students engage in reflection and discernment about their callings. This may be more obvious in some of the traditional disciplines, in which the pathway to a specific career is less clear; departments of classics, philosophy, and English know that most of their students will need to do some discernment as to the directions their lives will take after they complete their degrees. But the applied fields have a related problem: many of them have only come into existence in the last few decades, and most are related to professions that are changing faster than can be absorbed by their practitioners (let alone by the academic programs that try to prepare people for these professions). Students in these fields may already know who their first employer will be; but will they be ready to think through their next career move, five or ten years in the future? Will they be able to navigate the inevitable shifts that will occur as their field evolves, as a result of various economic, political, technological, and sociocultural changes? Or will they look back at their undergraduate degrees as something that prepared them well for a five- or ten-year career, but not so well for everything that occurred after that? Across the disciplines and applied fields, academic institutions have a stake in—and indeed, perhaps a responsibility for—forming their students in practices of vocational exploration and discernment that will sustain them throughout their lives.

A third point: the language of calling and vocation is relatively *elastic*, allowing it to be adopted by a wide variety of academic institutions, departments, and programs. As I have suggested throughout this introduction, these entities often differ from one another in significant ways. Indeed, many observers believe that the success of the Lilly Endowment's grant programs in this area was due in part to the wide latitude it allowed participating institutions to develop programs, language, and overall strategies of implementation that were specific to their contexts. Colleges with close ties to a particular denomination tended to stress the theological elements of vocation, while more secular institutions found the language helpful in encouraging students to think about the meaning and purpose of their lives. Departments and programs that funneled students into specific careers could employ the language to help students think about specialization within that field, and about how they might focus their energies beyond the workplace. At the same time, academic departments that focused on broader forms of preparation found the language of vocation useful for helping students think about their options after graduation, ranging from a specific career, to volunteer opportunities, to graduate and professional education. And across the whole spectrum of undergraduate education, many found that the language stretched well beyond the world of work; it was useful in helping students think about their future lives in the broadest possible terms.

Many institutions discovered the truth in the claim that, with respect to programs designed to help students reflect on their callings, "If you build it, they will come." The elasticity of the concept meant that institutions did not have to resort to requirements or mandates in order for students to participate in the work of vocational reflection and discernment. Many students were eager to engage in this work because they were already asking the kinds of questions that vocational discernment programs were designed to highlight. Of course, some students occasionally need to be nudged to face these matters directly; most of them, however, are all too aware that questions about their future lives cannot be put off forever. In the midst of the many academic requirements they must fulfill, the residential life regulations they have to obey, and myriad other hoops through which they must jump, college students often welcome the opportunity to engage the questions with which they themselves are most directly concerned.

This element, too, should make the process of vocational reflection of interest to educators and students across a wide variety of disciplines and fields. For faculty, it allows for the development of programs that suit the needs of their own fields of study, without needing to conform to a particular college-wide model. For academic staff, it can provide an opportunity to become more involved in the lives of the students who are enrolled in their departments and programs, perhaps bringing their own life experience as a resource. For students, it offers both an opportunity to deepen relationships with the faculty and staff in one's own department or program and a bridge to the questions that are being asked by fellow students, whether in their own fields of interest or in others. And for higher education in general, the language of vocation and calling is sufficiently malleable that it can be brought into conformity with each particular academic institution's own vision of its work—so much so that we may even be able to speak of the *vocation* of a college or university.[12]

---

12. For an extended treatment of this theme, see chapter 11 of this volume.

These three elements are not meant to be summative or exhaustive; they are only pointers toward vocation's potential to provide a new vocabulary for higher education. In particular, they all suggest that programs that focus on vocational reflection and discernment can truly range "across the academy"; they can have an impact on, and be useful to, a wide variety of scholarly disciplines and applied fields. These three terms will be taken up in varying ways by some of our authors, but their contributions will also add to this list; they will point to additional cross-disciplinary and college-wide advantages of programs that focus on calling and vocation. In order to prepare the ground for their contributions, the final section of this introduction offers a thumbnail sketch of the book as a whole.

## *Four perspectives on* vocation across the academy

This book is divided into four main parts, each of which offers a particular perspective on the importance of vocational reflection and discernment across the range of academic disciplines and applied fields. From the outset, the authors decided against writing a separate chapter on each of thirteen different fields of study. Even though this might have made at least one of the book's chapters essential reading for educators and students in that particular field, it would have also reinforced the tendency of academic disciplines to remain in their own silos. Instead, this book considers four different *pathways* or *approaches* through which the disciplines can come into conversation with one another: first, by emphasizing certain themes that are common to them all; second, by borrowing concepts from one discipline that can apply to many other disciplines; third, by focusing on the future lives of undergraduates, which is a matter of interest to everyone (regardless of field); and fourth, by considering some of the institution-wide obstacles that need to be addressed if the language of vocation and calling is to be perceived as relevant to all academic departments and programs.

Part one bears the title "Calling without Borders: Vocational Themes across the Academy." It focuses on three areas that will be of interest to nearly all academic disciplines and applied fields. In chapter 1, vocation is described in terms of *responsibility*—both as a response to an external summons and as an internally motivated ethical stance. Whether or not students have already discerned a particular career path, they need to consider their future lives in terms of the responsible use of their gifts. This chapter employs examples drawn primarily from the field of medicine, but its implications are relevant to students aiming at a wide range of professions—as well as those who are still discerning their future direction. We then consider, in chapter 2, a problem that besets students (and their teachers) across all fields of study: the fact that we so often feel called in varying directions, some of which seem to be incompatible with one another. How can students go about sorting out and prioritizing these multiple callings, and how can faculty and staff best help them do so? This chapter employs examples from a number of ancient stories and tales to illustrate the various ways of facing a complicated, and possibly incommensurate, range of callings. The focus on narrative is expanded in chapter 3, which considers it as a common theme in vocational reflection and discernment across the disciplines. While narrative may seem a more obvious category in certain academic departments and programs (such as those that study language or literature), recent commentators have argued for the narrative quality of a wide range of experiences; this makes it relevant to practically all academic fields. Given the presence of responsibility, conflict, and narrative in so much vocational reflection, a great deal of productive conversation can be fostered among the various fields of study by focusing on these three central categories.

Part two, "Calling in Context: Fields of Study as Resources for Vocational Reflection," demonstrates how vocational insights arising from a particular discipline can play an important role in other fields as well. We begin in chapter 4 by examining a key insight of sociology—namely, that vocational discernment takes place across the entire life course. Given the fact that college students face so many immediate concerns (employment prospects, potential mates, and a more definitive separation from the parental home), even the most farsighted undergraduates may have some difficulty considering anything beyond the next few years. Hence, all disciplines and fields have something to learn from a perspective that encourages careful consideration of the entire life course when thinking about vocation. In chapter 5, we turn to the fine arts, and specifically to the discipline of music, in an effort to consider the ultimate goals of our work. Is it primarily a form of self-expression? Is it designed primarily to arouse the emotions, so that those who experience our work will respond more positively to whatever we are offering? Needless to say, these questions are not limited to those students majoring in the arts; all students need to think through the relationship between their own motivations for pursuing a particular discipline and the motivations of those whom their work is intended to reach. In chapter 6, we turn to an applied field—business administration—to consider the communal aspects of vocational discernment. Too often, "finding one's calling" is assumed to be a task assigned to individuals; in point of fact, however, vocation is traditionally discerned with the help of others. Drawing on the insights of organizational theory and on the concept of covenant, this chapter suggests that students need not feel isolated and alone as they undertake the work of vocational discernment. Finally, chapter 7 provides the perspective of a scholar active in two fields of study that are often considered rather distant from one another (theology and biology). This chapter retrieves the ancient categories of *wisdom* and *conscience* as themes that have grown out of the humanistic disciplines, but are relevant across the entire spectrum of academic departments and programs, including the natural sciences. As such, this chapter provides a concrete example of the rich interdisciplinary conversations that can be fostered by a focus on the language of vocation and calling.

In part three, we shift into the future tense. Under the title "Called into the Future: Professional Fields and Preparation for Life," we consider how students and their teachers might think most productively about the world after graduation. That world will certainly include work, so we begin in chapter 8 with an examination of that surprisingly elusive concept. How has work been defined over time, and how do we understand it today? As noted above, the world of work is in constant change; this means that all academic programs have a vested interest in making sure students are prepared for their future work life in the broadest possible sense. In chapter 9, we examine undergraduate professional degree programs—that is, those that prepare college students for work in a particular field without the expectation that they will need additional graduate or professional training. The chapter primarily employs examples from the quickly growing field of engineering, but its insights apply equally well to other professional degree programs, such as nursing, computer science, and business management. We conclude this part of the book, in chapter 10, with a consideration of the relationship between the "what" and the "how" of a person's future life: not only the work that the individual will do, but also the kind of life he or she will lead. Vocational discernment is not limited to considerations about one's future paid employment, nor is it brought to completion in the small window provided by the college years. This chapter offers a number of examples from the field of law, and focuses on the theme of redemption as a means of helping us think about how even the most wayward vocational paths can sometimes lead to a fulfilled and fulfilling life.

Part four is titled "Vocation at Full Stretch: Overcoming Institutional Obstacles to the Language of Call." These contributions consider how various structures within American higher education may make some of the goals of this book more difficult to achieve; they then suggest how these obstacles might be addressed. We begin in chapter 11 by examining the degree to which the language of vocation applies to the institution as a whole. Do colleges have "callings"? If so, how does this language change the way an undergraduate institution might describe its own purpose and reason for being? If the institution were to shift into a more specifically vocational register when thinking about these issues, this might open up more opportunities for students to think about their own lives in terms of how they are being *called*, rather than simply what they choose to do. In chapter 12, we turn to some of the reasons that faculty and staff in all academic fields might be reluctant to engage in conversations with students about vocation. The sources of this reluctance range from large-scale cultural forces to very specific features of the professoriate; these are explored in detail throughout the chapter, which ends with recommendations about how academic conversations about vocation might be facilitated. Finally, in chapter 13, we take up the question of how this book's reflections might impact classroom teaching. To what degree should faculty across the disciplines be engaged in the *formation* of their students, such that questions about calling and vocation can arise within the classroom setting? Can "good teaching" be more than just a description of excellent techniques, but be broadened so that teaching is understood to be oriented toward *the good*? A number of recent commentators have raised doubts about such an approach, but this chapter argues that the undergraduate classroom can and should be a place for formation—both moral and intellectual.

The book concludes with a short epilogue, designed to suggest how various academic disciplines and programs might integrate vocational questions into their own work, and how this topic might become a subject of common conversation within the college community.

## A *new vocabulary*

American higher education is a great success story, but its complexities create problems and tensions that can impose obstacles to productive conversations among educators, students, and administrators. No single approach can hope to address this problem entirely, but a great deal of progress can be made by investing in *educational language that works*. Our advocacy of this "new vocabulary" for higher education is not offered merely for the sake of innovation; in fact, in many ways it is not new at all. We have already witnessed its success in the academy; it has gained traction across the entire range of disciplines, fields, and institutions where it has been applied. It has demonstrated to many observers that it is, in fact, "language that works." In an age in which higher education is under attack on so many fronts, and when the disciplines and applied fields are so tempted to retreat into their respective silos, anything that has the potential to draw them into conversation with one another is certainly worth exploring. We hope that many readers will be willing to accompany us on that journey. Even if we find ourselves returning to the some of the very places where we started, we may come to know them for the first time.

# PART ONE

*Calling without Borders*

## Vocational Themes across the Academy

The first three essays in this volume focus on considerations that will be of interest to students and faculty members in nearly all academic disciplines and applied fields. Whether a particular subject area focuses on the natural world or on human creativity, on social structures or individual behavior, its teachers and students will be faced with the three issues raised here: *responsibility, conflict,* and *narrative.* Given the resonances of these themes across the academy, this discussion could easily become abstract; these three authors, however, strive to keep the conversation as concrete as possible. Their chapters demonstrate the relevance of their claims with attention to specific majors, individual courses, and particular paths of discernment. It seems likely that educators and students in every field and discipline will have experienced many of the concerns and questions raised in the pages that follow.

As was suggested in the introduction to this volume, vocation and calling can serve colleges and universities by providing a common language—a language with a specific yet capacious vocabulary that can be employed across the traditional disciplines and the applied fields. The three chapters that follow examine three specific domains of terminology within that broader vocabulary, demonstrating that they enjoy a wide range of applicability across the academy. While we may be tempted to assign some of these terms to particular disciplines (*responsibility* to the field of ethics, perhaps, and *narrative* to the study of languages and literature), these authors convincingly demonstrate that the relevance of these terms is much more widely affirmed. Faculty and staff in all disciplines and fields have a vested interest in helping their students to grow into more responsible human beings, to negotiate the conflicting claims upon their lives, and to tell their stories truthfully.

Because these chapters range quite widely, they raise a host of questions that bear on the present state of undergraduate education. Among these questions are several that seem likely to be of particular interest to the readers of this volume:

- As undergraduate students seek to consider their future direction in life, what level of responsibility do they bear for their own choices? To whom are they primarily accountable, and to what degree do they recognize this reality and make it their own?
- How should students weigh the conflicting responsibilities that they will face? What tools will they need in order to navigate their futures in this regard?
- To what degree will students need to depend on particular ways of telling their own stories, such that they can grasp their various responsibilities and negotiate the conflicts that will necessarily arise?
- How will emerging adults face the temptation to tell their stories in ways that glide too easily over competing callings or that try to evade certain elements of personal and professional responsibility?
- Is the structure of undergraduate education, as students currently experience it, able to equip them with the tools that they will need to address these questions—not only during their student days, but also over the course of their entire lifetimes (when these concerns will undoubtedly recur)?

These are large questions; they cannot be adequately addressed by overly narrow accounts of the purposes of higher education (particularly those that focus only on headline-grabbing metrics such as a graduate's first-year salary!). But regardless of how a particular major field's social, economic, or political value is perceived, its faculty and staff will always have a vested interest in helping its graduates consider larger questions of meaning and purpose. Yes, these students hope to get good jobs; but they would also like to live good lives. We believe that everyone involved in this process—faculty, staff, and administrators, as well as students, parents, and alumni/ae—will consider those goals more achievable, and will be equipped to pursue them more successfully, if they become more proficient in employing the vocabulary of vocation.

# *I*

# *"Vocation Is Responsibility"*

## BROADER SCOPE, DEEPER DISCERNMENT

### *Margaret E. Mohrmann*

"VOCATION IS RESPONSIBILITY, and responsibility is a total response of the whole human being to the whole of reality."[1] These words, written by theologian Dietrich Bonhoeffer (1906–1945), help to raise the central questions of this chapter: What does it mean, and why does it matter, that we might construe vocation as *responsibility*—and then further construe responsibility as virtually boundless? How can this near-infinite expansion of both concepts help students think about their futures in meaningful ways, and help educators guide them as they do so?

This chapter explores the melding of vocation and responsibility in order to demonstrate how their connection might clarify and illuminate both concepts. It suggests that when these two concepts are drawn into mutual conversation, they can become more valuable—not only for students in the process of vocational reflection and discernment, but also for faculty members and others who advise students, and for deliberations about the curricular and pedagogical implications of an expanded level of attention to vocation and calling.

This chapter begins with a brief analysis of responsibility, attending to its definition and to its possible placement among the human virtues. It then considers, first, how a focus on responsibility *deepens* our understanding of the relations among vocational "call," personal abilities and inclinations,

---

1. Dietrich Bonhoeffer, *Ethics*, ed. Eberhard Bethge, trans. N. H. Smith (London: Macmillan, 1955), 258, translation slightly modified.

social needs, and career choice; and, second, how thinking in these terms also *broadens* the perceived scope of the vocational pull beyond the arbitrary boundaries of career and employment. This leads to a brief concluding reflection on how such an approach can generate and shape efforts by colleges and universities to nurture their students' sense of responsibility. Broadly speaking, this chapter seeks to demonstrate that, because responsibility requires a total response of the whole person, it is something for which students need equipping, encouragement, direction, and even formation.[2]

In the later parts of this chapter, most of the examples are about students who are exploring a vocation in medicine. This focus reflects my own profession and my experience counseling students considering a future in health care (within which there are multiple possible career paths). It also speaks to certain realities of vocational discernment in undergraduate education today: a significant proportion of entering college students say they intend to become physicians (at my university, the figures are consistently close to 50 percent). Most of these students, for one reason or another, will not do so; instead, they will find themselves re-entering, or entering for the first time, a process of vocational exploration and discernment. Thus, while the issues considered here are particularly salient within the health professions, they are germane to most other vocational trajectories as well—including law, teaching, business, architecture, military or government service, media and communication, the arts, research in the sciences or the humanities, and many others. Each of these has its own complexities, surprises, and relationship to the world—just as each student has his or her own particular gifts and desires. But all these professions, as well as the undergraduate disciplines that prepare students to pursue them, have a common denominator: responsibility.

## *Response, responsibility, and virtue*

How might we better understand responsibility in a way that explains and builds upon its relationship to vocation? We can begin by noting that responsibility may be usefully construed as *the reliable ability to respond.* This simple and obvious claim should not be taken as a mere linguistic tautology, but as a necessary move to reawaken us to what this (perhaps too familiar) term should convey. Responsibility is the ability to be

---

2. For more on this process, see chapter 13 of this volume.

*responsive*—to other people, to situations, and to the world ("the whole of reality," in Bonhoeffer's terms). It designates, therefore, the ability to recognize particular obligations, to deliberate about them, and to fulfill them *responsibly*—as well as learning to manage them appropriately (whether by accepting, declining, deferring, or delegating). These are obligations entailed not just by one's career or job, but also by one's very existence as a person—a person who is necessarily in relation with other persons and with the world.[3]

The Latin *responsus*, the direct ancestor of *response*, denotes not simply an answer or reply; it refers to a harmonious agreement or correspondence with someone. This is so because its root (*–spons*) refers to a promise or pledge, as can be detected in other English derivations (such as *sponsor* and *spouse*) that carry that sense forward. The verb form (of which *sponsus* is the past participle) is *spondeo*: to promise, to take a sacred vow, to contract in marriage. The addition of the prefix *re–* to the verb and noun forms intensifies the mutuality implied in promising or, especially, in marrying.[4] *Re–* introduces a sense of reverberation: not simply a return or an answering back, but a sustained movement back-and-forth between two or more mutually responsive actors. *Respondeo* indeed means "to answer" or "reply," but also expresses the idea that the responder agrees with, resembles, measures up to, or in some way corresponds—in reciprocal relation—to something else.[5]

## Responsibility as virtue

Note that the opening quotation does not say that vocation—and by extension, the discernment required for it—is merely *a* responsibility, as we typically use the term (connoting a task or obligation). Rather, both vocation and responsibility are spoken of as characteristics of a whole person that, in part, determine the moral quality of one's being in the world. It is

---

3. This explication of responsibility owes much to Margaret Urban Walker's discussions, both in her book *Moral Understandings* (Oxford: Oxford University Press, 1998), particularly chap. 4, "Charting Responsibilities," 77–100 (83–106 in the 2007 second edition), and her earlier (1991) essay, "Moral Luck and the Virtues of Impure Agency," reprinted in Margaret Urban Walker, *Moral Contexts* (London: Rowman and Littlefield, 2003), 21–34.

4. See the discussion (in chapter 6 of this volume) of *covenant*, a term deeply resonant with the mutuality of responsibility.

5. *Oxford Latin Dictionary*, ed. P. G. W. Glare (Oxford: Oxford University Press, Clarendon Press, 1982).

then possible, and helpful for this analysis, to think of responsibility (and indirectly, vocation) as having the nature of a *virtue*: a habitual disposition to perceive, deliberate, and act in certain excellent ways.[6] Responsibility— "being a responsible person"—can then be more fully defined, in the language of virtue, as one's settled disposition to discern, take on (or assign), and fulfill certain tasks or display certain attitudes that are perceived as something like obligations toward another or toward a situation—and to do so appropriately and well.

Some commentators understandably resist assimilating responsibility into the category of virtue. One might argue, for example, that the virtues are commonly understood to be primarily directed toward the introspective subject's character development, subsequent behavior, and ultimate flourishing, whereas responsibility's gaze is outward—finding its ethical premises and moral aims in the person and needs of the other and in the self's need to be fully and properly responsive.[7] The purpose of this section, however, is not to make the case for responsibility as a classical virtue; its purpose, rather, is to clarify some of what "being a responsible person" entails, regardless of how one classifies the trait of *responsibility*. To that end, there are two further points to be made about responsibility-as-disposition before proceeding to consider its relation to vocational discernment.

## Nuancing the argument

First, just as an appropriate expression of the virtue of courage may result in harm to oneself—even death—so enactments of responsibility may not always appear to contribute to one's flourishing.[8] Consider, for example, the

---

6. This approach has implications not only for our grasp of the concept but also for the roles and obligations of faculty and staff who participate in students' formation, as well as their education; on this point, see also chapter 13 of this volume. For more on the virtues and their relationship to vocation, see the chapters by Douglas V. Henry, Paul J. Wadell, Thomas Albert Howard, and Hannah Schell, in *At This Time and In This Place: Vocation and Higher Education*, ed. David S. Cunningham (New York: Oxford University Press, 2016), chaps. 7–10.

7. "Whereas . . . virtue theory focuses on patterns of self-formation and well-being, the ethics of responsibility pictures human beings as dialogical creatures existing in patterns of interaction." William Schweiker, "Disputes and Trajectories in Responsibility Ethics," *Religious Studies Review* 27, no. 1 (2001): 18–24, here 18.

8. See Lisa Tessman, *Burdened Virtues: Virtue Ethics for Liberatory Struggles* (New York: Oxford University Press, 2005) for an illuminating and provocative argument that some virtues— specifically, virtues required under oppressive conditions—cannot be said to result in the

author of the chapter's opening quotation, which was taken from his posthumously published *Ethics*. Dietrich Bonhoeffer was a German Lutheran pastor and theologian who was prevented from completing that book because of his arrest by the Gestapo and, two years later, his execution while in prison. The close linkage of responsibility and vocation in his ethical thought is exemplified in his own biography—including the fact that he had chosen to return to Germany in 1939, leaving the safety of the United States in order to be present with and for the anti-Nazi "Confessing Church" that he had helped found in 1934. Bonhoeffer's return and his subsequent participation in the opposition to Hitler were highly responsible as well as courageous acts that eventually led to his execution at Nazi hands. Given his particular faith tradition, this outcome might not be construed as destructive of his well-being from an "eternal" perspective; however, his actions required both his turning aside from certain obligations to and relationships with those close to him and his violation of his own firm commitment to nonviolence.[9] His enactment of responsibility thus seems undeniably virtuous; but in its contribution to his own personal flourishing, it remains ambiguous at best.

This example, of course, should not be taken to provide a reason to shy away from cultivating a responsible character; quite the opposite. Rather, it acknowledges that the lives of responsible persons are fully engaged and, thus, fully exposed to the terrible as well as the marvelous potential of human mutuality; it also reminds us that the nature of human flourishing is complex and communal.

Second, *responsibility* as a virtue-like aspect of one's character should be distinguished from *responsibility* used as a synonym for *task* or *obligation*. For example, philosopher of religion Jamie Ferreira, in a critical analysis of Emmanuel Levinas's thought on *welcome*, has written that "responsibility can be fulfilled grudgingly, hatefully"[10]—a claim she can make only if she

---

virtuous actors' individual flourishing, although they are essential for the oppressed community's survival and/or liberation.

9. The Bonhoeffer story is a particularly rich and poignant one for showing how responsible behavior can place one in a position of unresolvable moral conflict—in Bonhoeffer's case, the conflict between his deeply held Christian pacifism and his equally firm sense of responsibility to contribute to the elimination of Hitler. See chap. 13, "Killing the Madman," in Charles Marsh, *Strange Glory: A Life of Dietrich Bonhoeffer* (New York: Penguin Random House, 2014), especially 345–47: "Bonhoeffer did not try to resolve the paradox by assuming moral innocence but accepted the paradox by incurring the guilt born out of responsible action" (346). For more on conflicting calls, see chapter 2 of this volume.

10. Jamie Ferriera, "Total Altruism in Levinas's 'Ethics of the Welcome,'" *Journal of Religious Ethics* 29, no. 3 (2001): 443–70, here 447.

uses *responsibility* to designate a particular task or duty. In contrast, one cannot be a responsible person (that is, possess the attribute of responsibility) if one carries out one's obligations grudgingly or hatefully. Virtues are excellences of character; responsibility, insofar as the word refers to a settled disposition, names the (excellent) way in which one perceives and fulfills one's tasks or obligations—not only with the requisite skill but also with the focused attention and care implied in the word's connotation of mutual promise.

In fact, it seems unlikely that we would refer to one who fulfills obligations grudgingly as a truly responsible person, any more than we would refer to someone who reliably does evil as a person of integrity—despite that term's emphasis on consistency of motivation and behavior. As with the word *integrity*, the roots of which lie in a notion of a good original intactness (and thus ground its association with goodness),[11] the linguistic root of *responsibility*—in the mutual promising exemplified by marriage—supports our inclination to claim that a hateful response should not be credited as a manifestation of responsibility. It may be better described as a *reaction* rather than a response. Responsibility is a form of goodness; mean-spirited fulfillments of one's "responsibilities" may be more or less dutiful, but they are not enactments of the character trait we call "responsibility."

We can now build on this complex understanding of responsibility to further unpack the close relationship between responsibility and vocation. In the following section, I have found it useful to speak of two interrelated "parts" of the call: "inner" urges and abilities, particular to the individual discerner; and "outer" needs and obligations, arising in and from the world surrounding the discerner.[12] Nevertheless, given the inherent mutuality of responsibility—and, therefore, of vocation—this should be understood only as a heuristic distinction. Because of the constant reverberation between responder and that to which she responds, we should seek to resist any fragmentation of the wholeness of the person, of reality, of responsibility, or of vocation.

---

11. Margaret E. Mohrmann, "Integrity: *Integritas, Innocentia, Simplicitas,*" *Journal of the Society of Christian Ethics* 24, no. 2 (2004): 25–38; and "On Being True to Form," in *Health and Human Flourishing: Religion, Medicine, and Moral Anthropology*, ed. Carol R. Taylor and Roberto Dell'oro (Washington, DC: Georgetown University Press, 2006), 89–102.

12. For more on these two aspects of vocation, see David S. Cunningham, "Time and Place," introduction to *At This Time*, esp. 12–14.

## A consonant vocation:
### the fit between inner and outer call

The theological ethicist H. Richard Niebuhr (1894–1962) was an early proponent of "responsibility ethics": an understanding of the moral life that puts the ability to be responsive at the center of human community and of all our activities together.[13] Niebuhr argued that we are always in a stance of response, always responding to someone or to some state of affairs. Responsibility is the center of what we do and of who we are; our moral goodness depends on how well we do it. Our primary moral task, he argues, is to discern the response that is most appropriate to the situation at hand—that is, to find the *fitting* thing to do.[14] Perhaps more than any other understanding of responsibility, this sense of responsive *fit* may serve as the link to a discussion of vocation.

Vocation and responsibility both refer to the full response of a whole person to the whole of reality. The fact that responsiveness necessarily entails some level of mutuality or correspondence between the subject and the object of the response suggests, in turn, that vocational discernment entails a similar mutuality—between the reality that seems to be calling and the person who wishes to answer. The lens of responsibility thus enables us to look more deeply, both into the vocational call (beyond conventional depictions of certain jobs and professions) and into the one who is called (with attention to finding the appropriate degree of fit or fittingness).

There are, then, two fundamental aspects of vocation. One, we could say, is internal: an *inner* sense of attraction, even an insistent yearning, toward some way of being in the world and/or some sense of obligation toward that way of being. The other is external: recognition of an *outer* need, reception of an explicit request by another, and/or perceptions (more or less well informed) of the salient characteristics of certain possible futures. The former is an inward reaching, even a "push," toward a particular kind of work and life: an amalgam of one's talents, inclinations, and choices; deeply instilled family scripts, experiences, formation, and preconceptions; and many other influences (including, for some, a sense of divine indwelling that guides one's direction). The latter is an outward

---

13. H. Richard Niebuhr, *The Responsible Self: An Essay in Christian Moral Philosophy* (New York: Harper & Row, 1963).

14. Ibid., 60.

drawing, or "pull," exerted by certain kinds of work and life. This, too, is a blend of perceptions and assumptions, entreaties from others (the persons and situations one is prepared or situated to hear and acknowledge), and, for some, God's beckoning through the voices of need.

## The consonance of the calls

These two aspects were both distinguished and conjoined by Martin Luther (1483–1546), who is widely credited as the first Western thinker to delve deeply into the concept of vocation—expanding the term to include the work and lives of laypeople, and not just those of Christian priests, monks, and nuns.[15] One of Luther's early twentieth-century interpreters, Karl Holl (1866–1926), observed that Luther

> was of the opinion that God is experienced as reality in the fullest sense only where human beings at the same time take upon themselves life in all its totality, with its pressures, its disillusionments, and its oppressions. Then the moral task consists in this, that one understands in their consonance both the inner call, which one receives in the Gospel, and the voice which forces its way through to us from things themselves and their necessities.[16]

Here we find some of the likely roots of the Lutheran Bonhoeffer's linkage of vocation to the "totality" of life. But, more to the point, we hear the strong assertion that there are two kinds of calls embedded within the idea of vocation: the voice within, pointing one in certain directions, and the outer "voice which forces its way through to us from things themselves and their necessities." These two voices sound together, in "consonance" rather than in contrast. It is not only inner drives, gifts, or preferences that call us to our life's work; it is also the work itself and, more particularly, those whom the work serves.[17]

---

15. For more on this shift, see Kathryn Kleinhans, "Places of Responsibility: Educating for Multiple Callings in Multiple Communities," in Cunningham, ed., *At This Time*, 99–121.

16. Karl Holl, "The History of the Word Vocation (*Beruf*)," trans. Heber F. Peacock, *Review and Expositor* 55, no. 2 (1958): 126–54, here 154, translation slightly altered. The original is Karl Holl, *Die Geschichte des Worts Beruf* (Berlin: Verlag der Akademie der Wissenschaften, in Kommission bei W. De Gruyter, 1924).

17. For more on those whom we serve (as understood through the lens of the audiences for whom art is created), see chapter 5 of this volume.

Note that, for Holl as surely as also for Luther, both aspects of call are permeated with the divine; they do not place God's voice only in the Gospel-inflected inner call nor only in the needs of others. God, in this view, both pushes and pulls, pointing us toward our future and drawing us into it. This suggests that religious and non-religious accounts of vocation are perhaps not so different from each other. The divine aspects of each call are, for some, deeply embedded and paramount, whereas for others they are not; but in either case, the distinction between the two "orientations" of the call can still be useful for anyone undertaking vocational reflection and discernment—as well as for anyone who seeks to advise those who are doing so. (The remainder of this section thus assumes that, when encountering the language of calling and vocation, theological questions matter intensely for some; for others, not at all; and for still others, such questions are on the table but not as urgent.[18])

## Exploring the fit

Unquestionably, the two "calls within a call" are tightly linked; they are distinct, but ultimately inseparable. Evaluation of inner impulses is almost always undertaken in direct relation to whatever characteristics of a particular way of life draw us to it. The inner voice is awakened, informed, even *shaped* by the outer call. In turn, inward yearnings and prior assumptions largely determine which outer voices we are likely to hear and be drawn to—that is, which ones exert genuine pulls on our desires.

Such reciprocating influences may suggest a "fit" between inner desire and outer need that turns out to be only a superficial impression or even an illusion—easily shattered by more (or more accurate) information about one's abilities, the sources of one's inclinations, or the realities of the work. Some students, experiencing the "vocational crisis" that may result from such disillusionment, come to their advisors at a loss, entirely confused about what to do now and in need of clarification. Others come in firm certainty that their aim is true, seeking help with strategies for making their plans happen, and yet still in need (whether they know it or not) of some degree of redirection. Such students can be urged to ask questions of themselves and of their anticipated work—of the inner and outer aspects of their sense of vocation—and can be encouraged to undertake certain

---

18. On this point, see especially Cunningham, "Time and Place," 12–16; see also chapter 12 of this volume.

exercises in discernment. This work can ultimately help them to find a truer fit and, thereby, to pursue a responsible vocation that is both possible and satisfying.

Thus, although the two aspects of call are inseparable, for our purposes it is helpful to consider them serially—yet without losing sight of their interconnections.

## *The inner call: abilities, desires, and long-cultivated habits*

Derek, a sophomore who says he has always wanted to be a doctor, was surprised at how hard it was in his first year in college to stay afloat in his chemistry course; he got a low B the first semester, a C+ the second. He had to drop calculus in order to get through chemistry. Now he's taking organic chemistry and general biology, as recommended for pre-medical students, and retaking calculus. At the end of the first semester, he has a D in organic and Cs in biology and math. He's exhausted and scared. The only thing that has kept his GPA respectable (if not particularly med-school worthy) is that he has done well in his required writing classes and in the politics course he took just to fill a general requirement. He has also enjoyed those classes quite a bit, but he attributes that to their being such a relief from all the science. Derek loved his science classes in high school; now he dreads them.

Vocational discernment involves learning about oneself at least as much as learning about potential careers, and the self-knowledge sought includes not only likes and dislikes but also talents and aptitudes. There might be a host of reasons—social overengagement, financial pressure, depression, and substance abuse are all possibilities, among others—for Derek's poor performance in science and math. But it may also be the case that he has reached the limit of his ability to assimilate and work within scientific ways of thinking. It is a matter of careful discernment whether he should keep trying to bring his skills up to par (and work toward eliminating barriers to that task) or accept the grades as true information about his limitations.

If we understand vocation as *responsibility*, then it can never be the case that one is called to do something for which one truly has no aptitude; it would be entirely *irresponsible* to follow such a path. Some have suggested, not always in jest, that God looks to see what would be the most unlikely job for a person to do, then calls that person to it. The kernel of truth that may lie in that idea is that being asked (or compelled) to do what *seemed* impossible can, at times, reveal previously unrecognized skills, strengths, and interests—an explanation that assumes the existence of capacities there to be discovered and developed. But it is surely the case that we are not *called* to undertake a task or a career for which we possess no such capacities and at which we can only fail, or that will stunt us personally or lead to a lifetime of tedious desperation.

Admittedly, many people do have to take on certain jobs, whether for the short term or as lifelong work, for which they are ill-suited. Such tasks may be required by other calls: immediate survival needs, family obligations or pressures, or other circumstances beyond their control. And some may recognize, within such unwanted but unavoidable work, a call to respond to the situation with integrity and behave well, in spite of the temptation to despair.[19] But to consider them to have been "called" to that work would overturn our understanding of vocation and of responsibility (and, for some, the belief in God's concern for human well-being).

It should be immediately noted that this view, whether in religious or secular form, is a modern one. Luther was speaking to and about people who had little or no choice about their work and not much more about their nonwork lives. His discussion of the two aspects of vocation was not about discerning *which* work to do but, rather, about how to live within the place and the work one was born into by God's design. Luther's sixteenth-century situation of relative vocational immobility no doubt still applies to a significant part of the world's population, but many (not all) college students do have some real choices that lend a different, more expansive meaning to Luther's account of the consonant calls.[20] For such students, it may at times be appropriate to point out, gently but forthrightly, an evident mismatch between their aspirations—even when couched in a deeply religious sense of "call"—and their actual abilities.

---

19. For more on the relationship between the work itself ("doing") and the character of the worker ("being"), see chapter 10 of this volume.

20. On this point, see Kleinhans, "Places of Responsibility," as well as William T. Cavanaugh, "Actually, You Can't Be Anything You Want (and It's a Good Thing, Too)," in Cunningham, ed., *At This Time*, 25–46. For research documenting relatively low social and economic mobility in the United States for the past several decades, see ongoing studies by the Pew Trusts at www.pewtrusts.org/en/research-and-analysis/reports/2015/07/economic-mobility-in-the-united-states (accessed August 10, 2015).

## Examining the internal fit

Returning to Derek's case: a faculty advisor may well need to help him rethink his vocational conclusions in light of his possible academic limitations. A useful first question is: *What* is it that you feel called to be and to do? It is far from clear that anyone, ever, is called to "be a doctor" (or a professor, lawyer, CEO—these are all job titles, not vocations). A calling to a particular kind of work is more about activities to be undertaken and goals to be accomplished, rather than titles to be held or positions to be filled. Thus, one may be called to teaching, but it takes further discernment—weighing abilities and opportunities—to assess what kind of teaching, about what content, with what age or stage of learners. Perhaps Derek is experiencing a call to health care generally, to care for the sick and injured and dying or to help others preserve their health. Perhaps what he interprets to be a vocation as a physician arises from a desire to honor by emulation a much-admired relative or mentor. Maybe he has witnessed the significant health needs of his own community and wants to meet those needs in the most direct way he can imagine.

There are many honorable and meaningful aspirations that find medicine as their common denominator. Essays written by medical school applicants explain—often with great passion—the writer's certainty of a call to restore vision, make children happy, serve the indigent, give back to the community, or discover a cure for the affliction that took away a grandparent or sibling or best friend. Each is a laudable goal; none requires an M.D. to attain it. Even if entry into medical school is blocked because of the particular configuration of aptitudes in some students, this need not mean that they can never realize their vocations. What may be needed is a reconfiguration of their interpretations of their calls, seeking a fit between what is drawing them to medicine and what they are best able to do. The same is true for students with aspirations outside the medical field: the would-be architect whose ineptness at spatial imaging stands in her way can consider other avenues for responding to her desire to affect the built environment; the fledgling actor who simply cannot memorize lines can still be immersed in the world of the theater in creative ways.

After all, there is a difference between, for example, being drawn by a deep love of music and being called to *make* music. The former can be, and often is, fulfilled by attentive, appreciative listening—as well as attending, promoting, and supporting musical performances.[21] The possibility and

---

21. For a detailed discussion of music and vocation, see chapter 5 of this volume.

success of making music, particularly as one's vocation, depend upon talents that may or may not track with one's desires. In the case of a call into the medical field, something deep within may respond to the plight of the sick with a genuine urge to help. But what one may thus be called to do in order to provide help depends significantly on abilities and, often, opportunities. The empathic recognition of the needs of others is not enough; an honest and unflinching assessment of one's developed and developing intellectual capacities and emotional strengths is also required. This work can help a person determine how one's inner impulse may best match those needs—how it may best answer those calling voices. The most fitting response may be found in nursing or doctoring, ministry or advocacy, passing health-care laws or writing good policy or running a hospital, or even serving as a hospice volunteer while managing the family business (in response to different, and no less authentic, inner impulses and outer needs).

## *The outer call: the work itself and the pleas of others*

Sophie is set on becoming a physician—more specifically, a specialist in infectious diseases. She is eager to continue the string of medicine's triumphs over invading organisms by becoming an expert in diagnosis and treatment. She spends the summer after her first year in college interning in a clinic that serves persons who are HIV-positive, some of whom have AIDS. What she sees there are doctors, all specialists in infectious diseases, who spend most of their time trying to address problems related to their patients' inability to adhere to their medication regimens, failures to protect their sexual partners, poverty, hours-long travel to the clinic, inattention to good nutrition and self-care, lack of access to primary health care, and lack of fluency in the language in which treatment is administered and advice is given. The list of social, psychological, and financial impediments to health seems infinite—and the doctors there assure her that this is, indeed, what it means to care for persons with infectious diseases; HIV/AIDS, they observe, is not unique in this way. In the fall, Sophie comes to her advisor truly shaken in her sense of vocation: "I didn't realize I'd have to be a social worker, too!" she exclaims. "I just don't know any more if this is for me."

Matt, a year ahead of Sophie in college but interning in the same clinic that summer, had always dismissed the possibility of being a doctor. His attraction to work in health care, he said, is about the social-justice aspects of our care for the poor and marginalized. He's been planning on some combination of public health and legal education after college. He, too, is surprised to learn about the doctors' deep engagement in the social and psychological needs of their patients. For the first time in his vocational deliberations, Matt begins to consider the possibility of medical school. He wonders if being a physician might enable him to be not only on the "front line" of care but also in a position to effect real change, one person at a time. He comes to his advisor for help reworking his class schedule to fit in some pre-med requirements.

There is always more to any specific calling than one can see from the outside. The exploration of vocation requires of the explorers that they learn as much as they can about what the work actually entails, in order to recognize what it is about the career path they are responding to—and whether what seems to call to them is a true or false image of the work. We should note that, as a person seeks clarity about what is attractive about a particular career, that person is also investigating what it is (from within) that is reaching toward the work and the life that will encompass it. Both the mutuality of responsiveness and the "consonance" of the two aspects of call are highlighted by this further evidence; clearly, the "inner" and the "outer" are inseparable.

Many adults, well ensconced within one vocational path or another, are surprised to find themselves doing work they had not imagined when they set out. Sometimes this is a pleasant surprise, sometimes not. Discovering previously unrecognized skills in oneself, rising to unforeseen occasions in effective ways, allowing the demands of the work to expand one's experience of the world and of other people—all can be forms of positive growth within a career. On the other hand, finding little opportunity to do what one finds most fulfilling, being consistently asked to act outside one's abilities or against one's inclinations, or feeling closed off from sources of inspiration and support—all these experiences can lead to work that is haunted by a sense of deep dissatisfaction and incongruence.

I have counseled a few students in their final year of medical school who were desperate to find some way within medicine to do what they most wanted to do: take direct, hands-on care of patients. They had now recognized what most doctors actually do (and what their training had been preparing them to do), but they were in a panic about spending the rest of their lives doing that; this was not the kind of caregiving they had envisaged. One can make the case, in the abstract, that new processes of vocational discernment and resulting change are always possible, at any step in a career path. In practice, however, it can be exceedingly difficult to shift trajectory when one is carrying a six-figure educational debt and discovers that alternative paths will not be financially remunerated at the same rate as the one no longer desired. These are students who took an enormous, virtually irreversible step four years before, in response to something—but what they had responded to was not an accurate account of the profession they chose to enter.

## Examining the external fit

When undergraduates feel drawn to a particular vocation, they often rely on sources of information that do not correctly portray the nature of the path they are choosing. Some students drawn to medicine are avid fans of televised medical dramas and are nonplussed—some of them even bitter—when they find that most of medicine's actual patients have chronic problems, as well as tangles of physical and social afflictions, that cannot be resolved in an episode or a season (if ever). This predicament, of course, besets many potential career options—not just medicine. One can imagine the same sort of misunderstanding for aspiring lawyers, drawn to the field after watching countless courtroom dramas, who begin to see how little time lawyers actually spend in the courtroom and how much of their time is devoted to detailed research and calming their anxious clients. Many students yearn to become college professors because they imagine a life of reading good books, talking about them with smart people, and teaching students as eager and bright as they are—work that is interrupted only by long summer breaks. It turns out, of course, that the reality is something rather different.

Some students who want to become doctors participate in overseas medical-missions projects that lead them to overestimate the value, efficacy, and "heroism" of professional contributions to health care generally. John Lantos, a pediatrician and ethicist, addressed this problem with particular acuity in recounting his experience at a hospital in Nigeria after he was already in medical school:

> My time in Nigeria shaped my career, but not in straightforward ways. I saw how pitifully easy it would be to save lives. I realized that, if my goal as a doctor was simply to save as many lives as

I could, I should leave the United States and go almost anywhere else. There was no magic to it and not much skill. With a backpack full of tetanus toxoid or oral rehydration solution, I could trek through most countries in the world and save more lives in a week than I would save in Pittsburgh or Chicago in my entire lifetime. For the cost of one student's tuition for a year at an American medical school, I could probably save a thousand lives. Conversely, if I did not do that, if I stayed in the United States, *then my goal must be something else.*[22]

Lantos's challenging observation is a salutary reminder that one is never selecting simply a line of work, but is reaching toward (and being drawn by) a way of living significantly determined by the specifics of one's work. This includes its location, of course; the life and work entailed by practicing medicine in an African village is markedly different from that of a practice in an urban American medical center, or rural Appalachia, or the Upper East Side, or a Los Angeles barrio. The attractions of any one of these options do not necessarily map onto the realities of the others.

Vocational discernment thus demands an exploration of precisely what one is responding to (in focusing on a particular field), as well as determining whether one has gained an accurate representation of what such a career involves. From a perspective outside a particular job, it is often not possible to fathom fully what the task or position calls for, what demands are made, what constraints are in place. Students can be encouraged to place themselves in close observer positions, in ways that can challenge their assumptions about the nature of the call. This might require, for example, spending time with patients (instead of, or in addition to, shadowing doctors).[23] Students can also ask persons already in those careers about how the reality of the work has differed from their expectations.

---

22. John D. Lantos, *Do We Still Need Doctors?* (New York: Routledge, 1997), 67, emphasis added.

23. I have often recommended to pre-med students, sometimes successfully, that instead of shadowing doctors they seek the brief training required to become a Certified Nursing Assistant (CNA) or Patient Care Assistant (PCA). They would then have adequate credentials to be employed by hospital units and nursing homes in roles that require them to give direct care to patients—and thereby learn what it is to be in the presence of suffering, need, and helplessness, and to hear the voices—indeed, the pleas—of those to whom they wish to respond. Such roles offer a significantly different perspective from the one gained when students keep their eyes trained on the clinical practitioner they hope to emulate.

Students can also be encouraged to spend time with members of the communities whose health they wish to improve, in order to learn from their future patients about their needs and hopes. If a fit is to be found—in any possible occupation, not just medicine—between the student's "deep gladness and the world's deep hunger,"[24] then students must listen not to their imaginings and assumptions about what the needs are, but to the needy "world": the persons who are the only authentic identifiers of their own hungers.

What such investigation is likely to find is that within any occupation there are indeed voices—revelatory voices—that force their way through to us from people and their needs. The anticipated contemplative scholarly work of college and university faculty members, for example, is repeatedly interrupted, even derailed, by the needs of the institution, one's colleagues, and especially one's students; those seeking an "ivory tower" would be well advised to consider a different occupation. More broadly, many presumptions about what an occupation *is*, as well as what one does within it, tend to understate the inherent *responsiveness* of any vocation that has anything at all to do with people (that is, virtually all vocations).

Musicians have audiences, accountants have clients, salespersons have customers, producers have consumers, researchers have publics, most workers have colleagues, some have employees. The voices expressing the needs of those who share in or are affected by the work are an essential component of every "outer" call—and must be recognized as such if a responsive fit is to be found or fashioned. That fit can provide a seamless mesh between, on the one hand, what one desires or is able to do, and on the other, the needs of real human beings that demand precisely *that* drive and *those* skills.

## Attending to the voices

Of course, it is also true that the calls on one's responsiveness can seem limitless and insatiable. As Margaret Urban Walker reminds us, our responsibilities always outstrip our control.[25] Modes of responsible limit-setting are

---

24. I use the language of Frederick Buechner's phrase, which sounds throughout this book: "The place where God calls you to is the place where your deep gladness and the world's deep hunger meet." Frederick Buechner, *Wishful Thinking: A Theological ABC* (New York: Harper and Row, 1973), 95. See also Cunningham, "Time and Place," 12–13.

25. Walker, "Moral Luck," 26; see also chapter 2 of this volume.

fundamental tools of both pre-vocational discernment and intra-vocational awareness, efficacy, and satisfaction. Although an adequate consideration of those tools is well beyond the bounds of this chapter, it is important to note that a crucial ingredient in any consideration of such limit-setting is the active recognition that we are not alone in our responsibilities for the "whole of reality." Recognition of the complex communities within which we live and work—communities comprising persons with a variety of skills, calls, and contributions to make—allows us to see how the countless burdens of responsible living are and must be shared in order to be fulfilled.[26] Knowing that the burdens are shared enables us to recognize, without undue fear, that the scope of responsibility is considerably greater than we have considered thus far—especially given that the responsibilities within one's chosen occupation are not the only ones with legitimate calls on one's attention and abilities.

Throughout this discussion of the "inner" and "outer" aspects of the call (distinguishable but inseparable), we have focused on students' discernment of their future fields of work—and have risked losing sight of the breadth of meaning that "vocation" carries. The consonance of the calls indicates not only the fit between inner yearnings and outer needs, but also the inseparability of one's work and one's life. In the matter of limit-setting, it is too often the case that work responsibilities are given unquestioned precedence over those entailed by life outside the job. However, Bonhoeffer's expansive understanding of vocation—"a total response of the whole human being to the whole of reality"—argues strongly against such a facile and arbitrary arrangement of priorities. In the following section, we consider how recognizing vocation as responsibility broadens the meaning and purview of one's calling, which embraces the whole person as living in full engagement with the whole of reality.

## *Expanding the scope of vocation*

The "whole of reality," to which we are called to respond, clearly includes more than the work one does for so many hours a week or the way one "makes a living." What constitutes a "living" includes crucial relationships, activities, and obligations not entailed by one's occupation, although they

---

26. See the comments on the importance of communal discernment in chapter 6 of this volume.

may certainly be in more or less close connection with that work.[27] John
Lantos, after musing on geographical distinctions among the goals of a life
in medicine, wonders just what he did learn from that stint in Nigeria. He
tentatively asks whether it might be the case "that saving lives is easy, but
that living a life is much harder, and that medicine ought to be as much
about the way we live our lives as it is about whether or not we can or
should save lives."[28] In context, Lantos is referring to the less glamorous
but also vital role of doctors, in developed countries at least, as advisors
to persons wanting to live in medically healthy ways. But he could as well
have been speaking about vocation generally: choosing and working in a
particular occupation is easy compared to living a whole life. Consequently,
vocational discernment ought to be as much about *the way we live our lives*
as it is about whether or not we can work at the job we prefer, or for which
we think ourselves well suited.[29]

The lifelong tasks of being aware of, and of living within, the whole of
reality make continuous demands on our time, attention, effort, and care. In
addition to our mode of paid employment, we are called to be in responsible
relationship with friends and with family members, and to be in responsible
community with others—as members of a society (local and global), as citizens of a polity, and as participants in an environment. In each, we carry particular and often weighty responsibility. Whether and how we respond to all
the non-work-related calls that characterize living in the company of others
determines, to a large extent, the quality of our lives: whether we can, at the
end of the day, call ourselves happy, fulfilled, "successful." Students focused
on a future vocation construed simply as "the work they hope to do" should
be encouraged also to consider something of much greater scope: the kind
of life they wish to live and the kind of persons they intend to become—in,
through, and beyond their future occupations.

Students can be helped to consider how a singular focus on one's work,
narrowly construed, diminishes necessary attention to other parts of one's
life.[30] An article from many years back, in a "throwaway" journal distributed gratis to doctors in hospitals, is titled "Medicine: An Excuse from

---

27. For further reflections on this point, see chapter 8 of this volume.

28. Lantos, *Do We Still Need Doctors?*, 67.

29. See chapters 2 and 10 of this volume for further development of this crucial point.

30. See chapter 2 of this volume for some reflections on the ways that discernment of a
"higher calling" can sometimes blind us to the variety of vocational claims on our lives.

Living."[31] The authors tell us that those hearing this title often corrected what they thought was an error, certain that it must be about medicine as an excuse *for* living. On the contrary, this pithy essay, written by a married couple (a physician in academic medicine and a reading teacher), makes compelling claims about all the ways in which doctors—from the beginning of medical school onward—use the importance and urgency of their work to excuse themselves *from* obligations of family, friendship, and citizenship. Absence from the children's sports events and recitals, avoidance of jury duty, and even an abrupt departure from a difficult conversation made possible by a well-timed page: all are lapses of responsibility deemed excusable because of "more important" calls on the doctor's time and attention. Few doctors resist the temptation to misuse this get-out-of-obligations-free card.

Other vocational paths undoubtedly make certain excuses available to their practitioners as well; some of these may not be as readily accepted, but it is still relatively easy to claim that the demands of one's work are more important than other, "fainter" calls. This, too, should be a topic for vocational discernment: it is part of the broad scope, "the whole of reality," to which one is called to respond. The voices that force their way through to us are not restricted to those we have decided to hear by our choice of occupation. Vocation is a match between the inner call to respond and the outer call of need for response; when and whence these outer calls arise may be far less under our control than we might like, but our responsibilities remain nevertheless.

A second point made, more subtly, by this brief article—and very germane to our discussion here—has to do with the extent to which interpersonal relationships, social activities, and the fulfillment of civic duties should be credited with forming persons into better workers. That is, the sorts of characteristics that make it possible to carry out all sorts of occupations well (both effectively and happily)—traits such as care, responsiveness, conscientiousness, collegiality—are often crucially engendered, nurtured, and revived by encounters and activities outside one's occupation. Thus, the responsibility to attend to calls not directly related to work is at least binary: a responsibility to those calling, as well as a responsibility to continue to develop into persons who can carry out our occupations

---

31. Robert L. Brent and Lillian H. Brent, "Medicine: An Excuse from Living," *Resident and Staff Physician*, December 1978, 61–65.

well. The mutuality of responsibility is clear in this situation; that which calls us away from our chosen work also equips us, insofar as we respond well to those calls, to attend more carefully to the demands of the work.

These points may be obvious when thinking of the calls of friends and family, but less so when extended to the calls of the larger society—from needs of local communities to more global exigencies. But vocation is responsibility to and for the whole of reality—a realization that, as mentioned earlier, must be held in fruitful tension with the obligation to set responsible limits on how (and to what level) one responds to the myriad calls that reality constantly issues. Every occupation—no matter how hermetic it may seem, how limited its field of action—is an integral part of the greater human society of life and work. Occupations arise from the needs of society at least as much as from the inclinations of workers; they persist because these needs persist, and they remain accountable to society's demands—whether for good health care, well-made shoes, honest banking practices, or masterly musical performance.

Any student in the process of vocational discernment can be encouraged to ponder these questions: What do you think your life outside of work will be like? What should it be like? What do you want it to be? How do you understand your participation in this occupation to be a response to the world's needs? How will you keep yourself attentive to those needs? How will you meet all your responsibilities? In addition to gaining the skills needed to practice this profession, how are you educating yourself about the other responsibilities your life will entail? What is forming you? How else might you need to be formed and educated?

None of these questions has, or should be given, a clear, once-for-all answer. Rather, they are queries we all carry with us through life, checking ourselves against them from time to time. And they are all specifications of the broader questions that enable us to define ourselves as whole persons, living our singular lives: Amid all the varied and centrifugal "pulls," is my life coherent as a whole? How and where do I center my life?[32]

---

32. It must be noted that there remains a striking gender difference in the sorts and weights of responsibilities assigned and assumed, particularly those regarding the family, and a corresponding gender difference in the level of difficulty encountered in attempts to hold the tension fruitfully and set limits responsibly—often described, succinctly, as the problem of whether it is possible for *women* "to have it all." It would send a salutary message if faculty advisors were to ask male students the questions suggested in these two paragraphs as assiduously and comprehensively as they sometimes do of female students (many of whom are already pondering them), and encourage all students to include such considerations in their

## *Implications for colleges and universities*

This set of questions takes us beyond our reflection on the nature of vocation as responsibility; it asks us to think, even if only briefly, about the
resulting perspective on higher education, and especially about its role as
preparation for this kind of multiply responsible life. No doubt colleges
and universities have shown themselves quite able to prepare students for
a variety of occupations. Their graduates succeed in learning to be lawyers
and nurses and cellists, to run businesses and manufacturing firms, to sell
houses, raise crops, counsel troubled teens, teach school, carry out scientific research, and navigate the intricacies of the tax code. But what about
all the other responsibilities that students will be taking on? These may be
chosen or not, desired or otherwise: broad obligations of responsiveness
within their vocations, expansive responsibilities of family life and friendship, of citizenship in the community, the nation, and the world. Perhaps
our thinking about the tasks of higher education should also be deepened
and expanded—along with our thinking about vocation.

Colleges and universities, understanding themselves to be "vocational
schools" in this newly expanded sense, could rethink their approach to the
education needed by all undergraduates, in professional schools as well
as in the liberal arts, and regardless of their future job plans.[33] Life in a
democracy *calls* students to learn and practice thoughtful consideration
of issues and policies, as well as to cultivate the habit of voting. Life in
human society *calls* students to think deliberately about the nature and
formation of responsible adult relationships, at varying levels of intimacy,
from spouse to fellow inhabitant of the planet. And life in an occupation
*calls* students to consider all that affects both success and satisfaction in
one's work, as well as all whom the work affects.

The Greek word for "calling"—κλῆσις—has multiple, related meanings. In addition to its usual use in ancient texts to mean a calling (divine
or otherwise), it also can denote a summons to appear in court and an invitation to a feast. Just so, both vocation and responsibility entail a summons
to accountability. We must account, before the court of self and others, for
our assessment and use of our own abilities, talents, and desires—and for

---

investigation of prospective careers and employers. For more on this point, see chapter 4 in
this volume.

33. This point is taken up in more detail elsewhere in this volume, particularly in parts two
and three.

our attention to and care for the needs of others. Vocation, like responsibility, is a rigorous and demanding perspective on life. On the other hand, both are also gracious invitations—and, one could well argue, the only available admission tickets—to the bountiful feast of meaningful and fulfilling work, open and mutual relationships, and responsive, effective service to the world.

## 2

# The Conflicts in Our Callings

### THE ANGUISH (AND JOY) OF WILLING SEVERAL THINGS

#### Jason A. Mahn

HERE'S A SITUATION familiar to first-year undergraduates—and to the educators who serve as their advisors and mentors:

A student sits in his advisor's office, leaning back and crossing his arms, as if he might stay a while. He's been here before—going over general education requirements, checking in about social life in the dorms, reporting that he's attended all his Chem 103 classes even though his midterm grade doesn't reflect it. Ostensibly, he made the appointment to declare a major in biology on the pre-med track; he's brought the form that has been filled in since first term. Yet his first-year advisor—let us say, a professor of anthropology—senses that he is not in a hurry for her to "sign off." So she again brings up the fact that he seemed to have enjoyed his first-year seminar on Homer and an elective on existentialism and film much more than his year of general chemistry. He attended the information session about study abroad in Japan. She also remembers the comment he made suggesting that becoming a doctor is at least as much his parents' dream for him as is his own. "Have you thought about taking some more courses in philosophy or Asian studies or classics before making this decision?" she asks. "Did you know that you can take the MCAT and go to med school without majoring in biology?" And then finally, risking quirky sentimentalism by paraphrasing a poem she heard some time ago, "What do you really want to do with this one wild and precious life of yours?"[1]

---

1. The original quotation reads: "Tell me, what is it you plan to do / with your one wild and precious life?" Mary Oliver, "The Summer Day," from *New and Selected Poems*, vol. 1 (Boston: Beacon Press, 1992), 94.

It's not only students like this one who feel pulled in different directions by various obligations and thrust forward by different interests. All of us have arrays of gifts and capabilities with which to respond to the many needs of our communities and the world. Many of us, too, want desperately for one push or pull to rise above the rest, or for the many to combine into one—or at least line up into an order of priority. When they do not, the strain is considerable; we find ourselves degrading unchosen options so as to curb some of the anxiety and grief brought on by thinking about them. This might be the case for our imagined student, were he to leave his advisor's office with the major declaration form signed—newly convinced that Homer, Sartre, and Asian studies may be fun, but that they do not make a career, and so are not worth his time. Educators risk the same compulsions of choice and retrospective evaluation. How often do they convince themselves that, for example, research is a luxury for careerist faculty who are not committed to teaching? Or that engaging apathetic students should not be the concern of accomplished scholars? How often do parents, stuck in a late meeting, assure themselves that kids really only need one parent at a time? Or that they should not take on projects for the common good, because this would infringe on their family life?

Unity of purpose and will are invaluable components of vocational reflection and discernment. At the same time, the willingness to name multiple and competing callings—and even to be open to them—brings edification of its own. This chapter is centrally concerned with the conflicting callings that lay in store for college graduates. I focus not only on the conflict among typical social duties—family, work life, civic responsibility, and friendships, among others—but also between all those callings taken together, on the one hand, and on the other, the one calling that emerges as "primary," "higher," or even "divinely ordained."

Those who work in higher education should not only prepare their students for life's dilemmas and difficult choices, but should also help them to see the "learning and development"[2] that comes by risking action even when all options are sullied, or by holding onto and negotiating two or more incommensurable callings. What is more, students need to discover that a life of integrity and purpose is actually more likely to *occasion*

---

2. Martha C. Nussbaum, *The Fragility of Goodness: Luck and Ethics in Greek Tragedy and Philosophy* (Cambridge: Cambridge University Press, 1986), 44.

competition and conflict among callings, and even to be accompanied by existential suffering—even if such a life also helps them develop the "grit"[3] necessary to push through these things. Finally, to the degree that our institutional settings and personal beliefs enable us to speak theologically about the divine will and its claims on the lives of students and of their mentors, even here we should resist suggesting that clarity about that ultimate calling transcends or solves our daily dilemmas and multiple commitments. Hearing a "higher" call still requires us—and perhaps enables us—to face the conflicts in our callings.

## Between singularity of purpose and fragmentation of self

Education for vocation has, in recent decades, proved to be an important approach to humanistic education in the liberal arts. This is true largely because vocation directs our attention not only toward *doing* but also toward *being*. Ineluctably, vocational questions push past the immediate and pragmatic questions (What should I do with my time and skills?) to ones constitutive of personhood, agency, purpose, and meaning as such: Who am I? Why am I here? How shall I live? Moreover, those questions of personhood and purpose require answers that cohere with one another; they urge us, happily, to a more complete view of our own lives.[4] One cannot adequately respond to *who* and *why* questions simply by offering a diverse list of activities, skill sets, interests, and career options. The existential questions that surface in discussions about vocation thereby tend to invite something like *purity of heart* or *unity of will*—a largely coherent life that is plotted forward, lived well, and reflected upon along the way.

### Vocation and virtue

The language of vocation thus has many resonances with philosophical and theological accounts of *virtue*. There are many vocations, just

---

3. Angela L. Duckworth, Christopher Peterson, Michael D. Matthews, and Dennis R. Kelly, "Grit: Perseverance and Passion for Long-Term Goals," *Journal of Personality and Social Psychology* 92, no. 6 (2007): 1087–1101. See also connections to vocational discernment in Tim Clydesdale, *The Purposeful Graduate: Why Colleges Must Talk to Students about Vocation* (Chicago: University of Chicago Press, 2015), 222–23.

4. For more on this point, see chapter 10 of this volume.

as there are a number of virtues; however, each is authentic and can be distinguished from various imitations insofar as the vocation or virtue becomes a person's second nature—drawing her or him further toward a final and singular end.[5] This is why the virtues *qua* virtues must come in clusters, with the Christian tradition adding that charity is the form of all the other virtues.[6] It follows that if students decide to train for perseverance but not for self-discipline, they thereby demote their otherwise-laudable determination into a mere skill or pragmatic technique. They are aiming only for a more limited good—perhaps advancement from private to sergeant, or a good score on the LSAT. By contrast, various activities can become what Alasdair MacIntyre calls *practices*—and character traits can become *virtues*—only when they point beyond themselves to some higher good or a complete account of genuine happiness: something that can unite all of a person's gifts and efforts.[7]

The same is true for various vocations, and for vocation as a concept. I may hear a number of discrete callings during any one chapter of my life, not to mention over my life's narrative as a whole. But no one of these various callings—as scholar, teacher, department chair, or father—would seem to count as *my life's calling*, precisely because the complete flourishing of any one of these seems to threaten to leave the others out. One's vocation must somehow include these discordant callings within a single life, yet without subtracting from their specificity or ignoring the way they compete for one's attention at any given moment.

While the "unity of the virtues" must not be forgotten, an overly narrow "singularity of vocation" may lead to various distortions of the concept. When, for example, the goal of vocational reflection is described

---

5. For Aristotle on the virtues and their simulacra, see his *Nicomachean Ethics*, trans. Terence Irwin, 2nd ed. (Indianapolis: Hackett, 1999), I.13 and III.8. See chapters 1, 7, and 13 of this volume, for further discussion of virtue and vocation; for a more comprehensive account, see the whole of part 3 of David S. Cunningham, ed., *At This Time and In This Place: Vocation and Higher Education* (New York: Oxford University Press, 2016), 189–254.

6. For St. Thomas Aquinas's account of the unity of the virtues and charity as its final form, see his *Treatise on the Virtues*, trans. John A. Oesterle (Notre Dame, IN: University of Notre Dame Press, 1984), Question LXV. See also chapter 13 of this volume, as well as Douglas V. Henry, "Vocation and Story: Narrating Self and World," and Paul J. Wadell, "An Itinerary of Hope: Called to Magnanimous Way of Life," both in Cunningham, ed., *At This Time*, 165–88 and 193–215.

7. Alasdair MacIntyre, *After Virtue: A Study in Moral Theory*, 2nd ed. (Notre Dame, IN: University of Notre Dame Press, 1984), 187–89.

as a life of *integrity* or *authenticity*, this may unintentionally encourage students to avoid (or to hurry past) those circumstances where no one clear, single, and easily justified course of action presents itself. Such so-called tragic situations, in which incommensurable goods and unavoidable evils vie for the agent's attention, often lead to moral paralysis and a loss of integrity—as they do following "Sophie's choice" in William Styron's novel of that name.[8] At the same time, tragic situations sometimes also lead to moral growth, as well as to what we might call "vocational growth." They can prevent one penultimate good or one specific virtue from being elevated to the status of the final and complete goal of life. Moreover, they can dissuade a person from debasing unchosen options and unfulfilled obligations simply because one could not choose them. Such "roads not taken" may still have moral claims on a person, rightfully eliciting regret, remorse, remembrance, or a renewed sense of possibility. Finally, naming and claiming tragic situations can prevent one from narrowing one's moral focus to those people and goods that match one's predetermined sense of giftedness or line up with one's own will.[9]

## Oneself and the other

To find one's calling is to find one's self. Nevertheless, that self includes, at best, many others who impose on it.[10] To "have" a vocation is thus to be interrupted by, and made open to, unbidden others; for some, this might also include the divine Other. According to Emmanuel Levinas, even this distinction—between being called by God and by the needy neighbor—tries to keep distinctions too tidy and to order them too rigidly. For Levinas, "every other is the Other"; that is, God (or some other source of a "higher calling") is revealed in those who we encounter, and particularly in those who suffer. By their very presence, these "others" make moral claims on

8. William Styron, *Sophie's Choice* (New York: Modern Library, 1998). The main character repeatedly "plunge[s] into carnal oblivion and a flight from memory and grief" (576), to mention just one description of her loss of self in the wake of unavoidable evil.

9. Michael J. Sandel, "The Case Against Perfection," *The Atlantic Monthly* 293, no. 3 (April 2004): 51–62. See also Jason Mahn, "Called to the Unbidden: Saving Vocation from the Market," *The Cresset* 76, no. 1 (Michaelmas 2012): 6–17.

10. For further reflection on this point, see chapter 6 of this volume.

the rest of us.[11] This account is rooted in Levinas's own Jewish tradition; it also comes to flower in Christ's command to serve and know the divine Other by serving and knowing the others who suffer among us: the hungry and thirsty, the alien and the naked, the sick and the imprisoned (Matt. 25:31–46). If, then, a fragmented life and unreflected self is incapable of acting with consistency and unity of purpose, so too may be an overly reflected-upon life—one already "fully baked," so to speak. Those with too clear a sense of what remains inside and outside their own will and domain of responsibility may also fail to respond to the dynamic nature of the world and the changing needs of others.[12]

There is something of a Scylla and Charybdis here. Imagining that we can meet the needs of others without knowing the spiritual core of ourselves—without letting our singular lives speak—proves to be a recipe for overcommitment, disappointment, and resentment.[13] On the other side, thinking that my primary call is to preserve my authenticity, to remain "true to myself," often works to muffle the pleas or even legitimate the suffering of those seemingly outside my sphere of responsibility.[14] Moral philosophers have set up a parallel framework for considering selfhood as such: At one extreme is the substantive, solid self (produced by modernity, and usually male), whose received *identity* (from *idem* = to be the same) is self-reflexive and self-consistent. In this account, the self is so central that its relationships with others are seen as nonconstitutive; thus, "he" can always divest himself from them. At the other extreme is a postmodern, fluid, fragmented self, one whose playful performance within numerous personal/social/political spheres makes it unnecessary, and indeed

---

11. Emmanuel Levinas, *Totality and Infinity: An Essay on Exteriority*, trans. Alphonso Lingis (Pittsburgh: Duquesne University Press, 1969), 180–83; Levinas, *Otherwise Than Being or Beyond Essence*, trans. Alphonso Lingis (Dordrecht: Kluwer, 1991), xlii. Jacques Derrida helped popularize the claim that *tout autre est tout autre,* or that "every other is wholly other—is the Other." See especially Derrida, *The Gift of Death*, trans. David Wills (Chicago: University of Chicago Press, 1995).

12. See particularly chapter 1 of this volume, concerning responsibility as response to the moral summons of another.

13. Parker Palmer, *Let Your Life Speak: Listening for the Voice of Vocation* (San Francisco: Jossey–Bass/Wiley, 2000), 9–30.

14. On responsibility, see chapter 1 of this volume; on authenticity, see Hannah Schell, "Community and Commitment: The Virtue of Loyalty and Vocational Discernment," in Cunningham, ed., *At This Time*, 235–54.

unwelcome, to speak of a single, unchanging self.[15] Some have sailed
between Scylla and Charybdis by considering the "storied self" or "narrative identity"; we are capable of giving a coherent account of ourselves,
but this account comprises many subplots, supporting characters, and
dramatic turns and tensions.[16] Later in this chapter, I will return briefly to
narrative—suggesting that this category may best enable students to recognize and reflect on the significance of conflicts for their lives. For now,
I only note that the vocational equivalent of the "storied self" must also
steer between an endless multiplication of callings and commitments, on
the one hand, and on the other, an unflinching disregard for these conflicting callings—even when carried out under the banner of "singularity of
purpose."

## *The winding (and sometimes stony) paths of college graduates*

If then, in Frederick Buechner's famous terms, finding one's vocation
entails locating that spot (only one?) where one's "deep gladness and the
world's deep hunger meet,"[17] it also seems true that we must all ultimately
contend with our gladness*es* (plural) and the competing need*s* (also plural)
of a hungry world. Connecting these multiple "dots" will result in a much
messier and open-ended picture—not a single midpoint on a straight line.
A recent study of alumni from my own college demonstrates this rather
vividly.

    In 2014, the institutional research office of Augustana College (Rock
Island, Illinois) began its "Winding Path Study," a survey and questionnaire

---

15. Catherine Keller, *From A Broken Web: Separation, Sexism, and Self* (Boston: Beacon,
1986), 7–46; Jane Flax, *Disputed Subjects: Essays on Psychoanalysis, Politics and Philosophy*,
3rd ed. (New York: Routledge, 2013), 92–110; and Judith Butler, *Precarious Life: The Powers
of Mourning and Violence* (London: Verso, 2004). Charles Taylor traces the separate, selfsame, or "radically-reflexive" self to St. Augustine's command to "not go outward; [but]
return within yourself. In the inward man dwells truth." Augustine, *De Vere Religione*, as
cited in Charles Taylor, *Sources of the Self: The Making of the Modern Identity* (Cambridge,
MA: Harvard University Press, 1989), 129.

16. See Joseph Dunne, "Beyond Sovereignty and Deconstruction: The Storied Self," in *Paul
Ricoeur: The Hermeneutics of Action*, ed. Richard Kearney (London: Sage, 1996), 137–59; Judith
Butler, *Giving an Account of Oneself* (New York: Fordham University Press, 2005). For direct
connections to vocation, see chapter 3 of this volume; see also Henry, "Vocation and Story."

17. Frederick Buechner, *Wishful Thinking: A Theological ABC* (New York: Harper and Row,
1973), 95.

sent by email to graduates of the college and returned by nearly 2,800 alumni/ae.[18] The study was modeled on life course theory,[19] a sociological model that describes the life course of an individual as a series of trajectories, transitions, and turning points. The survey asked about the number of job changes, relocations, and other major transitions that the participants had experienced, as well as professional and personal factors that influenced them. The data quickly confirmed what the title of the study seemed to suggest: that "many if not most Augustana alumni have . . . led adult lives that look more like winding paths than straight lines."[20] The payoff for a college such as mine is equally apparent; it requires us to "continue to design a college experience that prepares every student to carve through life after college—no matter what comes out of the woodwork."[21] Colleges that emphasize general education and the liberal arts will be quick to point out that a versatile degree supporting multiple careers may be more valuable—financially and otherwise—than is professional training for a single line of work.

Less predictable was the detail and discernable emotion with which alumni answered the two open-ended questions about, first, experiences that led to substantial changes in the graduate's life path; and second, additional details that provide glimpses into his or her life story. Alumni wrote about falling in love, marriage, divorce, grief, job loss, unexpected opportunities, chronic illnesses, religious conversion, loss of faith, and the deaths of parents, spouses, and close friends. One wrote about getting the "adventure bug" to hike the Pacific Crest Trail and how the experience changed her work–life balance. Another wrote of being severely injured while at college and then leaving for two years to have surgery and recover financially. "Long story made short," the participant wrote, "this was a blessing in disguise: I started dating a fellow student whom I later married. My experience forced me to reflect on my goals which led

---

18. Described at "A new (and maybe better) way to understand the impact of an Augustana education," Augustana Institutional Research and Assessment Office, www.augustana.edu/blogs/ir/?p=1152 (accessed July 25, 2016).

19. See chapter 4 of this volume, which uses the life course model more centrally.

20. Mark Salisbury, "Hey: What's This I Hear about the Winding Path Study?," *Delicious Ambiguity: Using Evidence to Improve Student Learning at Augustana College Blog*, Institutional Research at Augustana College, www.augustana.edu/blogs/ir/?p=1320 (accessed April 15, 2015).

21. Ibid.

to greater success when I returned to Augustana."[22] Many, in fact, wrote of how seemingly chance encounters or circumstances changed the course of their professional and personal lives, only to look back and sense that there was something providential throughout:

> My father passed away four years ago, and it was shortly after that point in time that a lot of opportunities started to fall into place. I think it was for two reasons—God wanted me to be around to have a strong relationship with my father and family before his passing, and second, after his passing I had more emotional availability for my craft.[23]

Others waxed philosophical about what they have learned from life's winding path. I quote here a response at length:

> My postgraduate story is so long and diverse with a variety of reasons behind all of my location and job moves. I had and still have no idea what life holds for me and I've learned when you come to expect or plan, things change drastically. Since graduation I have done everything from singing the national anthem solo for President Bush, competing for Miss America, driving a forklift for my parents' business, tutoring at-risk children, setting up and managing on-site mock trials around the country . . . and now starting an etsy store. . . . Life has so many twists and turns and I never saw any of them coming! I've learned through much frustration of trying to figure out life that it is best for me to embrace and adapt rather than to attempt to manipulate and plan. . . . Maybe I'm just along for the ride, but I wouldn't have it any other way. It's a great adventure![24]

Still, it is one thing to be able look back on a winding path through life and see how it all makes sense (or celebrate the fact that it doesn't); it is another thing to be in the middle of difficult transitions and not know

---

22. This and the following quotations, lightly edited, were from Augustana alumni/ae who graduated between 2002 and 2008, seven to twelve years before the survey was taken. "Winding Path Study," used by permission of Mark Salisbury, Augustana Institutional Research.

23. Ibid.

24. Ibid.

how (or whether) the pieces will fall together, giving way to a sense of destiny, of redemption, or—what is synonymous for many—of *vocation*. Many alumni/ae also wrote about such difficult times of loss and forced choices, nostalgia for dreams deferred and grief for plans interrupted. But no comment was as sore as this one:

> Well, I was so strapped with debt after leaving Augustana but completely untrained in anything but writing endless papers that I had to join the military to pay off my massive student loan debt. This allowed me to deploy twice to a war zone and nearly die on at least 8 different occasions. I also took two IED blasts and suffer the aftereffects to this day. So going to your [expletive] school nearly killed me.[25]

Educators can learn a good deal from graduates who won't be featured in alumni magazines. The agonizing words of this one are presumably an attempt to counter (what the writer takes to be) the answer the researchers were looking for—namely, confirmation that the institution has helped develop "qualities of mind, spirit and body necessary for a rewarding life of leadership and service in a diverse and changing world," as the school's mission statement has it. How could we have served him better? It is hard to say, but perhaps we did not adequately speak of our own vocations as places of ambiguity and ambivalence, or even regret or remorse. Perhaps besides too many assigned papers, this student was told too many success stories—retrospective accounts of how one got from there to here, either because one made all the right choices or because Fate or Chance or God was working all things through for the good. Grief, disappointment, doubt, sorrow, and patient suffering are human capacities or dispositions that *can be learned*. They are not just emotional reactions, but also carry cognitive power—no less than do hope, faith, courage, and celebrations of success. By teaching and modeling the entire range of these dispositions, college educators might prepare students to become more fully human, while also more pliant and porous. Instruction in the proper response to tragedy may be the right place to start.

---

25. Ibid.

## *Tragedy without evasion*

*Tragedy* as a genre of drama displays instances of profound human suffering and loss in order to inspire moral learning and invoke cathartic release in its viewers and readers. *Tragic conflicts* or *tragic circumstances* more generally refer to everyday situations where decisions must be made but where competing and incommensurable goods vie for one's attention—or where some harm appears inevitable or necessary. Against overly simplified worldviews that presuppose moral clarity, rank options by clear criteria, and presuppose a person's unencumbered freedom to choose among them, a *tragic worldview* attends to moral constraints, misfortune, and the inevitability of loss. Attending to such features through literature and in "real life" enables people to develop dispositions (or virtues) that are easily missed in more glibly optimistic and moralistic accounts.

In a 1988 interview with Bill Moyers, moral philosopher Martha Nussbaum spoke of the continuing importance, in the contemporary world, of tragic heroes such as Agamemnon (in Aeschylus's tragic play of the same name). Facing a horrible dilemma—either to sacrifice his daughter Iphigenia (in order to allow for the survival of his people and nation), or to protect her from harm and destroy his country—Agamemnon was forced to choose between two competing goods and was thereby forced to commit at least one evil act. While Agamemnon's ordeal is exemplary in its intensity, Nussbaum argues that parents who must choose between an important meeting and their child's music recital face a choice with the same tragic structure. Whatever they choose, they will "have to neglect one of those commitments and neglect something that's really ethically important."[26] To use the language of vocation, we might say: they will hear a number of relevant calls, but may not be able to respond to all of them.

Nussbaum observes that the existential difficulty of such "undecidable"[27] moments is fully felt only by those whose ethical vision is wide and

---

26. Martha Nussbaum, quoted in Bill Moyers, *A World of Ideas* (New York: Doubleday, 1989), excerpted as "Interview with Martha Nussbaum," in *Leading Lives that Matter: What We Should Do and Who We Should Be*, ed. Mark R. Schwehn and Dorothy C. Bass (Grand Rapids, MI: Eerdmans, 2006), 309–10.

27. I use this word in the fairly technical sense of having no stable criteria by which a decision can be made; one must decide without such justification and thus become maximally responsible. See Derrida, *Gift of Death*, 53–81. "Undecidability" need not involve indecision, as Nussbaum makes clear: "The correct perception of a conflict need not entail indecision, since there can be such conflicts even where the claims are not evenly balanced.

who are aware of its complexity. If I decide in advance that family always comes first, or that decisions that have institutional ramifications in the working world are more important than interpersonal support, then I've slipped out of this potential quandary in advance. By contrast, the more fully I face a wide range of commitments—the more deeply I care about more than one thing—the more likely tragedy becomes.

For Nussbaum, as for Levinas, facing tragedy entails *suffering*; recalling that the Latin word for suffering is *passio*, we needn't be surprised that it tends to accompany anyone who is *passionate*. Indeed, through pain, "you understand better what your commitments are and how deep they are. That's what Aeschylus means when he says that through suffering comes a kind of learning—a grace that comes by violence from the gods."[28] Even when the claims are not equally balanced—when one option seems like the obviously "right" one—the processes of deliberation, decision, and defense will be no less agonizing. In the end, Agamemnon realizes that he must sacrifice his daughter; the nation cannot be destroyed for the sake of one life (and in any case, if the nation dies, Iphigenia will die with everyone else). Where he errs is in assuming that once the "right" choice has been made, he can sit comfortably, assured of being morally justified.[29] For Nussbaum, such impassive confidence in having chosen correctly entails a "peculiar optimism"—a shift in attitude toward his decision (once he brings himself to make it).[30] Agamemnon arranges "his feelings to accord with his fortune," and "omits the sorrow and the struggle" that he *should* feel, both before and after his decision.[31] "May all turn out well," he declares, giving voice to his passionless disassociations. The Chorus thinks he is mad; at a minimum, he is less fully human than one who, even if forced to make such a decision, would continue to feel the full force of his daughter's claim on him.[32]

---

Indecision by itself does not appear to be a virtue or decisiveness a deficiency." Nussbaum, *Fragility of Goodness*, 43.

28. Nussbaum, in Moyers, "Interview," 312.

29. Nussbaum, *Fragility of Goodness*, 30.

30. Ibid., 35.

31. Ibid., 36. Indeed, it is his decisiveness—not the actual sacrifice—that marks his moment of failure as a tragic hero. From this moment on, he treats his daughter as no more than an animal victim to be slaughtered.

32. Ibid., 35–39; Nussbaum in Moyers, "Interview," 312.

Aeschylus's *Agamemnon* would have its reader learn a complex set of appropriate feelings or dispositions that the protagonist himself fails to exhibit. One should properly lament, even while making the "right" choice; one should refuse to convince oneself that moral relevance is exhausted once the decision is made. We need to learn to act, to decide, and thus to close off other options—but also to remain "open" to them. That openness is cultivated by grief, suffering, lament, vulnerability, empathy, and remembrance. It requires a "hope against hope" that those unchosen options (which are also deep loves) are somehow still with us. As the *Bhagavad Gita* has it, one should act without being excessively attached to the fruit of one's actions;[33] one should make decisions, but should not use this decisiveness as a means of self-protection.

Whereas Agamemnon teaches this only by way of negative example, other tragic heroes provide a path more worthy of emulation. They act decisively, but still refuse to take refuge in the conclusiveness of their decisions or the assumed rectitude of the action. Take, for example, the title character of Sophocles's *Antigone*. She must decide what to do with the body of her brother Polynices, who was a traitor against the city-state; as such, he may not be buried inside or near the city, according to the decree of Creon (Antigone's uncle and the new ruler of Thebes). Nevertheless, Antigone chooses to defy her uncle's decree in order to honor her deceased brother. According to Nussbaum's analysis, both Creon and Antigone "narrow their sights" or "engage in a ruthless simplification of the word of value" on either side of the tragic situation—Creon in favor of civic duties, Antigone in support of religious and familial ones.[34] And yet Antigone emerges as the more sympathetic character, insofar as there remains—even within her single-mindedness—a vulnerable openness to face and recognize the very duties she rejects. I quote from Nussbaum's careful analysis:

> Antigone remains ready to risk and to sacrifice her ends in a way that is not possible for Creon. . . . There is a complexity in Antigone's virtue that permits genuine sacrifice *within* the defense of piety. She

---

33. *The Bhagavad-Gita*, trans. Barbara Stoler Miller (New York: Bantam, 1986), II.44–47: "Be intent on action, / not on the fruit of actions; / avoid attraction to the fruits / and attachment to inaction!"

34. Nussbaum, *Fragility of Goodness*, 52, 63.

dies recanting nothing; but still she is torn by a conflict. Her virtue is, then, prepared to admit a contingent conflict. . . . From within her single-minded devotion to the dead, she recognizes the power of these contingent circumstances and yields to them. . . . This vulnerability in virtue, this ability to acknowledge the world of nature by mourning the constraints that it imposes on virtue, surely contributes to making her the more humanly rational and the richer of the two protagonists: both active and receptive, neither exploiter nor simply victim.[35]

Antigone's virtue and calling to care for her family remain remarkable—not *in spite of,* but *because of* the fact that they are rendered fragile by the lasting relevance of unchosen goods. She chooses *well* (which is not necessarily to say "correctly"), insofar as she strives toward a particular, limited end while remaining open to other callings that impinge on her.

## *(On not saving students from tragedy*

Nussbaum suggests that passive dispositions—vulnerability, openness to suffering, the ability to grieve and to be moved by the anguish of others—are essential to human flourishing and to humanistic education. Reading Greek tragedies can form dispositions that acknowledge and withstand conflicting callings, before and after decisions must be made. Teaching tragedy need not be the domain of departments of classics or English alone; psychology, anthropology, religion, philosophy, and history departments might teach tragedy as well. A course on medical ethics or leadership training could include *Agamemnon* or *Antigone* as required reading; vocational exploration programs might ask alumni to recall situations of real loss, inevitable conflict, and dispositions of forbearance when speaking with current students.[36] Educators may also need to model such attention to conflicting circumstances in their own lives, and to abide with students when they find themselves called in differing directions.

---

35. Ibid., 67.

36. For more on the positive value of tragedy in the classroom, and especially the significance of seeing it in performance, see David S. Cunningham, "Tragedy Without Evasion: Attending [to] Performances," in *Christian Theology and Tragedy: Theologians, Tragic Literature, and Tragic Theory,* ed. Kevin Taylor and Giles Waller (Farnham, England: Ashgate, 2011), 213–32.

Having said this, I am painfully aware of my own shortcomings as an educator in this regard. Too often I have tried to save students from tragic situations and the conflict of their callings rather than helping them into and through them. An example is Christina,[37] a politically progressive, spiritually attuned young woman who recently graduated from my institution. While on campus, she was involved with the Interfaith Understanding group and a member of Micah House, an intentional religious community of college students dedicated to servanthood, hospitality, community, and prayer. She wrote a senior project on cross-cultural ministry among area Burmese refugees, with whom she also worked as an intern through World Relief. She also completed an honors capstone project, constructing an original work of mixed-media art that played with images of sainthood, transgression, and family memories.

Her senior year introduced predictable questions: What would she "do" with her nonspecialized liberal arts degree? Who would she be outside of school? How would she live out her calling(s)? Having tapped into several intentional communities and grassroots political movements through coursework, extracurricular activities, and friendships, Christina felt drawn toward participation in radical politics and life in community after graduation. She was creative and innovative; she was also ambivalent at best about bureaucratic structures, ecclesial powers, and prescribed authority. She wanted to *make* community and help *forge* political resistance, rather than simply "finding" employment with a preexisting organization (no matter how progressive and committed to social justice).

At the same time, Christina also had done enough work with World Relief and similar organizations to know that slow, structural social transformation often requires the efforts of organizations and institutions. Moreover, both she and her parents felt that she should get a "real job" with enough income to begin paying back student loans. She struck what seemed like a good balance: she applied and was accepted into the Lutheran Volunteer Corps (LVC) "gap year" program. She would live in community and work with Hmong and Latino/a populations in Minneapolis/St. Paul—living simply, serving marginalized people faithfully, and also deferring student loans. She accepted the position but had ongoing reservations. This was

---

37. The student's name has been changed. I am here working from my own memories and notes, but I checked them against Christina's and received permission to tell her story with these details in a phone interview, April 22, 2015. Reviewed and approved by the Augustana Institutional Review Board, March 2015.

a "middle course," which, positively considered, could be seen as reflecting Aristotle's account of virtue as a mean between two extremes. But was she really just evading difficult decisions? Or, worse, was she enacting a too-easy reconciliation of opposing forces in her life that ought to remain in tension?

My own tendency, and perhaps that of other older adults, was to find ways of minimizing vocational conflict for Christina, whereas she insisted on enduring it. Near the final deadline for withdrawing from the LVC program in Minneapolis, Christina asked to accompany me on a day trip to the New Hope Catholic Worker Farm in LaMotte, Iowa, where another student and I had done research. We spent the day talking with the eight members of the Catholic Worker movement on the farm, learning about how they raise most of their own food, why they protest against fracking and the prison-industrial complex, and how daily prayer and weekly reconciliation services helped to sustain their relationships with one another and with God. For Christina, such homegrown communities live and work intentionally and authentically in ways that corporations and even non-profit organizations cannot. I assumed that, for Christina, the difference between the two paths forward amounted to a difference between limiting oneself to defined tasks and the sense of freedom and authenticity that comes with resisting formal organizational arrangements. I also assumed that Christina understood herself to be revisiting her choice between what she perceived as a year of ready-made tasks and obligations and the beginnings of a seemingly freer and radical life "off the grid."

I was wrong about Christina's dilemma on two accounts, as I began to learn on the car ride home. For her, it was not a choice between responsibility and realism, on the one hand, and freedom and nonconformity, on the other. Rather, she saw a difference in two different kinds of commitments—to a relatively faceless organization, or to individuals and individual responsibility (where her commitment would need to be deeper and more binding). Or again, whereas I saw her as nervous about assuming obligations in the workaday world, Christina was actually concerned that that "real world" would not ask enough of her. It seemed all too easy for her to do that work well; the more open-ended, interminable callings of grassroots politics and homegrown communities could not be clocked in and out of, and Christina felt called to such a challenge.

In addition, I was wrong in assuming that Christina was deliberating about a choice in the first place. Based on my assumptions, I felt the need to assure her that the pain of the decision could be mitigated by choosing the option that kept other options open, at least for some time. I suggested that working with LVC for a year wouldn't rule out the possibility of something like a Catholic Worker community in the future, whereas the inverse might not be true. But when I asked her, a week later, what she had decided, she replied matter-of-factly—"Oh, yeah, I'm still going to LVC"—suggesting that, for her, choosing between the two options wasn't really the point. Christina was less concerned about *whether* she would travel to Minneapolis for a gap year program, than with the attitudes and assumptions she would carry with her when she went. Would she reject (or put on hold, or even disparage) other "options," in order to convince herself that her decision was the right one? Alternatively, could she, would she, be able to leave for Minneapolis and fully invest in that program, while continuing to hear callings that she would be unable to answer at present?

Needless to say, the low-level heartache with which Christina left for LVC was nothing like the anguish that Agamemnon should have felt when, having sacrificed his daughter, he stepped back onto the warship. Still, Christina's choice carries something of the tragic structure that we have been exploring here. For example, it has certain parallels to Antigone's struggle: the decision to sacrifice one set of callings while still listening for and readying oneself to respond to them. Christina resolved to hold onto divergent callings, not as rejected alternatives or future possibilities, but as a way of doing the work that needed to be done—while also undergoing a painful but necessary expansion of her moral vision, accountability, passions, and affections.

## A *higher calling?*

Thus far, I have been making four claims. First, tragic conflict between divergent callings arises for college graduates and their mentors, no less than it does for ancient Greek heroes and heroines. Second, we often seek to ameliorate such conflict, especially by justifying decisions and "dis-remembering" past possibilities and lost loves. Third, we would be wise to resist these tendencies toward a too-easy resolution of conflict. Humanistic learning and moral maturity often require cultivating one's capacity to bear—rather than to "solve"—the grief, regret, and ambiguity that follow from willing (and loving) more than one thing. Finally, I have been claiming that stories showcasing vocational conflict—especially those complex and universal enough to be called *classics*—can help us to lean into and endure our multiple and sometimes conflicting callings. They help us to resist the temptation to size up and resolve every dilemma.

But we need to consider another possibility. What if such tragic conflicts among our callings really are mitigated, not by inauthentic resolutions of the will or by debasing unchosen options, but because one of these callings really does present itself as the clearest, highest, or most authorized? Would not clearly hearing and heeding such a "higher" calling save one from the anguish of choice, the vulnerability of virtue, and the burden of contingent circumstances? Aren't the conflicts in our callings less troubling to those who are most religiously attuned, or specially elected, or truly authentic?

To designate a calling as "religious" or "higher," and to profess to have clearly heard or finally found it, emphasizes one's openness to receiving a call from without. It thus accentuates the receptive, passive, and vulnerable dimensions of vocation, for which this chapter has been arguing. At the same time, such language can quickly render particular vocations impervious to the ongoing questions and claims of unbidden others. When I was in seminary, I heard classmates speak of all kinds of hardships and doubts about their capabilities for ordained ministry, often followed by: "But God has called me to the ministry, so who am I to argue?" This particular combination of being beleaguered and self-assured might be more pronounced among those called to lay or ordained ministry, but it also affects others called to various forms of meaningful, difficult work.[38]

How might one testify to these "higher" callings, and to the felt unity of purpose that they seem to imply, without undercutting one's receptivity to others (and perhaps to the Other) that these callings are meant to affirm? Here again, narratives can help (though they also introduce complexities of their own). When Jesus calls the disciples to put down their nets and follow him, they do so immediately, leaving every other obligation behind. While that order of priority seems clear enough, other stories explore the real variance and ambivalence that arise when called to the "religious" life. For example, the gospels also tell the story of the rich young man (Mark 10:17–31 and parallels); he has kept all the commandments, but Jesus tells

---

38. See the comments in chapter 1 of this volume, on the problem of discerning a calling to undertake work for which one has no real capacity.

him that he should also sell all his possessions, give the money to the poor, and then "come and follow me" (v. 21). The man is disheartened and goes away. While some interpretations blame the man for his lack of resolve or his attachment to material goods, the story indicates that Jesus loves the man rather than condemning him. Jesus also acknowledges the difficulty, and perhaps the *impossibility*, of following one's deepest calling outright— at least when doing so depends only on human effort. For those pulled in different directions, he suggests, only God can lead us out of the quandary (Mark 10:27).

Perhaps the most graphic depiction of conflicting callings in the Bible is the so-called binding of Isaac. According to Genesis 22, Abraham hears a command from God to travel to Mount Moriah and offer his own son as a burnt offering. The reader knows that it is a test (v. 1), and Abraham seems to pass it; he arises early, travels for three days, binds Isaac, and draws the knife. Only then is Abraham relieved of this "special" calling by the voice of an angel, who tells him to sacrifice a nearby ram instead (Gen. 22:12–13).

Here, then, is a story about a summons—directly from God—that comes into conflict with (what most people might describe as) a more universal call for parents to love and protect their children. Many Jewish and Christian interpretations of this passage tend to set aside the potential violence of the scene, commending Abraham's faith in God and willing obedience—even at the expense of his commitment to Isaac. While some support can be garnered for this interpretation (see Gen. 22:17), it seems to miss the true pathos (and deeper purpose) of the entire account. Admittedly, part of the reason Abraham becomes "the father of faith" is his success in passing this extraordinarily difficult test. But in order for him to pass it well, he must do more than choose God over Isaac. Abraham's worthiness lies in his refusal to whittle down his love for his son, his apparent lack of interest in convincing himself that he is acting rightly or in taking undue comfort from the divine origins of the command. His faith resides not only in making the "right" choice, but also in properly undergoing and *bearing* (rather than too easily setting aside) the accompanying anguish.

I am helped here by a famous interpretation of Genesis 22—that of nineteenth-century philosopher Søren Kierkegaard. In his creative retelling, Kierkegaard underscores how easy it is for overly familiar readers to hurry past the "fear and trembling" that Abraham must have felt in being called in two opposing directions—to love and protect his son and to sacrifice him in obedience to God. The story makes it relatively easy for readers to skip quickly from Abraham's state of being *before* this dreadful test, to his circumstances after he has passed it. "What is left out of the Abraham story," says Kierkegaard, "is the anguish."[39]

Part of the difficulty is the common assumption that a clear calling from God simply surpasses and supplants all other callings—suggesting that this prioritization allows Abraham to escape his dilemma. But this is too easy a resolution. As Kierkegaard argues, Abraham is caught between two very real claims on his life: the "ethical" (Abraham's calling to love Isaac) and "the religious" (his calling to obey God's command):

> The ethical expression for what Abraham did is that he was willing to murder Isaac; the religious expression is that he was willing to sacrifice Isaac; but in this contradiction lies the very anguish that can indeed make one sleepless; *and yet without that anguish Abraham is not the one he is.*[40]

Without that anguish—without faithfully abiding in the incongruity between two callings (ethical and religious, universal and specific)— Abraham's faith is nothing. An authentic response to God's special calling does not entail choosing one option, labeling it the "higher," and thereby convincing oneself that one has been faithful. Rather, it entails a genuine acknowledgment of the very real pulls in both directions—and then choosing to act anyway, with fear and trembling. Responding faithfully doesn't necessarily mean finding a place to stand with assurance; it may mean, rather, groping one's way forward in faith and trust.

Naming certain callings as "religious" or "higher" or "special" does not protect us from the immediate burden of choice and the ongoing hardship of our multiple responsibilities. Rather, part of answering a clear call from God—or from the depths of one's conscience—entails becoming increasingly aware of the whole field of conflicting callings, and then acting anyway. Even when wrestling with our higher callings, we need to maintain this level of awareness and struggle as we reflect on and discern our various vocations.

---

39. Søren Kierkegaard, *Fear and Trembling*, trans. Alastair Hannay (London: Penguin, 1985), 58.

40. Ibid., 60, emphasis added.

## *Open to joy*

In his book *God, Medicine, and Suffering*, Stanley Hauerwas suggests that "it is odd, but I think true, that most of us are almost as ill-prepared to receive joy as we are suffering."[41] Both the oddity and truth of that remark can be made clear by returning to the stories of this essay—those of Abraham, Agamemnon, Antigone, and Christina—and by considering how openness toward conflicting callings might also become an opportunity to cultivate dispositions of joy.[42]

Notwithstanding all his attention to anguish, Kierkegaard surprisingly asserts that the real marvel of Abraham's faith is his readiness to hear the angel's subsequent commandment *not* to sacrifice Isaac. Abraham remains ready to receive Isaac back, "with more joy than the first time."[43] Kierkegaard explains that most people would have to give up loving Isaac in order to sacrifice him; it follows that they "would have been at a loss had [they] got Isaac back again." Or again: "What Abraham found the easiest of all would for [them] be hard, to find joy again in Isaac!"[44] The real miracle of faith is not the unwavering resolve to choose one thing, especially if that necessitates minimizing our love for whatever we have convinced ourselves to do without. "Faith" is, rather, the hope against hope—something closer to reflective, delicate trust—that even those desires that *cannot* be fulfilled, even those callings that *cannot* be heeded, are worthy of one's love. Abraham loves two seemingly irreconcilable others (God and Isaac); he listens for two callings. Only thus—and by acting without putting all his trust in his own action—does he ready himself for joy.

Nearly the same point is made in Nussbaum's discussion of Greek tragedy, despite the very different culture that generated those stories. We observed that Agamemnon fails as a tragic hero precisely because he curbs and "contains" the pain generated by the conflicts in his callings. Assuring himself of having chosen correctly, he puts all his "faith" in his own impeccable will, leaving himself practically no space to respond to the claims of

---

41. Stanley Hauerwas, *God, Medicine, and Suffering* (Grand Rapids, MI: Eerdmans, 1990), xiv.

42. For Aristotle's reflections on *eudaimonia* as the highest good, and how this final end includes (but is not synonymous with) worldly pleasure and good luck, see his *Nicomachean Ethics*, I.1, 7–11 and VII.11–14.

43. Kierkegaard, *Fear and Trembling*, 65.

44. Ibid.

his daughter and others. He remains comfortable and contented, failing to embrace the sorrow and struggle of the trial;[45] but this "comfortable" condition leaves him much less expectant, hopeful, and capable of receiving joy. Having reduced his child to a lamb for slaughter, he would have been at a loss to get her back—even if the gods were to have permitted it. Antigone was no less confident in her decision to bury her brother; but in contrast to Agamemnon, she does not absolve herself of the conflict. Through her own imaginative double movement, she "remains ready to risk and to sacrifice her [own] ends."[46] This opens her to deeper levels of suffering, but also makes her capable of receiving more joy. In her vulnerability, there is something joyful—not merely cheerful or self-satisfied, but a deeper and more authentic form of contentment. She might even be described as *ecstatic*, in that word's original sense: transcending one's own needs and desires, being grasped instead by something beyond oneself.

## Stories for an unscripted future

A year after graduation, vocational conflict remains for Christina—as does her eagerness to find true joy. In a recent phone conversation, she spoke of being torn in various directions and the difficulties this creates. "I don't think I can do it all," Christina confessed, referring to various commitments to her work with marginalized groups, to being intentional with her community, and to living simply—as well as hanging onto the hopes that were "suspended" (her word) when she moved to Minneapolis. She observes that a perfectly balanced life seems something of a pipedream, concluding that "I don't want to be a 'well rounded person' if that means working forty hours a week, having close friendships, doing my art, and everything else—I just don't believe that all of that is possible."[47] While it might seem that Christina is thus narrowing her moral scope by setting certain callings aside, I think it is truer to say that she is still facing a complex of potentially conflicting vocations while resisting the temptation to imagine that she can "do it all." But Christina is also aware that duties shouldn't be fulfilled only to be dutiful, nor does everyone enjoy serving others simply because their needs are great. She admits that she doesn't

---

45. Nussbaum, *Fragility of Goodness*, 36.

46. Ibid., 67.

47. Phone interview, April 22, 2015, edited slightly for clarity.

always enjoy her work and that she increasingly takes those feelings seriously. While serving others is arduous, so is discerning what truly makes one happy. In Christina's words, "this is learning humility, too."[48] I would add that Christina's readiness for joy—and the joy itself—are more capacious and durable, exactly *because* she is currently working through multiple conflicting callings.

Christina's story—as well as Greek tragedies, biblical narratives, and the stories of other students and graduates—can help us examine the promise of "vocational growth" that accompanies the conflicts in our callings. But stories such as these also pose a number of risks. Narratives are always told backwards, after the fact; thus, insofar as life is lived forwards, vocational stories can sometimes evade the messiness and the conflicts among our callings. Unlike the stories that we tell about it, the actual process of vocational reflection and discernment often proceeds without a clear sense of beginning, middle, and end.[49]

Still, through their variety and their breadth of reference, certain stories can help. The tragedies of Agamemnon and Antigone, as well as the testing of Abraham, help illuminate dispositions of patience, vulnerability, and responsibility—experiences of sorrow and of hope against hope. They belong not exclusively to philosophy, literature, and religion departments, but to intellectual inquiry as a whole. More contemporary "postmodern" stories that work between genres, or that play with narrative fissures, can also help us with the process of vocational reflection and discernment; we may come to identify with characters who actively resist being "scripted" in a single way.[50] Such reflections are important for all students across all departments and fields, because they are themselves preparing to enter an increasingly unscripted future.

Ideally, the undergraduate years will allow students to become acquainted not only with classic and contemporary tales, but also with the half-finished and often conflictual stories of their own mentors and of the students who have gone before them. If so, these students will be experiencing vocation at its fullest—and cultivating the dispositions that make human beings the ambiguous, fragile, and beautiful creatures they are.

---

48. Ibid.

49. Paul Ricoeur, *Oneself as Another,* trans. Kathleen Blamey (Chicago: University of Chicago Press, 1992), 160–61; compare MacIntyre, *After Virtue,* 214–16.

50. A favorite of mine to teach is Jeanette Winterson, *Oranges Are Not the Only Fruit* (New York: Grove Press, 1985).

# 3

## Called to Tell Our Stories

### THE NARRATIVE STRUCTURE OF VOCATION

*Shirley Hershey Showalter*

*We tell ourselves stories in order to live.*
—JOAN DIDION

IT'S 6 A.M. in Punxsutawney, Pennsylvania, and meteorologist Phil Connors, played by Bill Murray, reaches over to turn off the alarm. He opens his eyes and hears these words: "It's Groundhog Day!"[1]

I suspect that most educators, as well as many students, have sometimes felt as though they were living inside this classic film—stuck like Phil Connors in never-ending déjà vu. Teachers may be particularly susceptible to the theme of repetitive and mundane work, because their expectation for meaning is high. They know that other professions offer more economic rewards; consequently, they hope—even expect—that certain psychological and spiritual benefits will compensate for the occasional "sameness" of their experience. Students, too, can sometimes experience undergraduate education as something of a time warp, in which they feel as though each new semester brings only more of the same. Students and teachers want to believe in the inherent value of undergraduate education; thus, when they are no longer sure about that worth (or when they are unable to experience it fully), they suffer twice. This vulnerability can lead to boredom, cynicism, or even depression.

When our stories seem "stuck," the answer is not to retreat, but to create more and better ones. When stories connect educators and students to each other, they strengthen the vocations of both. Vocation, with its

---

1. *Groundhog Day*, directed by Harold Ramis, featuring Bill Murray and Andie MacDowell (Columbia Pictures, 1993). www.imdb.com/title/tt0107048/?ref_=ttfc_fc_tt (accessed March 2, 2016).

meaning derived from the Latin *vocare* (to call), sets up multiple stories by definition: it requires a call-er, a call-ee, and a purpose or goal. Applied across the curriculum, vocation consists of stories—our own stories, student stories, and stories about our disciplines. Out of these connected stories arise new narrative identities; these in turn can help us to hear new and renewed callings.

This chapter considers the significance of story and storytelling for framing conversations about calling and vocation. The approach extends across the academic disciplines, in the sense that it is not limited to those fields that explicitly use narrative as a primary element of their content and pedagogical method. After some initial reflections on the nature of story in general, the chapter examines three types of stories relevant to all classrooms and to all teachers, regardless of discipline: the teacher's story, the students' stories, and the story that is created by the classroom encounter. The goal of this chapter, then, is to demonstrate the degree to which more conscious attention to story can help to develop greater connection to larger questions of meaning and purpose, and can simultaneously invigorate the teaching and learning life. In addition, as educators and students become more reflective about their particular vocational journeys, they become better at helping others find and tell their own stories as well.

## *How stories work: some basic observations*

Consider, again, Phil Connors and his vicious cycle of repetition, reaction, and remorse in the movie *Groundhog Day*. Every day is February 2 and it begins with Sonny and Cher singing "I Got You, Babe." After the initial confusion and shock of daily sameness wear off, Phil tries to make use of his circumstances to pursue various forms of hedonism, defiance, and deception. He uses the knowledge that he gains to put himself in a better position to get what he wants from those he encounters, only to discover that this strategy seldom works out as he had planned. Many characters teach him lessons, but the one who helps him the most is one who never says a word: the old man whom Phil passes by, over and over again. (He doesn't actually have name in the film, though Phil variously calls him "Pop" or "Dad" or "Father.") Phil finally learns to see "Pop" as a human being when the man collapses on the street. Taking advantage of the repetition of his days, Phil tries everything: feeding him a good meal, taking him to the hospital, and generally making use of his odd circumstances—the fact that he must continuously relive the same day—to try to save the old man from death. Phil had claimed to be a god because of his power to start over and erase all his mistakes every day, but in this case his powers fail him. Only when he admits defeat—bending over the man as he takes his last breath—does a new story dawn in him.[2]

When he accepts death as his teacher, Phil finds the key that unlocks his own "stuck" story. Phil's heart is changed by this encounter and by listening to the stories of everyone in the town (and especially to that of his producer, Rita). We know his transformation is complete when—in place of his usual hatred of winter, of small towns, and of Groundhog Day itself—Phil offers a new story to his television audience. "When Chekhov saw the long winter," says Phil on his final Groundhog Day, "he saw a winter bleak and dark and bereft of hope. Yet we know that winter is just another step in the cycle of life. But standing here among the people of Punxsutawney and basking in the warmth of their hearths and hearts, I couldn't imagine a better fate than a long and lustrous winter."[3]

Phil has learned one of the deepest and best lessons of life: that we can compose, reframe, and reimagine our own stories. He emerges from his time warp, grateful for the love of his beautiful boss Rita Hanson, as well as that of many others in the town he had previously despised. He also recognizes freedom in the strangest of places: human mortality. His encounter with death breaks the control that hedonism and egoism had held over his life. Moreover, he no longer focuses his career ambitions on finding a way to leave small towns forever and head for the lights of the big city. He's still a weatherman, but he has come to view his work less as a career and more as a vocation.

Spiritual and philosophical teachers of many traditions have used this film in their sermons and meditations. At the base of this story stands an ancient spiritual ritual of psychic death and rebirth. In fact, out of precisely this kind of movement—from life to death and back to life—arose the classic structure of the narrative. In his *Poetics*, Aristotle analyzed the structure of tragedy, and specifically the structure of its story (plot, *mythos*):

Now a whole is that which has beginning, middle, and end....
A well-constructed plot, therefore, cannot either begin or end at

---

2. Lisa Schnelbach, "*Groundhog Day* Succeeds by Breaking the Rules of Every Genre," *Tor.Com*, February 2, 2014, www.tor.com/blogs/2014/02/groundhog-day-bill-murray-time-travel-spirituality-romantic-comedy (accessed March 5, 2015).

3. *Groundhog Day*.

any point one likes; beginning and end in it must be of the forms just described. Again: to be beautiful, a living creature, and every whole made up of parts, must not only present a certain order in its arrangement of parts, but also be of a certain definite magnitude. Beauty is a matter of size and order.[4]

If story is indeed universal, embedded in nearly every human activity (and therefore not just the province of literature departments or humanities divisions), what role does it play in helping both teachers and students to discern their vocations?

To answer that question, we can turn to the emerging movement focusing on the *narrative study of lives*. "The central idea in this movement is that human lives are cultural texts that can be interpreted as stories."[5] Psychologist Dan McAdams has studied the lives of Americans whom he describes as highly *generative*. He defines that term as "the adult's concern for and commitment to promoting the welfare and development of future generations."[6] The way generative people tell the stories of their lives creates a *narrative identity*; that identity can have lasting consequences on the lives, and narratives, of educators and of students.[7]

Story builds upon and reinforces the notion of a common humanity. Story therefore can be found in every discipline, and all of us construct stories from our earliest experiences in school until our last.[8] The question "What did you learn in school today?" is the invitation to a story.

---

4. Aristotle, *Rhetoric and Poetics*, 1426–38, English trans. Ingram Bywater, Modern Library Edition (New York: Random House, 1954), 233. Many writers have elaborated on Aristotle's three-part structure, attempting to show the universality of certain stories. Joseph Campbell describes twelve segments of the hero's journey; professor and screenwriter Tristine Rainer develops nine; Parker Palmer favors the four seasons; and dramatist Gustav Fretag places five sections into his pyramid structure.

5. Dan McAdams, *The Redemptive Self: Stories Americans Live By* (New York Oxford University Press, 2006), 14.

6. Ibid., 4.

7. For further reflections on the relationship between narrative and vocation, see Douglas V. Henry, "Vocation and Story: Narrating Self and World," in Cunningham, ed., *At This Time*, 165–91.

8. For an overview of narrative across the social science disciplines, for example, see www.colorado.edu/ling/CRIL/Volume20_Issue1/paper_MERRILL.pdf (accessed August 15, 2015). Neuroscience findings about brain structure are filtering into the communication fields. See Scott Schwertly, "The Secret to Activating Your Audience's Brain," March 4, 2015, https://blog.slideshare.net/2015/03/04/the-secret-to-activating-your-audiences-brain/ (accessed

Both students and teachers will learn more if they become proficient in answering that question. And throughout their careers, they will be asked to do so—first in the form of dinner-table conversation and handwritten essays, and later in the form of applications, lectures, speeches, courtroom arguments, and research. Inside the narratives we construct are the elements that can guide us into teaching and learning, into leadership, and into a life of continual growth from which we never "retire." And, as Phil Connors discovered in *Groundhog Day*, when we are stuck, we can learn to tell our stories anew; as a result, we have greater capacity to help others renarrate their lives as well.

## *The educator's story*

Every teacher stands in front of a class as the result of a set of stories. The stories contain clues to the big questions that students often have, as they examine the teacher's words and evaluate them against the open or closed expression on the teacher's face: "Who are you? Where did you come from? Why are you doing this?" This scrutiny takes place at a particular time and in a particular context. Teachers get to tell some version of their life stories every time they step into a classroom. Anthropologist Mary Catherine Bateson says that self-introduction is itself a creative genre, in which we can compose short stories using different emphases for different contexts.[9]

The first time I stood in a classroom, fresh out of college in 1970 (at the very peak of the Vietnam War), I introduced myself as "a member of a group that believes it is better to accept death than to kill another human being." I didn't expect to say those words, and I was unprepared for the thickness in my throat and moisture in my eyes as I spoke them. My teaching story was new and not quite assimilated; but I never forgot the stillness in the room. I learned that introductions had the potential for telling bits of story that set the stage for more questions and more stories. I became thoughtful and intentional about beginning the class with very short stories about my background, my values, and my desires for the class.

---

March 11, 2015). Data stimulates two centers in the brain (Wernicke's Area and Broka's Area, both related to language). Stories stimulate those same areas but add five others: the visual cortex, olfactory cortex, auditory cortex, motor cortex, and sensory cortex and cerebellum.

9. Mary Catherine Bateson, *Willing to Learn: Passages of Personal Discovery* (Hanover, NH: Steerforth Press, 2004), 66–74.

As I moved into higher education, I became aware of an unspoken prohibition against telling personal stories in the classroom. Literature professors, who teach stories, have more license than most; however, all educators have certain opportunities for legitimate storytelling, and many students crave knowing teachers' stories, told well. In fact, in the absence of information about a professor, imaginative students often enjoy making up their own stories. Like nature, the classroom abhors a vacuum; a "narrative vacuum" can be created when professors focus solely on content, or when students are expected to limit their attention to ideas and facts. Course content can fill a mind, and sometimes open it; but the right story can *transform* it.

What stories are most important to the vocation of the teacher and the student? First, educators can tell the story of how the subject first engaged them. Second, they can tell the story of why they teach—including a description of those who influenced them and the intellectual desires that were engaged in them, and even the challenges they faced, while they were still students.

Both of these types of stories have influenced my own teaching. I have sometimes encouraged students to think about their own relationship to a particular theme by inviting students to recall a childhood memory regarding that topic. Regardless of field of study, a teacher can ask students about stories of previous experiences—whether to honor them or to uncover hidden mythologies. Regardless of their majors, most students discover some past connection to the subject of the class. Good questions can evoke surprising bits of self previously hidden in students; they can also create classroom "buzz" as a community of learners begins to form.

## Stories told in many ways

Not all stories need to be voiced. Like an author who creates a backstory for each character, a professor may choose an invisible story as a guide to tone of voice, attitude toward students—even choice of wardrobe and posture. I never told my students, for example, about Mrs. Lochner, my sixth-grade teacher; but when I wrote my own memoir (in which I was deliberately searching for early signs of my own calling), I discovered that her physical and intellectual presence had left a deep impression.

If Shakespeare had observed Mrs. Lochner, he would have said she "bestrode our narrow world like a Colossus." A tall woman, she wore her gray hair pulled back in an attractive bun, which on her looked regal rather than plain. I noticed her carriage, first of all. It wasn't haughty, but it was not humble either. I sensed a way of being in the world that rooted down deep and then spread out wide, an embracing stance that would not bend with the wind, but merely sway gracefully and rhythmically.[10]

Educators create their narrative identities in part from their observations of other teachers, just as students are looking to them for pieces of stories they wish to adapt into their own. The unconscious impressions may be as important—or more important—than the conscious ones.

Academe has some conscious traditions that can flower into narrative if we think more intentionally about them. For example, Ph.D. graduation parties often celebrate intellectual genealogy, either formally or informally. A major professor may even go so far as to give the gift of a "family tree" to the newly minted doctor, showing the relationship of teacher–student influence that goes all the way back to an eminent pathfinder in the field such as Charles Darwin in biology or Karl Marx in economics or Marie Curie in chemistry. (Did the inclusion of Curie seem a little strange? Rachel Shteir has illustrated the too often patriarchal nature of this practice.[11])

One of the narratives that teachers owe to their students is the story of the discipline itself (at least in overview), as well as an account of the professors, authors, and other mentors who have influenced this particular teacher. The purpose of telling these stories is not to create clones of the professor, but rather to make invisible influences more visible— and therefore to make one's theoretical grounding more transparent. Undergraduates often have little or no comprehension of what forces go into the making of the subject before them.

Teachers' stories need not be long. In fact, many of the stories I remember from my own professors were short, but they had a disproportionately great influence. Little tidbits about research or their own graduate study

---

10. Shirley Hershey Showalter, *Blush: A Mennonite Girl Meets a Glittering World* (Harrisonburg, VA: Herald Press, 2013), 117.

11. Rachel Shteir, "Taking the Men Out of Mentoring," *The Chronicle Review, The Chronicle of Higher Education*, January 23, 2015, B20. This article offers a scathing critique of the way gender and hierarchy interact in higher education, "which, for all its promise of social mobility, ultimately remains both dynastic and as stratified as *Downton Abbey*." The author describes herself as mentorless and points out that many women academics share this plight.

or famous people they have known in the field—these apparently minor details made it possible to catch glimpses of the initial excitement that attracted my teachers to their fields and initiated the strange quest that had held their attention for years.

Other times, something pulls us out of ordinary time and a story takes center stage. For example, I was taking a class on American politics as a graduate student at the University of Texas in Austin when former president Lyndon Johnson died. My professor, Elspeth Rostow—who was married to Johnson's national security advisor, Walt Rostow—met the class as usual and asked if we wanted to talk about the president. I was no great admirer of Johnson, but this invitation taught me more than the standard lesson plan for the day would have. As a pacifist opposed to Johnson's actions in expanding the war, and very aware that Walt Rostow had advised the president to take them, I listened intently for clues about how good intentions went wrong. My professor wasn't in a confessional mode, but I recognized in that moment that what we call *history* happens because real people with real stories either read or misread the story of their times.

I don't even remember any specific words Professor Rostow spoke. Instead, I remember the faraway look that came into her eye when she talked about living in Washington and being part of two presidencies. From that one look I could imagine her as a young bride interested in politics and married to a political economist at MIT who joined the administration in a time of supreme optimism about America's place in the world. I sensed not only sadness about losing Lyndon Johnson, but perhaps grief also for those vanished days of supreme national self-confidence.

## TMI: too much information

Clearly, there is such a thing as too much personal storytelling in the classroom. If stories substitute for the hard work of content preparation, students quickly lose interest in the topic and respect for the professor. Students use the (usually pejorative) term *war stories* to describe the kinds of lengthy digressions into the intricate details of personal life that are sometimes taken by an ill-prepared or bombastic teacher; these can, of course, often come at the expense of the actual subject matter. Good stories should always draw the student's attention *to* the subject, not away from it. They should be used as judiciously as PowerPoint slides or video clips.

Postmodern theory instructs us in other dangers of storytelling. Stories often reinforce dominant power structures, sometimes without the conscious knowledge of either speakers or listeners. Details that don't fit into a storyteller's intended master narrative are often dropped. Other details might be exaggerated, while shadows, doubts, and ambiguities might be expunged. One should listen to stories—both one's own and others'—with a "hermeneutics of suspicion,"[12] and should bring an especially critical perspective to stories that contain no ambiguity or shadow. As Mark Edwards reminds us, the first-person narrative should not necessarily be taken at face value; we need to be self-aware and self-critical in assessing our own accounts of our lives, and those of others.[13]

What other hazards should educators avoid? The classroom is not the place for therapy, especially not the teacher's therapy. That doesn't mean that discrete mention of a personal crisis is never appropriate. In fact, if a spouse is dying, or one's house burned down, or a friend killed himself, or the instructor is facing a divorce, a cancer diagnosis, or clinical depression, then students may well be owed some kind of explanation—and in certain cases, follow-up reports about how and why the class will either proceed as usual or need to be altered in some way. The focus, again, is on the class itself and on student learning. Students will treat necessary information with respect when they themselves feel respected.

My own teaching narrative contains one especially large shadow. Like Dante, when I was midway through the journey of life, I found myself in a dark wood, having lost the straight pathway.[14] More specifically, I experienced a brief period of clinical depression in the middle of my career. I had to dig deeper for the big picture of my life in order to reconnect with the meaning I knew was there: I understood ruefully why these experiences characterized Dante's experience of the *Inferno*. My dean reassigned two classes to others and I continued teaching one class. I took the risk on the first night of telling the students that I was not feeling well (on a small campus, they knew that I had dropped two classes), that I was getting

---

12. This phrase, usually attributed to Paul Ricoeur, has influenced thinking about narrative throughout the academy, most especially in the humanities. See, for example, Paul Ricoeur, *Freud and Philosophy: An Essay on Interpretation* (New Haven, CT: Yale University Press, 1970), 32–36.

13. Mark Edwards Jr., *Religion on Our Campuses: A Professor's Guide to Communities, Conflicts, and Promising Conversations* (New York: Palgrave Macmillan, 2006), 72.

14. Dante Alighieri, *The Inferno*, trans. Michael Palma (New York: Norton, 2002), 3.

help, and that I loved this subject and this course. I would place my commitment to them and to our work together as my primary goal for the semester.

After that, I never mentioned my own health again—until the last ten minutes of the last class, when I thanked them for helping me recover myself by paying attention to texts, by writing with care and insight, and by showing interest and concern for each other in the class. Using quotes from the books we had studied and other favorite poems of my own, I told them what I had learned from them. I felt a sacred trust—and the students felt it also, as many of them said in notes they wrote after the class ended.

Years later, a number of students have told me they remember this class; now, of course, they have more of their own stories. One of them, Karin Larson Krisetya, became a teacher, and now works in the Philippines. She recently reflected on the impact of the course:

> Learning, suddenly, had a greater purpose than simply to understand the big ideas of the world; learning together could heal. I saw what a community looks like in education. As a community we could serve each other. That epiphany has shaped the rest of my life and the way I live out my own understanding of vocation. Without it, I could not be the teacher that I am today, creating learning spaces, vibrant with the excitement of discovering the unknown together.[15]

## *The students' stories*

I have always assumed that every student is taking my class for a reason, and that part of my task as a professor is to move that reason from its previous location on Maslow's hierarchy of needs to the next level.[16] Often, for example, my opening ritual includes the question, "Why are you taking this class?" I expect some of the answers to be "because it's required" or "my advisor suggested it" or "it meets at 10 A.M."

---

15. E-mail correspondence from Karen Larson Krisetya, a teacher living in Manila, Philippines, used by permission, August 18, 2015.

16. Abraham Maslow, *A Theory of Human Motivation* (Eastford, CT: Martino Fine Books, 1943, 2013), 67. Also at https://docs.google.com/file/d/0B-5-JeCa2Z7hNjZ lNDNhOTEtMWNkYiooYmFhLWI3YjUtMDEyMDJkZDExNWRm/edit (accessed August 16, 2015).

Most professors teach undergraduates who have no intention of majoring in their subject. Students may have had negative experiences with previous classes in the subject, or they may be taking the class only because it is required. These students can be among the hardest to engage in class discussion. Their sullen expressions, preference for the back row, surreptitious use of smartphones, and churlish answers when called upon make them seem immune to listening to stories. I've had a few such students during twenty-one years in the college classroom. Some of them I had to simply let go of, assuming that some other professor in some other discipline would have to light the spark. Some, however, opened up a little over time. And, at least once, a miracle occurred.

In an introductory literature and writing class intended to help students make the transition from high school to college, I assigned Chaim Potok's *The Chosen*,[17] thinking it would provide characters with whom they might identify. I asked students what role silence played in the education of the main character, Danny, whose father decides not to speak to him. One student, "Jeff," who had not volunteered to speak in class, wrote in his journal that he could not address this subject. To understand him, he told me, "You will have to read between the lines."

I took that statement as both challenge and invitation. Jeff was not an English major; he didn't say a lot in class. When he showed up for an individual advising session, however, I told him I wanted to learn to read between his lines. I wanted to know what he knew about silence. Slowly, haltingly, he told me the story of how he had lost his father in a boating accident while the family had been on vacation eleven years earlier. At age seven he had become "the man of the family." Where his father's voice had been, there was silence. He had not recognized the depth of his loss until he read about the silence between Reb Saunders and his son Danny in *The Chosen*. As I listened, I searched for words that might reduce his pain and ignite his calling. I tried to help him see that his silent suffering hadn't been in vain. I pointed out that, alongside his preparation for his chosen career in engineering, he had the capacity, like Danny, to do his work with a compassionate heart—made stronger and truer by the silence of suffering.

---

17. Chaim Potok, *The Chosen* (New York: Ballantine Books, 1967).

## Moving beyond the classroom

An educator's office provides abundant opportunities for constructing, offering, and examining narratives. Consider these office-centered roles just for starters: course selection, advising on plan of study in the major, and advising students about applications for future opportunities (graduate school, international study, or postgraduate awards). In conversations about these important decisions, mentors and advisors will do well to ask questions—listening carefully for signs of a student's most passionate interests, hopes, and fears. Educators may choose to tell bits of their own narratives in order to identify with students, encourage them, or challenge them to build a larger framework for their thoughts and plans.

Applications for postgraduate opportunities provide an especially important avenue for students to tell their stories. These programs typically require applicants to write essays on why they want to enter a particular field, attend a particular institution, or embark on a certain adventure (such as teaching English abroad or interning at a major firm). Professors can help students recognize that these essays are opportunities for telling the right story and telling it extremely well. When faced with the blank page, students often fall back on old habits; they want to begin with birth and make one long list of their accomplishments. Or, leaping to the other extreme, they may reach for abstract polysyllabic platitudes in the hope of sounding profound. Writing this type of essay—essentially a short memoir—demands the same kind of reflection and discernment in a young person that memoir writing requires at any age.

What single moments have guided me? What questions refuse to let me go? These are the kinds of questions that can elicit deeper stories. Some students may want to take recourse in a narrative that deprives themselves of agency ("I did nothing; God does it all"); but they can also be nudged toward a deeper examination of self and a more complex narrative without abandoning their religious beliefs. For some, what may be most lacking is unfettered time, as well as a free and ordered space, for thinking through these matters. In some cases, introducing meditation, yoga, or practices from the Ignatian or Benedictine traditions may give students new ways to access their stories, and fresh language for the quest. With or without religiously based practices, however, students all have access to their own experiences of wonder, fear, and shame: they have a trove of memories, which may well contain the kind of authentic story that helps them discover a new layer of selfhood. Nothing is more electrifying to the reader than happening upon an insight that surprised the writer. Socrates's time-less dictum says it best: "The unexamined life is not worth living"—and an unexamined essay is not worth submitting.

Does every student seeking to write an application for graduate school need to become initiated into deep spiritual formation? No. But every student who understands the means others have used over the centuries to get closer to the answer to the question "Why do I exist?" or "What is my purpose?" will at least begin to recognize when he or she is getting closer to (or further from) a truthful answer to that question.

Writing the short memoir essay is also a skill. It can become an opportunity for self-discovery, clarifying purpose, and connecting to the needs in the world. It demands thorough interior and exterior exploration, followed by careful word choice, structure, and judicious use of metaphor and illustration. Needless to say, it can also become an opportunity for manipulation—guessing what the judges are looking for and serving up stories designed to confirm whatever they believe and admire. Stories are not morally neutral; they are used every day, not only to help others develop and grow, but also to sell dubious products and to advance dangerous causes. When students find themselves tempted to create a false self for instrumental purposes, mentors need to help them revisit and revise these accounts, so that what is unique and praiseworthy about a particular individual is not replaced with a mere façade.

## Stories arise when others ask questions

Another frequently overlooked opportunity for narrative awareness is the academic advising session. Professor Shirley Roels recounts a time when she noticed something in the body language of a student and asked him a question that may have changed his life:

> In late October, "Jack" entered my office for the standard 15-minute academic advising session. My task was to review his academic plan for the spring semester, but Jack looked troubled. So I asked, "Is something bothering you about these choices?" Jack said he wasn't sure he wanted to be a business major.
>
> It had been the family presumption when he left his small-town home for college that he would major in business and then return home to help his father in leading the family jewelry store. But Jack said, "When I came to college and began to take economics courses

as part of my business major, I learned that I love economics. I think I want to go to graduate school in economics; but that would be so disappointing to my father." So I asked, "Have you discussed this with your dad?" He hadn't.

Several months later I saw Jack in the classroom hallway with a smile on his face. He said, "I asked my dad about this. He said it's OK if I want to go to graduate school in economics instead."[18]

The two questions asked by Professor Roels—"Is something bothering you about these choices?" and "Have you discussed this with your dad?"— freed a young man to see possibilities in his life that he had foreclosed prematurely. His story opened up because the questions removed his certainty that his parents had already written the script of his vocation. Asking questions—real ones, open-ended ones, like the ones described here[19]— can be the greatest gift one person can give to the narrative of another. If the goal is for the student to develop a worthy and viable narrative, this is much more likely to arise from the kinds of inner examination stimulated by good questions, than from the mere projection of someone else's story onto the student, or from well-meaning but generic advice dispensed from a supply of bromides on the shelf. It took me too long to discover the power of asking questions instead of merely offering potential solutions.[20]

While some disciplines make significant use of stories, not all teachers in those disciplines are skilled in the art of soliciting and using *student* stories. At the same time, professors in a wide range of disciplines— including those that do not usually rely heavily on narrative—may find themselves quite adept at bringing students' stories into the classroom.

18. Shirley Roels, personal correspondence from February 9, 2015, slightly edited.

19. Such questions might also include those suggested by the structure Parker Palmer adapted for teachers called the "clearness committee": a two-hour process in which one person describes a challenge in his or her life and other people ask open, honest questions that allow the person to hear his or her own inner wisdom. Parker Palmer, *The Courage to Teach* (San Francisco: Jossey-Bass, 1996), 152–56.

20. I am grateful to have been mentored by author and business leader Max DePree. While I was president of Goshen College, I taught a class (influenced by psychologist Robert Coles) called "The Literature of Spiritual Reflection and Social Action." One of the texts was DePree's *Leadership Is an Art* (East Lansing, MI: Michigan State University Press, 1987); the author agreed to visit the class and take questions from the students, and later agreed to serve as my mentor. He has never told me what to do, but he has asked a lot of questions. Some of his favorites are: Who do you intend to be? What makes you weep? What do you owe to others and to yourself?

The use of the journal—something I first encountered as a faculty leader of student groups (from many majors) studying and serving abroad—can be a teaching tool in any discipline. Student conferences and advising sessions (which are also available to all faculty, even when not required) can provide many opportunities to listen, ask questions, and demonstrate the connections between a course's content and the meaning and purpose of the student's own life—something that students may not yet see for themselves.

## *Our story: the story of* this *classroom and* this *subject*

In a good class, the teacher and the students together are sharing stories, even as they learn new things about the subject; they are gathering insight into the great questions "Who are you?" and "What do you love?" In a *great* class, the professor guides the students into a place of awe—not necessarily by being a great personal storyteller, but by listening to the story told by the subject matter of the course, and by helping students listen to and learn from that story.

By now the example of Nobel Laureate geneticist Barbara McClintock's phrase "a feeling for the organism" has become familiar even to nonscientists. The phrase has stuck because it's a mini-story—a story about how passion and precision can be combined in a calling. McClintock's intense degree of observation was described by her first biographer, Evelyn Fox Keller, as "intimate knowledge" and as "mystic" knowing. Keller compares McClintock's epistemology to that of other scientists influenced by Eastern philosophy, especially to physicists Niels Bohr and Robert Oppenheimer.[21] Within this way of doing science, a relationship between the organism and the observer is paramount, and each such relationship is different from all others. McClintock herself described her "feeling" for corn by using the idea of story: "I start with the seedling, and I don't want to leave it. I don't feel I really know the story if I don't watch the plant all the way along. So I know every plant in the field. I know them intimately, and I find it a great pleasure to know them."[22] Scientists are still contending over the

---

21. Evelyn Fox Keller, *A Feeling for the Organism: The Life and Work of Barbara McClintock* (New York: Freeman, 1983), 198–204. See also the reflections on McClintock's work in Henry, "Vocation and Story," 184–85.

22. McClintock, as quoted by Keller, *A Feeling for the Organism*, 198.

McClintock legacy,[23] but the idea that science and love are compatible will likely continue to be associated with McClintock because of the felicity of the phrase Keller chose to highlight: "a feeling for the organism."

## Connections between the teacher and the topic

The face of the professor is a place where students look to understand what it means to love a subject. In moments of exquisite attention, a correspondence between the story of the inner life of the teacher and the story of the inner life of the subject lights up the room. This can be true of a bird's nest, a rock, a work of art, a history, a holy book, a poem, or a doctor's rounds in the hospital.

I remember, for example, the story told to me by one of my mentors at Goshen College, Mary Eleanor Bender, a professor of French. She said she pauses at the threshold of each class she enters to remind herself of her calling to teach and of the sacred place of the classroom, as well as the history and culture of the French as represented in their language. When she said these words, her face seemed to be illuminated from within. That image of her face as she stood for a moment in a doorway—intentionally slowing down instead of rushing into the classroom—has stayed with me all my life.

So, too, the great teacher Jaime Escalante looked upon his subject of mathematics with awe. He was able to locate a story that served two purposes: it illustrated how important certain concepts are to the human capacity to comprehend the mysteries of math, and it connected the discovery of a critical concept to the teenagers in his classroom itself. In the movie about Escalante and his students, *Stand and Deliver,* one of the most memorable scenes occurs near the beginning. Escalante (played by Edward James Olmos) tells an origin story for the subject that completely transforms the way students look at math: "Did you know that neither the Greeks nor the Romans were capable of using the concept of zero? It was your ancestors, the Mayans, who first contemplated the zero. The absence of value. True story. You *burros* have math in your blood."[24]

---

23. See Carla Kierns's review of Nathaniel C. Comfort, *The Tangled Field: Barbara McClintock's Search for the Patterns of Genetic Control* (Cambridge, MA: Harvard University Press, 2001) in *American Science* 90, no. 1 (January–February 2002), www.americanscientist.org/bookshelf/pub/demythologizing-mcclintock (accessed March 6, 2015).

24. *Stand and Deliver,* directed by Ramón Menéndez, featuring Edward James Olmos (American Playhouse, Olmos Productions, Warner Brothers, 1988). Cited at www.imdb.com/title/tt0094027/quotes (accessed March 6, 2015).

The story of the subject at hand can bring teachers and students together as equal beneficiaries of a higher goal: to continue the work of discovery begun by others, and to put knowledge within the grasp of more people. This is especially true when the learning process helps to overturn false ideas that are imported from outside the classroom, helping to fill the vacuum created by ignorance with deeper and richer forms of knowledge. The relevant words for such a learning community include *curiosity, reverence,* and *gratitude.*

We all have subjects that have eluded us. Perhaps we blame poor teachers; perhaps we felt nauseated by the smell of formaldehyde or quaked in fear when it was our turn to walk onto a stage. We may never excel at such subjects; after formal schooling ends, we may not have much need to do so. But for those who love a subject, it continues to expand as they discover more of its secrets. The one thing any professor can try to do—even for students who struggle—is to describe the nature of the subject vividly and to offer more than one vantage point. Our ways of knowing may be divisible by type (quantifiable methods vs. qualitative; theory vs. experience; imagination vs. empiricism), but the subject itself can transcend any individual approach—and even help those who seek to integrate more than one method.

I remember, for example, discovering Annie Dillard's book *Pilgrim at Tinker Creek* when I was a young professor. Along with my husband, I was leading an international service-learning semester in Haiti. We had a paperback library consisting of books students brought with them to read during their six weeks of service in villages and then left behind for other students to read when they arrived. I remember sitting in bright tropical sunshine reading Dillard's description of a powerful experience of nature that continued to affect her long after it occurred. It led her to compare herself to a bell, which makes no sound until it is encountered by something external to itself: "I was still ringing. I had been my whole life a bell and never knew it until at that moment I was lifted and struck."[25] When I read that passage, particularly when I was living in that location, I knew exactly what Dillard meant. There, in a foreign country, where my previous educational experiences paled in comparison to the immediacy of my new environment, I felt "lifted and struck" by reading this passage.

---

25. Annie Dillard, *Pilgrim at Tinker Creek* (New York: Harper's Magazine Press, 1974), 34.

How can educators help their students experience their own lives as a bell—as something that could find its voice through an encounter with another? One option, of course, is to share a great writer's approach to a subject; students might examine the poetic way that Dillard describes the natural world. But the real challenge will be to try to investigate a writer like Dillard from an entirely different perspective. For example, what would it mean to analyze her work from the perspective of a neuroscientist? From that of a social scientist? Might other fields eventually help us understand what makes some of us feel "lifted and struck" by a particular experience? And what would practitioners in other fields gain by examining the principles under the poetic language? The key is likely to be found in learning to look—really look—at what is visible before us. In the words of the poet Rilke,

> If you trust in Nature, in what is simple in Nature, in the small things that hardly anyone sees and that can become huge, immeasurable; if you have this love for what is humble and try very simply, as someone who serves, to win the confidence of what seems poor: then everything will become easier for you, more coherent and somehow more reconciling, not in your conscious mind perhaps, which stays behind, astonished, but in your innermost awareness, awakeness, and knowledge.[26]

If we allow ourselves to look deeply into a subject—guided by good questions and by stories of awakening and persistence—we may experience the best story of all. That story tells of our own transformation: away from a mere compliance with educational requirements and necessities, and toward an engagement of our own deepest desires for beauty, awe, and joy. When this happens, a vocation may be born. The key for both professor and student is the ability to *pay attention* in a way that allows us to capture the unfolding narrative.

## Beginning, middle, and end

When one pays attention, one sees that certain segments of a college course matter greatly. First, the beginning: the syllabus itself is a story and

---

26. Rainer Maria Rilke, *Letters to a Young Poet*, trans. Stephen Mitchell (New York: Modern Library, 1984), 33–34.

requires great care. If the subject were a person, how would we describe its origin and history? By selecting some details from the past (just as we always do in introductions), we can look for connections to the present. The whole class, from the first to the last week, becomes the middle part of the story as the community of learners (which includes the teacher) tries to uncover as much as possible about what we now know.

The last class period provides a special opportunity for reflection on what the community has learned together. Teachers should design this last meeting with care. Too often, both the first and last classes resemble business meetings more than intentional narratives: hand out syllabi and answer questions in the first session; fill out forms and evaluate results in the last. Narrative attention calls for more than just transacting the business of the course.

Ritual can play a role, especially at the end. What symbol is strong enough to contain what we together have learned? The idea of the "last lecture" has now entered into pedagogical history after the phenomenal achievement of Randy Pausch at Carnegie Mellon University (CMU). Those who have watched Pausch's lecture in the last months of his life—or who have read the book that resulted from that lecture—have witnessed not only a moving tribute to the calling to teach, but also a farewell that elevates the subject he loved to its ultimate significance. Pausch made the decision to keep on doing what he had always done—lecture—and to treat death itself "like an engineering problem." He didn't get to choose the option of continuing to live; nevertheless, he could consider all the givens, and then use all the tools at his disposal to create the very best solution possible. Anyone who watched him speak—either in the Last Lecture itself or in the "charge" he gave to CMU graduates in 2008—witnessed a great example of a man who pursued his dreams until his last breath.

Today on the CMU campus, a pedestrian bridge connecting the Gates Computer Science building and the Purnell Center for the Arts is named the Randy Pausch Bridge: a symbol of the way one professor linked two great subjects.

## *Encore*

Over a lifetime—whether it is relatively short, like Randy Pausch's forty-eight years, or much longer—the most important fact that educators and students alike will face is the one Phil Connors eventually faced: death. Professors who have included their awareness of their mortality in their concept of vocation exude the kind of humility combined with will that calls students to do the same. This is why, in *Dead Poets Society*,[27] Mr. Keating takes his students out to the trophy case; he shows them pictures of smiling, muscular young men, now long deceased, and fiercely whispers, *Carpe diem!* Every discipline challenges young people to seize the day in some way; it's a calling that resonates across time and space. Professors who endeavor to contribute to knowledge as well as convey knowledge, and who do so urgently but not anxiously, will always call forth the devotion of the young.

To be sure, death eventually comes for the professor as well; but before that, in the usual sequence of events, comes retirement. Some professors declare they will never retire. Some "retire" while still on the job; others look forward to retiring as soon as economically possible. Ideally, however, the vocation continues even after the career ends. Indeed, young professors may well imagine themselves as elders, and then live into the questions that will make them wise—ready for the meaningful work that they design for themselves to undertake *after* the retirement party.

For the sake of convenience, I sometimes say I am "retired"; still, the word seems wholly inadequate.[28] I prefer Marc Freedman's "encore career" or Sarah Lightfoot's "third act." I respond even more positively to Mary Catherine Bateson's phrase: "composing a further life."[29] Bateson views aging as an "improvisational art form calling for imagination and willingness to learn."[30] We actually need a new phrase for this new phase. I advocate the term "encore vocation"—emphasizing the generative nature of our narrative identities and allowing teachers, and indeed members of any profession, to continue to carry out their vocations in creative, new

---

27. *Dead Poets Society*, directed by Peter Weir, featuring Robin Williams, Robert Sean Leonard, and Ethan Hawke (Touchstone Pictures, in association with Silver Screen Partners IV, 1989). www.imdb.com/title/tt0097165/?ref_=ttco_co_tt.

28. To retire means to retreat or to withdraw to some place, "especially for the sake of privacy"; this usage is recorded from the 1530s. The sense of "leave an occupation" first appears in the 1640s. As a transitive verb (to retire some particular thing), it appears in the 1540s, meaning "to withdraw or lead back" (i.e., a military brigade); the meaning "to remove from active service" is first attested in the 1680s. *Oxford English Dictionary* (New York: Oxford University Press, 1989, 1998), s.v. *retire*. The strong connection between this word and military language is worth consideration.

29. Mary Catherine Bateson. *Composing a Further Life: The Age of Active Wisdom* (New York: Random House, 2010).

30. Ibid., 19.

ways. Isabel Allende recommends the Spanish word *jubilación*—the word for retirement in Central and South America.[31] Instead of retreating into the past, a wise elder continues to walk into the future—jubilantly.

Our vocations continue even after the paychecks stop. And even well before that point—in the stage that Bateson calls Adulthood II, beginning at approximately age fifty—we may get to compose the best stories yet. Bateson describes the task with the kind of verve and imagination that comes straight from her own story and those of many she has interviewed:

> I like to think of men and women as artists of their own lives, work-
> ing with what comes to hand through accident or talent to com-
> pose and re-compose a pattern in time that expresses who they
> are and what they believe in—making meaning even as they are
> studying and working and raising children, creating and re-creating
> themselves.[32]

How is this major cultural change relevant to undergraduate education, and in particular to the faculty, staff, and students who carry out its work? The change that we are experiencing is a profound one, and its impact will be felt throughout the life cycle.[33] The "extra" thirty years beyond age sixty-five that many of us will experience are not just years tacked onto the end of a career; they are practically another life.

Bateson offers the suggestion that these years are like a room unexpectedly added to one's house. It isn't just a shack tacked on to the back; it's a well-integrated addition, which actively transforms the entire house. "The way you use all the rest of the house, the way you live and organize your time and even your relationships, will be affected by the change."[34] The implications of this change for the idea of vocation are enormous.

A story that sustains a life until the end must be both resilient and flexible. Whether we stay in our professions for five years or fifty, the major themes of our lives will likely cycle in and out, choosing a slightly new path for every iteration. These cycles differ from the endless repetitions of

---

31. Isabel Allende, Ted Talk, filmed March 2014, www.ted.com/talks/isabelle_allende_how_to_live_passionately_no_matter_your_age?language=en (accessed August 15, 2015).

32. Bateson, *Composing a Further Life*, 24.

33. For more on vocation across the life course, see chapter 4 of this volume.

34. Bateson, *Composing a Further Life*, 11.

*Groundhog Day*, but the key to giving them meaning is the same for us as it was for Phil Connors. We can fight against the weight of time, or we can accept our mortality and devote ourselves to generativity. The undergraduate educational environment is a marvelous place to share this faith: here, a community of learners composes its own life across time, struggling to build ever more commodious stories that will echo into the future. And we do so, knowing that when stories are given away in pure love—love of our subject and love of our fellow learners—they will live forever.

# PART TWO

---

# *Calling in Context*

## Fields of Study as Resources
## for Vocational Reflection

As noted in the introduction to this volume, its authors originally considered writing one chapter each from thirteen different academic disciplines and applied fields. In the end, we felt that this might obscure the
degree of integration that the language of vocation and calling can potentially offer. At the same time, however, we felt that it was important that
a few chapters in the book arose from particular fields of study, and this
for two reasons. First, we wanted to emphasize that vocational language
is not limited to particular academic departments or programs, and that it
is not exclusively the province of the humanities (even though it receives
a great deal of attention from humanistic fields such as philosophy, literature, and religion). Second, we wanted to propose that the specific *ways* in
which various subject areas have employed the language of vocation may
be of interest to a much wider range of academic enterprises, across the
range of traditional disciplines and the applied fields. This second section
of the book showcases four such instances.

In order to cast the net widely, we here provide examples from the
social sciences, the arts, the applied fields, and the natural sciences. In
each case, a scholar whose work is focused within that particular academic
division offers an indication of how vocational thinking plays a role in her
or his discipline. In addition, each author offers some reflections on how
that particular discipline's approach might be of value for students and
educators who work in other academic departments and programs. The
questions they address include these:

- How does a sociological perspective that attends to the entire life course
  provide additional insights into vocational reflection and discernment

among college students? How is this process affected by categories such as race, class, and gender?

- To what degree are students in the fine and performing arts motivated by romantic notions of self-expression, and what alternatives to this view are presented by a vocational perspective? How might the artistic relationship between performer and audience be mapped onto other fields of study and forms of work? Can artistic categories such as meaning, interpretation, context, and materiality help to reframe the relationship between a student's own enthusiasm for a particular kind of work and the needs of those who are served by that work?

- How are students affected by the problems of academic specialization and disciplinary silos as they explore their potential vocations? Does the broader academic community play an adequate role in an individual student's vocational reflection? How can the field of business, and in particular the study of organization theory, help us better understand these problems, as well as providing indicators as to how they might be addressed?

- How can students in the natural sciences best be introduced to the work of vocational reflection and discernment? Can the "supercomplexity" that they will face in their professional lives be addressed by traditional vocational terms such as *wisdom, prudence,* and *conscience?* How can the sciences and the humanities work together to address some of the world's most pressing problems?

In each case, certain concerns that are specific to a particular field take on a larger degree of significance, demonstrating a relevance beyond that particular field and thereby serving as a potential resource for vocational reflection in other disciplines. In addition to addressing this need, the chapters in this part of the book encourage us to think about interdisciplinarity more generally. What are some of the concerns about undergraduate students that should be common to all academic majors? How can the traditional academic disciplines and the applied fields remain in conversation with one another? To what degree does the language of vocation and calling encourage and facilitate such discussions? We believe that, when the following four chapters are read with such questions in mind, students and educators from all sectors of the college or university will have considerable wisdom to contribute to an interdisciplinary conversation about calling and vocation.

# 4

## Calling over the Life Course

### SOCIOLOGICAL INSIGHTS

*Catherine Fobes*

UPON ENTERING COLLEGE, students may imagine that over the next few years they will discover what their future will bring. Indeed, many hope to develop a career plan that will remain constant for their entire lifetime. This chapter presents an alternative perspective: namely, that the process of discerning one's future path is typically not a one-time event, but an ongoing process over the course of one's life. My own life story provides us with an initial illustration of this reality.

As I graduated from college with a major in psychology, I knew that I wanted to work with people; beyond that, however, I didn't have a clear sense of a calling. To explore career options, I held several jobs throughout my twenties, from a one-week experience at the front desk of a rental car company to a four-year stint in a college development office. In this last position, I went on a series of silent retreats, during which I discerned a call to attend divinity school. After I had made that move, one of my faculty mentors asked me whether I had ever thought of going on for a doctorate. I had not; at age twenty-nine, wasn't I too old? I delayed making a decision for several more years while caring for a family member, but eventually I began a graduate program in the sociology of aging. There, I was introduced to the *life course perspective*—a theoretical approach to understanding how social factors shape individual, familial, and work lives from birth to death.[1] This perspective,

---

1. Jill Quadagno, *Aging and the Life Course*, 6th ed. (New York: McGraw–Hill, 2014). Starting in the 1960s and building on studies in developmental psychology, sociologists have used

combined with my own experience along my vocational path, has convinced me of the need to expand our notion of vocational discernment.

While vocational choices made during the years of young adulthood can be formative, human beings can and should undertake meaningful and purposeful engagement in vocational questions during all the stages of our lives. This point is driven home by a variety of twenty-first-century social forces,[2] particularly as they impact vocational reflection among the members of younger age cohorts.[3] How might undergraduates come to think about vocation as something that continues and evolves over the entire course of one's life?

To explore this question, I begin by introducing the history, key figures, and concepts in the life course perspective. Then, I will apply two life course concepts to vocation. First, examining a variety of vocational *transitions and turning points* helps capture the dynamic nature of social roles and relationships throughout our lives. Second, exploring *the accumulation of social advantages and disadvantages* illuminates how factors such as race, gender, and social class can play a major role in shaping vocational discernment, making decisions about one's future, and developing perceptions about self-actualization. Throughout the chapter, we will discover

---

the life course approach to study the interrelationships of age, cohort, and historical and social contexts in the trajectory of an individual's life, during which transitions and turning points shape later life outcomes, accumulating advantages and disadvantages based on race, social class, gender, and other factors.

2. Work and family life are shifting in the contemporary life course, owing to shifts in population trends, a fluctuating global economy, technological advances, increasing life expectancy, vicissitudes in social policies, and micro-sociological changes in daily life. Although the full dimensions of these social forces are beyond the scope of this chapter, they are helping to usher in two new life stages that are relevant to questions about vocation. The first is an elongated path to adulthood; see especially Jeffrey Jensen Arnett, *Emerging Adulthood: The Winding Road from the Late Teens Through the Twenties*, 2nd ed. (Oxford: Oxford University Press, 2015). The second is termed *encore adulthood*, during which individuals in their fifties, sixties, and beyond pursue meaningful and purposeful engagement in educational, volunteer, or paid-work arenas, or in more informal contexts. See Dawn C. Carr and Kathrin S. Komp, eds., *Gerontology in the Era of the Third Age: Implications and Next Steps* (New York: Springer, 2011). On the latter point, see also the closing section of chapter 3 of this volume.

3. Social gerontologists identify six birth cohorts in the twentieth and early twenty-first centuries: swing generation (1900–1926), silent generation (1927–1945), baby boomers (1946–1964), baby busters (1965–1976), echo boomers (1977–1994), and millennials (1995–2005). See Quadagno, *Aging and the Life Course*, 9.

a number of strong arguments in favor of understanding vocational exploration and discernment to be a lifelong enterprise.

## *The life course perspective*

The life course perspective is a theoretical and methodological approach to understanding how social factors shape individual and familial lives from birth to death. Five basic tenets govern this perspective:[4]

- All persons continue to change and develop across the life span.
- Individuals have *agency*, the capacity to act on their own behalf and on behalf of others.
- The timing of key life events and transitions influences their impact on a person's life.
- Human lives are linked, influencing one another's transitions and trajectories.
- Historical, political, and economic contexts frequently impact later life outcomes.

With respect to the last tenet, these contexts play a particularly important role when they occur during key life transitions. For example, wars and economic disasters typically accelerate whatever changes are already occurring within a life course.[5]

Social changes following World War II ushered in many innovative ways of thinking about life and society. Social dislocation (brought about first by the Great Depression, then by postwar affluence) led scholars to pose novel research questions about the impact of economic and historical contexts in shaping individuals' choices, actions, and outcomes. The shifting age composition of society—driven in part by the large baby boomer cohort and by policy changes stemming from the Social Security Act of 1935—suggested an increased level of awareness and thoughtfulness about the

4. Glenn H. Elder Jr., "The Life Course and Aging: Some Accomplishments, Unfinished Tasks, and New Directions," presented at the annual meeting for the Gerontological Society of America, Boston, Massachusetts, November 11, 2002.

5. This section draws from Catherine Fobes and Megan M. McCullen, "The Life Course Perspective," in *The Wiley Blackwell Encyclopedia of Family Studies*, ed. Constance L. Shehan (Hoboken, NJ: Wiley, 2016), 1300–1305.

adult life course. Social problems in middle and late adult life—including, for example, the disproportionate percentage of elders living in poverty before 1935—encouraged sociologists to examine how early life experiences influence later life outcomes. These historical events helped lay the conceptual foundation for the emergence of the life course perspective.

Starting in the 1960s and building on studies by developmental psychologists, sociologists began studying varying aspects of age, aging, and the role of historical context in social groups. Two main foci emerged, forming the theoretical underpinnings of life course studies in sociology: the "sociocultural" and "cohort-historical."[6] The sociocultural approach, developed by Bernice Neugarten, maintains that the life course is governed by *age norms*: informal rules that stipulate age-appropriate behavior and roles.[7] She discovered that rules governing age-appropriate behavior were so deeply ingrained in the cultural fabric of society that they function as a *social clock*, indicating when we are "on time" or "off time" for familial and educational life events. For instance, remarks such as "It's about time he got married" or "Isn't it a little early for them to be having a child?" revealed individuals' awareness about (and perceptions of) age norms. The social clock orders major life events by influencing when people might go to college, marry, obtain a professional job, have children, or retire.

The cohort-historical approach, proposed by Matilda Riley, focuses on the role that historical events have on age cohorts.[8] Riley and her collaborators argued that people age in a range of ways, shaped by their varied exposure to social change.[9] Further, she pioneered the theory of age stratification—the idea that society tends to rank people based on age, as well as on other social categories such as gender, race, and wealth.[10]

Glen Elder's 1974 book *Children of the Great Depression*[11] has been viewed as the premiere sociological work that synthesized both approaches into

---

6. Elder, "The Life Course and Aging," 4.

7. Bernice L. Neugarten, Joan W. Moore, and John C. Lowe, "Age Norms, Age Constraints, and Adult Socialization," *American Journal of Sociology* 70, no. 6 (May 1965): 710–17.

8. For a list of these cohorts, see note 3.

9. Matilda White Riley, "Social Gerontology and the Age Stratification of Society," *The Gerontologist* 11, no. 1, part 1 (Spring 1971): 79–87.

10. Matilda W. Riley, Marilyn E. Johnson, and Anne Forner, eds., *Aging and Society, Volume 3: A Sociology of Age Stratification* (New York: Russell Sage, 1972).

11. Glen Elder, *Children of the Great Depression: Social Change in Life Experience*, 25th anniversary edition (Boulder, CO: Westview, 1999).

the life course perspective. Through his longitudinal research on a cohort of children born in 1920–21 (who were therefore adolescents during the Great Depression), Elder showed that those young people whose families experienced greater stress also developed an array of coping strategies and skills that benefited them later in life. In a second and extended edition of his work, Elder compared a cohort of children born in 1928–29 with his original research cohort, discovering that the Depression had a more deleterious impact on the younger cohort (i.e., those who had experienced it as young children).[12] Elder's work illustrates that the *age* at which one experiences an event—and not the mere fact of having lived through it— shapes the life course. In more recent years, these research questions have gained greater prominence, as the life span of Americans has increased and baby boomers have started to enter retirement.

As we now turn to examine the details of the life course perspective more closely, we will quickly discover how significant this approach can be for conversations about vocation.

## *Transitions and turning points*

Sociologists employ conceptual lenses through which to view the life course. Every individual has a parallel and intertwined series of trajectories associated with different aspects of life, including employment, family, and health. Each of these trajectories is made up of a series of transitions and turning points. *Transitions* mark a change from one social role to another (from single to married or from nonparent to parent); these changes may have a major impact on our callings. For example, new parents may choose to leave (or refuse) employment and other opportunities that might require working at night or extensive travel. *Turning points* are specific types of transitions that are unalterable, such as the change in status from being a high school graduate to becoming a college student, losing a parent, or receiving the diagnosis of a chronic and progressively debilitating illness. In the cases of both transitions and turning points, these significant alterations of one's life course can have a profound

---

12. Ibid. For instance, younger boys from economically vulnerable families were less likely to visualize promising futures and to develop aspirations for themselves. In contrast, male adolescents during the Depression often performed military service during World War II, so they accessed housing and educational benefits from the Servicemen's Readjustment Act of 1944 (popularly known as the G.I. Bill).

impact on vocational discernment. A future plan that seemed best in one set of circumstances can easily be forestalled, and new vocational options may seem more compelling in the light of shifting priorities.

How can students better envision and prepare for the vocational transitions that may occur throughout their lives, and how can educators help them to do so? We might begin by attending to a particular exemplar, following the transitions and turning points in that person's own life course. Consider, for example, the case of Dorothy Day, co-founder of the Catholic Worker Movement, who went through a number of transitions in her work, family, and religious trajectories. Already at the age of sixteen, she was speaking of her future in vocational terms, observing that the "plight of the poor, of the workers, . . . of the destitute, the very fact that *The Jungle* was about Chicago, where I lived, whose streets I walked, made me feel that from then on, my life was to be linked to theirs, [and] their interests were to be mine; I had received a call, a vocation, a direction to my life."[13]

Day enrolled at the University of Illinois and joined the Socialist Party, believing that religion would only hinder her work. After leaving the university at age eighteen, she went to work for the *New York Call*, a socialist daily paper. She left that job to join other suffragists in picketing the White House, whereupon she was arrested and jailed; she then engaged in a hunger strike for eight days. Over the course of the next decade, she worked as a freelance writer, a nursing assistant, a clerk at a department store, a restaurant cashier, and a model for art classes; still, she kept coming back to one focus. "A longing to write, to be pursuing the career of a journalist, swept over me," she observed. "Even though I loved the work at the hospital, I felt that it was my second choice, not my vocation."[14]

After selling her first novel, Day moved to Staten Island, where she transitioned from being single to living as the partner of Forster Batterham, a biologist (and anarchist). During this period of her life, she was surprised to find herself starting to pray daily and to attend Mass regularly on Sunday mornings. While pregnant, Day experienced a call to baptize her child in the Catholic Church and then to convert to Catholicism herself. Her religious inclinations meant that Day wanted to be officially married, but Batterham was not interested; thus, her call to become a Catholic would require her to make the difficult decision of leaving her partner.[15]

---

13. Dorothy Day, *The Long Loneliness* (New York: Harper Collins, 1952), 38.

14. Ibid., 93.

15. For further discussion on conflicting callings, see chapter 2 of this volume.

Day's conversion marked a significant turning point in her life. She moved back to Manhattan, where she met Peter Maurin, a former monk who was devoted to the Franciscan ideal of poverty. Together they founded the Catholic Worker Movement; they published a newspaper (printed in her kitchen); they maintained a series of houses of hospitality; and they engaged in nonviolent direct action on behalf of the poor and the homeless. She continued to protest, write, and serve the poor until her death.

Dorothy Day's life course illustrates the fluidity in the vocational trajectories of work, family, and religious life; in her case, all these followed a zigzag course that no one could have predicted. Day did not set out to start a social movement; but she was willing to listen and to leave room for the unexpected. As a result, she allowed her vocations to evolve and intertwine over time, through a number of significant turning points and transitions. Day's vocational journey exemplifies Parker Palmer's dictum, "Before you tell your life what to do with it—listen for what it intends to do with you."[16]

I have taught Dorothy Day's story in my own courses, but a straightforward biographical study is not the only means by which students can become more aware of the transitions and turning points that they are likely to face. In a travel-study course to England called "Women, Work, and Calling," we studied Dorothy Day, Cecily Saunders (founder of St. Christopher's Hospice), and Virginia Woolf. We read original writings by each woman, examined and discussed the ways in which their vocational paths unfolded, and engaged in field trips—working at The Catholic Worker Farm in Hertfordshire,[17] participating in a workshop at St. Christopher's Hospice,[18] touring Bloomsbury, and traveling to Woolf's childhood summer home in Cornwall. Throughout this experience, students were encouraged to apply findings and insights from the course to their own vocational journeys; they wrote papers applying a particular aspect of vocation to the life of the historical figure, to their hands-on experiences, and then to their own lives.[19]

---

16. Parker J. Palmer, *Let Your Life Speak: Listening for the Voice of Vocation* (San Francisco: Jossey-Bass, 2000), 3.

17. For further information see The Catholic Worker Farm, http://thecatholicworkerfarm.org/ (accessed August 5, 2015). For a list of Catholic Worker communities worldwide, see "Directory of Catholic Worker Communities," www.catholicworker.org/communities/directory-picker.html/ (accessed September 10, 2015).

18. For further information, see www.stchristophers.org.uk/ (accessed August 5, 2015).

19. I use Frederick Buechner's essay "Vocation," in *Leading Lives that Matter: What We Should Do and Who We Should Be*, ed. Mark R. Schwehn and Dorothy C. Bass (Grand Rapids,

This kind of pedagogy does not necessarily require students to leave the country. A similar course could be offered on campus by supplementing the readings with documentary films and speaker panels that present the lives of people called to similar kinds of work. Moreover, this approach can be applied across the disciplines by engaging in dialogue with the life stories of interesting exemplars in that particular field. For example, students of anthropology, biology, or environmental science could explore the life course of Jane Goodall, who began as a primatologist in the Gombe Stream Chimpanzee Reserve in present-day Tanzania. While she continues to study and write about primate behavior, as well as providing ongoing support for field research on wild chimpanzees, she has since transitioned to writing about mindful eating and to addressing environmental concerns as a conservationist. Her story illustrates how one may be called to multiple linked vocations over a lifetime.[20] Students in chemistry, biology, physics, political science, or peace studies courses could examine the contours of Linus Pauling's sequential turning points as winner of the Nobel Prize in Chemistry and then the Nobel Peace Prize. Wallace Stevens, an insurance executive and poet, offers interesting material for majors in either business administration or English—especially as an example of someone whose apparently disparate endeavors were simultaneous rather than serial. From any of these cases, students can develop a sense of how their own lives may be affected by transitions and turning points, including many that they cannot yet imagine.

## Accumulated advantages and disadvantages

A sociological approach to vocation also recognizes the ways in which various forms of social inequality can endure across the life course.[21] Race,

---

MI: Eerdmans, 2006), 111–12, Sharon Parks's notion of meaning-making in *Big Questions, Worthy Dreams: Mentoring Young Adults in their Search for Meaning, Purpose, and Faith* (San Francisco: Jossey–Bass, 2001), and Parker Palmer's ideas in *Let Your Life Speak*.

20. See Jane Goodall with Gary McAvoy and Gail Hudson, *Harvest for Hope: A Guide to Mindful Eating* (New York: Time Warner, 2005); and Paul Tullus, "Jane Goodall Is Still Wild at Heart," *New York Times*, March 13, 2015, www.nytimes.com/2015/03/15/magazine/jane-goodall-is-still-wild-at-heart.html?gwh=8C4E21EC8E17512A9CD36D00BD3C6961&gwt=pay&assetType=nyt_now (accessed May 31, 2015). Especially well-suited for a class on vocation is Jane Goodall's memoir (with Phillip Berman), *Reason for Hope: A Spiritual Journey* (New York: Time Warner, 1999).

21. Phyllis Moen, "A Life Course Approach to the Third Age," in *Gerontology in the Era of the Third Age: Implications and Next Steps*, ed. Dawn C. Carr and Kathrin Komp (New York: Springer, 2011), 19.

gender, and social class can privilege the process of vocational exploration and discernment for some individuals while constraining, or even extinguishing, the vocational journeys of others. College students in general may already inhabit (or at least be moving toward) certain advantageous positions in terms of social class, regardless of their circumstances of origin; educators, too, tend to occupy predictable rungs on the ladder of social stratification. But we would be unwise to treat either students or faculty in undifferentiated ways; whether acknowledged or not, the specific details of both students' and educators' social locations shape the discussion of vocation.

Across the disciplines, examining vocational advantages or disadvantages from a life course perspective serves at least three purposes. First, it can help educators to understand more deeply their own social disadvantages or privileges—not just in their present social location, but as an aggregation over time. Second, they can better understand their students, given that they all come to college with an accumulation of privileges and disadvantages; this in turn can help them offer better guidance. Finally, students who attend to questions of social location are better able to understand not only their own accumulated privileges and constraints, but also the world that they will enter as college graduates—which may be very different from the world in which they spent their pre-college years.

All these elements can have a profound effect on how a student carries out a program of vocational exploration and discernment, regardless of the student's discipline or field of study. Moreover, attention to these matters can have a dramatically positive effect on the personal lives of all students, whatever their backgrounds. It can help those who grew up with fewer advantages to make their way in a world in which privilege plays a key role; it can also help advantaged students awaken to the realities of the lives of those who inhabit a less privileged world.

## Racial inequality

To help illuminate the cumulative construction of how racial privilege and disadvantage shape vocational discernment, I borrow the term "sedimentation of racial inequality" from sociologists Melvin Oliver and Thomas Shapiro. According to these authors, the processes of asset accumulation for some (and peonage for others) have become layered along racial lines, magnifying inequality over time and across generations.[22] This

---

22. Melvin Oliver and Thomas Shapiro, *Black Wealth, White Wealth* (New York: Taylor & Francis, 1995).

accumulated layering is amplified by occupational, educational, and housing segregation (among other factors), and by the intergenerational transfer of assets (or lack thereof).[23] Wealth provides one empirical indicator of
racial sedimentation; in 2013, for example, the average African-American
household had just $11,000 in median net worth, compared with $13,700
for the median Latino/a household and an astounding $141,900 for the
median white household.[24] Although establishing and perpetuating racial
inequality may no longer be the overt intention of the law, such inequality
has certainly not disappeared.

Life course theory emphasizes that a person's social location is not
adequately revealed by a snapshot of where that person is now; we need to
examine how various structures have gotten each person to this place over
time. While students of color face challenges of identity and vocational
discovery that are similar to those of other emerging adults, their journeys
may be complicated by the fact that these explorations take place within a
society that in many ways is hostile toward them. Many teens in marginalized racial groups will never make it to college, whether for cultural or
financial reasons, or because they lose their lives on the streets.[25] Although
news headlines and societal perceptions tend to focus on these issues as
one-time events in the lives of marginalized persons, the life course perspective emphasizes the degree to which these social disadvantages accumulate over time; this magnifies their impact and creates an even greater
disparity between perception and reality.

Teachers and academic advisors need to keep in mind that pre-college
life for students of color may necessitate, among other things, developing a set of survival strategies to navigate institutional and individual racism on a daily basis. For example, in a letter to his son, Ta-Nehisi Coates

---

23. These might include major financial transfers, such as receiving an inheritance or getting help from one's family to make a down payment on a house; or they might take the form
of smaller but still significant transfers through wedding or graduation gifts, or through
payments for one's college education, vacations, or summer camp.

24. Pew Research Center, "Wealth inequality has widened along racial, ethnic lines since end
of Great Recession," December 12, 2014. Household net worth was measured by subtracting
debts from assets. See www.pewresearch.org/fact-tank/2014/12/12/racial-wealth-gaps-great-
recession/ (accessed December 14, 2015).

25. As this chapter was being written, tensions concerning race on college campuses have
been intensifying, in part sparked by the death of numerous African-American teens and
young adults at the hands of police officers. In response, a number of global activist movements have emerged; for one example, see www.blacklivesmatter.com/ (accessed December
28, 2015).

described the street code he developed as a fifteen-year-old growing up in Baltimore:

> When I was about your age, each day, fully one-third of my brain was concerned with who I was walking to school with, our precise number, the manner of our walk, the number of times I smiled, who or what I smiled at, who offered a pound and who did not—all of which is to say that I practiced the culture of the streets, a culture concerned chiefly with securing the body.[26]

For students of color, the challenge is not just to discern the kind of people they wish to be, but also to spend time and energy in protecting one's body and mind—and learning how to reject and overcome the societal assault of racial epithets and racist actions. As the poet Claudia Rankine recently observed, "The notable difference between black excellence and white excellence is white excellence is achieved without having to battle racism. Imagine."[27]

The racism experienced by students of color may result in harmful physiological and psychological effects, such as depression, anxiety, helplessness, social isolation, fear, trauma, and exhaustion.[28] Students of color convey a disproportionate number of physical ailments linked to stress, such as headaches, high blood pressure, and fatigue.[29] Such inveterate exposure to prejudicial attitudes, negative stereotypes, and acts of discrimination accumulates into "racial battle fatigue," which endangers social, psychological, spiritual, academic, and physiological

---

26. Ta-Nehisi Coates, *Between the World and Me* (New York: Spiegel & Grau, 2015), 24. The term "pound" refers to an informal greeting using fists that can signify a bond, familiarity, positive affection, respect, and/or a general greeting. Offering a pound suggests being on good terms, whereas withholding a pound may indicate ill will. I am indebted to Ted Thornhill, scholar in sociology and African-American studies, for this explanation (email correspondence, December 24, 2015).

27. Claudia Rankine, "The Meaning of Serena Williams: On Tennis and Black Excellence," *New York Times Magazine*, August 25, 2015, www.nytimes.com/2015/08/30/magazine/the-meaning-of-serena-williams.html (accessed August 28, 2015).

28. See Stacy Anne Harwood, Shinwoo Choi, Moises Orozco, Margaret Browne Hunt, and Ruby Mendenhall, *Racial Microaggressions at the University of Illinois at Urbana–Champaign: Voices of Students of Color in the Classroom* (Urbana: University of Illinois, 2015),2. Available atwww.racialmicroaggressions.illinois.edu/files/2015/03/RMA-Classroom-Report.pdf (accessed August 5, 2015).

29. Ibid., 2.

well-being.[30] Furthermore, such experiences are so complex and numerous that "the cumulative burden of a lifetime" can "contribute to diminished mortality, augmented morbidity, and flattened confidence."[31]

Colleges and universities can no longer ignore the impact living in a racialized society has on the lives of its citizens.[32] In fact, this time and place can provide teachable opportunities to develop multipronged approaches that acknowledge racial inequity as a core component of twenty-first-century society. It can simultaneously allow us to work toward providing safe spaces on campus, as well as routes for students to explore racial identity while dialoguing about difference.

Davidson College provides a positive model for others to follow. Its strong institutional commitment to diversity[33] is evidenced, in part, by a racially and ethnically diverse curriculum.[34] The college actively recruits and retains faculty of color, providing (among other structural supports) a Faculty of Color Affinity Group that meets monthly. Its multicultural life is vibrant, providing over a dozen student organizations, peer mentoring, themed housing, and a wide variety of multicultural support resources for students of color. Davidson has also found ways of addressing a problem faced by many colleges and universities: how to foster meaningful conversation between students about social constructs of difference. The college seeks to prioritize such exchanges by using campus organizations and

---

30. Ibid., 2.

31. Paula J. Caplan and Jordan C. Ford, "The Voices of Diversity: What Students of Diverse Races/Ethnicities and Both Sexes Tell Us about their College Experiences and Their Perceptions about Their Institutions' Progress Toward Diversity," *Aporia* 6, no. 3 (2014): 30–69, here 35. One empirical indicator of diminished mortality is the life expectancy gap by race. For example, on average, white men live to 76 years of age, while African-American men's average life expectancy is 71. See Quadagno, *Aging and the Life Course*, 89. Second, there is a sharp disparity in age-related patterns of suicide, with a rise in suicide rates for white men with age, while the suicide rate for African Americans is highest during emerging adulthood. See Jeffrey J. Arnett and Gene H. Brody, "A Fraught Passage: The Identity Challenges of African American Emerging Adults," *Human Development* 51, no. 5–6 (December 2008): 291–93, here 292.

32. Sherry K. Watt, "Situating Race in College Students' Search for Purpose and Meaning: Who Am I?" *Journal of College and Character* 16, no. 3 (August 2015): 135–42, here 140.

33. See Davidson College's website, "Multicultural Life, Institutional Commitment," www.davidson.edu/student-life/multicultural-life/institutional-commitment (accessed December 14, 2015).

34. This includes, for example, Africana, Arab, Chinese, East Asian, French and Francophone, Hispanic, Latin American, Studies, and Middle East Studies Programs. "Majors & Programs," www.davidson.edu/academics/majors-and-programs (accessed December 14, 2015).

off-campus trips to foster conversations between Caucasian and African-American students, between atheists and religious students, and among students from varying political backgrounds.[35] A context such as this would allow an institution to build vocational discernment programs that foster multilayered learning environments and teach vital skills. As Sherry Watt argues, learning to "exist and function responsibly in a racialized society will increase the possibility" that all community members "will make positive contributions to society as citizens."[36]

## Gender inequality

Conversations about vocation must account for the competing and, at times, conflicting responsibilities of paid work and family life. Despite the fact that 57 percent of women in the United States participate in the paid labor force,[37] many work–family conflicts remain "deeply gendered in that women, more than men, continue to shoulder domestic and family responsibilities."[38] Historically, middle-class Caucasian women's and men's vocations were societally prescribed by gender norms that generally assigned women to the domestic sphere and men to the public sphere in the role of the economic provider.[39] Though the majority of women continue to navigate some form of employment in addition to family responsibilities, others "routinely cite work–family conflicts as a reason for 'opting out' of the paid labor force" (if they can afford to do so).[40] From a historical perspective, vocation, paid work trajectories, and family responsibilities have not only been highly intertwined; they are also shaped by gender norms.

Because we too often associate the language of vocation only with decisions about the workplace, we typically forget that the particular forms of

35. Frank Bruni, "The Lie About College Diversity," *New York Times*, December 13, 2015, SR3, www.nytimes.com/2015/12/13/opinion/sunday/the-lie-about-college-diversity.html?emc=eta1&_r=0 (accessed December 15, 2015).

36. Watt, "Situating Race," 140.

37. U.S. Department of Labor, "Women's Bureau," www.dol.gov/wb/stats/stats_data.htm (accessed December 24, 2015).

38. Kristine De Welde and Andi Stepnick, *Disrupting the Culture of Silence: Confronting Gender Inequality and Making Change in Higher Education* (Sterling, VA: Stylus, 2015), 103.

39. Jessie Bernard, "The Good Provider Role—Its Rise and Fall," in *Public and Private Families: A Reader,* 2nd ed., ed. Andrew Cherlin (New York: McGraw–Hill, 2001), 54–69.

40. De Welde and Stepnick, *Disrupting the Culture of Silence*, 103.

family life to which we are called are also essential elements of our vocations. This calling is particularly strongly related to gender and gender
identity. Clearly, the heterosexual nuclear family structure (mom, dad,
and the kids)—once assumed to be the norm—is no longer the dominant
family form.[41] This shift, however, does not reduce the degree to which
a call to a particular form of family life is deeply related to gender. The
women's movement, Title IX, the increase in women's economic independence, and a rise in no-fault divorce laws have enabled women to
leave marriages that were unsatisfying or in which they and/or their children were being abused. Since 1960, the percentage of divorced or separated people has nearly tripled, while the percentage of never-marrieds
has almost doubled.[42] More recently, the marriage equality movement
has made it possible for same-sex couples to marry. Economic impacts
and cultural traditions also strongly affect the degree to which people
feel called to marriage[43] or called away from it.[44] Broadly speaking, the
vocation to marry has historically been deeply related to gender, sexuality,
race, and class.

Though there has been progress in women's labor force participation
rates and women's movement into higher education and managerial positions,[45] sexism, heterosexism, and gender discrimination remain rampant;
these conditions particularly impinge on women's and LGBTQ students'
collegiate careers and vocational journeys. For example, students are
often explicitly or implicitly steered toward or away from certain majors,
based on their biological sex or gender attributes. Female students report
"feeling out of place in classrooms and majors where there are few

41. Pew Research Center, "The Decline of Marriage and the Rise of New Families," November
18, 2010. From 1960 to 2008, the percentage of marrieds declined from 72% to 52%, the percentage of divorced or separated rose from 5% to 14%, and the percentage of never-marrieds
rose from 15% to 27%. See www.pewsocialtrends.org/2010/11/18/the-decline-of-marriage-
and-rise-of-new-families (accessed April 20, 2015).

42. Pew, "The Decline of Marriage." Also see Eric Klinenberg, *Going Solo: The Extraordinary
Rise and Surprising Appeal of Living Alone* (New York: Penguin, 2012).

43. Shirley A. Hill, "Why Won't African Americans Get (and Stay) Married? Why Should
They?" in Cherlin, ed., *Public and Private Families*, 108–12.

44. Kevin M. Roy, Nicolle Buckmiller and April McDowell, "Together but Not 'Together':
Trajectories of Relationship Suspension for Low-Income Unmarried Parents," *Family
Relations* 57 (March 2008): 198–210.

45. Barbara J. Risman, "Finishing the Gender Revolution: Re-aligning Economic and
Caretaking Work," presented at the annual meeting for the Society for the Study of Social
Problems, Chicago, Illinois, August 28, 2015.

women, because they feel they are not taken seriously and/or they fear confirming the stereotype that, for instance, women do not belong in physics or engineering."[46] In addition, microaggressions in the hallways, bathrooms, offices, and classrooms can also constrain vocational reflection, particularly when students find their intelligence demeaned or when their appearance is considered their most significant attribute. And of course, sexual assault, harassment, hate crimes, and rape cases on campuses are well documented.[47] Academic institutions most clearly demonstrate their commitment to matters of gender and sexuality as elements of vocational reflection when these issues are present in the curriculum.

Macalester College in St. Paul, Minnesota, is an excellent example of a liberal arts college that affords opportunities for exploring these questions at the institutional, community, and small-group levels. Its major and minor in Women's, Gender, and Sexuality Studies offers over thirty courses on a rotating basis. In addition, Macalester's vocational discernment programs provide opportunities for reflection, service, and civic leadership and engagement; they also offer internships with a variety of organizations, enabling marginalized students to access professional mentors in the larger community who have faced some of the same issues regarding gender, sexuality, and gender identity as have the participating students.[48] Faculty and peer mentoring is built into these programs, which can aid the vocational discernment process as well. A number of Macalester student organizations are devoted to providing safe and supportive spaces for women and for LGBTQ students and their allies, and to promoting awareness about gender equity as a human rather than a women's issue.[49]

One component of Macalester's vocational reflection program, known as Embody the Change (ETC) circles, aims to "provide a safe courageous community for students to have authentic space to talk about things that matter."[50] Such spaces are not limited to a focus on gender and sexuality; they address a wide range of circumstances through which students have

---

46. Caplan and Ford, "The Voices of Diversity," 55.

47. See De Welde and Stepnick, *Disrupting the Culture of Silence*.

48. Macalester College, "Reflection and Vocation Programs," www.macalester.edu/cec/reflectionandvocation/ (accessed December 14, 2015)

49. Macalester College, "Clubs and Organizations," www.macalester.edu/lifeatmac/clubs/ (accessed December 14, 2015).

50. Macalester College, "Embody the Change," www.macalester.edu/cec/reflectionandvocation/etc/ (accessed December 14, 2015).

experienced the gradual accumulation of privilege or disadvantage over the life course. Estee Hernandez argues that these "counter-spaces" allow for marginalized populations to create their own safe and trusted locations, within which their experiences and contributions can be validated as important knowledge—be it through face-to-face encounters or virtual communication (for example, via social media).[51] Greater attention to virtual or online opportunities can sometimes provide an important means of access for marginalized student populations, and should be receiving more attention from those who work in vocation reflection and discernment programs.

## Social class inequality

Many theorists, emphasizing the accumulation of advantages and disadvantages across the life course, maintain that inequities based on social class are sustained not only by structural conditions (such as wealth inequality) but also by cultural boundaries. These boundaries are constructed around the possession of *cultural capital*, which is, in part, transmitted across generations through the family. The concept of cultural capital was originally articulated by Bourdieu and Passeron;[52] in the present context, it reminds us that college students begin their undergraduate careers with widely varying accumulations of advantages and disadvantages. When students from the dominant social class enter college, they are already able to process certain key social and cultural cues; many working-class and first-generation students, on the other hand, must find a way to acquire these skills *while they are in college*, in order to negotiate their educational experience.

In general, educational systems treat elements of cultural capital as signs of intelligence; these elements range from personal style and linguistic competence to expertise in business or travel and familiarity with elements of high culture (books, music, art). Educational systems are not passive in this process; in fact, they play a significant role in increasing the value of the cultural capital that is already held by the dominant social class.

---

51. See Estee Hernandez, "#hermandad: Twitter as a Counter-Space for Latina Doctoral Students," *Journal of College and Character* 16, no. 2 (May 2015): 124–30.

52. Pierre Bourdieu and Jean Claude Passeron, *Reproduction in Education, Society and Culture* (Beverly Hills, CA: Sage, 1977).

Implicit or explicit classism—which is often coupled with assumptions about race and gender—tends to specify a limited range of knowledge as socially worthy; it simultaneously tends to exacerbate the alienation experienced by those students whose knowledge is not recognized as valuable. One of the most important facets of Bourdieu and Passeron's theory is the notion of cultural capital as "a basis for exclusion from jobs, resources, and high status groups."[53] If what is deemed to be "intelligent by definition" marginalizes or even eliminates one's particular social or cultural group, then this will only serve to restrict access to the world where this knowledge is valued. Students who are unable to develop sufficient cultural capital are unlikely to achieve the grades, garner the recommendations, and participate in the networking opportunities that might otherwise have opened certain vocational paths for their consideration.

Two specific mechanisms by which colleges and universities reproduce social class inequality are via admissions criteria and campus activities.[54] First, admissions requirements that favor travel abroad, learning enrichment activities, legacy students, and high SAT scores tend to privilege students from wealthier class backgrounds, as these students are more likely to possess such attributes. Further, skyrocketing tuition costs and fees, combined with a perception that this may lead to a heavy debt burden, have constrained poor students from pursuing higher education. (In reality, many academic institutions have worked hard to make college affordable to students with fewer financial resources, and to avoid saddling them with unreasonable levels of debt; unfortunately, however, this reality is not always transparent to students and parents.) In addition, some students with fewer financial resources may be dissuaded from participating in campus activities, services, and programs that generally require expensive fees or early payments, such as internships and global travel opportunities. As Will Barratt explains, "Leadership experiences, out of school volunteer experiences, school-related activities, summer workshops, years spent abroad are all factors that enhance an application to a highly selective college. Participating in these experiences that build cultural capital

53. Michelle Lamont and Annette Lareau, "Cultural Capital, Allusions, Gaps and Glissandos in Recent Theoretical Developments," *Sociological Theory* 6, no. 2 (Autumn 1988): 153–68, here 156.

54. Jon C. Dalton and Pamela Crosby, "Widening Income Inequalities: Higher Education's Role in Serving Low Income Students," *Journal of College and Character* 16, no. 1 (February 2015): 1–8.

takes money and time."[55] Money and time are scarce resources for poor and working-class students, who are typically juggling the responsibilities of a paid job—and often more than one—in addition to academic and familial responsibilities.

A case study from the *New York Times* highlights how distinctions in cultural capital can play out, illuminating the social class gap in vocational exploration.[56] It describes the marriage of two people, Cate Woolner and Dan Croteau, who came from different social class backgrounds and who both had children from previous marriages. Cate's sons were educated at a private preparatory school; they report no clear idea of what they want to do in life. One of them left college to study in India for a few months and then attended massage school before returning to his undergraduate program. He dreams about opening a "brewery-cum-performance-space, traveling through South America or operating a sunset massage cruise in the Caribbean," and knows he will have the financial backing to do so. In contrast, Dan's daughters are first-generation students, the only ones among twelve cousins who went to college. For both of them, money is continually tight, constraining their vocational options. One of the daughters wanted to begin an internship with a human rights group, but she needs a paid summer job; when she graduates, her debt will push her toward a job with a law firm rather than with a nonprofit. So when one of her stepbrothers "teased her as being a sellout, she reminded him that it was a lot easier to live your ideals when you did not need to make money to pay for them." This example reminds us again of the accumulated nature of privilege and disadvantage; even a new marriage (and thus the combining of economic resources) did not necessarily create a rising tide that could lift all boats.

Employing social class as a way of grasping student needs can furnish beneficial insights into the types of educational and vocation programs that kindle success. We can gain much insight about how to accommodate low-income students from Berea College, where the strategic plan's goal of "comprehending our distinct backgrounds as well as our common American culture" is given flesh by intentional recruitment of low-income

55. Will Barratt, *Social Class on Campus: Theories and Manifestations* (Sterling, VA: Stylus, 2011), 51.

56. Tamar Lewin, "A Marriage of Unequals: When Richer Weds Poorer, Money Isn't the Only Difference," *New York Times*, May 19, 2005. All future citations regarding the Woolner-Croteau family are from this article.

students, a need-blind admission policy, and a tuition waiver based on a student work program.[57] Further, Berea provides many instructive examples of how to recruit and involve marginalized students into vocational programs within the social context of residential living and the liberal arts. For example, its Labor Program and its Center for Excellence in Learning through Service (CELTS) both require students to synthesize deep and disciplined learning, meaningful work, and personal growth—as well as to "develop intellectual, physical, and spiritual characteristics into committed action."[58] Similar programs are in place at other "work colleges" such as Blackburn College and Warren Wilson College, both of which have been active in ongoing national conversations about vocational reflection and discernment.

Though most colleges and universities do not provide students with enough work opportunities to replace tuition costs, they can still find ways of paying closer attention to the impact of social class on student learning and attainment. They can also develop other compensating arrangements so that learning enrichment experiences are more accessible to low-income students; this, too, can aid in tackling the problem of widening income inequality on campus.[59] Programs for vocational exploration and discernment can help institutions of higher education to acknowledge, understand, and remedy social and economic inequalities, and thereby prepare all students to promote a common societal good.

## The weight of accumulation

The basic sociological approach to stratification views inequality as a product of social processes, not innate differences among individuals. Our campuses exist in a racialized, gendered, and classed society. Thus, social inequalities are not just static outcomes of the moment; they accumulate over time.[60] Higher educational organizations need to situate "big questions

---

57. Berea College, "Being and Becoming: Berea College in the 21st Century, The Strategic Plan for Berea College" (Revised May 2011), www.berea.edu/cisrk/files/2012/08/being-and-becoming-june-2011.pdf (accessed December 12, 2015).

58. See Berea College, "Learning, Labor, and Service," www.berea.edu/lws/ (accessed December 12, 2015).

59. Dalton and Crosby, "Widening Income Inequality," 6.

60. For example, women and members of racial and ethnic minorities have lower incomes and higher rates of poverty in old age than do white males because of earlier life experiences,

and worthy dreams"[61] within this social context, moving toward more equitable institutional policies while providing resources on the ground to help develop and strengthen needed skills among faculty, administrators, staff, and students. Such work can go a long way in helping to offset some of the weighty differences between those who have accumulated privileges and those who have accumulated disadvantages over the course of their lives. It may also have an even broader impact: helping academic institutions contribute responsibly toward improving race, gender, and class relations throughout the twenty-first century.[62]

## *Vocation for the long haul*

The life course perspective provides a lens through which we might broaden and deepen conversations about vocation across the disciplines, helping us better understand the process of vocational exploration and discernment as a lifelong enterprise—regardless of a student's major field of study or professional direction. It emphasizes that a student's or an educator's social location is not adequately revealed by a snapshot of a moment in time on campus; various transitions and turning points, as well as accumulated advantages and disadvantages, provide key indicators of how we arrived at a particular place and time, as well as where we might go in the future.

Vocation is not just an individual choice or a caprice of health; it is also shaped by patterns of work and family at large in society, as well as the particular historical era into which we are born. Understanding the nuanced social forces affecting the twenty-first-century life course should play an integral role in our efforts to employ the language of vocation and calling in higher education today.

---

less access to occupations that provide health care and pensions, and constrained opportunities over the life course. See Quadagno, *Aging and the Life Course*, 365.

61. See Parks, *Big Questions, Worthy Dreams*.

62. Watt, "Situating Race," 140. For further reflections on the relationship of vocation to race, class, gender, gender identity, and sexual orientation, see Caryn Riswold, "Vocational Discernment: A Pedagogy of Humanization," in *At This Time and In This Place: Vocation and Higher Education*, ed. David S. Cunningham (New York: Oxford University Press, 2016), 72–95.

# *To Whom Do I Sing, and Why?*

## VOCATION AS AN ALTERNATIVE TO SELF-EXPRESSION

*David Fuentes*

IN THE CREATIVE arts, many assume that the motivation to sing or to dance, to paint a canvas or to write a novel, is a highly personal one: that the artist creates entirely for herself, finding and following her own unique inner voice. According to this view, artists operate with the conviction that their talents set them apart; they work to integrate art-making with their personal stories and seek to make art in their own individual ways. This account echoes Oscar Wilde's claim that "art is the most intense mode of individualism that the world has known." Being an artist is thought to require developing one's own rules for life—as though ordinary civic and interpersonal responsibilities would impinge excessively one one's ability to speak in the free and intensely emotional ways that only true visionaries can.

This conception of the artist may be something of a caricature; certainly, many truly successful artists take a far more down-to-earth approach to their work. Nevertheless, the Romantic ideal of self-expression has an intense pull on our imaginations; it permeates not only the public sphere but also our schools of art and music. These views also reflect the broader individualistic tendencies that are woven throughout our culture. As such, they raise significant questions—not only about the vocations of artists and musicians, but about the vocations of those in other fields as well. In *Habits of the Heart*, Robert Bellah coined the term *expressive individualism* to describe the notion that "each person has a unique core of feeling and intuition that should unfold or be expressed if individuality is to be realized."[1] This pervasive cultural mindset was nicely encapsulated by Steve Jobs, who gave the following advice at Stanford University's 2005 commencement: "Don't let the noise of others' opinions drown out your inner voice. And most important, have the courage to follow your heart and intuition. They somehow already know what you truly want to become."[2]

This raises some interesting questions for vocation. Can one be "called" by one's own voice? And what sort of call would this be? A call merely to express oneself, or perhaps to *transcend* oneself? Should we attend to our own inner voices to the exclusion of all others, or might we be called to contribute our voices to a larger conversation? Unless we more carefully examine our assumptions about this "inner voice" and its drive for self-expression, the language of *vocation* can easily become little more than a way to justify one's own desires—even if these are described less egoistically, as ways of developing and using one's talents and gifts. For students in the arts, the problem is even more acute; our culture's assumptions about creativity and self-expression can undermine the establishment of habits and attitudes that lead to a lasting and meaningful vocation.

Fortunately, educators and students can challenge such assumptions and realign our thinking about the relationship between self-expression and vocation. When students understand that their primary motivation to study a particular field is to become part of the larger human project, they are more likely to aim for a vocation centered on enriching their fellow human beings. They learn to embrace their particular discipline—not because it produces ecstatic experiences or draws attention to themselves, but because it is one of the most human things they can do.

This chapter will suggest how such a shift is possible, and will highlight the role of certain concepts that are associated with the language of *vocation* and *calling* as offering alternatives to narrowly focused accounts of self-expression. I begin with a vignette that illustrates the degree to which students are already uncomfortable with the idea that self-expression provides an exhaustive account of their creative energies. A second section

---

1. Robert N. Bellah et al., *Habits of the Heart: Individualism and Commitment in American Life*, with a new Preface (Berkeley: University of California Press, 2007), 334. (It should be noted that Bellah was highly critical of this perspective.)

2. Steve Jobs, Stanford University commencement address, delivered June 12, 2005, http://news.stanford.edu/news/2005/june15/jobs-061505.html (accessed March 2, 2016).

provides a deeper historical and cultural account of the dominance of self-expression as an artistic paradigm; this is followed by a section offering three strategies as viable alternatives. A concluding section offers another illustrative vignette, demonstrating the kind of thinking that students can do when they are released from standard cultural assumptions about self-expression.

## *Supply and demand*

On the first day of a gateway course for music majors and minors, I pose a question that my students rarely consider: "Why do people listen to music?" I list their responses on the whiteboard:

> because it's fun
> to relax
> to intensify emotions
> to change emotions
> to express oneself
> to set a pace and attitude for exercise
> to feel connected with other people
> to block out bad thoughts

Now, a new question: "Why do musicians make music?" I move over a few feet to start a new list:

> to make people happy
> because it feels right to do it
> to make money
> to express ourselves
> to use and develop my talent
> to connect with other musicians
> to glorify God
> to get attention

Now, we're ready for some fun: "Why don't these two lists match?"
Silence.
I continue: "Should musicians adjust what we do based on what audiences hope for when they listen?" More silence. "Wouldn't that put us in a better position to sell our products and services to potential customers?"

At this point, a conversation breaks out. Though a few students hedge their bets by offering qualified agreement with this description, most try to build arguments that support the idea that music is about something more than emotional gratification—and that musicians are more than entertainers. Still, considering the two very different lists on the board, it can be a hard case to make. So I offer some help.

"What might we make of the fact that both lists mention self-expression? Isn't it a bit strange for a *listener* to say that music helps her 'express herself'? After all, she doesn't make any sound (and may not even move her body) when she listens. How can just listening count as expression?" My students answer with no hesitation. "The music 'says something' that the listener can't say on her own."

"So music has meaning?"

"Of course."

"Even when there are no lyrics?"

A much less energetic "of course . . . ."

"How about from a musician's side of the equation? When you play or sing, are you expressing yourself, or something bigger than yourself?"

We spend some time prodding at the implications of both options. When a singer-songwriter tells us about how he feels about a tumultuous breakup, is he expressing something bigger than himself? Does a musician express herself while she plays a Beethoven piano sonata? Whose emotions are conveyed: hers or Beethoven's? I remind the students that we're not drawing conclusions just yet, that we'll investigate these issues throughout the course. Still, this is something they want to talk about, especially when I ask, "Is it possible for artists to over- or under-express themselves when they perform? What might each extreme look like? And how might an audience react?" Answers are likely to include some variations on these themes:

> If it's not emotional enough, the audience will get bored.
> The music needs to have that certain "spark."
> Your job is to knock the audience out, to make people feel something.
> You don't just learn an instrument, you learn to play a crowd's emotions.

I then ask, "How does a performer learn to create emotional intensity? By registering for 'Knocking Out the Audience 101?'" Polite chuckles.

One student responds, "The more control you have over your instrument, the more you can let your own emotions come through."

So I ask, "What if they come through too strongly? Can a performer's emotions overpower the 'meaning' of the music?" We have now returned to the point where the listeners are using music to help them express themselves.

Music has function; we "use" it as we drive, exercise, cook, and relax. But it also has meaning: music reveals, shapes, and affirms what people feel, experience, desire, and believe. Music not only helps us feel; it also helps us know. As Martin Luther King Jr. put it, "When life itself offers no order and meaning, the musician creates an order and meaning from the sounds of the earth which flow through his instrument."[3] In class, I use this quotation as a bridge to a final exercise.

"Martin Luther King Jr. was a preacher and a civil rights leader. Who else ought we to hear from in this course? What other experts might offer a unique perspective on why people listen to music?" There's still room on the board for one more list:

filmmakers
conductors
songwriters
philosophers
kindergarten teachers
athletic trainers
psychologists

I then point out that "all the types of people you've just mentioned have a lot to say about what music *can* do; several will even offer ideas about what music *should* do." And with a minute left, I wrap up. "I know this is just the first day of class, but let me tell you about your final paper. One question: What do you hope will happen when you walk on stage?"

In the several years I've taught this course, those final papers have never included a single mention of personal satisfaction or finding and expressing one's own unique voice. Many students cringe at their (now former) craving for thunderous applause. Instead, they talk fervently about a new-found desire to perform in a way that helps others receive the many benefits of music they've discovered throughout the course. Another theme

---

3. Martin Luther King Jr., "On the Importance of Jazz," Opening Address of the 1964 Berlin Jazz Festival, http://wclk.com/dr-martin-luther-king-jr-importance-jazz (accessed March 2, 2016).

frequently pervades these final papers: students begin to think of their practice as *service*, rather than a means of self-improvement—a radical shift in a pervasive perspective.

## Expression meets self-expression

For most of human cultural history, the arts have been understood to convey something immensely larger than the individual concerns of the artist who created or performed a particular work. Art could stir the emotions, yes; but its greater aim was often to awaken the mind and the soul to appreciate beauty, truth, and reason. Those who listened to music or viewed art only to indulge their emotions were deemed morally reckless and weak. In the case of music, its crowning glory was its ability to *tune the soul*; it captured, manifested, and instilled the selfsame order underlying the whole universe. Broadly speaking, this way of thinking dominated music from Pythagoras through Mozart.

Since the nineteenth century, however, the continuing dominant role of Romanticism has meant that music's ability to create intense emotional experiences has tended to overshadow its role in promoting order, beauty, and truth. Here, all fingers point at Beethoven, whose early compositions had followed in the classical practice of his immediate predecessors, Haydn and Mozart. Their music emphasized drama, frequently juxtaposing contrasting themes and moods within a single movement; this challenged listeners to follow the course of its main elements—chiefly melodic ideas, in various guises—in the same way that one might scramble to anticipate the fate of a protagonist when reading a novel. Always the innovator, Beethoven pushed every element of classicism much further, leading to an outcome that superseded what anyone might expect: more sudden emotional mood swings and more convoluted narratives.

The response of those listening to Beethoven's music frequently extended beyond mere feelings into what seem to be metaphysical experiences. While a passage by Haydn or Mozart might well capture an emotion that we recognize, Beethoven's music often seems to put us in touch with the unnamable—embodying suffering, joy, yearning, or awe, yet at the same time transcending any of these experiences. And this was no accident. Beethoven called music "the one incorporeal entrance into the higher world of knowledge which comprehends humanity but which humanity cannot comprehend." As such, he believed that "music is a higher revelation than all wisdom and philosophy. Music is the electrical soil in which the spirit lives, thinks and invents."[4]

Starting with Beethoven, then, "the search for transcendence turned inward. Divinity was to be found in the spirit of man, not in a remote and theoretical cosmos.... This earthward shift resulted in a paradox: as the emphasis was transferred to the human scale, the human agent—the artist—came to be regarded as superhuman."[5] While we are unlikely to use the term "superhuman" for an artist today, we do expect one special gift: the ability to locate his or her own unique emotional or spiritual core, and to let it sing. In the same way, those who resonate with a particular artist's output often do so because it helps them find and express *their* own unique emotional or spiritual core. In this sense, a "great" artist is not necessarily a person who has astounding technical abilities; greatness belongs to those who can consistently create emotional experiences that are powerful, even transcendent.

## Strong emotional experiences

The issue of transcendent experiences brings us back to an earlier question: "Does music express something bigger than myself?" Here, we ought to mark a difference between *"communicating* about something bigger than myself" (addressing concerns that we all share) and *"creating* the sense that I can connect with something bigger than myself" (that is, some profoundly overwhelming "force"). This second sense of expression has been explored in a study done over several decades that records over 500 accounts of what have been termed "strong experiences with music" (SEMs).[6] These are instances when listening to or making music resulted in weeping or euphoria, sensations of flying, dizziness, light, or inner warmth, physical and psychic healing, convincing experiences of leaving one's body, and (in two participants) the feeling of being "wrung out like a dishcloth."

---

4. This quotation is attributed to Beethoven in, for example, Nat Shapiro, *An Encyclopedia of Quotations About Music* (New York: Springer Science & Business Media, 2012), 6–7. In its published form, it is actually a description of Beethoven's perspective by his friend Bettina von Armin (Brentano), in one of her letters to Goethe. See William Kinderman, *Beethoven* (Berkeley: University of California Press, 1995), 147.

5. Jamie James, *The Music of the Spheres: Music, Science, and the Natural Order of the Universe* (London, England: Abacus, 1993), 196.

6. Alf Gabrielsson, *Strong Experiences with Music* (New York: Oxford University Press, 2011).

I, too, have had strong experiences with music, though I must admit I don't know how to re-create them within myself—nor teach my students how to produce them when performing. But the very terminology has implications that should concern us: many people believe that unless they have an SEM, they are not truly experiencing music in all its fullness. But if we expect every musical encounter to register a maximum reading on the emotion meter, we not only set ourselves up for frequent disappointment; we also likely reduce, rather than strengthen, our encounter with music. Too exclusive a focus on the emotions disregards the capacity of a work of art to grant comfort, inspire perseverance, affirm the worth of certain virtues, and awaken new perspectives on the human condition. Perhaps even more tragic is that this emphasis on personal artistic experience—using art to retreat into one's own very private world of thoughts and moods—has, for many people, practically replaced its traditional (and far richer) role of drawing us *together*.

## Wowing the audience

Is it possible to locate the point where appropriate musical expression (whether by the performer or listener) transgresses into self-expression? Performing "with expression" (for which we often use the word *musically*) involves adding inflection to certain notes in the same way that speakers use pitch, volume, and timing to clarify the intent of their words. It is hardly coincidental that a speaker's pitch, volume, and timing are all musical elements; without them, human beings couldn't communicate fully. We use music to shape the meaning and gravity of our words—which helps to explain why email correspondence is so frequently misunderstood.

However, playing *emotionally* is considerably easier than playing *musically*. An emotional musician uses passionate feelings to create excitement; a musically expressive musician uses nuance and inflection to convey conviction. Emotions can be conjured, faked, overinflated; musicality, however, requires insight. The emotions are still in play, but they are far richer and have more lasting impact when they arise organically from a response to the content of the musical gestures, rather than being manufactured to impress an audience.

Audiences do not only *love* intense emotion; they typically expect it, even demand it. And this is not only true for the arts. Who would dare think of bringing an idea or product into any arena without strategically considering the audience's emotional response? What mode of presentation will pack the biggest punch? Which single element should I emphasize to give me an edge over my competition? Once I have people's attention, how will I keep it? Such concerns are so ubiquitous that even people with exceptional musical insight can fall into playing the game. Consider Michael Tilson Thomas's reflections on fellow conductor Leonard Bernstein:

> He felt that we wasn't really doing his best unless he was swaying on the precipice of his endurance. Whether he was conducting Mahler or playing a Haydn trio it was the same; oceans of sweat, fluttering eyes, hyperactive athleticism. He'd get a bemused far-away look that seemed to gaze off beyond the horizon into the spirit of the music itself.... Whatever he had to do to achieve it, maintain it, he did. The public loved it, understanding it was all part of the supreme sacrifice of himself he was making for them.

How much of this is necessary? Can a musician execute an effective crescendo without oceans of sweat or hyperactive athleticism? Can someone shape a sweetly tender phrase without fluttering eyelids, or convey longing without a bemused far-away look? Although this description was meant as praise, it also implies that Bernstein's stature was not a product of his extraordinary musical gifts alone; he freely employed a number of "showbiz" elements as well. By placing undo focus on whatever performers might do to elicit an emotional response from their audiences, might we be encouraging others to devalue the actual merit of the work? Have we created a culture of two-year-olds opening presents at Christmas—more interested in the shiny wrapping paper than the contents of the box?

## Self-expression beyond the arts

The arts are not the only place where strong emotional experiences are expected to forge a connection to "unnamable" domains. People in any field are apt to say that they find a strong sense of purpose, identity, and meaning from their work. When we look closer, though, we will often find that these results often depend less on the work itself than on the emotions that are associated with it. Recognizing the inherent relationships between work, personal fulfillment, and emotional rewards, we should also recognize that the various ways we might prioritize these elements will lead to very different approaches to vocational reflection and discernment.

What if we were to return to that Christmas present wrapped in shiny paper, and to think of this as a metaphor for vocation? The present might be quite appealing in its current (wrapped) state, but at another level we know that its essence lies underneath the packaging. We might ask ourselves what part of this vocational "package" gets us most excited. Is it the work that I will be doing, or the personal fulfillment and emotional rewards I derive from doing it? Is it the possible benefits of my vocation for others, or is it the excitement of bringing my gifts into the public arena? These questions raise additional issues in turn. Is my work meaningful because I find it emotionally rewarding, or do I reap emotional rewards from committing to work that I already recognize as meaningful? Is my work meaningful because it lets me fulfill my ambitions, showcase my gifts, and indulge personal preferences? Or do I find personal fulfillment from committing to work that *others* will recognize as meaningful?

There is nothing inherently selfish about hoping for work that is emotionally rewarding and personally fulfilling, just as there is nothing necessarily inherently selfish with hoping for strong emotional experiences through music and the other arts. Much depends on how desperate we are to fulfill these desires, and what we might be drive to sacrifice or overlook in order to do so. In this respect, people in any field are just as likely as a musician or other artist to lapse into self-indulgence and self-importance.

As an example, let me point to a personal temptation I face when I teach. If someone asks, "How did class go today?" I too easily base my response on how it felt to deliver the lecture or lead the discussion: how effortlessly and powerfully my words flowed, whether I thought my own on-the-spot analogies were clever, whether the students appeared engaged and impressed. Experience has proved, however, that none of these emotional rewards indicates whether much actual learning occurred. When I focus too narrowly on these matters, I fail to focus on my vocation as a teacher—which includes the question of what my own audience is experiencing, and in particular, what they are learning. I, too, need to think about those to whom I sing—and why.

## *Alternatives to self-expression*

Once my students become aware of the characteristics of self-expression that I have just described, they seem appalled by their own tendencies to indulge it—though to be fair, they feel trapped by a culture that touts passion and authenticity as abiding among its highest virtues. "How can I ever hope to move an audience if I don't throw everything I have into every performance?" "Why should I become a musician if I don't have something original to say?" In the rest of this chapter, I examine specific approaches to recalibrating purpose and value in ways that dependably lead to a richer and more nuanced manner of expression for both performer and audience. Though the focus is on the role of intuition and imagination in musical performance, I believe that the types of reorientation advocated here can have implications throughout the disciplines and applied fields.

## Reclaiming meaning and interpretation

The most important issue in resisting self-indulgence is that we redirect our focus from the musician's persona to the content of the music itself. By "the music itself" I mean that musical notes "do" something—that all the various ways they might move (or linger) have meaning and significance to us human beings, such that we somehow "get" what each musical gesture is "about." In saying this, I recognize that this notion is not universally accepted. For example, many are persuaded by arguments that music can have no commonly understood meaning (or even that music has nothing like meaning at all). But advertisers and filmmakers know otherwise; they can use music to convey powerful impressions about identity, convictions, fears, and dreams in fractions of a second. Indeed, their skill in this regard helps them make billions of dollars each year.

For teachers, the trick is finding ways to talk about musical meaning so that it becomes apprehensible to the performer (and, for that matter, to the audience as well). The most effective approaches recognize that music is not so much a language of clear thoughts as it is one of multi-layered impressions. Of the several approaches I use in various courses (whether for musicians or nonmusicians), I have found one—cause and effect—to be particularly helpful; it provides specific goals, engages the imagination, and opens up clear options for interpretation. It also has the advantage of being fairly simple; it involves pointing out that the work we do—in my case, making music—isn't magic. Every time we notice an effect (in those who experience our work), we can also find a cause. In the case of music, it may be something in the way that the melody hesitates, or the bass thumps, or the harmonies lean.

Consider a recent cause-and-effect session for "The Rain Song" by Led Zeppelin. As usual, I begin with a broad question: "What mood does the introduction set?" Not surprisingly, the first response is, "I feel raindrops."

So I ask, "Is that because of the title, or something in the music?"

Another student offers, "The cascading opening chord, plus several that come later, seem to spill like rain." Then I play the first bit of the song again.

"Did anything seem different this time?"

Another student, "I could really hear what Lisa described." Aaron—always engaged, but having established permanent residence at the back of the room—says, "It reminds me of my first girlfriend." (I once forbade all personal associations, but then I discovered that sometimes, these can actually stem from elements in the music. The rule in cause and effect is that nothing is out of bounds, so long as the student can explain how the music creates the impression that he or she describes—and do so in a way that others can experience the connection, too.) Aaron adds, "The way the syncopated part seems to swirl reminds me of the way my first girlfriend used to sway and spin in slow motion when she danced."

I use Aaron's description to point out that so many of music's gestures not only emulate but actually embody physical movements (like walking, leaping, reaching) or physical sensations (like our breathing or heartbeat). So, I teach the students another helpful question—"Where do you feel the music in your body?"—which not only keeps cause-and-effect from turning into a mere a mental exercise, but also teaches the students to listen with all of their senses.

As students continue to contribute observations, I discourage them from trying to sew the various ideas into a single story; any unified account that we invent will railroad the more intuitive course that the music is likely to take on its own. Actually, the various gestures and impressions within one piece of music tend to be assembled (by the listener) as though they were impressions in a dream; lingering with them in that way is better than trying to tie everything up into a neat package. The goal is not to figure everything out once and for all, but to discern possible meanings and implications. So, the impressions we collect during a cause-and-effect exercise—mental, physical, emotional—don't uncover the literal meaning of the music, but they do allow us to get to something even more important. They remind us that music operates on (at least) two levels: it has overt meaning, conveyed by lyrics, a title, or association with images, and it also has covert meaning, conveyed through gestures, tone, and rhythm. This is what I referred to earlier when I suggested that music conveys the meaning of our words—the ways we read each other, and the basis of our responses to each other.

In courses for musicians, I ask the students how they might perform the elements of "The Rain Song" they have identified. "What might you do to make the cascading chord seem to 'splash' more?" "How might you shape each subsequent chord a bit differently?" "How could you use tempo to give the syncopated chords a wider spin? A more inward-directed sense of spinning?" As the students share their ideas for all these questions, they can't sit still. Their arms, bodies, and faces are moving—acting out the music.

## Restoring context

Many reputable musicians have recognized a dangerous tendency to sequester music into various silos—academic, highbrow, artistic, niche—rather than considering its broader and more vital roles across all of human culture. We can also become so fixated on the technical aspects of the art form—the "how to" elements that are, of course, a part of every field and discipline—that we can lose track of its wider significance. A helpful guide here is the composer Elliott Carter, whose extraordinarily long career[7] benefited from his deep roots in other fields—mathematics, physics, philosophy, and Greek. He taught all these subjects just before World War II. In 1944, he wrote that

> music departments are too often staffed by professionals with little capacity to see their subject in a broader light than the teaching of special technical demands.... The thoughtful student who is no virtuoso finds little to his taste in a department that teaches skill without an appeal to reason, that attempts to demonstrate many styles but fails to take up the basic question of style itself, of philosophic and historic meaning. The purely practical approach is largely responsible for the low estate to which music, as a vital part of our intellectual equipment, has fallen.[8]

---

7. Elliott Carter continued composing until just before his death at 104. In energy alone, the oeuvre of the last decade of his life rivals that of composers in their 20s or 30s. The solo piano work "Catenaries" is a case in point. When I play it for students, they have a hard time believing that it was composed by a man in his 90s!

8. Elliott Carter, "Music as a Liberal Art," in *Elliott Carter: Collected Essays and Lectures, 1937–1995*, ed. Jonathan W. Bernard (Rochester, NY: University of Rochester Press, 1997), 309–13, here 309.

Carter's objection here is in agreement with what others have said when recognizing a shortcoming of professional training: "trained persons are taught *how* to do something; educated persons also know *why* they do it."[9] This "why" element was further addressed by Henry Fogel, dean of the Chicago College of Performing Arts, when he spoke at the 2009 National Association of Schools of Music Annual Meeting:

> The tired old cliché that the music we believe in is universal, and that it has transformative powers on human beings, is a tired old cliché because it is true. But too few of the people who actually perform that music understand the cultural and social context in which they are currently functioning, and thus do not think about much beyond the art of performing the music. . . . Some schools of music are definitely beginning to address some of these issues. However, I think they are in the minority and those efforts are still in their relative infancy.[10]

Fogel's ideas were picked up, in turn, in the keynote address at the 2010 National Meeting of the College Music Society, given by board member David Myers, chair of the music department at the University of Minnesota:

> I would submit that the greater cause is our shared conviction in the value that music may bring to the universal condition of being human, to being in relationship with one another in an increasingly diverse and too frequently polarized world, and for encouraging creative, intuitive and empathic understanding in a global and interdependent society. In the words of novelist and painter Henry Miller, "Art is only a means to the life more abundant. It is not in itself the life more abundant. It merely points the way, something which is often overlooked by the artist. . . . In becoming an end, [art] defeats itself."[11]

---

9. William F. May, *Beleaguered Rulers: The Public Obligation of the Professional* (Louisville, KY: Westminster John Knox Press, 2001), 8.

10. Henry Fogel, "Keynote Address to the National Association of Schools of Music," November 2009, http://nasm.arts-accredit.org/site/docs/ANNUAL%20MEETING%20 PAPERS/FOGEL_NASM%20SPEECH%20NOV%202009.pdf (accessed March 2, 2016).

11. David Myers, "Music and the Public Good," *College Music Symposium*, September 24, 2010, http://symposium.music.org/index.php?option=com_k2&view=item&id=10303:

Myers, Fogel, and Carter recognize that educators can do a far better job helping students establish a foundation of understanding and depth that will inform and direct their burgeoning technical abilities. In most circumstances, this won't require changing the curriculum, since most disciplines and applied fields include coursework in the history and methodology of the enterprise; most students also take general education courses in other academic departments and programs. Nevertheless, achieving this goal will require more intentional effort on every instructor's part to help students see the relevance of classroom courses—not only on their field as a whole, but, more importantly, on the larger human culture within which these students will live and serve. Posing an open-ended question can prompt students to make such connections themselves. For example, "How does this piece of music open you up to something bigger than the feelings you get while listening to it or playing it?" Here are a few of the avenues down which such an approach might lead.

What might a love song, a dirge, or a call to battle teach about what it means to be a fallible yet responsible member of our human society? (Songs challenge us to know about and understand not only our neighbor, but also people from other times and other cultures.) What are some of the experiences, desires, and convictions present in this piece? How are they complementary, and how do they contradict each other? (Learning how others have tried to make ethical, spiritual, and intellectual sense of the world challenges us to reconsider our own perspectives and assumptions.) Which convictions are embodied in this music? (Through demonstrating the nature and significance of reason, wisdom, courage, patience, and compassion, various fields of study also *foster* these virtues.) How are the overt claims made through the lyrics reinforced or contradicted by the covert suggestions made through the music? (To fully understand anything requires that we weigh evidence skeptically, remembering that there is always more than one side to every issue.)

Questions like these can help students recognize the rich, significant voice that their own field of study might contribute to intellectual work across the disciplines—an aspect of vocation that is frequently undervalued or neglected entirely. Here, it is both illuminating and motivating to

---

music-and-the-public-good-can-higher-education-fulfill-the-challenges-and-opportunities-privileges-and-responsibilities-of-the-21st-century? (accessed March 2, 2016).

point out the unique role that students' creative work might play in awakening intuition, which is so essential in approaching the many important
questions we face. This connection has been noted by many observers—
including Albert Einstein, who commented that "If what is seen and
experienced is portrayed in the language of logic, then it is science. If it
is communicated through forms whose constructions are not accessible
to the conscious mind but are recognized intuitively, then it is art."[12] As
one specific instance among many, Einstein once eagerly told Shinichi
Suzuki, the inventor of the Suzuki method of music education, that "the
theory of relativity...occurred to me by intuition, and music was the
driving force behind that intuition.... My discovery was the result of
musical perception."[13]

If the arts can help people grasp constructions that are not accessible
to the conscious mind, it should be clear why so many people recognize
the "spiritual" dimension of these fields. This may involve a claim that that
the arts themselves exert supernatural power, but it need not do so. For
example, Christian theologian Stephen Guthrie, in speaking of the relationship between the arts and the Holy Spirit, reminds us that the senses
are broadly connected to a more general sense of spiritual capacity and the
fullness of human life:

> In music, painting, and the other arts, our senses are engaged and
> enlarged, our physical experience both refined and broadened. We
> attend carefully to both the world and to our own physical experi-
> ence of it. We gain practice in those very capacities that together
> indicate life and health—sight, hearing, attention, and responsive-
> ness to touch. We become, in a very real sense, more fully embod-
> ied, more fully incarnate. In this regard, the arts mirror the work of
> the Spirit. The Sprit's work is to make us responsive. Conversely,
> those who are spiritually dead have quite literally lost their senses.
> The biblical descriptions of their conditions are a litany of sensory
> deprivation.... They are blind, deaf, and mute (Isa. 43:8); eyes that
> do not see and ears that do not hear (Ezek. 12:2; Mark 8:18); they

---

12. Albert Einstein, *Menschen* 4 (January 1921), letter to the editor. Cited in *The Expanded
Quotable Einstein*, ed. Alice Calaprice (Princeton, NJ: Princeton University Press, 2000), 271.

13. Shinichi Suzuki, *Nurtured by Love: A New Approach to Education*, trans. Waltraud Suzuki
(New York, New York: Exposition Press, 1969), 90.

have become calloused (Matt. 13:15), hardened in their hearts, and have lost all sensitivity (Eph. 4:18–19).[14]

When artists embrace these connections, they can ignite their audiences' imaginations in ways that help them engage more responsibly—both with the art that is created for them and with the broader issues raised by those works.

Evoking this level of engagement in the audience is an indispensable aspect of the artist's vocation. Focusing on excellent technique alone will never achieve this—not even when combined with excellent expressivity. Indeed, we might do well to question our natural enthusiasm for the word *excellence*—a word which appears prominently in the majority of mission statements for arts departments across the country. Too often, this word grants excessive authority to those who have achieved some (arbitrarily defined) mark of technical ability, and who display those abilities in emotionally impressive ways. As an alternative to *excellence*, we might consider a word like *faithfulness* or *service*.

## Responding to the material

Finally, I want to suggest that whatever we offer to others through our vocations—whether tangible or otherwise—is ultimately a very *material* offering. Particularly in the arts, but in other fields as well, it is tempting to think of our offerings as mysterious, esoteric, and not really subject to the limits of the material world. This, too, is part of the legacy of Romanticism. As John Freeman notes,

> Romanticized ideas of the artist's otherness, of art arising out of inspirational leaps taken by the innately creative, remain common currency in our general (in)comprehension of the creative process. As well as providing a somewhat misleading idea of art making, they fuel the belief that creativity is beyond analysis; that the ways of making art are instinctive rather than reflective, and that its processes should remain shrouded in secrecy.[15]

---

14. Stephen Guthrie, *Creator Spirit: The Holy Spirit and the Art of Becoming Human* (Grand Rapids, MI: Baker Books, 2011), 69–70.

15. John Freeman, "First Insights Fostering Creativity in University Performance," *Arts and Humanities in Higher Education* 5, no. 1 (February 1, 2006): 96.

Escaping from this shroud of secrecy is difficult, but it can be done. When Chilean poet Pablo Neruda describes his art making, he likens it to the very *material* mystery of ironing laundry. His first images come out of the washing tub, "wrinkled, all in a heap." They must be wrestled onto the ironing board, where "the hands keep moving, moving, / smoothing out the sacred surfaces." That, he tells us, "is how things are accomplished."[16]

This is not an exercise in false humility. The ordinary, everyday elements of any artist's work, like that of someone who washes clothes, requires extricating elements from the swirling, chaotic foam of the cosmos. These must be wrung out, stretched, ironed, and formed into something that can be deemed "good." Perhaps the composer happens upon a bit of material that catches her fancy—a chord, a rhythm, or a snippet of melody. In the rough, the material has good potential, but it is undeveloped; it needs shaping, smoothing, stretching, trimming, and just the right placement. So, the composer responds to it and forms it until it feels "exactly right." She "knows"—*senses*—when it pops into place—when it sounds "in tune."

When something is truly in tune, it can't be made more in tune; any change will knock it out of tune again. Once the creator of the piece is satisfied, she passes it off to a performer—for whom, on first encounter, it may well again feel "wrinkled, all in a heap." So, the performer also must practice it, respond to it—making adjustments in this riff, in that crescendo—until the music feels "in tune" to him as well. The audience responds, resonating with the order that the performer has found in the composer's music.

As we attend to the material from which our work is constructed, and as we bring it in tune, we are making "faith statements"—intuitive ones— about our sense of what the world is supposed to be like. We might not recognize this every time we hear a lullaby or an advertising jingle, but it does occur; moreover, our calibration of what makes something "in tune" is shaped by a multitude of factors. Some can be identified: our own formation and training, various personal experiences, and a rich, complex stew of cultural influences. But other shaping forces are more ephemeral— including the unnamable desires, fears, convictions, and delights that are more easily captured by gestures than by words. We not only strive to bring

---

16. Pablo Neruda, *Fully Empowered*, trans. Alastair Reid (New York: Farrar, Straus and Giroux, 2001), 37. [English translation of *Plenos Poderes*, 1962.]

out work "in tune"; we also seek to respond to the wider world—groaning, as St. Paul suggests, in chorus with the noisy ongoing song of creation:

> The creation itself will be set free from its bondage to decay and will obtain the freedom of the glory of the children of God. We know that the whole creation has been groaning in labor pains until now; and not only the creation, but we ourselves, who have the first fruits of the Spirit, groan inwardly while we wait for adoption, the redemption of our bodies. (Rom. 8:21–23)

Musicians and other artists are often singled out for their ability to look at a broken, disheveled world, to reimagine it without wrinkles, and to craft a song or painting that makes hope and freedom tangible for the rest of us. But what Paul indicates in this passage is that this motivation is not limited to one particular field or vocation; it is just as true for the plumber and the professor as it is for the potter and the police officer. We all groan—first, as we become aware of everything that needs our attention; and then, as we use our unique gifts, training, and intuition to unearth and bring forth everything that is innate, possible, and best. This requires action on our parts, but it also requires resisting the temptation to impose our own will onto the material or situation at hand.

Our calling, then, is the discovery and articulation of order. Consider what might happen if we were to broaden the notion of responsive work beyond the scope of music into the arts more generally, and indeed to every field in which something is created or done for others. The shared space between performer and audience has parallels with other shared spaces: between worker and customer, teacher and student, researcher and research community. Hence, the process of "responding to the material" plays a role in everything we create: songs or sculptures, knowledge or skills, products or services. Starting with a deeply instilled sense of the human value and purpose of the work we do, we use talent and training to respond meaningfully to the materials at hand—not abstractly or in ways that serve our egos or emotional needs, but in ways that also respond to the true needs of our neighbor. This can take place through a concise mathematical equation or a foolproof recipe for peanut brittle, a multifaceted high school production of *Hamlet*, an elegant earthquake-resistant suspension bridge, or a peaceably monitored protest rally.

Responsive work, then—rightly done and rightly directed—liberates both the worker and those whom the work serves. And if we began to name and explore all the ways that our work moves and awakens us and others as we offer it, I submit that this will not only inspire us to reimagine why we do whatever we do; it can also radically reorient our vision of vocation.

## Connecting our performances with our audiences

In a sense, we have come full circle. This chapter began by describing the artist's work as an intense expression of thoughts and experiences, and it may seem that we find ourselves in a similar situation once again. But there is a clear difference, and it revolves around *motivation*. To the extent that making art centers on the person making it, it becomes a means of gratifying the artist's emotional or egotistic needs. In contrast, art that remains centered on the material at hand opens space for the audience to delight in, work out, bemoan, or simply ponder the many experiences, desires, and convictions we all share. When the focus is too narrowly on self-expression, art is likely to aim for emotional intensity rather than emotional depth. Artists easily create the "wow" factor by appealing directly to the audience's emotions through exaggerated displays of passion or by using manipulative, self-adulating theatrical tricks. In contrast, the thoughts and feelings that arise from encountering the actual content of a work of art prompt insight, contemplation, empathy, and resolve.

Here, the role of education is integral, as teachers can demonstrate methods for exploring content (as we saw with the cause-and-effect exercise), and can engender habits of reflection and engagement that connect art and music to the larger concerns they embody. And how does this embodiment occur? The ways that the artist brings the basic materials of her craft into order betray her deepest intuitions about everything that is right and wrong in our world. In this sense, the utterly material work of the artist is at the same time deeply spiritual. Indeed, the selfsame impulses for order-making motivate all manner of responsive work across the trades and disciplines.

The true significance of an artist's work, then, doesn't originate from within the artist herself but, rather, draws its substance from experiences and concerns common to us all. In this way, our struggle is not a struggle to express ourselves so much as it is a struggle for meaning, for clarity, for light. And the more faithfully we groan or exult as we sing or make art, the more readily our audiences will recognize their own voices in ours, and the freedom in our notes might liberate our neighbor, as well.

With this in mind, I'll close with another exercise from my music course designed to get at some of these very issues. I invite students to compare ten versions ("covers") of "Over the Rainbow." We start with Judy Garland's original rendition from *The Wizard of Oz*. Students describe her performance as melancholy, dreamy, resigned. When I ask which musical features might produce these impressions, they point to Garland's lazy rubato, her subdued tone, the smooth sound of the swing orchestra, and the bouncy but somewhat lazy pattern in the bass. I take notes on the board, and tell the students that they're free to revise or add more comments after hearing other versions.

Next, I present a gypsy jazz rendition, much faster, with a highly ornamented variation of the melody tune and a sunny, energetic guitar accompaniment. Here, students frequently mention an urge to dance (or at least engage in vigorous foot tapping). I follow this with a much more drawn-out version by Placido Domingo. The introduction itself takes over a minute, and is more serene than either of the earlier versions (placid, as one punster once added). But as soon as the voice enters, we're more amazed than moved. Such perfection! Students categorize it as "so perfect that it's hard to believe that he's longing for a better life."

Then I play a version by Bob Schneider: no orchestra this time, just an acoustic guitar and a raw, gravelly baritone. His voice cracks and strains to hit the notes; sustaining anything seems out of the question. This version evinces little energy (except in brief bursts) and no reverb; yet there's something utterly compelling here. I've done this presentation now well over a dozen times, and the students' reactions to this version always run the same way. They picture a father, broken and world-worn, singing to his child. Here, the song's central message—dreaming for a better life—is not the personal experience of the singer; it is, rather, his hope for his child. This isn't singing for the pure self-satisfaction of singing; Schneider's version is so much more than an autonomous experience.

After hearing this version, I ask the students why they didn't think of the audience in the previous versions. They have a hard time answering, but when pressed, they can imagine the setting of each of the performances, even though the musicians don't seem to have the same sort of connection with their audiences. And then a few more covers. Tori Amos's voice also cracks and strains, but the students don't buy it; most say that it's completely manufactured, an attempt to seem emotionally vulnerable.

Then the jazz piano virtuoso Art Tatum, where students are torn: they marvel at his technique, but are baffled (some are angry) as to why he obliterates the meaning of the song. A short discussion about "showing off" ensues: students recognize that fast fingers, perfect vocal technique, and heart-wrenching feelings can serve either the music or the performer's ego. Sometimes the discussion goes even further, with students outlining conditions where showcasing talent is most and least appropriate.

I will admit that the first time I gave this presentation, I was surprised that students were willing to take such strong positions on what was effective and what was not. Our culture tends to expect uncritical acceptance of others' musical tastes and practices; anything that even lightly smacks of judgment is considered a despicable vice. But given the right opportunity—in this case, side-by-side comparisons—students will enthusiastically argue that style and technique are not only about the performer. They either communicate or obfuscate something essential—something we all need to hear. And it turns out that this is what they, too, want to happen when they walk on stage.

# 6

## Coordination, Community, Covenant

### INSIGHTS FROM ORGANIZATION THEORY

*Michael E. Cafferky*

IN 2015, WHEN the United States was playing against Japan in the final game of the FIFA World Cup, Carli Lloyd sealed the victory by scoring a hat trick. Lloyd is a midfielder; those who play this position are expected to be skilled at passing the ball to the forwards, who are the specialists at striking at closer range. But Lloyd is also known for her ability to strike the ball accurately from a long distance, as though she were a forward. Other players on the team had developed more than one specialty as well: Julie Johnston, a defender, also participated as an offensive striker when the ball entered play from a corner kick. Her abilities were well known to opposing teams, but they still had difficulty stopping her from scoring.

These are examples of highly skilled specialists at work. Team sports demand such specialization; however, the greatest teams are those in which individuals are able to go beyond their own special assignments and to participate in something larger. Even if a team boasted excellent players in every position, and even if each player had honed her specialty to perfection, something would be missing. Teams are strongest when their specialized players have secondary skills and talents that overlap with those of their teammates; the most effective teams are those in which these various abilities are well integrated into a whole. Success is more likely for teams with a well-thought-out organizational structure—one that integrates the specialized roles of its individual players, who in turn bring a wider range of strengths.

Higher education faces the same structural challenge as does the soccer team. Faculty, staff, and students are specialists in their various fields and roles—developing expertise in various specific areas of the curriculum, offering and utilizing specialized support services in both academic and extracurricular enterprises, and keeping abreast of new developments in their various fields. Ideally, however, all these individuals would also be seeking a broader use for the specialized knowledge they gain and the practices they develop, such that these various specializations can be integrated into a more coherent whole. Needless to say, however—given the various pressures on higher education to produce experts in fairly narrow fields of study—these latter goals too often fall by the wayside.

This problem has had a particularly significant impact on business education. Often, undergraduate majors learn accounting from one instructor specializing in that field, marketing from another, and management from a third. Similarly, business law, economics, and finance are all seen as their own subfields; each is often taught by its own specialist instructors and learned by students in separate courses. The more highly specialized these fields of study have become, the greater is the need for intentional efforts to integrate them into a whole—preferably through teaching–learning experiences that allow students to understand how these various fields relate to one another. And if the students in each subfield fail to develop secondary specializations (as did the championship soccer team), they will not be able to contribute as fully to the organizations that they will eventually serve.

Extreme forms of specialization can also have a detrimental impact on the work of vocational reflection and discernment. Faculty become excessively specialized, and students develop similar tendencies; in the end, neither is able to provide the kind of balanced assistance to others that is so well demonstrated by a successful soccer team. Specialists who focus too narrowly on their own fields cannot be so easily integrated into the work of an organization as whole; this remains the case whether the setting is a university, a for-profit company, a governmental organization, or a nonprofit agency. Those who discern their vocations too narrowly (or too individualistically) may find it very difficult to carry out that vocation in the real organizations in which they are likely to work.

While the problem of vocational overspecialization cannot be solved in a single stroke, this chapter will argue that the field of organization theory offers certain insights that may be helpful in rethinking our current circumstances. While vocational reflection and discernment can be important elements of undergraduate education, their benefits can be easily vitiated by academic overspecialization. This is a structural problem, having to do with the way colleges and universities are organized; it is therefore amenable to a structural solution.

This chapter begins by employing the terms of organization theory to consider how persons are differentiated from each other and yet integrated for achieving group goals. This structural account allows us to see vocational discernment both as a specialized individual function and one that needs to be integrated with other community-building processes. The second section examines the structural tensions inherent in organizations: tensions between individual interests and community interests, as well as those between self-identity and group identity.[1] Managing these structural tensions is a complex process; thus, in the third section, we turn to the concept of *covenant* and consider its potential as an integrating influence within larger organizations. A final section considers some ways that institutions of higher education might develop better forms of vocational reflection and discernment, in which individual "specialists" are willing to go beyond their narrowly defined fields to contribute to a more integrated whole.

## *Organizations and specialization*

In the business disciplines, many scholars have examined how the organizational and structural dynamics of a goal-oriented social group can best be managed.[2] One can, of course, come to a better understanding of these groups by exploring the specific characteristics of their members—examining, for example, intrapersonal, psychological, and interpersonal

---

1. These three interrelated sets of structural tensions (specialization and integration, individual and community, self-identity and group identity) form a threshold concept for understanding the vocational discernment process. For more on the notion of threshold concepts, see chapter 7 of this volume.

2. Important work in this field over the last half century includes that by Amitai Etzioni, *A Comparative Analysis of Complex Organizations: On Power, Involvement, and Their Correlates* (New York: Free Press, 1961); Peter M. Blau and W. Richard Scott, *Formal Organizations: A Comparative Approach* (San Francisco: Chandler, 1962); Paul R. Lawrence and Jay W. Lorsch, *Organization and Environment: Managing Differentiation and Integration* (Homewood, IL: Richard D. Irwin, 1969); W. Richard Scott, *Organizations and Organizing: Rational, Natural and Open Systems Perspectives*, 5th ed. (Upper Saddle River, NJ: Prentice Hall, 2002); and Mary Jo Hatch and Ann L. Cunliffe, *Organization Theory* (Oxford: Oxford University Press, 2006).

influences. Such approaches are certainly valid, but they also have their limitations.[3] A structural perspective can help to compensate for some of the deficiencies of other viewpoints; it can help us see how organizations are shaped by larger and broader concerns that may not be reflected in their individual members.

Human beings arrange their relationships structurally to accomplish certain goals; their work often has a direct impact on others. We call these goal-oriented groups *organizations* precisely because the individuals and subgroups within the larger entity are more or less *organized* for fulfilling commitments to various stakeholders. Organizations typically carry out their work by assigning their members various specialized tasks; the more complex the environment in which an organization operates, the more such specialization occurs.[4] Similarly, more complicated tasks generally call for a higher degree of specialization among members. For example, in certain businesses, purchasing agents inside the organization obtain materials that are used by specialists within various operating units; these specialists use the materials to make things that are sold by sales professionals and distributed by specialists in logistics. Over time, the task-related knowledge of these specialists increases.

Specialization tends to increase efficiency; however, it also results in organizational "silos" that can tend to operate independently of one another. Specialization may begin as a response to complexity in the *external* environment, but it also contributes to the *internal* complexity of the organization.[5] Specialization can, therefore, have an unfavorable impact on the effectiveness of the organization as a whole in fulfilling its commitments.

## Integration and coordination

To address the problems created by specialization, organizations rely on *integration* and *coordination*. We might say that these strategies sit at one end of a spectrum, in dynamic tension with specialization, which lies at the

---

3. Lee G. Bolman and Terrence E. Deal, *Reframing Organizations: Artistry, Choice and Leadership*, 3rd ed. (San Francisco: Jossey-Bass, 2003), 25–44.

4. In many organizations, specialization takes the form of differentiation of tasks or division of labor.

5. Peter M. Blau, Wolf V. Heydebrand, and Robert E. Stauffer, "The Structure of Small Bureaucracies," *American Sociological Review* 31, no. 2 (1966): 179–91.

other end. Each force pulls in a somewhat different direction with respect to the organization as a whole, each counteracts the deleterious impacts of the other, and—if not properly managed—each is at risk of undermining the other. Ideally, however, integration and coordination can balance the more typical organizational tendencies toward excessive specialization.

*Integration* is fostered through a shared desire for accomplishing organizational goals and mission; it focuses on shared mental and emotional responses to common problems, as well as shared moral assumptions.[6] For example, when players on a sports team understand the strategy for the upcoming contest with their rival, or when they share knowledge about the weaknesses of their opponent, this keeps them focused on a common approach to the game. Players self-monitor and adjust their own behaviors while keeping in mind the group's overall strategy. Similarly, when an organizational goal is clear to members of a sales team, they tend to make a more concerted effort to accomplish that larger goal, rather than focusing on their individual sales quotas.

*Coordination*, which is closely related to integration, involves the use of direct contact between supervisors and subordinates, direct contact among employees, and the careful joint management of schedules, plans, policies, procedures, liaisons, committees, task forces, and teams.[7] So, for example, when a restaurant server writes down an order and delivers it to someone in the kitchen, this written or spoken order is a simple coordinating device. For instructors and students, the course syllabus is a coordinating mechanism; it provides information that the entire class can use in preparation for assignments, discussion, and assessment.

Some coordinating devices also serve as integrating influences. For example, the syllabus is a coordinating mechanism (if it contains a schedule of due dates and other expectations), but it is also a tool that brings about integration by, for example, clarifying the course's learning objectives. Much as a company policy manual does for employees, the syllabus communicates the rules and values that the instructor expects the class to embody.

6. John Child, *Organization: Contemporary Principles and Practice* (Malden, MA: Blackwell, 2005), 79–110; Dan E. Schendel and Charles W. Hofer, *Strategic Management: A New View of Business Policy and Planning* (Boston: Little, Brown, 1979), 258–59.

7. Schendel and Hofer, *Strategic Management*, 258–59; Richard H. Hall and Pamela S. Tolbert, *Organizations: Structures, Processes and Outcomes*, 9th ed. (Upper Saddle River, NJ: Pearson Prentice Hall, 2005), 34–44.

Organizational leaders have the responsibility to oversee the tension between specialization, on the one hand, and integration and coordination, on the other. In fulfilling this oversight role, leaders are also serving the needs of the larger society to which the organization is linked, which can lead to greater personal and communal flourishing. Nevertheless, the structural choices that leaders make come with tradeoffs. Opting for a particular organizational plan will mean forgoing opportunities that could have been enjoyed by organizing in a different way; leaders typically must make adjustments to manage the less desirable results of those particular organizational choices. Often these negative elements will not be immediately revealed; only over time will all of the weaknesses of a particular structural choice become apparent. For example, some start-up family businesses are structured along traditional functional lines, in which workers are divided according to assigned tasks and the owner maintains close centralized decision-making authority. As the business grows, however, employees will eventually need more autonomy to make decisions. If a decision-making authority is not shared by the owner with managers, the organization will find it difficult to continue growing.

## Implications for vocation

From these structural elements we can discern certain implications for thinking about vocation in the undergraduate setting. A college or university is also an organization, and it has its own tendencies toward specialization; moreover, academic institutions want to encourage their members to develop their own talents and skills and to provide meaningful service to others. As these institutions continue to develop programs for vocational reflection and discernment, they need to be attentive to the hazards of specialization. If these programs can be coordinated with one another and integrated into a coherent whole, they can participate in the same kinds of advantages that these strategies accrue in other organizational settings. And to whatever degree they can take some of the burden of this integrative work off the shoulders of the individual student, the more likely they are to achieve their intended results.

For example, most undergraduate institutions encourage students to participate in various forms of career counseling.[8] The goals of this work

---

8. Virginia N. Gordon, *Career Advising: An Academic Advisor's Guide* (San Francisco: Jossey–Bass, 2006).

include attending to the student's temperament and personality traits, improving self-awareness and self-acceptance, helping the student shape an educational plan that is consistent with his or her career goals, and evaluating progress the student is making. This kind of help can certainly be beneficial and can serve as an efficient form of feedback; still, the focus is on the inner cognitive decision being made by an individual student, who is still considered the "specialist" in finalizing these decisions. Moreover, career counseling can focus on helping students find "that one job" that matches their abilities, without reference to the kinds of secondary specializations that are in high demand today (and in all kinds of organizations, not just in soccer teams!). While the person–job match is an important consideration, by itself it lacks the elements of integration and coordination that are so important in the complex process of vocational discernment. The career counselor can thus represent something of an organizational silo for vocational discernment—one that may or may not have any meaningful contact with other related parts of the institution.

Vocational reflection might also be prompted by a student's conversations with a residence hall staff member, a coach, or another person who has had the opportunity to develop a fairly clear sense of how the student engages with others (and the role these traits might play in the student's future). Much can be gained by this process, particularly since some students seem largely unaware of their impact on others. And of course, any conversation with a trusted advisor could certainly help a student think about careers to consider, how to position him- or herself with prospective employers, and how to engage in other meaningful activities that will lead to a life of fulfillment and purpose. At the same time, these kinds of conversations can contribute to the problem of specialization, since individual mentors necessarily observe students from their own limited perspectives. If one mentor is not in conversation with others who might be advising the student, the burden for integration returns on the shoulders of the individual student.[9]

Finally, students may be in conversation with faculty members, who may encourage students to consider a particular career—particularly if that career aligns with the faculty member's discipline or field of expertise. This allows the advisor to provide information about the true nature

---

9. This is not meant as a negative judgment on mentoring in general, which can be an important element of vocational discernment. However, it may be at its best when it is deliberately communal in focus; I will return to this point below.

of the profession or career, to explain its benefits and its drawbacks, and to describe the type of work that it involves and the avenues it provides for career advancement. Perhaps more importantly, it provides an opportunity for the student to learn about how this kind of work shapes the rest of one's life: how it affects one's secondary engagements, avocations, and leisure time. But like the other advisors mentioned here, the faculty member typically has access to only certain elements of a student's overall profile—usually the intellectual elements, or those based on observation of the student in the classroom or the laboratory. This may or may not square with the picture gained by a staff member who sees the student outside those environments, or the career counselor who has access to other data about the student's talents and capacities. And of course, while faculty members can speak to these issues in their own disciplines, they are rarely in a position to compare their own experiences with those of colleagues in very different fields of study or professional work.

As the chapters in this book illustrate, the work of vocational reflection and discernment among undergraduate students takes place in an extremely complex environment. If our hope is that these students will find the place in society where they can flourish, then we would be unwise to think of them as the "specialists" in this work of discernment—particularly since they are likely to be the least experienced persons in the equation. But this is precisely what too many institutions have been willing to do; as a result, the academy can begin to mirror the modern Western elevation of individual choice and self-expression.[10] In essence, we ask students to become integrators and coordinators with respect to a task (vocational discernment) with which they often have little experience. This remains true even in those cases in which someone else (perhaps a parent or a pastor) plays an important role in guiding a decision about vocation. The highly specialized nature of institutions of higher education makes integration a challenge. Moreover, as the introduction to this volume suggests, these institutions experience their own internal tensions, including those that can make it difficult to integrate learning *across* the various disciplines and applied fields. And this only covers the academic side of the equation; we need to add the various roles of other divisions of the institution, including

---

10. On choice, see especially William T. Cavanaugh, "Actually, You Can't Be Anything You Want (and It's a Good Thing, Too)," in *At This Time and In This Place: Vocation and Higher Education*, ed. David S. Cunningham (New York: Oxford University Press, 2016); on self-expression, see especially chapter 5 of this volume.

student development, career services, residential life, and athletics. If each of these various programs attempts to help students undertake vocational reflection and discernment—and if they do so without integration and coordination—then all the problems of specialization will be loaded on to the shoulders of the student. No surprise, then, that an atomistic and overly specialized approach to vocation renders it an individual, cognitive process—thereby leading students to think of it primarily in terms of self-fulfillment, or even just as "finding a job." From the student's point of view, it is easier to retreat into this language than to juggle the various (and frequently competing) bits of advice received from myriad sources.

## *Individual and community in tension*

The structural perspective that we have been exploring here, derived from organization theory, has two counterparts in the field of social psychology. The first of these is best described as the tension of individual and community; the second is the related challenge of achieving both self-identity and group identity. These counterparts are structurally at the root of academic disciplines such as philosophy, psychology, and sociology; they are also fundamental to social experiences in families, in the workplace, and in many other settings in which human beings relate to one another: business, politics, ethics, and leadership studies. We therefore need to explore these tensions in greater detail.

Finding meaning *in* life—as well as its first cousin, finding one's calling *for* life—both need to be acknowledged as social and communal experiences. While we cannot deny the intrapersonal dimension of vocational discernment, the discernment of one's calling—and the expression of that calling in a meaningful life in relation with others—occurs in a social context. We reflect on our vocational journeys with the people around us (in the present), with or because of other people who have been important to us (from the past), and with still other people in view (for the future).[11] Vocational discernment requires attending to one's own circumstances, but also to the needs of the larger communities of which our vocations are a part.[12]

---

11. The issue of community has been effectively explored in Peter Block, *Community: The Structure of Belonging* (San Francisco: Berrett-Koehler, 2008). For a somewhat older perspective, see Roland L. Warren, *The Community in America* (Chicago: Rand McNally, 1972).

12. Other resources include Steward R. Clegg, *Management and Organization Paradoxes, Advances in Organization Studies* 9 (Amsterdam: John Benjamins, 2002); Uichol Kim,

From the perspective of organization theory, this tension is the "basic and enduring problem."[13] It is closely related to the fundamental paradox of our lives in relation to others around us: human beings desire to relate to others, and also to be distinctive from the groups to which we belong.[14] Similarly, vocational discernment encourages a person to express his or her individual identity, but this is never completely autonomous; our membership in various groups provides a context within which we can make distinctive contributions, even as we assimilate the claims of the group into our individual identities. This does not mean that individual needs are fulfilled only at the expense of community needs (nor the opposite); vocation is not a zero-sum game. Rather, precisely because individual and community are so integrally related, so must our vocations be attentive to the simultaneous fulfillment of individual needs and the needs of others.[15]

When vocation focuses too narrowly on the individual, this only deepens the tendencies toward isolation in contemporary life. We move seamlessly and quickly from one social role, one social institution to another in the routine of our lives. In such circumstances, any real sense of "belonging" may remain fairly superficial. Even volunteer service tends to be taken up on a temporary basis only, so that the volunteer is free to make connections elsewhere on short notice.

Ultimately, one's calling is inseparable from the larger community; it can never be autonomous or purely individual in its expression. In fact, the community often presents or transmits the vocational call; it is usually the vehicle, and may sometimes even be the source, of the callings that we discern.[16] Communities are the repositories of wisdom, the transmitters

---

Harry C. Triandis, S. Cigdem Kagitcibasi, Sang-Chin Choi, and Gene Yoon, *Individualism and Collectivism: Theory, Method and Applications* (Thousand Oaks, CA: Sage, 1994); Kenwyn K. Smith and David N. Berg, *Paradoxes of Group Life: Understanding Conflict, Paralysis and Movement in Group Dynamics* (San Francisco: New Lexington, 1997); and Stephen Young, *Moral Capitalism: Reconciling Private Interest with the Public Good* (San Francisco: Berrett–Koehler, 2003).

13. Charles Perrow, *Complex Organizations: A Critical Essay*, 3rd ed. (New York: McGraw-Hill, 1986), 66. Other scholars who have identified this paradox include Emil Durkheim, Henri Fayol, and Talcott Parsons.

14. Tom Postmes and Jolanda Jetten, *Individuality and the Group: Advances in Social Identity* (Thousand Oaks, CA: Sage, 2006).

15. For further reflections on this relationship, see chapter 1 of this volume.

16. See, for example, some of the elements of community described in chap. 2 of Etienne Wenger, *Communities of Practice: Learning, Meaning, Identity* (Cambridge: Cambridge

of good practices, and the shapers of moral conscience and virtues. If persons do not participate in the communal sharing of wisdom about each other, their understanding of how they can contribute to society will be severely limited. Hearing a call thus involves noticing and interpreting the signals from others around us with respect to determining which needs are most important to a community, as well as how we can best address these needs.[17]

In vocational reflection and discernment, the role of the community can take many forms. For example, campus leaders or student groups sometimes bring to campus guest lecturers, artists, or other professionals who can share the stories of their own vocational journeys. In my own context, one seminar is built around weekly sessions that feature the narrative of a person who uses his or her calling to serve in a business or nonprofit organization. These guests are not part of the campus community, but they represent the wider communities that students are preparing to enter upon graduation. Those who attend these events have the opportunity to visualize themselves in new situations or roles, where their own deep passions will connect with needs of others.

A greater focus on the community might encourage us to ask, "What am I called to be so that others in my community—or others in a community of which I am not yet a part—can fulfill *their own* callings?" Asking this question provides a means of inviting the community to play a more significant role in helping its members discern their callings. This requires that persons in community be encouraged to provide feedback to one another, which can help to shape the callings of individuals and of the community as a whole.

Every semester I observe one or more students who have the gift of identifying core issues and then articulating these to fellow classmates. Others have the ability to ask a key question that highlights a central issue and sparks further conversation. I usually have a personal conversation with such students, asking them if they have thought about where they might use this gift to serve others. Sometimes the question is, "Have you thought about preparing to serve by honing these gifts in graduate school or advancing your intellectual development in a doctoral degree?" To

---

University Press, 1998). In addition, almost every chapter in this book offers examples in which a person's calling is heard, shaped, and discerned in community.

17. Warren, *The Community in America.*

encourage the student to think beyond just a job or career, I ask, "Have you thought about how you might serve others by being an advocate? What might be the options for you to develop your talents and abilities?"

Finally, the community is the setting in which higher-order concerns are discerned so that all members of that community can respond to them. In the world of business, for example, this means that some people become passionate about creating objects that can contribute to a flourishing life. Among this group are those who have a certain degree of foresight and courage that allows them to take entrepreneurial risks on behalf of society. They plan, organize, arrange, and coordinate their way through the community, pulling together resources that can be beneficial. Similarly, a community seeks to preserve the physical health and social harmony of its members. This encourages some individuals to pursue the technical training they will need to become doctors, caregivers, educators, therapists, and counselors. Others advocate on behalf of vulnerable and marginalized members of society. Still others foster safety by committing to serve and protect. At the same time, community relationships remind us that calling involves more than simply doing one's job; it involves engagement with the domestic, social, and political spheres, and it shapes how one thinks of avocations and leisure.[18] In all these ways, we are responding to the higher-order concerns of the community by discerning vocations to which we can dedicate our lives.

## *From community to covenant*

Community provides a space within which we can attempt to manage the tensions between specialization and integration, and between individual needs and the needs of the group. In essence, community poses the question: What is necessary for members of society to thrive together? The answer is found in the cluster of deep commitments that persons make to one another, which form the basis of civil society. They are at work in myriad times and places: when people join together to accomplish certain tasks; when families form to share a household and perhaps to raise children together; when strangers enter an established community and become a part of it. These commitments lead to the formation of organizations; these organizations, in turn, combine to form educational systems,

18. For more on this point, see especially chapter 8 of this volume.

health-care systems, civil government, and systems that respond to crises and threats to well-being. All this is possible because of the commitments that individuals make to one another.

These commitments can be best understood as various kinds of *covenants*. A covenant provides a way for human beings to overcome the basic ontological problem that we all face: namely, that we are separate beings, yet we need and want to live together in community. The language of covenant is designed to attend to the needs of individuals while also bearing responsibility for the larger community and the needs of the whole. In terms of organization theory, covenant is a fundamental influence supporting efforts toward integration; it might even be considered the backbone of all integration efforts.

A historical account of covenant would need to start with the ancient world, and especially with the Hebrew Bible, in which the relationship between God and the people of Israel was expressed in terms of covenant. This account may be particularly familiar to some readers, and I will return to it briefly at the end of this section. For present purposes, however, it may be best to forgo any detailed historical account of this phenomenon (which in any case is available elsewhere[19]), and to concentrate on the use of the term in the contemporary context, where it is actually more common than many people might assume.

A covenant involves making a commitment or forming an agreement with another person or group. While a covenant includes an agreement or pledge, it goes deeper by including one or more provisions that protect or provide for both parties contributing to the relationship. For example, one party might offer a guarantee to the other party that will be fulfilled regardless of circumstances; or, one group might agree in advance to seek mediation if a dispute arises. Guarantees and agreements of this sort are, in the best cases, designed to be attentive to the long-range interests—not only of oneself, but of the other party as well.

Covenants are broader and deeper than contracts. A contract creates a structure for individual transactions; a covenant expands to outline broader

---

19. See, for example, G. K. Beale, *A New Testament Biblical Theology: The Unfolding of the Old Testament in the New* (Grand Rapids, MI: Baker Academic, 2011); T. Desmond Alexander, *From Eden to New Jerusalem: An Introduction to Biblical Theology* (Grand Rapids, MI: Kregel Academic & Professional, 2008); Walter C. Kaiser Jr., *The Promise-Plan of God: A Biblical Theology of the Old and New Testaments* (Grand Rapids, MI: Zondervan, 2008); Scott J. Hafemann and Paul R. House, *Central Themes in Biblical Theology: Mapping Unity in Diversity* (Grand Rapids, MI: Baker Academic, 2007).

duties that foster the bond in the relationship. Contracts are specific, laying out the expectations for each party individually, whereas covenants tend to embrace a general concern for the well-being of the relationship. Contracts are often short-term and time-limited; covenants tend to involve long-term or even permanent responsibilities. A covenant "becomes part of one's history and shapes in unexpected ways one's self-perception and perhaps even destiny."[20]

We sign papers that incur debt which must be repaid. The lender helps us with cash flow now; we agree to a repayment plan that takes care of the interests of the lender later. At one level, this appears to be a simple contract, but there is a difference: both parties have an interest, not just in getting whatever the document indicates that they will get, but in preserving the *relationship* between the parties as well. For this reason, we speak of these obligations as "promises," which may include provisions that protect both parties and that seek to keep the relationship functioning, even if one of the parties fails to keep a promise. In some covenants, the borrower promises to protect assets that serve as collateral for the loan. Other covenantal provisions may proscribe the borrower from taking an action that diminishes the value of the relevant asset or from encumbering the loan in a way that increases the risk of the bond to the borrower.

Covenants are also encountered in the academic setting. A basic agreement is established when an instructor publishes the course syllabus and students agree to enroll in the course; in this sense, it can be considered a contract, and at some institutions this language is employed quite explicitly. But at a deeper level, other commitments are being made that go well beyond contractual exchange. Instructors commit to be fair when administering assessments, not just from a sense of duty, but also because they have the well-being of the students in mind. Students commit to contributing to the teaching–learning process, not just because they "have" to do so, but also because they want that process to be successful. Similarly, when students participate in a small-group assignment, group members often develop a covenantal agreement to work with each other, to coordinate their efforts, to resolve differences that arise, and to manage group conflict. For some students, the language of covenant may describe a deeper

---

20. William F. May, *Beleaguered Rulers: The Public Obligation of the Professional* (Louisville, KY: Westminster John Knox Press, 2001), 139.

relationship with an athletic coach, with the leader of a musical group, or perhaps with a major professor or advisor.

Marriage is sometimes described as a covenant relationship, but covenants in other settings (such as in business) need not require the degree of emotional and physical intimacy that characterize the ideal marriage. Covenantal relationships may simply involve loyalty to another person or group of persons, or even to the wider community. In the case of a profession such as medicine, covenant involves a solemn pledge or oath to society for all patient-care relationships that the physician enters into in the future. The attorney–client relationship can be seen as based on a covenant.[21]

As mentioned above, another perspective on covenant is provided by ancient Hebrew culture, as recorded in the Bible. The ancient Hebrews used the language of covenant as a way to communicate the ethical framework that results in a flourishing, long life for persons and for the community as a whole.[22] Covenant is an enduring, loyal commitment to the relationship with oneself, to one's family, to work associates, to the broader community. A covenant is an agreement or a promise to contribute something of value to a long-term relationship that results in a better life for all involved. Covenant relationships are not merely individualistic but also communal in scope; they are designed to benefit both individuals and the entire community. They are preferred over casual, temporary relationships.

The language of covenant suggests some important implications for the vocational discernment process. It describes the commitment that students, faculty, staff, and administrators should make to one other, in order to engage in the difficult, ambiguous tasks of helping one other in the process of vocational reflection and discernment. When educators begin to think about this process as part of their covenant with students, they are taken beyond the minimal contractual obligations of their particular position as members of the faculty or staff; they focus instead on the larger ramifications for various communities as students discern their vocations through advising sessions, classroom conversations, and extracurricular

---

21. Joseph Allegretti, "Lawyers, Clients, and Covenant. A Religious Perspective on Legal Practice and Ethics," *Fordham Law Review* 66, no. 4 (1998): 1101, 1112–15.

22. Michael E. Cafferky, "The Ethical-Religious Framework for Shalom," *Journal of Religion and Business Ethics* 3, no. 1 (2014): article 7.

activities. Similarly, the language of covenant might bring administrators to the place where they would ask: How can we organize in such a way that genuine vocational development occurs while the student is in our learning community?[23] A contractual way of thinking measures progress only by asking how many students took advantage of career counseling, preference tests, and meetings with advisors. A covenantal way of thinking asks a different question: *to what depth* have these various programs and services taken students, as they seek to discern their vocations?

## *Coordination, community, and covenant in practice*

Undergraduate education, by its very nature, creates transitory communities: each year, about a fourth of the students are new arrivals, while another fourth have graduated and have joined other communities. In some ways, the natural cycle of higher education contributes unwittingly to the notion that transitory communities are an acceptable way to live life. This can also make it difficult for institutions to develop truly communal processes of vocational reflection and discernment, since it may take a year or two just for the deeper conversations to get started. For some students, such conversations may not take place at all; if they do occur, it may not be until late in the senior year, when other pressures (such as securing a job) can obscure the goals of deeper reflection.

Hence, to develop the coordinated, communal, and covenantal elements of vocational reflection and discernment, colleges and universities need to be intentional about how they structure and organize these efforts. In this last section, we consider some of the ways that they might do so.

### Existing resources

We turn first to opportunities that are likely already in place at most colleges and universities. Through a slight change in emphasis, certain institutional resources can be helpfully directed toward communal and covenantal forms of vocational discernment.

---

23. For further reflections on the advantages of employing the language of vocation on an institution-wide basis, see chapter 11 of this volume.

## *The role of the faculty and staff*

Our comments about the tension between individuals and the community may, at first glance, raise questions about the role of any particular educator in the discernment process. It can be easy to characterize the role of such persons as individual mentors, engaging students one on one and bringing the focus back to each student as a unique individual. But faculty and staff are also part of a larger learning community, the members of which are on a journey toward a better understanding of their own callings and those of their colleagues. Educators need not allow their roles to lapse into an individualistic focus; they can work to relate their own calling to that of the entire community. Some institutions, for example, have experimented with "mentoring communities," which help reduce the burden on one individual and simultaneously bring a wide range of voices into the conversation.[24]

Educators are interested in bringing the best, most current knowledge of the discipline to students. But they also realize that there is not enough time available in a degree program to cover all areas of knowledge, even when the discipline is quite circumscribed. Taking time away from covering content in order to address deeper issues of calling may, for some instructors, be seen as a high opportunity cost they are unwilling to incur. Those who work with students outside the classroom have similar constraints; there are simply not enough hours in the day to address reflectively all of life's problems.

Still, faculty and staff should avoid passing along all responsibilities in this area to the college's career center or another campus office. In addition to compounding the problem of specialization as noted earlier in this chapter, such a course of action makes it difficult for students to understand their concerns as truly woven into the fabric of the institution. If students do not find a certain level of interest in the deeper issues of life in even one faculty member in their field, or one staff member who works with a program in which they are deeply involved, they will lack role models for this part of the process. And if students sense that the institution as a whole is less than fully committed to thinking and acting in vocational terms, they will be less likely to do so themselves.[25]

---

24. Here, see above all the work of Sharon Parks, *Big Questions, Worthy Dreams: Mentoring Young Adults in their Search for Meaning, Purpose, and Faith* (San Francisco: Jossey–Bass, 2001); for specific examples of such programs, see Cynthia Wells, "Finding the Center as Things Fall Apart: Vocation and the Common Good," in Cunningham, ed., *At This Time*, 25–46.

25. For more on this point, see chapter 11 of this volume.

Educators, like students, are on a journey of discerning and expressing their own callings. This fact, however, is often opaque to undergraduate students, for whom faculty and staff members often appear to be firmly anchored in a specific field. Educators may be better prepared to enter into communal processes of discernment if they engage in conversations about their own callings, including the ways that they have needed to work beyond their own specializations for the good of the whole. By experiencing the power of community dialogue about such matters, faculty and staff may feel better able to engage students in similar sets of questions. Narratives about the vocational journeys of faculty and staff may provide an integrating mechanism, modeling for students what vocational reflection might mean. For example, Nebraska Wesleyan University offers a program that emphasizes the importance of improving one's skill at telling one's own story and listening to the stories told by others. The feedback received when others listen to the narratives both offers aid to one's own discernment and provides a spark of community awareness regarding the importance of calling.[26]

### Emphasis on integrating structures

For the work of helping their students enter into covenantal and communal vocational discernment, many institutions may have more resources at their disposal than they realize. Long before the current explosion of interest in calling and vocation, most colleges and universities already had programs in place to help students develop a greater awareness of their future plans or to help them make career choices.[27] In addition, in courses with titles such as *Introduction to Business* or *Careers in Health Care*, students are afforded the opportunity to explore various occupations, comparing their own personality, interests, and aptitudes with the expectations of this work. While both these approaches might tend to offer a more individualistic, career-oriented account of the student's future life, it would not take much to shift their focus toward how this work contributes to better-functioning

26. See www.nebrwesleyan.edu/press-and-media/news/national-humorist-storyteller-help-kick-nwu-storytelling-project (accessed February 7, 2016). For further reflections on the importance of such storytelling, see chapter 3 of this volume.

27. Thomas J. Halasz and C. Byron Kempton, "Career Planning Workshops and Courses," in *Career Counseling of College Students: An Empirical Guide to Strategies that Work*, ed. Darrell A. Luzzo (Washington, DC: American Psychological Association, 2000), 157–71.

organizations and to the public good. Those who are responsible for these services and programs need only ask a few additional questions: Who most needs whatever it is that workers in these fields have to offer? How do these consumers (or these receivers of services, or—to use the language of chapter 5 of this volume—these "audiences") judge the value of whatever they are being offered? How can their lives be improved through the work being considered?

Other institutional structures may have significant potential for exploring the communal dimensions of calling. Colleges that offer specialized residence halls or apartment complexes (focusing on a particular major or area of interest) already have a structured, ongoing setting for developing vocational conversations within the communities that these living arrangements provide. From a structural point of view, these are built-in integrating devices. At the liberal arts college where I studied, the modern language dorm provided a setting for students to practice language skills; it also created a more integrated community in which students were already invested in making the relationships work. Such communal living arrangements are an ideal setting for exploring the deeper elements of calling. Vocationally themed residence halls at some institutions provide one possible model for this kind of arrangement.[28]

At the university where I teach, the honors program has done well at developing the sense of community dimension to learning. Starting from the first year and continuing through the senior year, this community of scholars (which includes faculty) meet regularly, go on field trips in small groups, attend regional conferences, participate in and report on research, and take part in informal conversations about questions of meaning and purpose. Special convocations are offered that lead to conversations about what it might mean to contribute to the common good. Built into these processes is the opportunity to take the conversation to the next step by encouraging the community to provide members feedback. A program such as this can make an extraordinary difference in students' abilities to see beyond their own areas of specialization and to engage in less individualistic forms of vocational discernment.

---

28. See the description of one such project in Tim Clydesdale, *The Purposeful Graduate: Why Colleges Must Talk to Students about Vocation* (Chicago: University of Chicago Press, 2015), 75–79.

# New (or renewed) programming

In addition to those structures already in place, institutions can develop a number of low-cost, high-impact programs that can provide opportunities for coordinating various efforts toward vocational discernment, focusing on their communal elements and drawing both students and staff into covenantal relationships. Many of these have been successfully under-taken at a variety of institutions; more information on the specific features of these programs is available in both print and online formats.[29]

## *Retreats*

One useful approach to integration is to conduct a retreat for students where they are challenged to consider their callings and vocations. Retreats can be powerful experiences for students; for some, the opportunities for quiet reflection that a retreat offers may be just the atmosphere where an inner call can take shape in conscious thoughts or commitments. These events are not limited to particular disciplines or fields; they can range across the entire academic spectrum and may focus on a particular major field or on an interdisciplinary mixture of students.[30] Boston College runs an extremely successful program of this sort ("Halftime") that involves most of the undergraduate class between their sophomore and junior years.[31]

Such programs need to be structured with care; they can come to be seen as life *apart* from community, rather than life within the larger community. If the retreat is focused exclusively on the inner cognitive and emotional processes, where participants are encouraged only to distance themselves from others and to listen to God or to their own hearts, the communal and covenantal aspects of vocation may be marginalized. Properly structured, however, a retreat can encourage students to listen to

---

29. Information about programs dating back to 2001 is archived at www.ptev.org. Current programs are described at connect.cic.edu/NetVUE/; NetVUE also maintains a large Community Network Site for active member institutions, as well as a public blog at www.vocationmatters.org. See also Clydesdale, *The Purposeful Graduate*, for a description of some of the resources that various programs have produced.

30. See chapter 7 of this volume for an example of how this kind of program can work in the natural sciences, for example.

31. For a detailed description, see www.bc.edu/offices/formation/programs/Halftime.html; for a sense of how this program fits into the overall work of vocational discernment at Boston College, see the institution's entry on the archived PTEV website, www.ptev.org (both accessed March 7, 2016).

the patterns of discernment in the wider community; similarly, the community can be encouraged to provide feedback regarding how the student may best serve others. Furthermore, a retreat can point the way for ongoing conversations that can take place once the event is over and its profound impact starts to fade.

## Storytelling

Because of its deep roots in covenantal relationships and community, vocation can make use of narrative as a powerful integrating influence.[32] In addition to offering their own stories, educators can make a positive contribution by telling stories about those within the discipline who have made contributions to higher-order community functions. Stories about famous inventors, social activists, government leaders, researchers, and scholars abound; but it may also be important to tell stories about less well known individuals whose work is deeply integrated into the communities of which they are a part.[33]

In addition, mentors can encourage students and alumni/ae to tell their stories. As members of the learning community listen to these narratives, they can also provide reflective feedback to help students think deeply about who they are and how they can contribute to human flourishing. While a person's official "job description" may make the work sound highly specialized and narrowly focused, most stories of "life at work" make it clear that a variety of secondary specializations are almost always necessary, and that if a person wants to understand exactly what kind of work the job involves, this will require hearing from a number of people in order to gain the widest possible perspective.

## Community conversations about gifts

Despite the strong emphasis in this chapter on the communal dimensions of calling, we should not forget the legitimate value of individual gifts. Lest we allow the pendulum to swing too far from individuality, we need to remember that, without the expression of individual gifts, the community could not fully develop. Where do university students learn how to

---

32. For more on this point, see the discussion of narrative in chapter 3 of this volume.

33. For examples, see Charles Pinches, "Stories of Call: From Dramatic Phenomena to Changed Lives," in Cunningham, ed., *At This Time*, 122–42; see also chapter 8 of this volume for examples of less well known but deeply integrated work.

participate in community conversations about their own particular gifts? Where in the degree program do such opportunities exist for this type of training in each academic discipline? At present, too little time is devoted to practicing conversations about giftedness in the context of the higher-order functions of a particular field or discipline. This suggests the need to create structures in which small groups of students can describe what gifts they see in one another that might be put to use in service of the larger society.

Our goal here, and throughout this chapter, has not been to eclipse the individual; on the contrary, it has been to enhance the significance of individual actors by reminding ourselves of how deeply we are connected to the lives of others. Whether through membership in a sports team, employment in a company, volunteer service in a community or religious organization, or enrollment in an institution of higher education, all of us are deeply woven into one another's lives. The more we become aware of these connections, the more successful will be our efforts at vocational reflection and discernment.

## *The goodness and beauty of the frame*

If one's calling consisted of nothing more than finding a job or career, then vocational discernment could be managed by the academic department or program in which the student is preparing for that work, or by a career services office with little connection to the rest of campus. But if calling is something larger (as all the contributors to this volume suggest), then vocational discernment cannot be left to any single element of an organization's structure. Instead, programs need to be developed that attend closely to the relationship of individual and community; for those seeking to undertake this task, the structural perspective offered in organization theory provides an important resource. The traditional "specialist" in the vocational development process—the student—will need some assistance from the larger educational community for integrating disparate feedback messages gleaned from talking with advisors, counselors, instructors, chaplains, coaches, and others. Students will need to coordinate and integrate all this feedback, but they should not be led to believe that they are already experts in this work. In other words, vocational reflection requires shared leadership, which in turn requires that commitments go deeper than merely contractual arrangements; true discernment requires a covenantal commitment to work together for a common goal. This can provide the necessary time and space for each student to explore the broader questions of vocation—which are, of course, not limited to decisions about one's academic major, job, or career.

In order to offer such commitments, higher education will need to go well beyond the functional, practical goals that are too often assumed to be at its core. Indeed, programs for vocational reflection and discernment require us to attend to broad categories, including those that were once gathered under the heading "universals": truth, goodness, and beauty. It may seem surprising to mention such high ideals when speaking of abstract concepts of everyday practice such as specialization, integration, community, and identity. Nevertheless, the larger significance of these structural concepts may become clearer when we consider how they are instantiated in the organizations that we sustain and the people with whom we are in relationship. Understood in these terms, such concepts acquire a goodness and beauty not unlike the elements that we might recognize in a great work of art or an elegant mathematical equation.[34] They point to a productive tension which keeps a bridle on unrestrained self-interest, while completing the self in relation to others. To use a metaphor from the arts, vocation is a call to stitch a particular pattern within the tapestry of our lives; this can only be done within a frame, and that frame is held together by the interrelated tensions of community and individual, specialization and integration, self-actualization and covenant. As we find ourselves called to create a beautiful work of art within these tensions, we are also reminded of the goodness and beauty of the frame.

---

34. For more on connections to the arts and to the natural sciences, see chapters 5 and 7 of this volume.

# The Art and Science of Vocation

## WISDOM AND CONSCIENCE AS COMPANIONS ON A WAY

### *Celia Deane-Drummond*

IN THE AMERICAN context, undergraduates typically take at least some courses outside their major and minor fields. Different disciplines have different starting points, philosophies, and methods; moreover, despite valiant attempts to generate interdisciplinary centers or institutes, most academic fields operate largely in silos and compete with one another for authority. Students who work in more than one discipline are liable to find it difficult to sort out these differences. Even within any given discipline, battles rage as to whether, for example, an empirical or theoretical approach is the most effective way of arriving at answers to specific questions. Some newer fields (such as biochemistry or biophysics) represent an attempt to bridge disciplines, but these efforts can often lead to even more fragmentation and more specialization—as well as increasing the overall volume of information that students are expected to absorb.

As an example of these difficulties, consider the relationship between natural sciences and religious studies. Scientists often struggle with difficult issues that arise out of their scientific practice, which has increased the level of attention to professional ethics. But the models for ethical deliberation in the sciences tend to be heavily consequentialist, encouraging an approach that relies primarily on cost–benefit calculations. Ethical questions are also of great concern in the field of theology, but that discipline operates with a very different set of methods, sources, and norms. As a field of study, it has been squeezed out of university curricula in many parts of the world, on the premise that post-Enlightenment reasoning should not dabble in subjects that allow religious faith to contribute to understanding. Yet when scholars seek to grapple with some of the huge questions facing humanity, they may need to attend to what religious traditions can contribute. For example, prominent atheist philosopher Jürgen Habermas argues that Judaism and Christianity provided the basis for what later became a secular ethical framework for right action.[1] Similarly, atheist philosopher of science Thomas Nagel argues that when it comes to understanding the human place in the cosmos, a reductionist scientific account is inadequate to the task; scientists have to take proper account of questions about meaning and purpose, and perhaps even about the transcendent.[2]

Undergraduate students who find themselves wading into these deep waters might be forgiven for feeling somewhat overwhelmed. Nevertheless, the world that they will face when they graduate is likely to become yet more complex. In fact, Ronald Barnett has described this situation as one of *supercomplexity*.[3] Graduates will encounter unpredictable combinations of knowledge; finding a way to take responsibility in such situations requires robust preparation, as well as tools that will enable the possibility of decision making. Barnett suggests that higher education should not try to deny supercomplexity, but should prepare its future graduates to live purposefully in its midst. The differing approaches to knowledge that students encounter in their coursework will help to prepare them for the complex societal contexts that they will eventually face.

All of this has significant implications for reflection on and discernment of one's vocation—particularly when that work is defined (as the chapters in this volume have sought to do) as more than simply a process of deduction based on a person's particular skills. The language of vocation suggests something more profound about a person's orientation toward future practices, as well as that person's calling in relation

---

1. He claims that secular ideas of egalitarianism, autonomy, and individual morality of conscience are "the direct heir of the Judaic ethic of justice and the Christian ethic of love. To this day there is no alternative to it." Jürgen Habermas, "An Awareness of What is Missing," in *An Awareness of What is Missing: Faith and Reason in a Post-Secular Age*, trans. Ciaran Cronin (Cambridge: Polity, 2010), 18.

2. Thomas Nagel, *Mind and Cosmos: Why the Materialist Neo-Darwinian Conception of Nature Is Almost Certainly False* (Oxford: Oxford University Press, 2012).

3. Ronald Barnett, "University Knowledge in an Age of Supercomplexity," *Higher Education* 40, no. 4 (December 2000): 409–22.

to a specific community. An undergraduate education provides an excellent opportunity to consider these questions, regardless of whether this takes place within a particular religious tradition (where employing the language of vocation may reflect its own deep religious history[4]) or in a more secular context, focusing on questions of meaning and purpose. In any case, students who face these questions will be in need of companions to help them navigate a rapidly changing world.

This chapter begins with a more thoroughgoing analysis of the differing methods operative across (and even within) differing fields of study, suggesting how the language of vocation can help us transcend some of these field-dependent methodological differences. It then introduces two specific "companions" that can aid students in the process of discernment, whatever their field of study: *wisdom* (including both *speculative wisdom* and *practical wisdom*; the latter is also known as *prudence*[5]) and *conscience*. The chapter concludes by describing a particular instance in which some of these concepts and tools were employed among students, in order to illustrate their importance for vocational exploration and discernment.

## *Differing fields, differing methods*

I begin by considering why the different disciplines and fields of study tend to require students to undertake confusing mental gymnastics. Consider the challenges for science students in a course that I have regularly taught on global bioethics. Some of these students aspire to be health professionals, often with the eventual aim of becoming doctors in challenging health-care settings; others eventually want to conduct more biologically focused research on, for example, the genetics of malaria or other tropical diseases. All have a background in a biological science of some kind; they also share aspirations to use their science in ways that will benefit wider society. However, many find it difficult to think outside a scientific discipline in the ways that are demanded by other fields, such as ethics. At the same time, they recognize that studying this field will be crucial to do the kind of work they hope to do.

---

4. For an account of this history in the Christian tradition, see William C. Placher, ed., *Callings: Twenty Centuries of Christian Wisdom on Vocation* (Grand Rapids, MI: Eerdmans, 2005).

5. Prudence also includes an active, practical component, leading to action; thus its close relationship to *practical wisdom*.

## Ways of knowing

Different disciplines develop their own ways of knowing and specific practices that, according to anthropologist Marilyn Strathern, lead to *fractal* ways of knowing. By this she means ways of knowing that avoid strict divisions that separate these approaches into mutually exclusive categories: *either* rational or interpretative, *either* individual or communal. She uses an analogy from mathematics, *the fractal*, where (as in a snowflake, for example) the pattern laid down at an individual level repeats itself and emerges eventually as a complex structure.

Building on this concept, Strathern argues that there are viable and workable alternatives to what seem to be insoluble dichotomies or dilemmas. In the student context, this may translate into the tension between one's own desire for academic success, on the one hand, and society's needs for basic, often more practically orientated skills, on the other.[6] Developing a sense of vocation requires navigating this difficult territory, where the needs of both the individual and the community chime for attention at the same time.[7]

Different disciplines also have a powerfully shaping influence on the character of individuals. As they are gradually exposed to these worlds, undergraduates often begin to experience new sources of meaning. In my own experience as a biologist, and in my experience of teaching student scientists from a range of subject domains, the sense of loyalty that builds among those committed to the scientific search for truth is palpable. The laboratory is a society in microcosm, and successful labs are highly cohesive. Immersion in these reified yet highly practical investigative worlds has certain parallels to religious formation, including attention to the specific practices of scientific investigation.[8] So, as Strathern suggests, "People's identities are in part forged in the kind of knowledge practices that different disciplines engender. This is not just in terms of shared bodies of knowledge, but rests in the manner in which material is collected, evidence appraised, work criticized and results evaluated."[9] Knowledge

---

6. Marilyn Strathern, *Partial Connections* (London: Rowman and Littlefield, 2004). Matthew Crawford discusses the philosophical issues involved in the move away from practices in *Shop Class as Soul Craft: An Inquiry into the Value of Work* (London: Penguin, 2009).

7. For more on the relationship between the individual and the community, see chapter 6 of this volume.

8. For a historical account, see Andrew Warwick, *Masters of Theory: Cambridge and the Rise of Mathematical Physics* (Chicago: University of Chicago Press, 2003), especially 114–75.

9. Marilyn Strathern, "Knowledge Identities," in *Changing Identities in Higher Education: Voicing Perspectives*, ed. Ronald Barnett and Roberto Di Napoli (London: Routledge, 2008), 11.

cannot be separated from the particular practices that shape that way of knowing.[10]

## Threshold concepts

Another useful construct, slowly becoming established in the literature of higher education, is that of a *threshold concept*: a concept that is essential to one's introduction to a particular discipline, in order for its subject matter to be properly understood. In any given discipline or field of study, threshold concepts can evoke a deeper appreciation of a particular area of knowledge; they can also open up other areas of knowing that remain obscure without such concepts.[11] Without mastering a discipline's threshold concepts, students will remain confused about the point of a particular area of study.

This construct can be particularly useful to educators, since it enables them to identify what might be crucial in a given subject area in order for a student to make progress in learning. Rather than overburdening students with content, educators can concentrate their efforts on enabling undergraduates to focus on threshold concepts in each discipline; as a result, far more learning takes place.[12] In the natural and applied sciences, threshold concepts are often considered provisional rather than fixed; however, these fields are commonly taught (especially at more elementary undergraduate levels) *as though* their practitioners have discovered hard facts about the world that have been proven and "finalized" by experimental method.

In my own experience of teaching undergraduates who are majoring in the natural sciences, one such threshold concept is the idea that *science is value laden*—or even, at least in some aspects, socially and historically constructed. For many students, this comes both as a surprise and an occasion for further questioning; it creates a disturbance in one's equilibrium. The new knowledge gained seems alien; it unsettles previously held convictions about what was assumed to be the case. It can be termed *troublesome* knowledge[13] —sometimes unsettling deeply held and previously

---

10. Ibid., 11–20.

11. Glynis Cousin, "An Introduction to Threshold Concepts," *Planet* 17 (December 2006): 4–5.

12. Sarah Barradell, "The Identification of Threshold Concepts: A Review of Theoretical Complexities and Methodological Challenges," *Higher Education* 65, no. 2 (2013): 265–76.

13. Ray Land, "Crossing Tribal Boundaries: Interdisciplinarity as a Threshold Concept," in *Tribes and Territories in the 21st Century: Rethinking the Significance of Disciplines in Higher*

uncontested convictions that may stem from previous educational experiences in secular, religious, or familial settings.[14]

"Troublesome knowledge" is therefore a second threshold concept that is crucial when considering different disciplinary learning experiences. Such troublesome experiences have a profound impact on the lives of students with respect to the *ways* they know (the epistemic level) and with respect to their *sense of being* (the ontological level). As a result, it is more than just a platitude to say that students are not the same as they were before their experience of higher education. In the course of entering into troublesome forms of knowledge—or indeed, of mastering any kind of threshold concept—students enter a liminal phase in which they may oscillate between old and emergent knowledge states.[15]

Some studies on the experience of physics students provide evidence for this phenomenon in the learning process.[16] Students will often feel bewildered or confused when they encounter disjunctions between, for example, the analytical philosophy of science (which seeks to understand presuppositions behind basic scientific concepts) and science itself (which is premised on its representation of an aspect of material reality). This is very uncomfortable psychologically, even for those experienced in this kind of work; not surprisingly, then, undergraduates tend to resist the transformation that such new encounters require. Instead of true learning, they often try to find ways of mimicking the kinds of work done in the field, imitating either the teacher or some other source.[17]

I have experienced this first hand when teaching the global health students referred to above, all of whom have been trained in the empirical

*Education*, ed. Paul Trowler, Murray Saunders, and Veronica Bamber (London: Routledge, 2012), 175–85.

14. Strathern also compares interdisciplinary work with that of ethnographic disjunctions; both lead to transformative knowledge processes. Marilyn Strathern, "Disciplinary Encounters: Confident Comparisons and Uncertain Exchanges," keynote lecture delivered at "Transfusion and Transformation: The Creative Potential of Interdisciplinary Knowledge Exchange," Institute for Advanced Study, July 13–17, 2014, Durham University, United Kingdom.

15. Jan H. F. Meyer and Ray Land, eds., *Overcoming Barriers to Student Understanding: Threshold Concepts and Troublesome Knowledge* (London and New York: Routledge, 2006).

16. For an interesting study of this phenomenon, see Ibrahim Abou Halloun and David Hestenes, "The Initial Knowledge State of College Physics," *American Journal of Physics* 53 (1985): 1043–55; and Ibrahim Abou Halloun and David Hestenes, "Common Sense Concepts and Motion," *American Journal of Physics* 53 (1985): 1056–65.

17. Cousin, "Introduction to Threshold Concepts," 5.

sciences. Each year, a small handful of these students experience an almost visceral reaction to any inclusion of theological perspectives in the discussion. This is not simply a reaction to religion as such; it manifests a mistaken assumption that science is not already value laden and that it can be kept "pure" by excluding religious and ethical questions.

I suggest that nurturing a genuine sense of vocation among undergraduates is analogous to facilitating proper navigation of the liminal space of such troublesome knowledge: both require the teacher to take account of the risky psychological space that an exploration of vocation engenders. Here, new ideas about where students might decide to focus their energies sit uncomfortably alongside previously assumed roles from their background experiences. Educators must therefore be sensitive to the particular social and cultural contexts, both of undergraduates in general and of individual students in particular.

## The role of "grand narrative" accounts

For some students, certain assumptions about God and certain perceptions about their purpose in life may lead them to describe their vocation as a *divine calling*. Hence, students and educators (in all kinds of academic institutions) will often find themselves negotiating the relationship between a vocation (broadly understood) and religious belief. Some students may be strongly influenced by what might be called a "grand narrative" approach to the way God works in history—a particular overarching story about the world and the place of humans in it that has a definitive beginning, middle, and end. Those who hear and tell this story often see it as providing a wholly objective view of what is taking place. (It should also be noted that "grand narrative" accounts are not limited to those who approach these questions from a religious perspective; some atheistic worldviews are also of this type.) Under the influence of the grand narrative account, some may develop a strong belief that there can be only *one* particular vocational path and that it must be discovered and pursued regardless of any signs to the contrary. This view may lead to anxiety and to unnecessary restrictions on vocational exploration and discernment.[18]

There are other, more positive ways in which narratives can be fruitful for vocational reflection and discernment; in particular, they can offer a

---

18. For further reflection on situations in which students describe their own vocational trajectory as a "higher calling," see the discussion in chapter 2 of this volume.

way of gaining wisdom and insight through reflection on particular exemplars. Moreover, the stories we tell each other will impact the particular vocations that rise to the surface.[19] We *learn* our own stories and gain a sense of identity in interaction with others through observation, mimicry, and rehearsal; we become *socialized* into particular roles by our institutions; and gradually, we *internalize* such expectations and make them our own.[20]

All of this suggests that the assumed contrast between religious approaches to vocation and secular alternatives is not quite as stark as some might assume. Both are concerned with the generation of meaning and a sense of identity.[21] The authoritative claims of a particular religious tradition (such as magisterial teachings, tradition, and scripture) can, of course, be interpreted in different ways; but more univocal interpretations can lead to narrower guidelines about various matters—including a restriction on the options open to undergraduates who are seeking to discern their vocations. Sometimes these narrower guidelines are designed to point students toward specifically religious vocations.

But grand narratives are not confined to religious questions; such approaches are sometimes characteristic of traditions such as law, medicine, or engineering. There, too, univocal interpretations of the various authorities are sometimes used to funnel students into a specific field, creating an overall drive toward professionalization that may lead students to feel that fewer options are left open for them. Similarly, in molecular biology, research lineages become established, and future research is typically carried out according to norms characteristic of those lineages. For example, research on the *Drosophila* fruit fly established patterns of sharing information and cooperation that then drew others in and became a standard for the subfield.[22] These developments were largely positive, in the sense that the community was collaborative rather than antagonistic.

---

19. On the role of narrative in vocation, see chapters 2, 3, and 10 of this volume, as well as chapters 5 and 7 in David S. Cunningham, ed., *At This Time and In This Place: Vocation and Higher Education* (New York: Oxford University Press, 2016). See also Mark Edwards, *Religion on Our Campuses: A Professor's Guide to Communities, Controversies, and Promising Conversations* (New York: Palgrave Macmillan, 2006).

20. Edwards, *Religion on Our Campuses*, 31–62.

21. Ibid., 31–42.

22. Robert E. Kohler, *Lords of the Fly: Drosophila Genetics and the Experimental Life* (Chicago: University of Chicago Press, 1994).

But it also provides an example of how unitary interpretations are established, even in the sciences. The success of a particular approach can lead to the assumption that there are few alternatives.

Still, in spite of the temptation to construct grand narratives and to drift toward unitary interpretations, narrative can be a successful tool in the educational process. Stories can encourage students to consider what it might be like to do a particular task; stories can also raise particular issues that may not otherwise occur to undergraduates. Stories inculcate a form of wisdom, encouraging students to identify with particular exemplars and thereby helping them decide how to act. At the same time, I want to suggest that nothing can replace the wisdom that comes from actually getting involved in particular practices of that particular intended role. For example, practical teaching experience is crucial to the task of teacher training; similar examples can be offered across the entire spectrum of academic disciplines and applied fields. Discerning one's vocation is necessarily a *practice* of a sort; any form of decision making that is purely theoretical and detached from concrete experiential practices is more likely to be illusory. Even a theoretical mathematician needs to have some understanding of what it is like to *perform* the tasks that the profession involves; similarly, an experimental biologist needs to know what it means, in practical terms, to follow the agreed protocols of a scientific community in order to design and implement an experiment and to analyze its results. If stories and practices each give us certain insights, how might a student use this information to discern a vocation—particularly within a complex set of circumstances, in which the student faces many different and competing demands?

## *Practical wisdom and speculative wisdom*

To answer this question, we turn first to the concept of wisdom, and more specifically, to two of its more specific species: practical wisdom and speculative wisdom.

### Practical wisdom

The classical traditions speak of *practical wisdom* or *prudence* as an excellence of character that is concerned with matters of daily life: how to live well. Practical wisdom has three phases—deliberation, judgment, and action—all of which are relevant to vocational discernment. Even prior to the judgment phase, we need to develop the ability to learn from others, an accurate memory of experience, clear insights about what is the case, and a keen sense of what outcomes may result from our decisions. The judgment phase involves the use of reason and insight, making a decision in the context of a community of others. The action phase allows for small decisions to test a vocation in a given direction, and can also provide confidence in prudential reasoning.

Students need to make all kinds of deliberations and judgments, large and small, as they go about the process of vocational discernment; these will need to lead to action if they hope to align their training with the vocational paths that they have discerned. Hence, those who are able to cultivate a kind of practical wisdom will be better able to consider how their deliberations, judgments, and actions align, and how this alignment can help them continue on the path they are following.

For example, students who aspire to be scientists of a particular kind need to make prudential judgments about not just what might get them the best grades, but also what tools might be most useful to them in the future; they also need to be attentive to signs of growth and development in their field. Consider how the biological sciences have changed in recent years. When I trained as an experimental botanist, it was helpful, but not essential, to have some training in mathematics, and especially in statistics. Today, it is impossible to do this kind of work without higher-level mathematics. At the same time, students also need to find ways of resisting "fashions" in their fields. The new wave in research involving genetic modification of agricultural plants (GMOs) was integral to the scientific ethos in the field during the time I was a practicing scientist. But that wave of research has not been sustained, at least in Europe, partly due to cultural suspicion about eating genetically modified crops; similar concerns are developing in the American context. Practical wisdom, therefore, also tries to consider what is right at the deepest level of discernment, not simply what is most expedient.

Of course, practical wisdom can also be distorted and spoiled in all kinds of ways, so where truths are forgotten prudence no longer flowers into action, and becomes "blocked."[23] The role of the educator could be viewed as one that helps unblock potential barriers to practical wisdom

---

23. Aquinas, *Summa Theologiae* II–II.47.16, Blackfriars edition, vol. 36, trans. Thomas Gilby, O.P. (New York: McGraw–Hill; London: Eyre & Spottiswoode, 1974), 48–51.

acting in the lives of undergraduates. At the same time, gaining a sense of what these barriers might be (and helping to solve them) is a pastoral exercise, as well as an educational one.

What role will practical wisdom play when students consider a range of opportunities that all may be feasible? It can help them articulate what priorities are most important for a given set of circumstances; moreover, the judgment phase of practical wisdom requires us to make decisions of conscience. It would be ill-advised for a student to choose a career that goes against her or his conscience for the sake of, for example, higher economic rewards. Practical wisdom acts as a mean between extremes; hence, it can never be found in excess. This, too, applies to vocational discernment: if one tries to be too clever or to overanalyze, this may lead to a lack of dedication to a particular course of training. Similarly, if a person's over-inflated sense of courage leads to a failure to judge correctly the dangers of a particular activity (or one's lack of aptitude to undertake it), then this will mean a foolhardy approach to health and survival. By cultivating the virtue of practical wisdom, one develops a more *accurate* judgment of the relative risk of certain activities—and of the intellectual merits of a particular case.

## Speculative wisdom

Another aspect of wisdom will be relevant if a person's process of vocational reflection and discernment also brings *theological* questions into play. In that case, one's calling is often understood as a response to one's relationship with God. In the classical Thomistic tradition, the process of working out who we are—in relationship to others and in relationship with God—is described as the virtue of *wisdom as such*, existing alongside other virtues of speculative reason (understanding and science). This does not mean that there is no "wisdom" in fields other than theology; however, a theological perspective necessarily entails that the highest forms of wisdom will necessarily have something to do with God. The tradition of natural theology was always inclusive of other domains of knowledge, such that insights from the sciences represented a form of wisdom that pointed beyond these fields to the divine source of all things in God; still, as Divine Wisdom, God provides the measure of what that highest human form of wisdom entails.[24]

---

24. Aquinas, *Summa Theologiae* I–II.66.5, Blackfriars edition, vol. 23, *Virtue*, trans. W. D. Hughes (New York: McGraw–Hill; London: Eyre & Spottiswoode, 1969), 214–17.

Is it still possible to make such a claim in a more secularized educational setting? I suggest that it is; moreover, it is particularly important for educators to understand the origins of this tradition when working with students for whom religious beliefs are important. This perspective also reminds us that *ultimate* wisdom is never attainable—which is not to say that humanity should give up the search. Indeed, it is a search that can and must be shared among all persons, including those who do not hold an explicit religious belief. Proper attention to speculative wisdom can lead to insights beyond the day-to-day decision making that is facilitated by practical wisdom.

In my own contact with secular anthropologists at the University of Notre Dame, for example, the theological account of wisdom has proved fascinating as a topic for further empirical research. It accounts for certain features of deep human desires that are missing from the more observational mode of the social-scientific study of religion. Further, new scientific questions about the evolution of wisdom have arisen as a result of this exchange, opening up a paradigm for the study of human origins that differs from the perspectives typically held by evolutionary anthropologists. In this sense, considerations of speculative wisdom have worked to enhance, rather than to inhibit, social scientific research. Students who hold religious beliefs need to be encouraged not to separate those beliefs from their experiences in secular fields of study, nor to see the two domains as non-overlapping authorities. Instead, they should be encouraged to allow their religious and secular commitments to work together as they reflect on their callings.

Thus, for example, an undergraduate who wishes to be a natural scientist may decide, through various practices of vocational discernment, to focus her or his training on problems that have the greatest social impact, rather than those that attract the most funding. If theological considerations are important for that person, this decision may be affected by perceptions about how one is being called by God. If religious believers are not permitted or encouraged to take such matters into account, they may be less confident that they have made a good choice. Without wisdom, then, their conscience may be troubled—a topic to which I will return below.

## Allowing wisdom to play a role

Undergraduate students need occasions in their course of study when they have an opportunity for quiet reflection and contemplation, regardless of their religious background or personal beliefs, so that they can develop the kinds of practical and speculative wisdom described here. Traditionally, such wisdom could emerge in the context of a retreat setting. Others might encourage reflection through the study of sacred texts or through meditation. A number of institutions have developed programs that employ the spirituality of Ignatius of Loyola, which deliberately sets out to encourage the participant to imagine different scenarios for action that can be tied to particular vocational choices and to consider whether such experiences lead to consolation or desolation.[25] This ability to imagine ourselves in different roles or scenarios may also take place in silence, and/or through close engagement with texts. Often stories and scenes from these texts can be used in an imaginative exercise in order to trigger latent or hidden desires or feelings. All of these approaches offer ways of opening up the participant to a different kind of inner hearing that has a spiritual dimension. Based on the premise that God desires our highest good—and that, in coming closer to God, we become more true to innermost selves—accurate discernment is only reached in a detached rather than an attached state, where participants understand themselves to have surrendered completely to the will of God in obedience.

Consider a specific instance in which undergraduate students were encouraged to draw on the traditions of practical and speculative wisdom at the boundary between disciplines. This took place during a retreat for the students in a course that examined the relationship between ecology and Catholic social teaching.[26] This course included a mixture of students in the humanities and the natural sciences. The experience overall had a profound effect on the lives of this group; they were taken away from their everyday class context and allowed to spend time in reflection as part of the learning process. Students were encourage to examine texts on the topic, to reflect on the insights they had gained, and to engage in deeper reflection on the impact these reflections were having on their own learning

---

25. Ignatian spirituality does not deal only with a choice between good and evil, which are often obvious enough, but also choices between seeming parallel goods. These are often the kinds of choices that undergraduates face when discerning their vocation. For a practical guide with examples, see Timothy M. Gallagher, O.M.V., *Spiritual Consolations: An Ignatian Guide for the Greater Discernment of Spirits* (New York: Crossroad, 2007).

26. For a more detailed description of Catholic social teaching, and of its application to the concepts of work and leisure, see chapter 8 of this volume.

and vocational journey. Many had never encountered Roman Catholic social teaching on the environment and were surprised to see the extent of engagement with the science of ecology in these texts.

Many students reported that the experience had a profound impact on their sense of vocation, even though the class itself was not deliberately designed to promote such a result. Here are some examples of the stories that they shared:[27]

JANE: All of humankind does not just mean the humans of today. It is not fair if the humans of today, especially those in wealthier nations, are hoarding these resources. I feel like I need to do something! I want to give these readings to everyone on campus—no—to everyone in the world. And all people need to hold themselves accountable and decide on things that they can and should live without.

BILL: After this weekend, the appreciation that I already possessed for the natural world has grown to be even greater. I now feel prepared to make an ever more concerted effort to live my life in constant wonder and awe at God's magnificent creation. This will involve more than just a renewed love of the great outdoors; it will involve a greater recognition of our place in creation and the cooperative existence of people and the environment. Each contributes to the fulfillment of the other. I will take away from this weekend the mindset that my actions do in fact make a difference. I may be only one, but I am one.

JENNIFER: Although we didn't get into the scientific specifics of what exactly the problems are in terms of environmental issues today, I came away with a deeper understanding on a personal level of the importance of correcting that ignorance and making concrete changes in my own life in order to have a small but certainly not negligible impact on global society—the human family. A theme I've been contemplating recently in other aspects of my life came up in my thoughts again here—the idea of living intentionally, making every aspect and action of my life deliberately, with a clear goal, a clear purpose in mind. That doesn't mean being constantly busy and constantly productive, but also deliberately taking the time to reflect on, meditate in, and appreciate the intentional order and beauty of my environment, a true gift from God.

---

27. Statements have been edited for clarity; names have been altered, but they still reflect the gender of each respondent.

Clearly, it did not take much effort to create the conditions necessary for such reflection and discernment to flower at an individual and collective level. In any case, deliberation requires *both* individual and collective contemplation. This class provided a safe space in which individuals could envisage their futures in the light of particular texts they encountered.

What was perhaps most surprising, to me as an educator, was that even those who did not self-identify as religious found engagement with theological texts to be illuminating for their own decision-making process. While there is always the risk that students might be prone to mimicry in their encounter with threshold concepts that lie outside their discipline, that risk seemed minimal in this context; students were prepared to offer criticism on some elements of the course, as well as to speak up about aspects of the readings with which they disagreed.

By affirming the role of speculative and practical wisdom in the work of vocational discernment, educators help students enter into a process of *reflective becoming*. This is best understood as a deep learning through experiences of encounter. Such experiences are, to some extent, deliberately "staged" by the educator, but positioned in such a way that the students have the freedom to make that experience their own. Hence, while one mode of wisdom is speculative, it is built on specific experiences and careful reflection on them. If students are not given such opportunities to reflect, then it is unlikely that wisdom will be fully developed and nurtured in a higher educational setting. In the examples described above, speculative wisdom eventually leads to a commitment to practical wisdom, and to a deeper understanding of what needs to be done. It is the combination of the speculative and the practical that makes wisdom so powerfully relevant to vocation.

## *Conscience and judgment*

Conscience is perhaps best understood as an inner guide to right decision making; it is relevant regardless of particular religious belief. It is closely related to wisdom, and especially to practical wisdom; as noted above, in its judgment phase, practical wisdom requires not just prior deliberation but also a well-developed conscience.[28] This is particularly

28. I have discussed conscience in relation to freedom and in the context of decision making in genetics in Celia Deane-Drummond, "Freedom, Conscience and Virtue: Theological Perspectives on the Ethics of Inherited Genetic Modification," in *Design and Destiny: Jewish*

relevant for internal decisions that have to be made within a discipline, as well as the kinds of vocational reflection and discernment that students undertake with respect to their future field of study or type of work. Given the variety of possible vocations on offer for most undergraduates—assuming, that is, that they are not locked into a particular future path against their will—a vocational decision will also be a decision of conscience. It will include discernment of moral elements about what that calling entails, as well as the kinds of goods that result from its practice. An undergraduate may wish to become a theoretical physicist, but she also needs to be sensitive to what her conscience is encouraging her to do in making a decision about how that knowledge might be used. If conscience, desire, and practical wisdom are aligned, an authentic decision will result.

## Conscience and morality

Linda Hogan has pointed out that conscience has come to be associated with what it means to be good morally.[29] In the biblical tradition, conscience is normally associated with having *integrity*: a pure heart, a good conscience, and a genuine faith are bound up with one another.[30] But even those who operate from outside a specifically religious perspective can still experience the "whispering of conscience."[31] This notion is particularly useful for vocation, since envisaging a form of work may encourage the role of conscience as that which encourages us to act: I should do this, or I should not do that. When students have the opportunity to engage in particular practices, conscience may serve as a kind of witness: I have become involved by trying out a particular path, and my conscience is either affirming what I have done well or criticizing what I have done badly. All these senses of conscience come into play as different vocational possibilities come into view. In a technical sense, conscience does not direct action;

---

*and Christian Perspectives on Human Germline Modification*, ed. Ronald Cole-Turner (Cambridge, MA: MIT Press, 2008).

29. Linda Hogan, *Confronting the Truth: Conscience in the Catholic Tradition* (Mahwah, NJ: Paulist Press, 2001), 18–20.

30. An example is 1 Tim. 1:5: "the aim of such instruction is love that comes from a pure heart, a good conscience, and sincere faith." These phrases suggest synonymous meanings—that is, conscience is associated with having moral integrity.

31. Hogan, *Confronting the Truth*, 9–32.

still, in a practical sense, action follows its lead—insofar as the conscience will witness, incite, or confirm particular actions.

In many respects, the classical view of conscience was naïve in relation to our current understanding of human psychology and sociology of knowing. However, if conscience is situated more clearly back in the tradition as an element of practical wisdom, this may allow us to develop a more holistic understanding of the concept. Practical wisdom is an intellectual virtue that includes judgment, but also leads to action.[32] It can be developed and enlarged to include the wider human community; this aspect may be particularly relevant when helping undergraduates discern their vocations.

## Conflicting callings

Conscience is a particularly useful tool where the choices faced by students may lead to a sense of conflicting and competing calls—often in relation to goods of family and occupation, both of which may not be able to be satisfied. Martha Nussbaum argues that some of these cases are simply tragic dilemmas that have to be acknowledged as such, and accepted as unresolvable.[33] But conscience, I suggest, enables us to draw certain priorities, such that we can come to a certain degree of acceptance of the difficult choices we must make. This does not mean that such decisions are painless, nor that they can merely be brushed aside; Nussbaum rightly views these as inappropriate responses to the problem of conflicting callings. But conscience can provide a third way, in which we neither shirk

---

32. For further discussion on practical wisdom and its elements, see Celia Deane-Drummond, *The Ethics of Nature* (Oxford: Blackwell, 2004), 10–15.

33. Martha Nussbaum claims in an interview that "often when you care deeply about more than one thing, the very course of life will bring you round to a situation where you can't honor both of the commitments. It looks like anything you do will be wrong, perhaps even terrible, in some way." Martha Nussbaum quoted in Bill Moyers, *A World of Ideas* (New York: Doubleday, 1989), excerpted as "Interview with Martha Nussbaum," in *Leading Lives that Matter: What We Should Do and Who We Should Be*, ed. Mark R. Schwehn and Dorothy C. Bass (Grand Rapids, MI: Eerdmans, 2006), 309. The perception that there are difficult decisions to make where both would be wrong is also echoed in the theory of double effect; but this theory still assumes a choice is possible—namely, that in situations where both outcomes are considered wrong, the choice is for the lesser of two evils. Nussbaum is of the view that often a choice is impossible, and in such circumstances would lead to a permanently troubled conscience, though she does not use the language of conscience in this interview. See also Martha C. Nussbaum, *The Fragility of Goodness: Luck and Ethics in Greek Tragedy and Philosophy* (Cambridge: Cambridge University Press, 1986). For an extended discussion of Nussbaum's perspective, see chapter 2 of this volume.

our responsibility to come to a decision, nor simply accept its unresolvable nature.

What happens if an undergraduate discerns a vocation through conscience, but it opposes certain moral claims that the student considers authoritative? An example in the Roman Catholic tradition might be a decision to be a development aid worker who distributes condoms to those in AIDS-ridden regions, or a decision to become a medical researcher on embryos, for example. According to Thomas Aquinas, conscience (*synderesis*) is the habit of practical reason arising out of natural law—the first principle of which is to do good and avoid evil. Conscience refers to the way those principles, and especially the first principle, are applied in specific circumstances. This means that the rule of *synderesis* is very general; it would miss the point to see conscience as a mere application of rules. Rather, conscience attempts to take a range of factors into account before reaching a particular judgment. I believe that it is this *range* of factors that needs to be encouraged when advising undergraduates about their vocation.

If conscience is understood to be the rudder or moral compass that helps to steer vocational exploration and discernment, then students will be more likely to claim those decisions as *their own*, rather than submitting to peer or familial pressures. At the same time, the interpretation of conscience in religious or even scientific communities is one where conscience is shaped by a process of communal formation. Vocational decisions are complex; they require navigating the expectations of the community, along with individual sensitivity to what is right, as guided by the action of grace in the heart of the believer—"the still small voice." It is too easy for educators to reinforce the individualism that is such a dominant characteristic of Western culture; if, on the other hand, students are exposed to the perspectives of a whole community, as well as those of particular individuals, they are more likely to come to decisions that foster social and individual goods.

Conscience is also linked with the idea of making *responsible* decisions, where responsibility implies taking account of the societal impacts of those decisions.[34] Conscience should be seen, not just as an individual decision, but as situated in a community that helps to shape conscience and is shaped by perceived decisions of conscience. Different communities will

---

34. For more on responsibility, see chapter 1 of this volume.

also give higher priorities to the relationship between conscience and the formation of those virtues most closely allied with prudence, including justice, compassion, temperance, and fortitude. Undergraduates making important decisions about their lives do so in an academic community that has its own ethos; the prior implicit or explicit claims of that community will help to determine which options are most likely to come to the surface in specific judgments of conscience. The particular institutional pressure on individuals to make choices in given directions may either be intentional or unintentional; but in either case, students undertaking the work of vocational discernment need to be aware of this influence. For example, in many institutions, academic programs and institutes are dedicated to explicit issues of social justice and compassion for the most vulnerable members of society in a global context; the presence of such programs on campus is bound to impact the career choices of individual students.

Precisely how such influence impinges on the life of an individual will depend on a combination of conscience (which alerts the individual to given norms, either held individually or collectively), and practical wisdom (which offers a guide as to how to put those norms into practice). Conscience is like an inner moral compass, but it takes practical wisdom to know how to act responsibly.

## *Preliminary conclusions: prudence, action, and responsibility*

One of the key distinguishing marks of practical wisdom is that it leads to *action*; in this respect, it may be distinguished from conscience, which may or may not be "obeyed" in ways that lead to practical outcomes. Prudence, therefore, necessitates a *putting into practice* and a testing that is highly relevant across a wide range of disciplines, both theoretical and applied. I suggest that this aspect of prudence is particularly important for vocational choices across a wide range of disciplines, since different options can be "tried out" in educational and work contexts as part of the experience of learning.

During my time at the University of Chester, all second-year undergraduates from all departments were obliged to take "work-based learning" as part of their coursework. The six-week placement was transformative for many students in helping them discern their future careers. I helped facilitate this course on at least two occasions early in my teaching career, and many students found it an eye-opening experience to get out into the workplace. Deliberation with those who were actually faced with decisions integral to the work placement proved both challenging and rewarding for students. They were required to write up their reflection and comment on how it had impacted their overall learning experience. While some faculty members treated such experiences with a certain amount of condescension (asserting the supposed superiority of theoretical and traditional knowledge), it was clear that from a practical point of view such experiences were crucial in allowing a deeper form of knowing to develop—namely, practical wisdom or prudential reasoning.

Of course, not all work placements were a success. Some students found that they were unsuited to the particular position they had signed up for; on other occasions, employers exploited the student visitors and only gave them the most menial tasks to perform. Still, such examples were in the minority, and the feedback from students meant that where partnerships led to poor experiences, they were not sustained. This course also provided a model that could become particularly significant for those who are entering university from backgrounds where there has been no familial history of higher education.[35] The gap in skills now felt in many practical industries (such as engineering) is such that the ancient idea of the guild and apprentice may start to return. And such practice in the workplace is typically combined with coursework when students are preparing for professional fields such as medicine, law, engineering, or business.

The cultivation of practical wisdom can also be linked with encouraging a sense of responsibility—for both the individual and for the communities of which they are part.[36] For those students who understand God to be the source of their callings, this may include a desire to work in the world in a way that chimes with that perceived divine calling; they will resonate with Buechner's claim that "the place God calls you to is the place where your deep gladness and the world's deep hunger meet."[37] For students who do not share these assumptions, a wider sense of moral

---

35. For further reflection on the difference this makes, see chapter 4 of this volume, as well as Caryn Riswold, "Vocational Discernment: A Pedagogy of Humanization," in Cunningham, ed., *At This Time*, 72–95.

36. For a detailed account of the role of responsibility, see chapter 1 of this volume.

37. Frederick Buechner, *Wishful Thinking: A Theological ABC* (New York: Harper and Row, 1973), 95.

and social responsibility is often present; what they perceive as good may often be shared with those who take a more specifically theological perspective. Hence, learning the art of being a responsible chemist, biologist, or engineer may not differ very much, regardless of a student's religious background or perceptions.

In both secular and religious circumstances, vocation is not simply transactional; it is not simply as a matter of how one functions in a society and the role that one plays, as though this were a matter of logical deduction. Rather, there are likely to be *transcendental* elements in any sense of keen responsibility for others, whether these are acknowledged or not. The task of the educator is to discern what *kinds* of responsibilities are most appropriate as goals in the light of the particular decisions made in the vocational choices of undergraduates. The classical tradition, drawing on Aristotelian philosophy, stressed human flourishing as that which orientated particular decisions and served to build morally responsible agents.

Both practical wisdom and conscience are companions on a way: they help assist students in the process of discernment at a particular moment in their lives. In the natural sciences, discernment can be particularly tricky for undergraduates; decisions about further study, including one's choice of subfield, tend to lock careers into particular paths. It takes genuine courage for a highly trained physicist to be willing to work with a biologist, crossing into a new discipline after having been formed in a different one. Hence, the companions of practical wisdom and conscience are important across the academic disciplines and throughout the life course. Those trained in sciences at undergraduate and graduate level may subsequently have a change of heart and undergo new training. Although such transitions can be difficult and costly (financially and psychologically), they also open up the possibility of a "second chance" that may lead to an even more fulfilling vocation.[38]

How can one come to *know* that one is discerning rightly? The English Puritans relied on individual self-reflection to counter any self-deceptive tendencies.[39] Practical wisdom and conscience are closely related to that

---

38. For more on this point, see chapter 10 of this volume.

39. This is discussed in a helpful way in Nathaniel Warne, *The Call to Happiness: An Investigation of Happiness, Virtues, Commands and the Common Good in the Doctrine of Calling, through the work of Aristotle, Thomas Aquinas and Sixteenth and Seventeenth Century English Puritans*, doctoral dissertation, University of Durham, England, 2015. Warne also refers to Aristotelian practical reason in this context, in ways that are in line with my own attention to Thomistic versions of practical wisdom.

insight, as well as taking into account the communal aspects of decision making. While vocational reflection is important, students need to realize that the process of responding to their various callings will extend over a life course; the decisions that they make appropriately at one stage of life will be understood differently in the light of further experience.[40] Such choices represent *a* way, rather than *the* way; a degree of flexibility is required in making such decisions, and one can usually expect that other (and perhaps very different) opportunities will arise in the future.[41]

Decisions based on practical wisdom will never evoke the kind of certainty of mind that might be true for certain other decisions that we make; in this respect, vocation will participate in that uncertainty. Conscience and practical wisdom help navigate the increasingly complex factors that come into play as undergraduates are faced with new responsibilities and relationships once they leave college. In this respect, conscience and practical wisdom are implemented through particular decisions, even as they are formed in the process of that implementation. Vocation presupposes imagination; in this respect, it is an art, the particular expression of which will be unique for each individual as situated in a particular network of relationships. But this is not all: recalling that the Latin word *scientia* actually means "knowledge," we might observe that vocational discernment is also a science: a particular "way of knowing" that is sorely needed today, in the face of supercomplexity and rapidly multiplying fields of study. An educator, in this sense, can only hope to be a midwife—nurturing the art and science of vocation in the lives of undergraduates, to whom and for whom these faculty and staff bear a particular responsibility.

---

40. For more on this point, see chapters 3, 4, 8, and 10 of this volume.

41. For more on this point, see chapter 10 of this volume.

# PART THREE

# Called into the Future

## Professional Fields and Preparation for Life

As the authors of this volume considered the various ways in which the language of vocation and calling might have a role to play across all academic disciplines and applied fields, their thoughts turned very quickly to the *future*. In every institution of higher education, in every field of study, educators and students spend considerable time and energy thinking about what will happen after the students complete their undergraduate academic programs. Will they go directly into rewarding, well-paying jobs? Will they find the right forms of volunteer service or other "gap-year" programs before taking the next step in their vocational journeys? Will they be admitted to the graduate or professional programs that are right for them, and will they receive enough financial aid to make their further study viable? Will they look back at their undergraduate institutions in a positive light, having been well prepared for the world they are entering?

These questions are on the minds of everyone at the college or university. How they are answered will affect how faculty members evaluate their program's curriculum and the quality of its teaching, how offices of alumni relations and institutional advancement work with their constituents, how admissions offices advertise their school's offerings, and what kinds of promises academic staff can make to students considering the programs of study that they administer. Most significantly, their students' future paths will determine how they look back on their specific academic programs, their undergraduate institution as a whole, and perhaps even the entire enterprise of higher education.

Conversations about calling and vocation are necessarily oriented toward the future. They encourage us to ask where we are heading, how we will get there, and what kinds of challenges we are likely to encounter along the way. As a future-oriented form of language, vocation speaks directly to the interest that all academic departments and programs share in the paths that their graduates will take. Interestingly, this claim holds true regardless of whether a particular field of study is currently experiencing a period of high demand and full employment, or one of lower demand and economic uncertainty. It resonates across the lines of race, class, and gender. It is as true for programs that expect students to continue on to higher degrees as it is for those in which students typically enter the workforce right away. And the breadth of these future concerns go well beyond the realm of paid employment and career marketability; academic institutions are also interested in whether their graduates' whole lives turn out to be fulfilling and meaningful, whether they find their true purpose, and whether they will one day be able to look back—over the entire arc of their lives—and recognize something that is true and good and beautiful.

This surprisingly universal interest in the future lives of college graduates provides the motivating energy for the authors of the following three chapters. Each of them is concerned with tracing the contours of that future with attention to how it might affect vocational reflection and discernment among undergraduate students in the present moment. By focusing on broad themes such as the nature of work, the curricular structure of undergraduate programs, and the ways that our future lives can be redeemed by new opportunities, these authors raise a wide range of questions that map right across the disciplines and applied fields:

- How do we understand the concept of work, and how has that understanding evolved over the years? What is the relationship between work and leisure, or between the work that we do as paid employment and that which we undertake for other reasons entirely? Work may be important for our individual identities, but does it completely structure and exhaust those identities? Who are we, beyond our work?

- How should we evaluate undergraduate programs that prepare students directly for the world of work, in comparison to those that expect some further level of graduate education before the student is fully prepared for that particular career? What kinds of pressures are created in each case (on academic departments, on institutions of higher education, and on the students themselves)?

- Is education at risk of becoming a mere commodity? Does the current level of public expectation about the "value" of a college education distort our perception of various undergraduate departments and programs? What relative weight should we give to economic claims about the employability and first-year salaries of graduates in a particular field, as compared to their level of general satisfaction with respect to less tangible matters, across the entire span of their lives?

· How do all of these factors affect the future of the professions, including law, medicine, engineering, and business? Given that the professions are usually understood as both a means of livelihood and a contribution to the public good, what is the appropriate relationship between paid employment and other aspects of professional life? Do these questions differ, depending on whether a profession expects a relatively short period of postsecondary preparation (as do business and engineering), or many more years of higher education (as do law and some medical fields)?

· How can undergraduate institutions find the right balance of curricular and co-curricular offerings, such that its graduates develop not only marketable job skills and an adequate introduction to their particular disciplines or professions, but also the ability to read well, to think critically, and to write and speak in ways that communicate?

· To what degree can students be led through a program of emotional, moral, and personal development, so that they are both fully prepared to enter a particular profession or field, and sufficiently agile to make adjustments in their future trajectories that our quickly evolving and newly emerging circumstances seem likely to demand?

Clearly, the questions articulated here are broader and deeper than can be satisfactorily addressed in three short chapters. Nevertheless, we do believe that this part of the book contributes significantly to our primary goal: demonstrating that the language of vocation and calling can help educators and students to develop a productive conversation that transcends the boundaries of the traditional disciplines and the applied fields.

# 8

## Laboring in the Garden

### VOCATION AND THE REALITIES OF WORK

*Christine M. Fletcher*

ACADEMICS ARE UNDER pressure from administrators, government officials, parents, and the media to justify the costs of a college education.
The dominant narrative suggests that attending college should lead to a
well-paying job, which is essential to buy the things that define success
in a consumer society: a house, a new car, lots of clothes, and vacations
to interesting destinations. This narrative assumes, as most of our culture does, that work is synonymous with paid employment—and that paid
employment is the only work that is significant.

Given this context, it should not surprise us that the word *vocation* is
often employed in the self-help and "business success" literature to con-
note a kind of self-fulfillment through paid work. This helps to buttress a
corporate climate of work, demanding not only more hours from workers,
but more emotional investment as well—which in turn tends to devalue
the time that would be spent with family and friends.[1] This use of the language of vocation, however, is radically incomplete; rewarding paid work
may indeed be a *part* of one's vocation, but only one part. The unpaid work

1. Recent stories about the 24/7 work culture include Jodi Kantor and David Streitfeld,
"Inside Amazon: Wrestling Big Ideas in a Bruising Workplace," *New York Times*, August
15, 2015, www.nytimes.com/2015/08/16/technology/inside-amazon-wrestling-big-ideas-in-a-
bruising-workplace.html (accessed March 7, 2016); and Claire Cain Miller, "The Problem with
Work Is Overwork," *New York Times*, Business, May 31, 2015, BU4, revised version online at
www.nytimes.com/2015/05/31/upshot/the-24-7-work-cultures-toll-on-families-and-gender-
equality.html (accessed March 7, 2016).

of family, community service through voluntary work, and hobbies are equally a part of a purposeful life.

Undergraduate students are done a disservice if they are not helped to recognize the value of work that is done, not for money, but for the service of the family or the larger community.[2] Work that is undertaken for pay will be a central part of vocation, and the undergraduate years are an important time for asking the right questions about the kinds of work that students are considering. Nevertheless, they also need to ask broader questions about the roles that employment, family, and community will play in their *fully human* lives.

This chapter seeks to develop a broader understanding of work and vocation. Its argument is based on the claim that work should be understood as an activity of human beings that seeks to develop their potential and to affect the world around them. This broader definition recognizes that work integrates individuals into the economic system, but also into social, political, and familial modes of cooperation.[3] This broader definition is especially useful in a time when more and more jobs are being done by robots, or otherwise removed from the sphere of human activity through technological changes. In our contemporary era in particular, we need a better conception of work; and that new account will be essential for helping us develop a deeper understanding of vocation as a call to a meaningful life.

The chapter begins by examining work from a historical perspective, attending to the traditional division of work and leisure; it then turns to work as creative effort. It argues that work must be understood in a wider sense in order to critique two forms of idolatry: that of paid work as the singular all-encompassing space for the making of meaning, and that of leisure as the merely passive consumption of consumer goods and media. Both of these assumptions disconnect all human activity, whether work or leisure, from any idea of the common good. The chapter then turns to explore the effects of technology in an economy in which more and more jobs are being taken over by automation; this in turn underscores the need for a broader notion of work. Throughout the chapter, we will be reminded

---

2. Indeed, this misleading claim—that real work is restricted to paid employment—has a number of unfortunate results; it leads, for example, to students who tell their instructors that they were unable to do the reading for class because "I had to work."

3. Kathi Weeks, *The Problem with Work: Feminism, Marxism, Anti-work Politics and Post-work Imaginaries* (Durham, NC: Duke University Press, 2011), 8.

that vocation will still exist, even if paid work were to disappear altogether; work, in the broader sense advocated here, will still need doing.

## *Labor, toil, creation, leisure*

Two people are digging in a garden. Is this work or leisure? Their activity involves effort and skill; it can be done as employment, but it can also be a leisure activity. If the food from the garden were necessary for their survival, Karl Marx would call it *toil*, whereas Hannah Arendt would call it *labor*.[4] If they are digging because they are employed by the land's owner, they are experiencing paid employment; Marx would describe this as *alienated labor*, since its fruits are claimed by another.[5] Others might call it *toil* because it is primarily bodily rather than mental effort. On the other hand, our diggers might be homesteaders who are growing cash crops that they will sell for money to pay taxes on the property—they are still working, but they have chosen the labor and their work is not "mere" toil. Alternatively, these gardeners might be highly paid executives who are working on their hobby farm where they grow organic food as a luxury, not a necessity; they can buy all the food they need, and so their digging is leisure. In any case, simple observation does not tell us exactly how to label the activity—which in turn helps to illustrate the complexity of the issues surrounding work.

Work is human activity that demands effort; it gives human beings the pleasure of that exercise of their energies. This definition of work—as any activity, mental or physical, that involves effort—aligns with the physicist's definition of work: force that moves a body. It also has the advantage of including the work that often is not waged: children's play, students studying, housework, child care, and elder care. Work is a world-structuring, meaning-making enterprise that gives our lives content, social identity, and status.[6]

In our time and place, paid employment is seen as giving us our primary identity. The question upon meeting someone is not "Where are you from?" or "Who is your family?"; instead, we ask "What do you do?" or, even more explicitly, "Where do you work?" These questions imply a

---

4. Hannah Arendt, *The Human Condition* (Chicago: University of Chicago Press), 7.

5. Karl Marx, *Economic and Philosophical Manuscripts of 1844*, trans. Martin Milligan (New York: Prometheus, 1988), 22.

6. Darby Kathleen Ray, *Working* (Minneapolis, MN: Fortress, 2011), 7.

distorted vision of what it means to be human; after all, we are (or should be) more than our jobs, however important and satisfying those jobs may be. Thus, while paid work plays a role in the vocation of many people, it is not essential for a life of meaning and purpose; such a life can be lived by someone who is wholly unable to earn money and who is totally dependent on others.

The problem of work changes as human ingenuity creates new ways of doing things; this further complicates the boundaries that divide work from leisure. In the ancient and medieval world, work was activity for survival; this distinguished it from leisure. Whether one was a worker or leisured depended on birth; *vocation* became the word for those who left either of these states in order to take up work in the church. Joseph Pieper reminds us that "the Greek word for leisure is the origin of the Latin *scola*, German *Schule*, English *school*. The name for the institutions of education and learning mean 'leisure.' "[7] Leisure, not work, was sought; philosophy and learning were activities of leisure. Pieper therefore translates Aristotle's dictum on work as follows: "We are *not-at-leisure* in order to *be-in-leisure*."[8] We work in order to have time for other pursuits.

In *The Human Condition*, Hannah Arendt accepts this ancient distinction between work and leisure. She goes on to distinguish three fundamental human activities: *labor,* activity to support biological life; *work,* activity which provides the artificial world of things (i.e., differentiated from our naturally occurring surroundings); and *action,* the activity that goes on directly between people, without the intermediary of material objects.[9]

For Arendt, labor leaves no residue; the result of labor is almost as quickly consumed as the effort is spent. This characteristic may explain why housework is so undervalued. The products it produces—an orderly house, clean clothes, and regular meals—disappear almost as soon as the worker creates them. The day's work needs to be done over and over again. In the ancient world, this work was, if possible, done by slaves, because of the "slavish nature of all occupations that served the needs for the maintenance of life."[10]

---

7. Joseph Pieper, *Leisure, The Basis of Culture,* trans. Gerald Malsbary (South Bend, IN: St. Augustine's Press, 1998), 3–4.

8. Ibid., 4.

9. Arendt, *The Human Condition,* 7–8.

10. Ibid., 83.

Work, for Arendt, creates the material objects—"the sheer unending variety of things whose sum total constitutes the human artifice."[11] Workers are tool makers, who lighten the burden of labor; the ideal they pursue is usefulness, and their public realm is the market. While the laborer (*animal laborens*) serves nature, the worker (*homo faber*) subdues it; the logic of human making transforms nature from a gift into raw material. Work produces things that "possess a durability Locke needed for the establishment of property, the 'value' Adam Smith needed for market exchange, and they bear testimony to productivity, which Marx believed to be the test of human nature."[12] Action, Arendt's final category, refers to the exercise of human freedom in the world. Rather than sustain our bodies or add things to our world, action's effects are felt in the web of human relationships. In this realm, human beings act as responsible agents.[13]

Arendt's three categories are extremely useful in analyzing work. In actual practice, of course, they often overlap. A stay-at-home mother might start a small business by making and selling baby blankets; she *labors* in sustaining her own and her children's biological life, *works* as she sews the blankets, and *acts* when she takes initiatives not forced upon her by necessity nor prompted by utility.[14] Still, these three general categories are important for students seeking to integrate paid work into a fully human life. By recognizing the three spheres—work from necessity, work to make things, and work to sustain relationships—the work of the whole person can be brought into consideration. These categories suggest some obvious problems with the totalizing view that sees paid employment as the only real form of work; such a view tends to make those who are not employed for wages disappear from notice, from political debate, and from public concern.

In this totalizing view, employment is seen almost exclusively as an *end*—both for the individual and for the political system. Governments seek to manage the employment rate; most people consider it a measure of social well-being. Kathi Weeks, a contemporary political theorist, shows that the value of work as a social institution does not enter today's debates about political theory; it is considered beyond discussion. She maintains

---

11. Ibid., 136.

12. Ibid., 136.

13. For a detailed analysis of responsibility, see chapter 1 of this volume.

14. Arendt, *The Human Condition*, 177.

that this exclusion from theoretical questioning exists, first, because work has been privatized and individualized; and second, because worker-based activism within the political party system has declined precipitously. Ethical buying and consumer boycotts have become the primary avenue by which individuals can hope to have any significant impact on the economic system.[15]

Weeks identifies the problems of underwork (including unemployment), overwork (the way work monopolizes our time and energy), and what she calls *non-work*, which has two elements: socially necessary yet unwaged forms of work (such as housework and dependent care), as well as a more theoretical construct: our apparent inability to create a space for achievement and social reciprocity outside the framework of waged work. She observes the relatively recent genesis of this idea: "The value of work, along with its centrality to our lives is one of the most stubbornly naturalized and apparently self-evident elements of modern and late, or post-modern, capitalist societies."[16] In the seventeenth and eighteenth centuries, religious convictions helped to provide a motive for approaching work as the center of one's life; but in the nineteenth century, the "work ethic" had transformed into a discourse, not about the afterlife, but about self-improvement in this life. By the middle of the twentieth century, work began to be seen as part of a person's self-expression and creativity.[17]

## Devaluation of unpaid work

The traditional division of work and leisure tended to identify work as necessary to survive; work was largely limited to Arendt's category of *labor*. The activity of caring for others was rendered largely invisible, and therefore fell outside the common definition of work. With the industrial revolution, work for sustenance moved out of the home and became labor for wages. Men worked in order to provide the monetary support for dependents at home, while women remained in the home and provided "love's labor": direct care for these dependents. Men lived in the public sphere of the economy and politics, where money served as the defining standard of worth; hence, women's unpaid labor of caregiving was not treated as

---

15. Weeks, *The Problem with Work*, 3.

16. Ibid., 43.

17. On the complex relationships among these terms, see chapter 5 of this volume.

"real" work, but instead defined as women's special "vocation." Middle- and upper-class women's leisure became a status symbol: "my wife doesn't have to work."

One strand of feminism sought to have women's work in the home recognized in the economic system, regarding it as work that is socially necessary and dignified. Addressing this problem, some critics advocated for a family wage—a wage calculated not for an individual laborer but for the laborer and dependents. A second strand of feminism, typified by Betty Friedan, declared that a woman "can find identity only in work that is of real value to society—work for which society usually pays."[18] Neither of these approaches questioned the circumstances of work, which often included long hours and a system that distanced the worker from private and family life. In the twentieth century, many women left the home for paid work, which meant that no one was there to do the unpaid caregiving; consequently, these women had to work "the second shift," to use Arlie Hochschild's phrase. As more women followed this trajectory, caregiving was outsourced. Hochschild describes the result:

> Care work is a hot potato job. Many husbands turn over care of the young and old to their wives. Wives, if they can afford to, often turn it over to childcare and eldercare workers. In turn, many immigrant nannies hire nannies back home to help care for the children that they have left behind, forming a care chain.... Underlying this gender/class/national transfer is the devaluation of care. This is based on the idea that care work is "easy," "natural," and—like parenting—not quite real work. Part of what makes care work invisible is that the people the worker cares for—children, the elderly, the disabled—are themselves somewhat invisible. Strangers entering a room may tend to ignore or "talk over" the very young and old.[19]

The work of giving care has lower status because our culture tends to value *things-in-general* more than it does *people-in-general*—and especially those people who are dependent on others (the sick, the disabled, the very young, the very old). Eva Feder Kittay suggests that this mindset strikes at the very root of democracy; she points out that it challenges the

---

18. Betty Friedan, *The Feminine Mystique* (New York: Norton, 1963), 346.

19. Arlie Hochschild, *So How's the Family?* (Berkeley: University of California Press, 2013), 30.

"self-understanding of democratic liberal nations as an association of free and independent equals," describing her view as "the dependency critique of equality."[20] Her work seeks to recognize and validate the lives of the vulnerable and dependent, thereby challenging the claim that our social order is "derived from the voluntary association of equally situated and empowered individuals."[21] Kittay bases her theory on the equality that we all share (as "some mother's child"); she seeks social recognition for the work of caring for dependents (and the work of caring for those who care for dependents). Her work thus develops a significant counter-narrative to the claim that only waged work is real work.

Kittay identifies dependency work as qualitatively different from most work carried out among equal contracting parties. Dependency work requires the worker to have what Kittay calls a " 'transparent self': The perception of and response to another's needs are neither blocked out nor refracted through our own needs."[22] Full recognition of the importance of dependency work to a society would result in a principle of social responsibility in care, which Kittay phrases as follows:

> To each according to his or her need of care, from each according to his or her capacity for care, and such support from social institutions as to make available resources and opportunities to those providing care, so that all will be adequately attended in relations that are sustaining.[23]

This is work that must be performed by humans for other humans; it resists the logic of technology and automation. Unfortunately, however, when care work *does* become paid employment, it is one of the most poorly paid jobs; in our system, the highest pay goes to autonomous actors who satisfy "rational" preferences in an amoral marketplace. When we challenge the assumption that work equals paid employment, we are challenging a social imaginary that places things above people—and one that excludes those who are not autonomous.

---

20. Eva Feder Kittay, *Love's Labor: Essays on Women, Equality, and Dependency* (New York: Routledge, 1999), 4.

21. Ibid., 73.

22. Ibid., 53.

23. Ibid., 113; entire passage italicized in original.

## Disordered leisure

Our culture assumes that work exists to fund "not-work," but in a different sense than Kittay uses the term. For us, "not-work" is usually understood only as leisure or retirement; but these are seen as costly endeavors, so they ironically create more pressure for higher-paying work—no matter what it requires of us.

The great promise of technology was free time: there would be no more slavery to the labor of survival. Thomas More's *Utopia* had a social organization designed to maximize leisure. Farm work, the most essential for survival, was done by everyone at some point in their lives for two years; those who found this work congenial could continue in it indefinitely. At harvest time, people from the towns would come to help out. All the other work of the society was done in six-hour workdays. In Utopia, trading was limited because its people had limited wants (no fashion or jewelry, for example). The free time created by this plan was to be used for further education or recreation. "They never force people to work unnecessarily, for the main purpose of their whole economy is to give all people as much time free from physical drudgery as the needs of the community will allow, so that they can cultivate their minds—which they regard as the secret of a happy life."[24]

Our modern, technologically improved world has not achieved the same balance of work and leisure. Joseph Pieper contrasts leisure as a condition of the soul to leisure presented as "breaks," "time off," "weekends," or "vacation." For Pieper, work is activity, effort, and social function. Leisure is *not* activity; it is the stillness that provides us with the necessary preparation for accepting reality. It is a letting go—a form of contemplation. It is not effort, but "the condition of considering things in a celebrating spirit."[25] Finally, it is most definitely *not* merely a break, after which we can get back to work more efficiently and effectively. True leisure—contemplation—stands outside the paradigm in which "everything is work."

This understanding of the relationship between leisure and work has all but disappeared in our society. Leisure has become subservient to

---

24. Thomas More, *Utopia*, trans. Paul Turner (New York: Penguin Books, 2003), 59, translation slightly altered.

25. Joseph Pieper, *Leisure*, 12.

work—just another market where relaxation can be bought and sold as a positional good. (Lying on the beach in Tahiti is imagined to be much better than lying on the beach in New Jersey, so we are willing to work more in order to experience the former instead of the latter.) Shopping is described as a hobby, and we are surrounded by devices that school us in a form of leisure that requires heavy participation in practices of consumerism.[26] Pope Francis has described our economy as "a throw-away culture which affects the excluded just as it quickly reduces things to rubbish."[27] All of these problems are, of course, exacerbated by the increasing role of technology in our lives; this will be our focus in the next section.

## *Working in a wired world*

Technology has disburdened our leisure as well as our work. Instead of a family spending time together with one member reading aloud to the others (and thereby sharing the experience of the literature), the contemporary household is filled with a plethora of screens (televisions, computers, tablets, phones) that are available to each family member in isolation. Hence, in place of shared experiences, we have substituted the triumph of individual choice. Entertaining ourselves by playing charades or playing cards, in contrast, would require greater effort on the part of the participants; these activities draw out the communal vocabulary formed by common experience. Instead of feeling more tired, as one often does after being passively entertained by a glowing screen, game players typically find themselves energized.

Andrew Stanton's film *WALL·E* is an extended parable about technology, focusing on the waste—human and otherwise—brought about by a society of mass production and mass consumption. In this story, the earth has literally been trashed; human beings have departed the planet in large spaceships that coddle their passengers. Technology has provided every sort of creature comfort on a physical level; no effort is required to eat, drink, or be clothed in the latest fashion. Entertainment pours out of screens. The turning point of the film occurs when the captain of the

---

26. See William T. Cavanaugh, *Being Consumed: Economics and Christian Desire* (Grand Rapids, MI: William B. Eerdmans, 2008).

27. *Laudato Si!*, paragraph 22.

ship rediscovers the need to *do something*—to be forced to make an effort in order to achieve a real result. What had been lacking, for the captain as well as the passengers, was any real sense of purpose. The only characters with real purpose throughout the film are the robots, like *WALL·E* and Eva—which makes them the most "human" characters in the story.

We are close to achieving the world that *WALL·E* predicted—a world where most goods can be produced without human work, thanks to 3-D printers and artificial intelligence systems. Automation has been seen as a twofold threat to workers since the Luddites broke the power looms in the eighteenth century; it threatens human livelihood and it also threatens our sense of purpose in being productive. What would happen in a world in which most people were not needed as workers? This question is explored in Kurt Vonnegut's dystopian novel *Player Piano*.[28] In this world, people have acquired all the material goods and income that they need; homes are equipped with automatic washers, dryers, ironing machines, and cooking systems that prepare meals in minutes. No one needs to labor or work. Automation runs the production processes; the ruling class consists of managers and engineers who are selected by the machines, based on their IQ and aptitude scores.

The great mass of the population is employed in the army, or in the "Reeks and Wrecks"—the repair squads that carry out all laboring jobs, but have no real work to do. Vonnegut captures the human cost of a world in which no work is needed in a scene in which the protagonist's car—a relic he cherishes because it doesn't drive itself—breaks down.

> "Five minutes," said the tall man. He took off his hat and, with an expression of satisfaction, ripped out the sweatband. He took a penknife from his pocket, laid the cap of the fuel pump over the sweatband, and cut out a leather disk just the right size. Then he cut out the disk's center, dropped the new gasket in place and put the pump back together. The others watched him eagerly, handed him tools, or offered to hand him tools, and tried to get in on the operation wherever they could. One man scraped the green and white crystals from the battery connection. Another one went around tightening the valve caps on the tires.
>
> "Now try her!" said the tall man.

---

28. Kurt Vonnegut, *Player Piano* (New York: Charles Scribner's Sons, 1952).

Paul stepped on the starter, the motor caught, roared fast and slow without a miss as he pumped the accelerator. He looked up to see the profound satisfaction, the uplift of creativity, in the faces of the Reeks and Wrecks.[29]

The men are satisfied, of course, because their efforts have made a *real* change in the *real* world.

When we change material objects through our work, this in turn has an effect on our own identities. This point is well described by Matthew Crawford, whose essay (and later book), "Shop Class as Soulcraft," explores craftsmanship and the discipline of working with things.

The satisfactions of manifesting oneself concretely in the world through manual competence have been known to make a man quiet and easy. They seem to relieve him of the felt need to offer chattering *interpretations* of himself to vindicate his worth. He can simply point: the building stands, the car now runs, the lights are on.... Craftsmanship must reckon with the infallible judgment of reality, where one's failures or shortcomings cannot be interpreted away.[30]

Crawford's language here precisely describes the outlook of the above-mentioned characters in *Player Piano*: in spite of the pseudo-satisfactions of the consumer life, there is no substitute for the creative life. One of Vonnegut's particularly prophetic characters, Lasher, observes that, "Sooner or later someone's going to catch the imagination of these people with some new magic. At the bottom of it will be a promise of regaining the feeling of participation, the feeling of being needed on earth—hell, *dignity*."[31] Vonnegut constructs for his readers a parallel between the dissatisfactions of the workers and their made-up work, on the one hand, and, on the other, the dissatisfactions of the managers and engineers in a system that offers them status but seeks only efficiency and material comfort as ultimate goals.

---

29. Ibid., 61.

30. Matthew B. Crawford, "Shop Class as Soulcraft." *The New Atlantis* 13 (Summer 2006): 7–24; here, 9.

31. Vonnegut, *Player Piano*, 80.

For the philosopher Albert Borgmann, technology relieves us from certain burdens of work, but it also reduces our level of engagement. He argues that technological devices (such as, for example, a central heating system) tend to dissolve the coherent and engaging character of the world of things as they existed before the advent of that technology. With a device, the relatedness of the world is replaced by concealed machinery; the commodities which the device makes available are consumed or enjoyed without engaging in the work that the context would require. Cooking from scratch, learning to play the flute, and building a fire in the fireplace all burden us; nevertheless, they also initiate us into the world through a community of practice, requiring us to make use of our capacities for thought, memory, attention, and action.

Borgmann identifies key features of the device paradigm. First, the science of technological devices promises liberation; ironically, however, this liberation means not only fewer burdens but less engagement. "Enrichment by way of diversion is overtaken by distraction, and conquest makes way first to domination and then to loneliness.... Things in their depth yield to shallow commodities, and our one profound and manifold engagement with the world is reduced to narrow points of contact in labor and consumption."[32] Further, the scale of values of work is turned upside down: work with machines is thought to be at least semi-skilled, but farmworkers and housewives "who command exacting but partially or primarily pretechnological skills are considered unskilled."[33]

Nicholas Carr discovers a similar paradox with respect to the impact of computers on our lives: automation frees us from work, but we lose the purpose and meaning that otherwise helps to make us truly free. "The choices we make, or fail to make, about which tasks we hand off to computers and which we keep for ourselves are not just practical or economic choices. They're ethical choices. They shape the substance of our lives."[34] Carr urges us to reconsider how we organize work and automation in order to change our goal—which he believes should be, not to maximize efficiency, but to cultivate a truly human life. As Carr notes, "to put it into uncharitable but not inaccurate terms, many doctors may soon find

---

32. Albert Borgmann, *Technology and the Character of Contemporary Life: A Philosophical inquiry* (Chicago: University of Chicago Press, 1984), 76.

33. Ibid., 119.

34. Nicholas G. Carr, *The Glass Cage: Automation and Us* (New York: Norton, 2014), 18.

themselves taking on the role of human sensors who collect information for a decision-making computer."[35] The same process is affecting auditors, traders on Wall Street, lawyers, and business executives.[36]

Academic institutions are not exempt from this trend; unfortunately, however, as students and educators become more reliant on technology, their engagement with learning often suffers. The presence of technology in the form of laptops and cell phones gives students a chance to multitask during class; they check social media, text their friends, surf the web. Such multitasking reduces the capacity for learning—not only for the student who is attempting to multitask, but also for everyone else in the room, and particularly those who can see an active screen.[37] Lectures are recorded, notes are pre-posted in the learning management system, or notes are typed into the laptop; faculty members are thus tempted to duplicate the same material for every class, and students do not give the material the degree of attention that would have been needed in order to listen and to make handwritten notes of significant points. UCLA cognitive psychologist Robert Bjork has identified the use of less technologically oriented teaching practices (such as demanding handwritten notes) as "desirable difficulties"—tasks that make students' brains work a little bit harder in the short run, but that pay off in terms of better long-term memory.[38]

These investigations into the effect of automation confirm Vonnegut's insight that human beings need to be *engaged*; they need to put forth a certain amount of effort in order to exercise true agency. The increasing speed

---

35. Ibid., 115.

36. Barbara Ehrenreich, in a book review in the *New York Times*, writes, "It's impossible to read 'Rise of the Robots'—for review anyway—without thinking about how the business of book reviewing could itself be automated and possibly improved by computers." Barbara Ehrenreich, "Welcome to Your Obsolescence," *New York Times Book Review*, May 17, 2015.

37. Faria Sana, Tina Weston, and Nicholas J. Cepeda, "Laptop Multitasking Hinders Classroom Learning for Both Users and Nearby Peers," *Computers & Education* 62 (March 2013): 24–31,www.sciencedirect.com/science/article/pii/S0360131512002254 (accessed August 29, 2015). Similar studies were summarized in Anne Murphy Paul, "You'll Never Learn! Students Can't Resist Multitasking, and It's Impairing their Memory," *Slate*, May 3, 2013, www.slate.com/articles/health_and_science/science/2013/05/multitasking_while_study-ing_divided_attention_and_technological_gadgets.html (accessed August 29, 2015).

38. "The Surprising Secret to Better Student Recall," *Pedagogy Unbound* blog, September 10, 2014, https://chroniclevitae.com/news/697-the-surprising-secret-to-better-student-recall (accessed April 2, 2015). Similar results have been summarized in Pam A. Mueller and Daniel M. Oppenheimer, "The Pen Is Mightier than the Keyboard: Advantages of Longhand Over Laptop Note Taking," *Psychological Science* 25 no. 6 (June 2014): 1159–68 (accessed August 29, 2015), doi: 10.1177/0956797614524581.

of innovation and advances in artificial intelligence, computing power, 3-D printing, and network availability mean that educators have little idea of what kinds of jobs will be available for their students in the coming years. They do know, however, that jobs requiring repetitive information handling are already being done, and done well, by computers. Students therefore need to develop higher-order thinking skills and creativity; these are the abilities that will be most valued in the new marketplace. This requires a fuller conception of vocation—one that attends to both waged and unwaged work, as well as to productive leisure.

## *Work and creativity*

Vonnegut's identification of work with both effort and creativity builds on a long tradition of thought about the subject in both Marxism and Christianity—two traditions that in many respects are antagonistic. However, both Marx and the tradition of Roman Catholic social teaching[39] agree that work, in addition to having an instrumental character, forms a person by drawing on his or her inherent creative powers; it also creates a relationship between the worker and other human beings. Marx's fundamental insight—the presupposition for all his future writing—was that labor is the essence of humanity, which is to be found "in the act of proving itself." Work, he argues, is the process by which we "come to be for ourselves" by developing our creative capacity.[40] Work is a mechanism, both of realizing both the individual's creative essence, and of building social relationships.

Similarly, the tradition of Roman Catholic social teaching has recognized that every worker is a creator. Pope John Paul II defined work very broadly:

> work means any human activity, whether manual or intellectual, whatever its nature or circumstances; it means any human activity

---

39. Catholic Social Teaching is the body of papal encyclicals (and work related to them) stretching from *Rerum Novarum* (1881) through, most recently at this writing, *Laudato Si!* (2015), all of which deal with questions of social ethics in a modern society. Catholic social thought is the wider category that would include theologians, ethicists, and practitioners reasoning about these encyclicals in practice.

40. Marx, *Economic and Philosophical Manuscripts*, 150. See also Weeks, *The Problem with Work*, 106.

that can and must be recognized as work, in the midst of all the many activities of which human beings are capable and to which they are predisposed by their very nature, by virtue of humanity itself.[41]

This creative element is also present in applied fields such as business administration: "The creative dimension is an essential component of human activity, even in the area of business, and it is especially manifested in the areas of planning and innovation. . . . Creativity and cooperation are signs of the authentic concept of business competition."[42]

For Jews and Christians, the creation story in Genesis tells us that Adam was to tend the garden—that was his assigned work. After the Fall, Adam *toils*; his work has become beset with difficulties. But work itself is part of human life; it reflects the image of the God who creates. This insight is emphasized in the work of Dorothy L. Sayers, best known for her "Lord Peter Wimsey" novels, who brought her experience as a creative writer to her reflections on the nature of work. For Sayers, good work should be thought of as "a creative activity undertaken for the love of the work itself"; we who are "made in God's image should make things, as God makes them, for the sake of doing well a thing that is worth doing."[43] Sayers contrasts the creative worker with the industrious apprentice, whose virtues were sobriety, thrift, cleanliness, and respectability, but who did not question the work itself (or the conditions under which it was done).

For Sayers, a key question is: "What work is fit for humans?" If work were viewed solely as a discipline, or as nothing more than punishment for sin, this question would make no sense. Any and all kinds of work would serve these lowly purposes; indeed, drudgery and monotony would be expected. According to Sayers, good work has two characteristics: it makes a good product, and the work *fits* the human worker. It is done at

---

41. John Paul II, *Laborem Exercens*, www.vatican.va/holy_father/john_paul_ii/encyclicals/documents/hf_jp-ii_enc_14091981_laborem-exercens_en.html (accessed December 19, 2014), introduction, translation altered.

42. *Compendium of Social Doctrine of the Church* (Vatican City: Libreria Editrice Vaticana, 2004), paragraphs 337 and 343.

43. Dorothy L. Sayers, "Why Work?," in *Leading Lives that Matter: What We Should Do and Who We Should Be*, ed. Mark R. Schwehn and Dorothy C. Bass (Grand Rapids, MI: Eerdmans, 2006), 192.

a human pace; the workers themselves control that pace, and the work engages the workers' knowledge, skills, and creativity. Sayers's idea of creativity recognized both the differences and similarities between the artist's experience of making and that of the dressmaker or the cook. In all these cases, the human mind engages with material realities to produce something—whether a loaf of bread, a dress, or a painting. All human beings have this capacity.

How we approach our work determines whether we are acting as free human creators or as limited servants of our technology. The difference lies in the approach to life. To the artist, life presents a series of opportunities to make something new; the technologist, on the other hand, sees life as a series of problems to be solved. The technologist solves the problem of pain and existential anxiety with Prozac; the artist, in contrast, writes *The Plague*. Sayers wants workers to have the opportunity to engage with experience and with their creativity, whether in their paid work or in their hobbies.

If we are able to understand work as necessarily involving effort and creativity, and to recognize that this effort is essential for human flourishing, we will quickly realize that people engaged in *crafts* have much to teach us. Peter Korn, a woodworker and teacher of woodworking, finds that often the people who come to his school to learn the craft are unsatisfied with their lives. "The banquet of work, leisure, and consumption that society prescribes has left some essential part of them undernourished. They are hungry for avenues of engagement that provide more wholesome sustenance."[44] He engages with the literature of craftsmanship, particularly that of Robert Pirsig, Richard Sennett, and Matthew Crawford (whose work was mentioned in the previous section).[45] All these authors agree that the key to a good life is the engaged pursuit of quality, and that our culture is defective in that it severs the satisfactions of individual agency from the things we actually do. "Pirsig faults the Aristotelian underpinnings of Western thought, Sennett faults the culture of corporate capitalism, and

---

44. Peter Korn, *Why We Make Things and Why it Matters: The Education of a Craftsman* (Boston: David R. Godine, 2013), 10.

45. Robert Pirsig, *Zen and the Art of Motorcycle Maintenance* (New York: Bantam, 1975); Richard Sennett, *The Craftsman* (New Haven, CT: Yale University Press, 2009); Matthew B. Crawford, *Shop Class as Soulcraft: An Inquiry into the Value of Work* (New York: Penguin, 2010).

Crawford faults the pernicious effects of the Cartesian mind/body divide on education and the workplace."[46]

For all three writers, the key to a good life is the engaged pursuit of quality. However, while Pirsig, Sennet, and Crawford pay little explicit attention to creativity, Korn makes it central to a life of meaning and fulfillment:

> The effort to bring something new and meaningful into the world—whether in the arts, the kitchen, or the marketplace—is exactly what generates the sense of meaning and fulfillment for which so many of us yearn so deeply. The dedication to quality that they prescribe is essential to productive creative engagement, but it is only a component, not the effort itself.[47]

This again recalls the perspective of Vonnegut's characters in *Player Piano*, for whom work becomes fulfilling only when it allows space for genuine creativity.

Matthew Crawford, himself a philosopher and a motorcycle mechanic, wants to draw out the discipline required by working with material objects; it is the inherent limits in the things themselves that test the capacity of the workers as they pursue their work. He also situates his work as serving a community—that of skilled riders. As a mechanic, he cannot use creativity in the way that Korn does when designing a new table, for example; but he does use his full mental powers, and physical senses, in order to get the task right. Crawford contrasts the satisfaction of his work with machines with the work he did as a "knowledge worker" (when he was required to read twenty-eight academic articles a day and write an abstract for each). He described that expectation as unsuited to the work itself; the work became purely instrumental, since it was impossible to do it in a way that honored the goods intrinsic to it.[48] He was a worker in the so-called knowledge economy, yet he had no time for *thought*. In fact, his job could probably have been done better by a computer.

Work that involves engagement, effort, and creative thought is work that is truly human. But this still leaves open the question of the ultimate goal or purpose of work; to this matter we now turn.

---

46. Korn, *Why We Make Things*, 12.

47. Ibid., 13.

48. Crawford, *Shop Class as Soulcraft*, 137.

# *Why work?*

Vocation involves a basic question: Does one "live to work" or "work to live"? To address this question in the classroom, I ask my students to compare Dorothy L. Sayers's essay "Why Work?" with an extract from Abraham Heschel's *The Sabbath*. Sayers sees work as something that "is not, primarily, a thing one does to live, but the thing one lives to do. It is, or it should be, the full expression of the worker's faculties," in which one finds "spiritual, mental, and bodily satisfaction."[49] She sees leisure as the intervals of rest, play and re-creation in order to go back to the work refreshed.

Heschel, on the other hand, writes of the Sabbath, which demands that we cease work. He disagrees with Philo, who presented the Sabbath in spirit of Aristotle (and Sayers): a time of rest to refresh us for more work. For Heschel, Sabbath means much more than this: "Six days a week we seek to dominate the world, on the seventh day we try to dominate the self."[50] In the contemporary context, we are enmeshed for (at least) six days a week in the technological civilization that is based on humanity's domination of nature in work to produce gain and goods. But this is not enough to fulfill us—nor would it be so if we were to work all seven days (or eight, if we could). Heschel maintains that the solutions to humanity's most vexing problems will be found, not in simply doing more work, nor in renouncing technical civilization, but in attaining some degree of independence from it.[51] Sabbath—with its requirement that we temporarily step away from commerce and work—creates a space to reclaim our identity as persons.

A further meditation on the important of the Sabbath comes from the pen of Oliver Sacks, who comments on its significance for those who are facing the end of life (as was he, when he wrote these words):

> And now, weak, short of breath, my once-firm muscles melted away by cancer, I find my thoughts, increasingly, not on the supernatural or spiritual, but on what is meant by living a good and worthwhile life—achieving a sense of peace within oneself. I find my thoughts drifting to the Sabbath, the day of rest, the seventh day of the week,

---

49. Dorothy L. Sayers, *Creed or Chaos* (London: Methuen, 1947), 194.

50. Abraham Joshua Heschel, *The Sabbath: Its Meaning for Modern Man* (New York: Farrar Straus, 1951), 13.

51. Ibid., 221.

and perhaps the seventh day of one's life as well, when one can feel that one's work is done, and one may, in good conscience, rest.[52]

The Sabbath regulations—which forbid work including using a phone, or switching on a light, or driving a car—place the human community of family and friends above the idols of work, gain, and consumption.[53] The Sabbath stands as a corrective to human pride and overcommitment to work. This overcommitment is seen, not just in corporate workaholics, but in a wide range of occupations; caregivers, for example, can lose a sense of proportion and give so much without caring for themselves that they burn out. Those who live to work, as well as those who work to live, need the true leisure that the Sabbath offers.

Of course, the question still remains as to precisely *what* work one should take up. Deciding on the right work for one's gifts can be a process of individualist seeking of self-satisfaction or a community-centered process.[54] Within the Christian tradition, Edward Hahnenberg describes vocation as a process in which "God calls me, through others, for others."[55] This open-ended and communal definition of vocation lends a space to evaluate how we will apportion the various kinds of work in a well-lived life: work for wages, work of caregiving, and the work of good leisure. If we hold fast to a larger concept of work—as human action which requires effort—we can provide each of these three elements a genuine place in the discussion about work and vocation. In addition, the communal nature of conversations about vocation can break open the isolation to which we are increasingly tempted, as technology progressively separates us from one another (even as it gives us the illusion of connection).

---

52. Oliver Sacks, "Sabbath," *New York Times* Opinion, August 14, 2015, SR1; also online at www.nytimes.com/2015/08/16/opinion/sunday/oliver-sacks-sabbath.html (accessed March 7, 2016).

53. A helpful introduction to the Sabbath regulations and their meaning is Christopher D. Ringwald, *A Day Apart: How Jews, Christians, and Muslims Find Faith, Freedom and Joy on the Sabbath* (Oxford: Oxford University Press, 2007). Pope Benedict XVI referred to Jacob Neusner, *A Rabbi Talks with Jesus* (New York: Doubleday, 1993), mentioning his discussion of the Sabbath discourse in Matthew as especially helpful. Benedict XVI, *Jesus of Nazareth* (London, Bloomsbury, 2007), 113–27.

54. For more on this point, see chapter 6 of this volume.

55. Edward P. Hahnenberg, *Awakening Vocation: a Theology of Christian Call* (Collegeville, MN: Liturgical Press, 2010), xiv–xvii. This phrase structures part 2 of his book.

Given the rapid evolution of the workplace and the home, we cannot know what work will be available in five or ten years' time; nevertheless, we do know what sort of people will be needed. We will need people who find meaning and purpose in being, and who can resist the lures of the consumer society; we will need people who know the limits of material goods in bringing about genuine happiness, so that they do not end up simply adding hours to their paid work in order to "buy" more goods and more leisure time. We will also need people who are capable of introspection, and who are willing to engage the world: mindful, self-disciplined, socially aware, and competent. They will be negotiating many identities and roles throughout their working lives. The foundation they need is the ability to read deeply, to think carefully and critically, to tolerate change, to work through difficulties, and to learn throughout life. In short, we will need people who have incorporated into their lives the traditional goals of liberal education, and who have reflected on the meaning and purpose of life as part of a process of vocational discernment.

Earlier in this chapter we considered the many possible accounts of work that might arise from observing two people digging in a garden. In fact, we can imagine the *same* two people having experienced, over the course of their lives, *all* the interpretations we offered. Perhaps at one point they were laboring (maybe for tuition money!); later, they may have been experimenting with living off the grid, home-schooling their children, and supporting themselves with their organic produce. Later still, they may have taken up gardening as a hobby; and as they entered retirement, they were perhaps working to supply the local food bank with fresh produce while enjoying the healthy exercise they need. In all these cases, they are participating in *work*—in the broader sense that we have suggested in this chapter. And in all cases, they can allow themselves to be led into this work through a thoughtful process of vocational reflection and discernment.

# Unplugging the GPS

RETHINKING UNDERGRADUATE PROFESSIONAL
DEGREE PROGRAMS

*Jeff R. Brown*

WHEN MY FAMILY and I moved back to my home state of Florida after spending eight years in southwestern Michigan, it was difficult to say goodbye to friends and family from the region. There was one small consolation: we had no difficulty convincing many of them to come and visit us—especially between December and April. Of course, our visitors would always have to visit Disney World and at least one or two of the other central Florida attractions. But if our guests had the time (or had run out of money), I would always recommend that they spend at least a few hours in what I consider the quintessential place for experiencing the natural beauty of Florida: Blue Spring State Park. The crystal-clear, 73-degree water rises steadily from its source at a rate of roughly 70,000 gallons per minute and flows through several hundred yards of unspoiled Florida wilderness before discharging into the St. Johns River. Historic oak trees arch over the water, draped with Spanish moss. In my view, Blue Spring stands up to any place in the world when it comes to natural beauty.

An interesting article about my beloved park recently appeared in the local newspaper.[1] It describes bewildered motorists who, relying on their trusty GPS devices, are regularly led down a dirt road on the edge of a

---

1. Dinah Pulver, "Where Are You Taking Me, Siri? iPhones Send Visitors Down Dead End," *Daytona Beach News-Journal*, June 15, 2015, www.news-journalonline.com/article/20150615/NEWS/150619672/0 (accessed October 8, 2015).

subdivision, then told to proceed along a double-track rough road to the park's long-abandoned entrance that was last used in the 1970s. As one driver reported, "I didn't think my car would make it." The actual route to the park entrance is well marked with the standard brown signs that one would expect to find for any state park or natural area; nevertheless, a significant number of drivers ended up lost. The author of the article reported seeing at least six misguided vehicles during a 45-minute period—on a weekday morning!

As it turns out, research into the effect of Global Positioning System (GPS) devices on drivers' ability to form cognitive maps of their environment dates back to the beginning of the widespread use of this technology in the mid-2000s.[2] My own experience with a GPS has always been that if I use it to get somewhere, I will never be able to get back without it. Apparently, once we delegate navigation to an external agent, we no longer experience the need to evaluate and respond to environmental cues (for example, those brown state park signs). And even though we may eventually arrive at our intended destination, we may not really know where we *are.*

All of this, I would argue, has something to tell us about vocational discernment. If we think of it as passive listening (to God, to our hearts, or to some external agent whose voice we seek for direction), we are essentially seeking the vocational equivalent of a GPS device. We would ideally like it to have excellent reception, advanced route-calculating algorithms, and a smooth and inviting voice (I prefer the Australian female). But in our desire to remain passive while we are led to our destination, what will we miss along the way? As an alternative, we might want to think of vocational reflection and discernment as requiring more active engagement on the part of the one who is called: engaging in practices that form our character and cultivate our talents, actively exploring the commitments we make, and learning to love the responsibilities we bear for those things that sustain us.[3]

In this chapter, I suggest that certain aspects of higher education are facing the same kinds of problems that greet drivers who rely too heavily

---

2. Gilly Leshed et al., "In-Car GPS Navigation: Engagement with and Disengagement from the Environment," *Conference on Human Factors in Computing Systems—Proceedings* (New York: Association for Computering Machinery, 2008), 1675–84, www.cs.cornell.edu/~tvelden/pubs/2008-chi.pdf (accessed July 27, 2016).

3. For a detailed discussion of responsibility, see chapter 1 of this volume.

on their GPS devices. I argue that undergraduate education in general, and certain kinds of degree programs in particular, might consider encouraging students to "turn off the GPS" that they are using to lead them through their coursework. By doing so, they can become more actively engaged in their own journeys of vocational discernment.

## *Directly from college to job*

My reflections begin with a focus on undergraduate professional degree programs (UPDs). These include engineering, nursing, education, social work, and accounting—any field of study where a specific bachelor's degree is considered the primary prerequisite for entry into professional practice. If a student's goal or ambition is to become an engineer, a nurse, or a teacher, the place to start is almost invariably a four-year degree program *in that field*. These degrees are noticeably different from those that prepare students for more traditional professions like law, medicine, and architecture; for these fields, although certain courses may be required or expected, students can effectively major in any discipline or field of study before pursuing the specialized forms of graduate work required to enter those professions.

Another defining characteristic of UPD programs is the highly prescriptive nature of their course requirements. Advisors constantly remind students of the importance of taking the necessary prerequisites in the appropriate order to ensure they stay on track for target graduation dates. This puts tremendous pressure on students to declare majors early and fill schedules to the point of bursting. The block diagrams that try to illustrate the course requirements for a bachelor's degree in some UPD programs are downright disorienting. Like drivers following the calm instructions of a GPS gone wrong, students begin to focus on little more than the next turn: the next requirement, the next exam, the next course in the sequence.

Faculty face similar hazards when trying to teach in these programs. Their problems typically begin when the professor who teaches, say, the third course in a disciplinary-specific sequence suddenly realizes that the foundational material covered in the first course is little more than a distant memory in the minds of students. They don't even know how to _____! Next, a slight sensation of panic may develop in the heart of the professor who *taught* that first course; the only valid response is to recount the number of class periods spent on that elusive topic that the students seem to have forgotten completely. In the midst of such curricular nightmares, it seems a rather tall order to expect faculty to develop a broader appreciation for questions of purpose and meaning, or to ask them to shift the discussion to matters of character formation.

Medicine provides an interesting foil for this discussion. My initial understanding was that students who wanted to go to medical school usually majored in biology, chemistry, or some kind of highly structured pre-med program, and that this provided the requisite knowledge base for success in medical school programs. In fact, of the fifteen core competencies that have been identified as necessary for entering medical school,[4] very few can be tied directly to any specific major or course of study. Ethical responsibility, cultural competence, social skills, teamwork, oral communication, and service orientation—these are only a few of the attributes that are considered critical for a successful career in medicine. These skills are clearly necessary in (and developed by) a whole range of fields of study; indeed, they might well be considered a summary of the skills that all aspiring professionals should possess. Only one of the specific competencies—"Living Systems"—is something at which, say, biology majors might be expected to excel as a result of their undergraduate experience.

If most of the core competencies identified by the AAMC are appropriate prerequisites for a wider range of professional practice, and if they can be developed through a variety of undergraduate majors, this raises interesting questions for undergraduate professional degree programs. How, specifically, do the curricula of these programs support—or subvert—the development of these broader competencies in undergraduate students? How do UPD curricula affect the students' commitment to and enthusiasm for the task at hand? To what extent are these competencies tied directly to one's sense of vocation and calling, and how do UPD programs either cultivate or elide vocational questions through their structure and their expectations?

## *Vocation, jobs, and ways of knowing*

Early research for this chapter led me to an often-used quotation that, I believe, points in a troubling direction for vocational discernment in

---

4. As determined by the Association of American Medical Colleges (AAMC): www.aamc.org/initiatives/admissionsinitiative/competencies/ (accessed December 21, 2015).

UPD programs: "Choose a job you love, and you will never have to work a day in your life."[5] Of course, it is tempting to imagine that finding one's true vocation will generate such unbridled passion that one's work will never feel like work. But students are being set up for disappointment and frustration if they come to belief that they won't have found their calling unless this is the case. This idea would seem to ring particularly hollow for students in UPD programs, from whom a tremendous amount of work is expected—all in the name of preparing them for a job that they *think* or *hope* they might love.

Frederick Buechner's classic definition of vocation elevates the discussion beyond how an individual might respond to work, pointing instead in the direction of purpose and meaning. He described vocation as "the place where your deep gladness and the world's deep hunger meet."[6] This definition is certainly richer; still, taken by itself, it also presents challenges in the UPD context. First, there is a general tendency to confound Buechner's term "gladness" with something different. In one anthology in which Buechner's comment appears, the editors ask the critical question: "By 'deep gladness,' do you suppose that Buechner means 'contentment,' or does he mean the kind of joy that can be present even in the midst of suffering?"[7] A similar question could be asked about the aphorism's turn toward "the world's deep hunger"; we seem to be willing to substitute the word *needs* for the word *hunger*, perhaps because most of us are all too certain about what we think the world *needs*. *Hunger*, on the other hand, is more personal and intimate. The world's *deep* hunger points to something that no one individual is capable of discerning or articulating without the help of others.[8]

Parsing Buechner's aphorism for its theological implications is an interesting endeavor, but it may not bear much fruit when discussing vocation in UPD programs. Fortunately, Buechner himself attempts to

---

5. Janet L. Yowell and Jacquelyn F. Sullivan, "Who Should Be an Engineer? Messaging as a Tool for Student Recruitment and Retention," *The Bridge: Linking Engineering and Society* 41, no. 2 (2011): 23–29. This quote is attributed to Confucius in an epigram for the article.

6. Frederick Buechner, *Wishful Thinking: A Seeker's ABC* (New York: HarperOne, 1993), 119.

7. Mark R. Schwehn and Dorothy C. Bass, *Leading Lives that Matter: What We Should Do and Who We Should Be* (Grand Rapids, MI: Eerdmans, 2006), 111.

8. See the further comments on this passage in chapter 1 of this volume, and in the introduction to David S. Cunningham, *At This Time and In This Place: Vocation and Higher Education* (New York: Oxford University Press, 2016), 12–13.

provide a more direct description of what vocation is and how those considering a profession might gain a sense of whether or not they are hearing a true call:

> The kind of work God usually calls you to is the kind of work (a) that you need most to do and (b) that the world most needs to have done. If you really get a kick out of your work, you've presumably met requirement (a), but if your work is writing cigarette ads, the chances are you've missed requirement (b).[9]

Cigarette ads barely exist today (at least in the United States), but that doesn't mean that we are off the hook. Ideally, educators should nurture the passions of their students while constantly collaborating to identify, at least in a general way, some of the world's greatest hungers. This is as true for those working in UPD programs as those in other facets of undergraduate education. Engaging this definition of vocation might even find traction in secular settings, so long as the conversation doesn't stop immediately after mentioning God.[10] In any case, UPD programs should, at a minimum, help students learn to nurture their passions through their work. More importantly, they should also engage students in determining and articulating their own views about which of the world's many "hungers" are among its *deepest*.

## The typical profile of a UPD student

Most of the first-year students whom I encounter during the initial stages of their engineering studies will articulate their motivation for studying engineering by pointing back to a strong affinity and aptitude for math and physics in high school. That is certainly helpful, and I can't imagine recommending engineering as a major for any student who didn't like these subjects.[11] But it is worth noting that at a very early stage in the process, students tend to gravitate toward areas where they feel comfortable—or

---

9. Buechner, *Wishful Thinking*, 118–19.

10. On this point, see the reflections on the evaluation of religious language among academics in chapter 12 of this volume.

11. Engineering is often defined as the application of science and math to produce artifacts that people find useful. My definition of engineering is "the intentional transformation of matter and/or energy to achieve some desired objective."

perhaps they are simply willing to allow their teachers to push them toward these areas.

Two other factors weigh heavily in students' decisions to enter UPD programs: economic considerations and the recent emphasis on promoting STEM subjects (science, technology, engineering, and mathematics) in high school and college. From a "return on investment" perspective, UPD programs appear to deliver. For example, in Florida, the five highest-paying first-year median salaries[12] for graduates from public universities are all connected to UPD programs (fire science, nuclear engineering, nursing, and two in electrical engineering) with a combined average median salary of $63,164. So far, so stereotypical. But while the degree programs associated with the five lowest-paying median first-year salaries by degree type (with a combined average of $20,130) includes two that might be expected (drama, along with Russian language and literature), the other three in this category are science programs: botany, entomology, and general physics. This suggests that even financial outcomes cannot be evaluated simply by distinguishing between STEM subjects and the humanities. One could certainly press these data harder, and first-year salary is clearly not the best metric for evaluating the worth of a college degree—though very few of those in positions of political authority seem to recognize the importance of this point. A number of bills introduced in Congress would have significantly elevated the availability of and attention to first-year salary data; and although the current approach of the U.S. Department of Education is somewhat broader, it still nudges the public toward an account of undergraduate education that is based largely on a financial calculus. The degree of publicity surrounding such data tends to focus students' and parents' attention on UPD programs.

Efforts to promote STEM subjects[13] in K–12 education have also gathered considerable steam over the past decade. Major reports by several national organizations released in the mid-2000s highlighted a growing need for enhancing the nation's investment in these fields, given the results of several longitudinal studies showing a relative

---

12. See https://stateimpact.npr.org/florida/2014/06/23/charting-florida-college-and-university-graduates-by-pay/ (accessed October 15, 2015).

13. Mark Sanders, "Integrative STEM Education: Primer." *The Technology Teacher* 68, no. 4 (2009): 20–26. According to Sanders, "STEM" was originally coined "SMET" by the National Science Foundation in the early 1990s.

decline in the performance of U.S. students in STEM subjects based on global comparisons. The America Competes Act of 2007 (renewed in 2010) provided considerable funding increases for new initiatives in STEM education across the entire spectrum of the education system (K–12 through post-doctoral research). Significant efforts have also been directed toward increasing retention in STEM programs at the postsecondary level.[14]

## STEM and the liberal arts

A recent episode of the NPR program *On Point*, with guest Fareed Zakaria, provides interesting insight into the ongoing debate about the future of higher education in the United States.[15] The discussion was framed, for the most part, along familiar lines of STEM versus the liberal arts, with Zakaria defending the traditional liberal arts model that is under considerable attack. The point was made, however, that the beginning and end of STEM—namely, science and math—are as foundational to the liberal arts as are literature and history.[16] Nonetheless, the "liberal arts" seem to be an easy target for politicians who are keen on tying higher education directly to economic benefits by promoting STEM subjects. As he was announcing plans to increase funding for STEM while decreasing funding for the liberal arts, Florida Governor Rick Scott said, "Is it of vital interest to the state to have more anthropologists? I don't think so."[17] If the very language of the debate is so ill-informed, is it possible that we are also missing additional context that might have very serious implications for our discussion on vocation?

---

14. A 2012 report by the American Society of Engineering Education (ASEE) highlighted best practices after surveying roughly 60 engineering schools across the country. American Society for Engineering Education, "Best Practices and Strategies for Retaining Engineering, Engineering Technology and Computing Students," August 27, 2012, www.asee.org/retention-project (accessed December 21, 2015). It would be difficult even to summarize the vast array of interventions and programs that the various institutions employed.

15. See http://onpoint.wbur.org/2015/03/30/liberal-arts-degree-fareed-zakaria-higher-education (accessed October 15, 2015).

16. See the introduction to this volume for comments on the place of some of (what we would today call) "natural sciences" among the "seven liberal arts" of the medieval era.

17. Zack Anderson, "Rick Scott wants to shift university funding away from some degrees," *Sarasota Herald-Tribune*, October 10, 2015, http://politics.heraldtribune.com/2011/10/10/rick-scott-wants-to-shift-university-funding-away-from-some-majors/ (accessed October 15, 2015).

The current debate concerning STEM subjects and the liberal arts points to a wider division related to "ways of knowing." C. P. Snow's seminal lecture from 1959, "The Two Cultures and the Scientific Revolution," described a growing divide between "literary intellectuals" at one pole and "scientists" at the other. According to Snow, our modern battle lines were formed, not by the seventeenth-century developments in the pure sciences and mathematics through natural philosophy (i.e., the science and math of today's liberal arts) but, rather, by the industrial application of science and math (the STEM version of science and math) in the second half of the eighteenth century. In many ways, Snow's lecture reads almost like a lament; he seems less interested in elevating one group than in somehow reconciling these divergent ways of knowing. "The clashing point of two subjects, two disciplines, two cultures—of two galaxies, so far as that goes—ought to produce creative chances."[18] Unfortunately, eleven years of debate on the matter left Snow convinced of the merits of science and somewhat less enthusiastic about the other camp:

> So we seem to have reached a clear divide between two cultures. One [the scientific culture] is cumulative, incorporative, collective, consensual, so designed that it must progress through time. The other [humanist culture] is non-cumulative, non-incorporative, unable to abandon its part but also unable to embody it. . . . It loses by its nature the diachronic progress which is science's greatest gift to the mind of man.[19]

Snow also provided an interesting analogy for this divide that is more relevant to the broader discussion on vocation:

> By the year 2070 we cannot say, or it would be imbecile to do so, that any man alive could understand Shakespearian experience better than Shakespeare. Whereas any decent eighteen-year-old student of

---

18. C. P. Snow, "Two Cultures and the Scientific Revolution," *Public Affairs* (London: Macmillan, 1971), 23. As noted in the introduction to the present volume, Snow would probably see today's academic environment as even more divided along the lines of particular academic cultures.

19. C. P. Snow, "The Case of Leavis and the Serious Case," in *Public Affairs* (London: MacMillan London, 1971), 96.

physics in that year will know more physics than Newton. . . . There is no built-in progress in the humanist culture.[20]

Dorothy Sayers had an excellent answer for C. P. Snow, though it predated his comments by almost two decades: "The fact that every schoolboy can now use logarithms does not lift him to the intellectual level of the brain that first imagined the method of logarithmic calculation."[21]

A mindset that is only comfortable navigating in the realm of STEM—particularly as it is currently perceived and portrayed, in a way that emphasizes skills development—will not bear much fruit for the work of vocational reflection and discernment. Even if STEM is where one gets one's kicks (which, in fact, I do), one should be willing to allow vocational discernment to remain "noncumulative"; it requires ways of knowing and being that must be thoughtfully engaged and re-engaged over the course of a lifetime.

## Charting a way forward

The academy is under tremendous pressure to deliver "the goods" on multiple fronts: society wants college graduates to be prepared for entry into professional fields, prepared for their roles as citizens, and prepared to recoup their investment of time and money. It will not be easy to add an emphasis on vocational discernment in UPD programs, either for the students who are navigating them or the institutions responsible for charting the terrain. Sweeping changes in either the content or the delivery of UPD programs are likely to be resisted by a tremendous level of inertia, and my sense is that the dominant cultural and political forces acting on these systems have little interest in accommodating anything else. Nonetheless, by reflecting on purposes of higher education and on the way that these programs transmit content and engage students, we may be able to transform UPD programs so that they can integrate more vocational discernment opportunities. This section begins with a discussion on the so-called banking method of education and my firsthand experiences with some of its dangers. Next, I address two approaches to possible solutions: re-examining the liberal arts in UPD programs, and exploring the value of service learning.

---

20. Ibid., 95.

21. Dorothy Sayers, *The Mind of the Maker* (New York: Harcourt, Brace, 1941), 44.

## The banking method

The second chapter of Paolo Freire's classic work on the philosophy of education, *Pedagogy of the Oppressed*,[22] describes what most educators would agree to be the wrong approach: the "banking" method of education. This approach treats knowledge as a series of discrete facts or packets of information that can only flow from the teacher to the student. The teacher's role is to disseminate facts and the student's role is to absorb them. After some period, the student regurgitates the facts and the teacher passes judgment.

As a Peace Corps Volunteer in Tanzania from 1998 to 2000, I had many opportunities to witness the banking method of education firsthand. Needless to say, many of its root causes can be traced to the legacy of colonialism and to the imposition of Western education models that are often in conflict with African epistemologies.[23] Still, watching these effects play out in my students' lives was nothing short of overwhelming.

Students in Tanzania complete their primary education in the national language of the country, Swahili.[24] When they enter secondary school, the language of instruction switches to English.[25] The challenges this posed to my students cannot be overstated. Imagine beginning a discussion on "vectors" with a group of ninth graders and being pleasantly surprised to learn that almost all the students already know what a vector is: "a quantity

---

22. Paulo Freire, *Pedagogy of the Oppressed*, trans. Myra Bergman Ramos, foreword by Richard Schaull, introd. Donald Macedo, revised 30th anniversary edition (New York: Continuum, 2002), 72.

23. Efforts by scholars to understand the full ramifications of colonization in Africa and its influence on education have been ongoing for decades; see, for example, the scathing critique in Walter Rodney, *How Europe Underdeveloped Africa* (Washington, DC: Howard University Press, 1974). While the example I provide from my experiences in Tanzania is decidedly negative, I also want to acknowledge the complexities and challenges confronting my students and colleagues who were working within a system with many flaws—most of which can be traced to the legacy of colonialism.

24. Swahili is often the second or third language for students entering primary school in Tanzania. This is most common in the rural areas, where the first (and sometimes second) language is the tribal language(s) of the students' parents. I once took an informal poll of students to determine how many languages could be spoken in our classroom of 30 students; we counted 11.

25. This policy was officially overturned in February 2015, and Tanzania will begin transitioning to Kiswahili as the primary medium of instruction through the 11th grade of public education. See www.thecitizen.co.tz/News/national/Bye-Std-VII-exams--English--Karibu-Kiswahili-in-studies/-/1840392/2623428/-/item/1/-/ws67ptz/-/index.html (accessed October 16, 2015).

that is described by a magnitude and a direction." Push the questions a little further, however, and you quickly discover that nobody has a firm grasp on what the word *direction* means. Of course, you don't really know the word in Swahili, but after a few diagrams on the board and some role playing, everyone agrees that the appropriate word for "direction" is *uelekeo*. Great! Everyone, student and teacher, is learning and making sense of the world together. Next, take that energy and shift the focus to *magnitude*. You ask, "Okay, class, can anyone tell me, in English, what do we mean when we say magnitude?" The star pupil, the one who can always be counted on to engage, raises his hand, stands up and replies, "a magnitude is a piece of iron that attracts another piece of iron."

Unfortunately, in the Tanzanian setting—where the cost of secondary education is so far out of reach for the average family, and where a student's opportunities for further education are wholly dependent on national exam results—simply knowing the *words* was a monumental struggle. The best that most students could manage was to recite the words that teachers wrote on the board. In most cases, those words came directly from the one copy of the textbook, to which only the teacher had access. This situation led to extreme forms of abuse—including teachers who purposefully withheld information from students during class time and then offered evening classes on a pay-for-access basis. Here, the banking method was on all-too-literal display.

Freire's critique of this approach points in two directions. First, the more that our students "accept the passive role imposed on them, the more they tend simply to adapt to the world as it is and to the fragmented view of reality that is deposited in them."[26] Any idealized visions that one might have of education as a vehicle for personal transformation or self-actualization are effectively stifled. Second, Freire's much harsher critique notes that "the capability of banking education to minimize or annul the student's creative power and to stimulate their credulity serves the interests of the oppressors, who care neither to have the world revealed nor to see it transformed."[27] Powerful forces and institutions in our culture have cultivated, whether intentionally or otherwise, a vested interest in the banking method of education; and to whatever degree we find ourselves

26. Freire, *Pedagogy of the Oppressed*, 73.

27. Ibid.

caught up in this approach, this can have a stifling effect on students' search for meaning and purpose in their studies.

In many ways, Freire's critique was simply a modernization of Plato's allegory of the cave.[28] For all the advances made by our culture through modernization and technology, Freire seems to be pushing back and saying, "No, you still haven't gotten it right . . . in fact, what you think you are doing to liberate people through education is actually having the opposite effect." Some good news on the matter is that the banking method of education, if not already dead, has at least gained the status of "barely defensible" in our modern educational context. It is not entirely clear whether this transformation has its roots in Plato, Freire, or the easy accessibility of information through the Internet. In any case, whatever power teachers once had—as a result of their access to knowledge or their ability to cite facts—has been almost completely neutralized by the revolution in information technology.

To update Freire's metaphor to something a little more relevant in the twenty-first century, perhaps we should caution against "the GPS approach" to education. For undergraduate professional degree programs in particular—which place an emphasis on applying knowledge to solve problems in the real world—the risk is not so much that students will develop little more than a capacity for rote memorization. Instead, we need to be concerned that, as the complexity of the problems to be solved increases (and it always does), the educational process will be reduced to a series of mere steps or procedures. Students can successfully follow these steps to solve a very narrowly defined problem; however, they sometimes also begin to assume that the solutions to all problems are reducible to a manageable series of predefined steps.

In some situations, of course, this is the best we can do. I teach a class on structural steel design that is built almost entirely around the 2190-page *AISC Manual of Steel Construction*. This book represents the collective wisdom of thousands of engineers who have been designing steel buildings across a span of more than 100 years. We obviously don't cover all the topics addressed in over 2000 pages; nevertheless, by the end of the semester, students have mastered some very specific tasks related to the design of steel buildings. The "GPS method" of teaching tends to isolate

28. Plato, *The Republic*, 514a–520d, English version edited and trans. Allan Bloom (New York: Basic Books, 1968), Book VII, 193–99.

each skill into a predefined process. When asked, students can demonstrate their mastery of these processes on an exam or a homework assignment. But if they become too dependent on following a series of steps to solve a problem, will they eventually limit their own vision to the kinds of problems they know they can solve?

The challenge is to teach these skills in such a way that they integrate with previous experiences, whether in other classes or in the wider world. On a deeper level, educators need to connect these skills, and the theory behind them, to their *value* in the world. The remainder of this chapter will examine ways of infusing the exploration of purpose and meaning in UPD programs—both through their curricula and through formal and informal interactions between students and faculty outside the classroom. In particular, I will consider the importance of the liberal arts and the promise of service learning.

## The liberal arts

Perhaps the greatest apologist for integrating the liberal arts into engineering education is Samuel Florman. Florman began his studies to become an engineer at Dartmouth in 1942. The original engineering program at Dartmouth, founded in 1867, was designed as a two-year professional degree that was to be completed after obtaining a four-year bachelor of arts degree with an emphasis in math and science. By the time Florman arrived in 1942, the entire program had been shortened to five years, with three years of undergraduate study (heavy in the liberal arts) followed by two years of engineering professional school. He finished the program in the spring of 1945 and was quickly called into service as a Navy Seabee near the end of World War II. His year of service was spent on a "deserted" island, working on construction projects and reading a lot of books. In his words, "On a Pacific Island, thousands of miles from what we call civilization, the decades condense and the urge for meaning wells up in the young wanderer."[29]

After returning to the United States and finding himself eligible for the G.I. Bill, Florman enrolled in a master's degree program in English literature at Columbia University. The first essay in his 1987 collection *The Civilized Engineer* bears the title "Concrete and Kafka: A Personal

---

29. Samuel J. Florman, *The Civilized Engineer* (New York: St. Martin's, 1987), 9.

Overture"; it describes the excitement and exhilaration he felt while exploring Kafka's literary criticism from an American perspective, as well as the
intense debates that would erupt during classes on the tragic view of life.
"This was totally different from anything I had ever experienced in an
engineering classroom."[30] Clearly, higher-level education in the liberal arts
was critical to Florman's formation as an engineer:

> I sometimes fancy that I am a Roman engineer travelling to the East
> with conquering legions. We bring with us skill and organization.
> We create roads and aqueducts, marbled halls and tiled baths. We
> improve "living conditions." Yet in this fantasy is strewn all about
> us the ruins of an earlier Hellenic civilization, traces of an art and
> architecture whose grace contrasts with our avowedly utilitarian
> works. What can we learn, I wonder—we who prize efficiency—
> from a culture that prized truth and beauty? Then, waking from
> my reverie, I ponder the grim fact that Greece, for all its art and
> philosophy, and Rome, for all its wealth and technology, both in
> the end toppled and fell. Perhaps a culture that weds competence
> to grace, and wisdom to know-how, would persevere and flourish
> where others have failed. Such a culture would have at its core a
> cadre of civilized engineers.[31]

Interestingly, Florman's earlier encounters with the humanities at
Dartmouth College did not inspire him at all. Indeed, it was actually the
math classes that captured his attention and enthusiasm: "the physical
world became an enchanted kingdom whose every secret seemed worth
exploring."[32] At the same time, Florman also admits that he unfortunately
started to measure the value of particular courses on the basis of their utility in supporting his future plans in engineering. If it weren't for that year
of reflection on the Pacific island, his story might have turned out very
differently. Even so, it brings up an interesting question: What is it about
the humanities that pushes young students away? And what is it about the
sciences and math that seems so compelling?

---

30. Ibid., 12.

31. Ibid., xii.

32. Ibid., 5.

E. F. Schumacher, best known for his international bestseller *Small Is Beautiful*, provides interesting insight into these questions in his less frequently read book, *A Guide for the Perplexed*. His chapter on "The Nature of Problems" establishes a fascinating dichotomy in which problems are divided into two fundamental types: convergent and divergent.[33] The example he provides for a convergent problem involves the development of a two-wheeled, human-powered form of transportation. The solution for this problem is something that everyone knows: the bicycle. And while there is no end to the possibilities for refinement and optimization that can be applied to this problem (carbon-fiber tubing, disc brakes), the general nature of the solution is a converging one: the basic design has become almost fixed.

Schumacher contrasts the convergent nature of bicycles with something more perplexing like education. Broadly speaking, two things are necessary for an educational model to function: order in the classroom and freedom of students to explore their own interests. A focus on order, to the exclusion of everything else, results in the creation of a prison. On the other hand, if student freedom is paramount and every other impulse is suppressed, the classroom becomes a circus. To further complicate the issue, little can be gained through efforts to somehow *optimize* the ratio of time spent in the classroom focused on discipline and drills, on the one hand, to time spent on open-ended exploration, on the other. Perhaps, borrowing from John Ruskin, "it would be so if the [student] were an engine of which the motive power was steam, magnetism, gravitation, or any other agent of calculable force."[34] As every teacher knows, however, the energy illuminating minds in a classroom cannot be controlled at will, and the "motive power"[35] of both teacher and student requires an ethic of care that cannot be prescribed. As with all divergent problems, solutions in education require an element of transcendence to achieve the desired effect.

Where might one find such transcendence? In the academy, we have nearly unrestricted access to a resource with intimate knowledge of divergent problems: the liberal arts. Advocates for the liberal arts in the modern academy have often attempted to justify their utility in terms that are more

---

33. E. F. Schumacher, *A Guide for the Perplexed* (New York: Harper & Row, 1977), 121–37.

34. John Ruskin, *"Unto this Last": Four Essays on the First Principles of Political Economy* (New York: John Wiley, 1866), 23.

35. Ruskin calls this the "Soul."

directly tied to "return on investment" and the valuable skills they can still provide for students. For engineers, this typically translates into the need for better communication skills and leadership capabilities. But this is not the only way in which the liberal arts are important to undergraduate professional degree programs. A recent article by Deborah K. Fitzgerald, a dean at MIT, does an excellent job of shifting the focus away from the mere development of skills, and toward matters of vocation and calling.

> The world's problems are never tidily confined to the laboratory or spreadsheet. From climate change to poverty to disease, the challenges of our age are unwaveringly human in nature and scale, and engineering and science issues are always embedded in broader human realities, from deeply felt cultural traditions to building codes to political tensions. So our students also need an in-depth understanding of human complexities—the political, cultural, and economic realities that shape our existence—as well as fluency in the powerful forms of thinking and creativity cultivated by the humanities, arts, and social sciences.[36]

One great irony in this discussion comes from an old anecdote about what engineers wish they would have seen more of in college.[37] The general outline is something like this: Ask an engineer right after he graduates from college and the engineer will wish he had taken more technical courses related to whatever project he is working on at the time. Ask an engineer who has been working for ten years as a professional and she will cite a desire for more coursework in business and economics. Finally, add another ten years to the timeline and he will wish he had spent more time studying the other liberal arts.

The trouble, of course, is that I would have a very difficult time convincing my students that, at this stage in their education, the liberal arts are worth even a sliver of their attention. I often try to engage students about something interesting they are studying that isn't related to math, science, or engineering; more times than not, I get a strong roll of the eyes followed by a heavy sigh. And here I was concerned about their apparent lack

---

36. See www.bostonglobe.com/opinion/2014/04/30/mit-humanities-are-just-important-stem/ZOArg1PgEFy2wm4ptue56I/story.html (accessed December 21, 2015).

37. Florman, *The Civilized Engineer*, 16.

of interest in my (more technical) classes! Undergraduate education needs to find ways of emphasizing that any form of technology, no matter how well applied, can become skewed when it no longer serves the (divergent) needs of human welfare. Most important, with regard to vocation and calling, too much emphasis on technical issues can completely overwhelm any attention to the search for transcendence in one's working life. One's whole outlook quickly becomes cloudy and seemingly overrun by a quest for the same certainty and stability that lie at the heart of convergent problems. The very motivation to work becomes skewed if it is no longer tied to the divergent needs of one's community.

Hence, although doing so will be difficult, UPD programs need to find ways of re-engaging students in the liberal arts. Doing so will lead to more "civilized engineers" (to use Florman's title), as well as more spiritually aware nurses, more creative computer scientists, and more reflective accountants.

## Service learning

Service learning is a valuable pedagogical tool that many UPD programs are using to increase student engagement. This model provides an interesting pathway for exploring William May's definition of authentic professional practice: "The professional's covenant, in my judgment, opens out in three directions that help distinguish professionals from careerists: the professional professes something (a body of knowledge and experience); on behalf of someone (or some institution); and in the setting of colleagues."[38]

UPD programs rarely fall short in achieving the first of these criteria: exposing students to a discipline-specific body of knowledge. Accreditation agencies seem to be effective at ensuring a specific UPD curriculum is properly aligned with industry expectations. Similarly, the third thrust—"in the setting of colleagues"—is also adequately achieved in a college or university context. Support on campuses for student organizations, both professional and interest-based, doesn't appear to be lacking.

As for the middle thrust of May's triad—"on behalf of someone (or some institution)"—most UPD programs have been less successful; and this is the goal that service learning is uniquely positioned to address.

---

38. William F. May, *Beleaguered Rulers: The Public Obligation of the Professional* (Louisville, KY: Westminster John Knox Press, 2001), 7.

Vocational discernment requires thinking about the presumptions of those *for whom* one works—which is closely tied to the larger goals or purposes *toward which* one works.[39] By facilitating an exploration of these questions through service learning, undergraduate professional degree programs can be infused with purpose and meaning in ways that are potentially transformative for students and for faculty. There may be no better way for students to discern "the world's deepest hunger."

Needless to say, various models of service learning can be fraught with potential pitfalls that might distort students' perceptions surrounding power and privilege.[40] Nonetheless, the potential effects of these experiences should not be underestimated. By providing students with direct applications of professional practice, as well as direct *engagement* with a community or other organization responsible for meeting community needs, service learning connects all three of May's defining characteristics for authentic professional practice.

## *Might we need an actual map?*

The GPS-gone-wrong example cited at the beginning of this chapter struck a chord with me—and not only because it involved a place that is dear to my heart. During the summer between my freshman and sophomore years of studying civil engineering at the University of Central Florida, I managed to land a full-time job with a land surveying company. For the better part of three months I worked as the rodman on a two-person crew that specialized in residential property surveys for real estate transactions. On a typical day we might survey three or four houses anywhere in the greater Orlando metropolitan area. The good thing about this particular type of surveying was that we didn't spend too much time working at any one site; anyone who has spent time in central Florida during the summer will understand why. I can still feel the relief that came with blasting the air conditioner as we drove from one jobsite to the next.

The time in the truck between jobs was not entirely quiet. My job was to navigate, and this being 1993, the primary tool I had at my disposal

---

39. Some parallels might be drawn here to the relationship between performer and audience as described in chapter 5 of this volume.

40. For an exploration of some of these matters, see Darby Ray, "Self, World, and the Space Between: Community Engagement as Vocational Discernment," in Cunningham, ed., *At This Time*, 301–20.

was a *Rand McNally Street Finder*. This book of maps was an incredible piece of technology, but it required a certain degree of care and attention to use it well. I began to discover that the *Street Finder* could only be of use to me if I maintained a constant awareness of where I was. If I couldn't properly locate our position on the map, then any future action that might have been planned based on a presumed location was suddenly suspect. Of course, I was just as reliant on technology using the *Street Finder* in 1993 as I would be today using a GPS; the difference, however, was that I was forced to pay attention to the space between where I was and where I was going.

The idea of "reading a map" is a tempting metaphor for vocation; more-over, undergraduate professional degrees lend themselves quite well to a "mapping" framework. For example, I cannot imagine a straighter line between adolescent dependence and functional adulthood than a UPD program. The model breaks down, however, when we expect the map to act like a GPS; we assume that we will receive real-time, updated directions that seemingly come out of nowhere. While the GPS is certainly effective (most of the time!) at getting people from point A to point B, it also allows them to disengage, to a frightening extent, from the place where they actually are. So it may go in UPD programs—and perhaps many other undergraduate programs as well.

Can the role of vocation in undergraduate programs be illuminated by this discussion of our relationship to maps, and how we might use them to find our way? If so, we may need to begin by considering vocational discernment as something akin to *mapmaking*. If we hope to add a specifically vocational dimension to our work of forming students for some future professional practice, and if we agree that all professions are ultimately practiced *on behalf of someone else*, then we have some of the elements we need to construct an adequate map. Some of the questions we might want to ask would include: How do we, through our professional work, draw lines of connection between ourselves and our communities?[41] How does the professional work itself shape the communities which it serves? Does the work support an integrated whole that leads to resilience through shared responsibility, or does it subvert community by strengthening some while ensuring that others remain weak?

---

41. See the discussion of the role of the community in vocational discernment in chapter 6 of this volume.

From this perspective, vocational mapmaking would require a keen awareness of existing relationships among people, places, and the things that sustain them. Vocational discernment then becomes a process of immersion within those boundaries that presently divide us, in both sacred and secular spaces, so that we might feel the tension between those forces that would try to pull us apart.[42] The point of this immersion is not to answer definitively the questions posed in the previous paragraph; its point is, rather, to engage with them repeatedly. Through this engagement we might develop new understandings of the world's deep hunger, as well as our own deep gladness. There is no reason to believe that UPD programs are incapable of engaging students in this journey; but if they are to do so, we may need to begin by turning off the GPS.

---

42. See the discussion of the tensions that result from conflicting callings in chapter 2 of this volume.

## *10*

# *Of Doing and Being*

BROADENING OUR UNDERSTANDING OF VOCATION

*Jerome M. Organ*

STUDENTS WHO ARE coming to the end of their college years face many decisions that are often a source of stress and concern. What should I do with my life? Should I spend a year volunteering, take a job in banking or marketing, or go directly to graduate or professional school? Should I return to the place where I grew up (and where I still have family and many friends), or should I move to a new city? Should I follow my significant other, in the hope that we might cultivate a life together, or should I take a job offer that would necessitate a long-distance relationship?

Regardless of how students might answer these questions, they are also faced with even broader and deeper questions about exactly what kind of person they hope to be. Do I want to live a life of concern for others, or should I focus my energies on my own self-development? Do I want to establish a reputation as a highly responsible individual, or am I less concerned about what others think of me? Should I devote all my energies to a specific goal or an important cause, or should I settle into a more regular routine of work and leisure?

This chapter seeks to develop a broad perspective on vocation that gives adequate attention to the breadth and scope of both of these sets of questions. This broadened account may help students—and those who seek to advise, guide, and mentor them—as they negotiate the stressful reality of thinking about *what they will do* and *who they will be*. In fact, the two words *doing* and *being* provide us with language for two different conceptualizations of vocation; the first is concerned primarily with specific actions, while the second focuses on character traits and a person's overall approach to life.

This chapter addresses both these elements. It suggests, first, that vocational conversations about *doing* may take place within too narrow a frame; they too often focus only on paid employment, and even more specifically, on the first job a student will have after graduation. We are called not just to a job (nor even to a career), but also to a *life*; this demands a broader account of what we might *do* with that life. These considerations lead naturally to this chapter's second area of focus: namely, that broader questions about *being* often get scant attention in the work of vocational reflection and discernment—even though these questions are, in the long run, of greater importance. More detailed attention to both of these elements, and to the relationship between them, may deepen our appreciation for the significance of calling and vocation in the lives of undergraduate students.

The chapter begins by focusing on the anxieties that students may face as they consider the shape of their future lives. It then examines the perspectives of *doing* and *being* in turn, noting that they are closely interrelated and that we need to develop a broadened account of each. With respect to *doing*, we need to be aware that even when our processes of vocational reflection go astray, we are often given a chance for redemption; this can reduce anxiety about "missing one's calling." With respect to *being*, we will note that *how we live* will play a much larger role in the shaping of our vocations than will all our decisions about what kinds of work we will do. The chapter then concludes with the story of a life in which both perspectives played a significant role.

## *How students face their future lives*

For many students, the framework for decision making, until and throughout college, has usually been one of maximizing one's options. Of course, most students recognize that, in keeping their options open, they will have missed certain opportunities for deeper exploration of particular paths; still, these costs often seem minimal, since so many opportunities are still available. Given that many college students are searching for things about which they are passionate and discovering different strengths and skills, it makes sense that they would approach decision making with a mindset of keeping their options open.

For those who have been oriented toward option maximization throughout high school and college, it can be daunting to engage in genuine vocational exploration and discernment. The options one is considering likely will require shifts in mindset and identity, as one moves from student to volunteer or worker; this can create a concern that perhaps one isn't going to make the "right choice."[1] The opportunity costs associated with choosing one option over others seem immense. Indeed, at one level, students faced with making a decision about what to do after college often find themselves going through something like a *grieving* process; they have to let go of any number of partially imagined dreams about what their future might have been.

This letting-go process can also generate doubts. Am I making the right choice? What if I put years into professional preparation and then discover that I hate my work? Do I really have the resources I need to do this? Students deal with this uncertainty, doubt, and evolving sense of identity in various ways. Some may be sufficiently uncomfortable with the state of "unknowing"—of having to live with and through multiple questions—that they try to make too quick a decision about what comes next. This "rush to judgment" approach may result in missed opportunities that are foreclosed before they have even presented themselves.

Other students may be so uncomfortable with having to decide what comes next that they avoid thinking about it completely, attempting to evade responsibility for their future. Of course, in doing so, they are still effectively *making decisions*. They miss deadlines to apply for jobs or graduate school, thereby limiting the opportunities from which they might choose. A student who is trying to choose between pursuing an MBA and working in finance may believe that, by waiting to make a decision, she is "keeping her options open"; but this too comes with a cost. Perhaps she doesn't apply to graduate programs on time, and also doesn't apply for some jobs that likely would have been very fulfilling for her. Ultimately, she may end up scrambling to find any job—or a combination of part-time jobs—simply to secure some means of generating income.

Finally, some students may want to "own" the opportunity to make decisions about their future, but find it genuinely difficult to do so. They may engage all of these questions with energy and depth, consulting faculty advisors, career office staff, friends, and family. They may employ all the resources of their faith communities or affinity groups to reflect on

---

1. As many chapters in this volume have suggested, the language of "choice" may not be the best one with which to consider vocational questions. Indeed, higher education (and our culture more generally) can create an "ideology of choice" that can be debilitating to those who are thoroughly ensconced in it. See William T. Cavanaugh, "Actually, You Can't Be Anything You Want (and It's a Good Thing, Too)," in *At This Time and In This Place: Vocation and Higher Education*, ed. David S. Cunningham (New York: Oxford University Press, 2016).

the choices before them. But this may only increase the internal struggles they experience, particularly when no single option clearly emerges as the "right" one. The consequences of making one choice (and absorbing the real opportunity costs of forgoing other options) may become overwhelming. These students may find themselves suffering from a "paralysis of analysis"—stuck in the process of considering various alternatives, each of which may seem comparably fulfilling (or unfulfilling).

For those considering further education in a graduate or professional program, the risks often seem even greater. Typically, such students experience a sense of "permanence" about such a choice; this produces its own anxieties, compounded by the fact that it will be many years before they take up the actual work the profession entails. Students often feel that, if they are about to invest several years (and significant amounts of money) in the pursuit of a professional degree, they are inalterably setting their future course without really being sure it provides a good fit and a real opportunity for fulfillment and flourishing.

These different types of students, of course, only give us a few touch points along a continuum of ways in which students engage with the responsibility of thinking about their future lives.[2] From these instances, however, we can perhaps distill two major elements with which undergraduates are wrestling. First, they tend to organize these questions under the heading of *choices* or *decisions* they must make, rather than as a life to which they are being called. Moreover, they often tend to think of these decisions as being once-and-for-all. Our cultural setting tends to promote the idea that whatever one chooses at a relatively young age will determine one's future in a permanent way; indeed, everything about one's life seems to depend on getting this one element of life *exactly right*.

In the face of these pressures on students, programs of vocational reflection and discernment can offer a worthy alternative. These programs can remove at least some of the tendency for students to think of their future careers solely as a choice or decision.[3] In addition, these programs

---

2. Of course, in deciding whether (and where) to go to college, students also worked through many questions about who they are, what they want to do, and who they want to become. But those decisions, too, were typically viewed as option-maximizing decisions; moreover, many students worked with their parents as partners in making those decisions. By contrast, as they approach college graduation, many of them are acting more independently for the first time, and their range of options may seem considerably narrower.

3. Again, a helpful analysis of this point may be found in Cavanaugh, "Actually, You *Can't* Do Anything You Want."

get other people involved, so that the weight of one's future does not seem to lie so heavily on one's own shoulders. Such programs often provide students with a wide range of resources, so that—when they do come to those places where the paths diverge and they have to make particular decisions—they are better prepared for their respective journeys. All these elements are present in the other chapters of this volume and in the vocation literature generally, but this chapter seeks to emphasize two points in particular. First, although vocation is indeed concerned with what a person will do, a student's initial decisions are probably less significant than most of them assume; people continue to develop over time, and vocational discernment is an ongoing endeavor that will reshape us throughout our lives.[4] Second, the greatest benefit of vocational reflection may have little to do with *what students will do* during their lives; its most profound implications are related to the question of *who they will be.*

## The school of the second chance

We begin by examining the questions that vocational exploration raises about we will *do*: where we will live, what work we will undertake, and which people will play major roles in our lives. What is the right job for me? Which graduate program should I pursue? How far away am I willing to move? With whom do I hope to work and live? These kinds of questions typically receive the lion's share of attention when the subject of vocation arises for undergraduates; indeed, students often experience considerable pressure from family, friends, and teachers to answer them. Given our academic context, however, we may tend to overemphasize the importance of answering these questions, especially since a student's first year or two after college is not likely to be determinative of his or her work life as a whole. Moreover, when graduates find that a particular job or a program of further education does not seem to have been the right path, most of them will be given a second chance (and a third and a fourth) to discover what they are called to do. Often, those alternatives cannot even be seen from the vantage point of the student who is about to graduate. By acknowledging that they will move on from college to "the school of the second chance," students may feel less stress and anxiety while working through the process of vocational reflection and discernment.

---

4. This point is explored in greater detail in chapters 3 and 4 of this volume.

The language of "getting a second chance" is related to the idea of *redemption*. This word is often employed in religious contexts, but the concept of redemption is also deeply embedded in American culture. Dan McAdams, a professor of psychology at Northwestern University, has written about our tendency to discuss our life journeys using the language of redemption—of second chances (and third and fourth chances, as well). He notes that "second chance" narratives have a privileged place within the canon of American life stories, and that many people of varied stripes— from politicians, to businesspeople, to former convicts—offer an account of their lives that is built on the theme of redemption.[5]

The broad range of the language of redemption makes it meaningful to many students, including those who do not espouse any particular religious perspective. However, for those who *do* embrace some form of theological worldview, the concept may have further implications. The Bible presents a series of stories of redemption—stories in which God's people went astray and were called back into relationship with God.[6] In stories such as the Prodigal Son (Luke 15:11–32) and of Paul's conversion (Acts 9:1–22), individuals are given second chances, allowing them to take a different path in life. For some students, these stories may provide a useful frame of reference—especially for those whose lives seem to be heading down paths that don't seem to fit, or that differ markedly from those for which they may have hoped and prayed. Such stories remind us that opportunities for redemption may well appear, and that they often redirect our lives onto a better path.

If students can imagine the possibility of redemption, this can change the way they think about the questions they are currently asking; it may diminish their worries about "making the right choice." Although vocational discernment is not something that should be taken lightly, students need not be overly anxious about measuring their progress against some imagined ideal of "correctness." If their vocational reflections lead them into work that is less meaningful or less fulfilling than they had hoped,

---

5. Dan P. McAdams, "The Redemptive Self: Generativity and the Stories Americans Live By," *Research in Human Behavior* 3, nos. 2–3 (2006): 81–100.

6. Some of these stories actually focus quite explicitly on vocation and calling, giving them an even greater degree of relevance for the present discussion. See Charles Pinches, "Stories of Call: From Dramatic Phenomena to Changed Lives," in Cunningham, ed., *At This Time*, 122–42.

there will almost certainly be opportunities to switch course and pursue a different path.

Some of the possibilities that students are considering will be the product of careful vocational reflection and discernment, but—as suggested in the first section of this chapter—others may be the result of inertia, poor guidance, or simple accident. Some of the actions that students take (and indeed, some of the actions we all take) are guided less by a robust sense of vocational discernment than by pursuit of self-interest, misguided affection, or a fundamental misunderstanding of who we are and how the world really works. Sometimes we are not entirely honest with ourselves about what considerations are guiding our thoughts about the future; we are reluctant to acknowledge the forces that might well take us away from certain potential callings. Moreover, we often set aside options that might have been more salient, had we been willing to engage in a more honest and reflective vocational discernment process.

In any case, a graduating senior's first opportunity out of college—whether volunteering, working for pay, going to graduate or professional school, or some combination of these—is unlikely to be the perfect fulfillment of any given student's sense of vocation. After all, students are still growing and maturing; they are still discovering more of their passions and gifts. Things they thought might be deeply interesting and fulfilling may turn out to be less meaningful than anticipated; areas in which they thought they might excel, given past experiences, may turn out to be more challenging in the real world. In addition, the student might be going through some transitions in identity. A student who had always been an athlete or musician, but who is no longer directing energy and time to soccer or to the viola, may find herself searching for ways to fill the void—and may be surprised at the degree to which these activities were necessary to affirm her place in the world. In some cases, students may be inclined to make decisions that are guided (or misguided) by personal relationships that may affect the student's vocational reflection process. Finally, the options available to particular students may be constrained by their modest academic performance, or by socioeconomic factors that are completely out of their control;[7] in either case, they may find limited opportunities in their areas of interest.

---

7. On this point, see chapter 4 of this volume, as well as Caryn Riswold, "Vocational Discernment: A Pedagogy of Humanization," in Cunningham, ed., *At This Time*, 72–98.

Still, new opportunities will almost always present themselves. We rarely fully grasp the set of possibilities that exist in the future. Indeed, there are times when the future presents opportunities that we actually could never have imagined and only discovered because of the situations that unfolded through previous decisions that we made. Here, I want to offer three such stories of redemption—stories about people who found themselves in circumstances that were hardly a perfect fit, and yet were offered the means to transform their situation and to take advantage of new opportunities. These are "second chance" stories; they give us a glimpse into the lives of people who found themselves in unsatisfying situations and took advantage of the opportunity to move into something more fulfilling and more meaningful.

## Undertaking a belated discernment process

Jenny graduated in 2009, in the midst of the economic recession. She was hoping to find a job that would allow her to use her degree in economics, but the market was tight. She felt fortunate to find a job with a for-profit educational enterprise that would allow her to cover her living expenses and begin to repay some of her educational loans. Her work included communicating with prospective students and recruiting them to take courses from among her company's offerings. She started the job with enthusiasm and a sense of responsibility. For several months, she worked diligently, learning about the various aspects of the job and becoming proficient at fulfilling her responsibilities.

Over time, however, Jenny became increasingly uncomfortable with the role she played in communicating with prospective students, particularly with respect to the degree to which they might need to borrow money for the education they were going to receive from a for-profit enterprise.[8] She wasn't sure the opportunities many thought might be available to them upon completing their course of study would actually materialize. She also noticed that she seemed more troubled about this question than many of her peers at the company. After several months, this became a significant

---

8. This is, of course, an endemic problem in for-profit education; worse still, it skews the data on student indebtedness generally, making the problem look worse than it is (at least for graduates of nonprofit educational institutions). For more on this point, see the extensive collection of data at the website "Securing America's Future: The Power of Liberal Arts Education," sponsored by the Council of Independent Colleges, at www.cic.edu/Research-and-Data/Liberal-Arts/Campaign/Pages/default.aspx.

source of stress in Jenny's life, making it hard for her to sleep at night and difficult to go to work each morning. She realized she needed to find some other form of employment—one that would allow her to work with integrity and to be of greater service to others.

Jenny had moved to a new city for her job, but she had some relatives there and had made new friends. Appreciating that it would be easier to find another job if she were still employed, Jenny did not quit her job; however, she did begin searching for other opportunities in earnest, including communicating with her network of family and friends about her desires. After a few months, using contacts through her network, she found out about a position as a consultant with an accounting firm. She applied for the position; during her job interview, she was able to explain what she had learned from her first work experience. She was eventually offered the position and has now worked with the firm for a few years, having been promoted twice over that period. This position was initially very exciting; it also involved a fair amount of travel, which allowed her to see the country and visit friends. However, Jenny recently got married and now is wondering whether the continued travel will be a challenge as she and her husband consider having children.

Jenny would not describe her initial position as one she garnered through vocational discernment. She needed a job and this job was available when she graduated during challenging economic times. But while in that position, she did engage in vocational discernment; indeed, it was more or less forced upon her, as she came to realize that her work was not only failing to provide meaning and fulfillment, but was in fact causing stress and unhappiness. A great many students like Jenny may find the work of vocational reflection and discernment to be difficult and time-consuming; they often try to put it off (which is made even easier if they receive an early job offer). It may turn out, however, that vocational discernment is finally unavoidable; indeed, most of us will find ourselves engaging in it repeatedly throughout our lives. Doing so may be particularly important when we are offered opportunities for redemption, and it will help if we've already had some practice at the work of discernment. In addition, simply acknowledging that vocational reflection is an ongoing (indeed, lifelong) endeavor may relieve some students of the pressure that they feel to "get it right the first time."[9]

---

9. For more on the lifelong character of vocational reflection and discernment, see chapter 4 of this volume.

## Recovering from errors in discernment

John graduated from law school in his home state and decided to move across the country to be with his girlfriend, who was preparing to attend graduate school. While he was a person of faith, he had not spent a great deal of time discerning whether this was God's call; he was in love, so this seemed to be the right thing to do to. Within a matter of months, however, John's girlfriend was no longer his girlfriend. He found himself living in a strange city for no particular reason, trying to figure out how to make his way in the legal profession.

Initially, life was not particularly easy. John wanted to work in the area of criminal prosecution, but because he had gone to law school in a different state, he didn't have a network of people with whom he was connected to help him in his job search. After passing the bar exam and getting licensed as a lawyer, he spent several months practicing what he described as "Steak and Ale" law: he worked part-time at a restaurant and part-time as a lawyer, representing people he met through his day job. Most of these people were dealing with landlord–tenant disputes, auto accidents, and charges of driving while intoxicated. It was not the professional life of his dreams.

However, after several months of doing this kind of work, building a network, and applying for several positions, John was invited to interview for a job as an assistant district attorney in a suburban county. He was able to draw on his varied experiences with clients and customers to demonstrate that he was capable of fulfilling the responsibilities of this new position. He got the job and moved out of the city to become part of a new community. There, he not only started on a career path that has led him to a position in the state attorney general's office; he also became part of a faith community, where he met his future wife. His vocation has now expanded beyond being a lawyer; he is also a loving husband and the father of two children.

John would probably admit that his initial decision to move across the country was not the best effort at discerning his vocation. He might have misread the foundation of the relationship, or chased after his own individual desires rather than thinking through the question of where he was being called. Like Jenny, he might have been better served had his educational institutions offered him more tools for the work of vocational reflection and discernment. Still, his initial error in judgment did not mean the end of his career; he adapted to a changed context, worked diligently to find his way toward a meaningful professional engagement, and eventually was presented with an opportunity for redemption. He also became connected with a faith community and a social community, where he could share his gifts in the service of others.

## Following a wandering path

Eric Betzig was the son of an engineer who owned a manufacturing business.[10] He studied physics at the California Institute of Technology and then went to Cornell to get a Ph.D. in applied physics. At Cornell, he started to work on trying to create high-resolution images of cells beyond what the best microscopes of that day could accomplish.

Inspired by the desire to solve this puzzle, he headed off to Bell Labs in the late 1980s, where he spent several years working on research projects and writing academic papers. Eventually, however, he became less enamored with several aspects of his situation. Not only was financial support dwindling; the institution's research was focused on generating more refined images of dead cells, rather than on his own interest in images of living cells. Frustrated by the strictures under which his research had to be conducted, Betzig decided to leave academic science. He became a stay-at-home husband, did some writing, and turned to his anticipated fallback plan: working for his father's manufacturing business (which he did for the next decade of his life).

During this period, however, Betzig's curiosity about how to solve various scientific puzzles never entirely dissipated. In 2004, he reconnected with a former Bell Labs colleague; both of them found themselves missing science and wanting to be back in the lab. Later that year, as new technologies continued to develop, the two men began working on an entirely new approach to microscopy. After two months of work and roughly $50,000 of their own money to buy the necessary parts, they constructed a new light-based microscope that facilitated images of small cells at resolutions that had never before been seen. With this new technology in hand,

---

10. This account of Eric Betzig is drawn from web pages that address various aspects of his path to the Nobel Prize, including www.britannica.com/EBchecked/topic/1996937/Eric-Betzig; www.freep.com/story/news/local/michigan/2014/10/08/ann-arbor-eric-betzig-nobel/16899395/; http://arstechnica.com/science/2015/04/quitting-failures-a-microscope-in-the-living-room-nobel-prize/; http://janelia.org/people/scientist/eric-betzig; and www.ibiology.org/ibiomagazine/issue-2/eric-betzig-and-harald-hess-developing-palm-microscopy.html (accessed January 16, 2016).

they found their way back into a research laboratory; in 2014, Betzig was awarded the Nobel Prize in chemistry.

## Redeemed lives

These stories share a common theme. All these individuals began a journey on one path, then found themselves doing things that weren't quite what they had hoped for or expected. But in the midst of frustration, or disappointment, or both, they were offered opportunities to serve others in a way consistent with their gifts and passions. For some, this was a journey of several months; for others, it required many years. The path may have been one of increasing accomplishment and fulfillment, or one of false starts and new beginnings. For all these individuals, however, discovering that they were not on the right path did not lead to a sense of failure. Rather, these disappointments were opportunities to learn, to further discover the ways that their interests intersected with the needs of the communities in which they lived, and to listen and watch for opportunities to meet those needs.

While these stories might offer a number of lessons, an obvious one is that a person's first job, or first experience of graduate school, or first volunteer position is unlikely to be perfect in every way. The first thing one does after college rarely offers that kind of fit. Indeed, in a study focused on the lives of former law students several years after they had graduated, most were found to have changed jobs two or three times, and to have found greater job satisfaction and personal and professional fulfillment with each job change.[11] This shouldn't come as a complete surprise. In that first position, we not only learn about what we like or don't like about the specific job; we also learn more about the nature of a particular career and of its possible work environments. As new opportunities present themselves, we are able to make more informed choices—both about the types of jobs and about the work environments that we find most fulfilling.

Students who are worried about what to do after graduation might be done the greatest service by those who can find ways of helping them not be quite so worried. Naturally, one hopes to make the "best" choice—to discern precisely what will fulfill one's sense of vocation and to allow one

---

11. Deborah J. Cantrell et al., "Walking the Path of the Law: How Law Graduates Navigate Career Choices and Tolerate Jobs that Fail to Meet Expectations," *Cardozo Journal of Law and Gender* 14 (2008): 267, 296–300.

to use one's gifts to serve the world in a unique way. However, for most students, the first situation after college will not be the fulfillment of a dream, but simply the next step on a journey—a next step from which one will better be able to see and understand what further steps might be in store.

For those approaching these decisions by searching for what God is calling them to do, there may be some comfort in understanding that God doesn't stop "calling" just because we haven't heard the call correctly the first time. God also called Samuel—three times, in fact—but Samuel didn't understand what was happening to him. Only after his mentor pointed out that he was being called was he able to respond to that call by saying, "Speak, Lord, your servant is listening" (1 Sam. 3:1–10). Samuel's story serves as a reminder that, first, we continue to be called and to be given opportunities to respond; and second, we sometimes need those around us to help us hear the call.[12]

Such stories remind us that we are all students in the school of the second chance. According to Dan McAdams, such opportunities are often particularly manifest in the stories of people with a "generative spirit"—a spirit directed toward making the world a better place for others.[13] The stories described in this section certainly fit this pattern; each person manifests the "generative spirit" of which he speaks. This provides a natural segue to the other concept of vocation on which this chapter focuses—that of *being*: how we will live and who we will be.

## *The good life*

The second element of vocational reflection focuses on the kind of people that we seek to *be*. Regardless of what we decide to do, we still have to think about *how* we will go about doing it—or, more particularly, the character traits that we will embody as we do our work and live our lives. This perspective emphasizes the importance of faithfulness, integrity, and authenticity; it focuses on the ways that we engage the world around us, regardless of where we live or what kind of work we are doing. For many students, these questions may appear to be of less immediate concern;

---

12. For more on the role of the community in vocational discernment, see chapter 6 of this volume.

13. For further discussion of McAdams's discussion of generativity, see chapter 3 of this volume.

nevertheless, they are the vocational questions that will probably make the most difference in a person's ability to flourish and to live a truly *good* life. When vocational discernment programs emphasize that *who we are* matters as much as *what we do*, they offer students a sense of peace and tranquility as they face complicated questions about the next steps of their journeys.

Clearly, this aspect of vocational discernment is not completely separate from the question of what we choose to do. All the stories in the preceding section touched on themes such as faithfulness, integrity, or authenticity; they have already alerted us to the fact that, regardless of what it is that we find ourselves doing, we can undertake this work in many different ways. While this is not the place for a detailed consideration of precisely what virtues we should strive for (and precisely how we should define them),[14] I do want to offer a few suggestions as to why the most important issues in vocational discernment are those that are focused on *being* rather than on *doing*.

## Vocational discernment: a "first world problem"?

In many respects, thinking about what we want to do is a privilege or even a luxury. In most of the world, these questions are decided in advance by social circumstances, political realities, economic conditions, and familial expectations. Even in the United States, for most of its history, most people had a fairly narrow range of choices regarding what they would do and where they would live.[15]

My maternal grandfather was a painter and my paternal grandfather was a plumber. Their spouses were stay-at-home wives and mothers. None of them had the benefit of a college education; my grandfathers received training as skilled laborers that allowed them to earn enough to support their families. They had few opportunities to engage in discernment as to whether they felt more called to plumbing than to welding, or to painting rather than to carpentry. This is not to say that questions of vocation played no role; certain forms of manual labor may be more gratifying to certain

---

14. This work is carried out elsewhere in the present volume (especially in chapters 1 and 7), as well as in chapters 7 through 10 of Cunningham, ed., *At This Time.*

15. On this point, see also Cavanaugh, "Actually, You *Can't* Be Anything You Want," and Kathryn Kleinhans, "Places of Responsibility: Educating for Multiple Callings in Multiple Communities," in Cunningham, ed., *At This Time,* 99–121.

people and may address a community's immediate needs more than others. But the range of choices for many people of my grandparents' generation was fairly limited. And this remains true today for billions of people around the globe whose opportunities are limited by the circumstances in which they find themselves. Hence, if we hope to think about vocational reflection and discernment as something more than just a "first world problem," we need to think of it as focused on more than just what we will do with our lives. It has to be more about who we want to be and how we want to live.

That was certainly the case for my own grandparents. While "just a plumber," my grandfather took great pride in his work and engaged his responsibilities with determination to do the job and to do it well. He had an innate understanding that he was serving others by providing them plumbing services that ensured running water without hassle and the need for constant repairs. But that is only part of the story. My grandparents loved their children and grandchildren and made a point of living their lives in a manner that demonstrated that love. They were at every grade school or high school concert and every birthday celebration; they hosted the entire extended family for Christmas and Easter. If my parents or one of my aunts or uncles needed help, my grandparents were there—doing what needed to be done. My grandparents were tremendous role models; they loved others and treated everyone with dignity and respect. While they didn't have a great deal of choice about what they did, they did have a choice about who they were and how they lived.

## The priority of being over doing

The importance of who one chooses to *be* manifests itself in other circumstances as well. Consider those among us who frequently garner significant media attention because of the profound skills they have in some athletic pursuit or artistic endeavor. Given their talent, discipline, and drive, these individuals likely had a clear sense of what they were called to *do*; most have devoted thousands of hours to honing their skill and refining their talent to make them truly among the best in the world. But many of the world's greatest athletes and artists may have had fewer opportunities to reflect on the aspect of vocation and calling that focuses on *being*.

In fact, for most of us, the more clearly we focus on what we should do, the easier it is to set aside questions about who we want to be and how we want to live. Certainly, many current or former athletes and artists did precisely this; stories of failure in this regard are all too frequent. For some, this lack of discernment manifested itself as a lack of faithfulness in relationships. For Tiger Woods, for example, this resulted in the dissolution of his marriage, the erosion of his reputation, and the loss of sponsorships. Others have used performance-enhancing drugs in an effort to increase their opportunities for success. Many have struggled with addiction to drugs or alcohol or gambling; some fritter away millions of dollars and find themselves bankrupt. Sometimes these actions impact a person's profession as a whole; many have seen their careers ruined and their reputations soiled. Sometimes, these individuals pay the ultimate price: the litany of artists and athletes who have died too young is long indeed. But even when those individuals who experience these struggles are able to continue in their careers, it is difficult to imagine that they are *being* the kind of people they hoped to be—even if they are *doing* what they hoped to do.

If we were to limit our understanding of vocation to the element of doing, then these celebrities would be positive exemplars of those who had found their callings. They discovered their athletic or artistic talent and worked hard to develop it. But vocation is not exhausted by doing; if these individuals fail to attend to how they should live and to who they should be, these matters are likely to cast a shadow over their many accomplishments.

## The interrelationship of doing and being

The stories in the first part of this essay, even though they were focused on what three individuals *did* with their lives, also provided examples of reflection on who they would be. Jenny and John, both of whom faced significant obstacles and needed to undergo additional vocational discernment, acted with integrity, authenticity, and faithfulness; they also gave attention to the needs of others, even as they struggled to take the next steps on their journeys. Similarly, Eric Betzig remained true to his passions and interests even in the face of frustration and adversity; he demonstrated a remarkable degree of patience as his life seemingly diverged from the path for which he had hoped.

These stories suggest that while what we do is important, we are fooling ourselves to imagine that this is the most important aspect of vocational discernment. When our plans run up against the inevitable complications that the world will put in our path, what will really matter is whether we have learned how to live in the midst of the disappointment and frustration. Part of the work of vocational reflection is to produce people who are well-grounded—who know the virtues and principles that they want their lives to manifest, and who will act with integrity in a manner consistent those traits.

## Coda: weaving it all together

I close with a story of vocational reflection and discernment that weaves together "doing" and "being" in interesting ways, and that might provide us with further insights about the importance of both elements in finding one's calling.

My colleague Mark Osler grew up in Detroit and studied history as an undergraduate. His first job after college was delivering flowers in inner-city Detroit. In need of more income, he answered an ad for a "young, resourceful person," and became a process-server—someone who delivers the summons and complaint to a person being sued. In this role, Mark discovered two things—one about the law and one about himself. He learned that the law tends to interject itself into people's lives in moments of great vulnerability; he saw the human side of the law in a way that made a lasting impression. He also learned that his interest was engaging people in their humanity. While many process-servers function as almost "faceless" people who deliver bad news and disappear as quickly as possible, Mark found himself deeply engaged in the work—talking with people and coming to understand their situation.

After a little more than a year as a process-server, Mark headed off to law school at Yale. The summer after his first year there, he worked in Chicago as an intern in the U.S. attorney's office and fairly quickly discerned a calling to criminal law—and, more specifically, to being a prosecutor. When he returned for his second year of law school, he took a class from Professor Dan Freed, one of the architects of the new federal sentencing guidelines. As someone who grew up in Detroit, and who was searching for order and fairness, Mark initially had a positive view of the new mandatory sentencing framework.

Upon graduation, Mark clerked for a federal judge and then took a job as an associate in a large law firm in Detroit. That first job was not tremendously fulfilling; he was especially struck by his own lack of agency at the firm. Still, he understood that this was a necessary step on his journey to the U.S. attorney's office. It helped him "learn the ropes" of practicing law and develop his legal writing and advocacy skills. While at the firm he got married; the Quaker ceremony included a period of reflection, during which those present could speak about anything that they felt called to share. His mother offered a passage from the prophet Micah—that we are called to do justice, to love mercy, and to walk humbly with God (Micah 6:8). This passage had a deep impact on Mark and has remained a guiding principle for him.

After a few years at the firm, Mark found his "dream" job, as an assistant U.S. attorney in Detroit. For the next five years, he saw himself valuing the limited discretion he had as a prosecutor and appreciating the extent to which his decision making involved moral engagement in considering whether and how to charge someone, as well as what sentence to seek. During this period, a significant portion of his caseload involved drug crimes—particularly cases involving the possession and distribution of crack cocaine, for which the federal sentencing guidelines mandated sentences 100 times more severe than for those caught with powder cocaine. He frequently encountered a federal public defender, Andrew Densemo, who religiously offered what Mark described as the "futile" speech: he asked for leniency in sentencing, based on the limited extent of wrongdoing involved, the ineffectiveness of this approach to the drug problem, and the tremendous discrepancy between sentences for crack cocaine and powder cocaine. As a prosecutor, Mark had a certain degree of discretionary power; but over time, he found himself called to exercise a different kind of power: that of a prophet, who might influence those in power rather than using it himself. Accordingly, he pursued work as a law professor.

He began teaching criminal law and trial advocacy at Baylor Law School, a Baptist institution where he could explore the relationship between his work in law and his Christian faith. He began writing about issues associated with the war on drugs and the federal sentencing guidelines, thinking back to the "futile speech" he had heard repeatedly. When he was invited to assist with a case involving several defendants caught in what appeared to be a racially motivated drug sweep in a nearby town, he became more engaged in the human reality of people dealing with injustice.

At about the same time, Mark was presenting some of his ideas regarding federal sentencing guidelines at a conference. In the question-and-answer period that followed, former President Jimmy Carter, who was sitting in the audience, asked Mark: "Who are you helping? What are you doing for those in prison?" These questions sat on Mark's heart and encouraged him to become more actively involved in helping to change the system.

He began working on pro bono cases focused on challenging the 100-to-1 sentencing disparity between crack cocaine and powder cocaine. Eventually, one of the cases on which he worked made it to the U.S. Supreme Court; in *Spears v. United States*, the court ruled that federal judges could ignore the lopsided sentencing requirements of the federal guidelines. That was great news for those facing charges, but was little solace for those already in prison. So Mark began a new venture, eventually founding the first Federal Commutations Clinic in the country. Over the last few years, Mark's efforts have largely been directed toward advocating for greater, more systemic use of the president's clemency powers, largely to help those who were convicted of minor drug offenses involving crack cocaine and who now find themselves in prison with long sentences. He worked to create the Clemency Resource Center, which is now reviewing hundreds, perhaps thousands, of cases of prisoners sentenced to long mandatory sentences for crack cocaine and other crimes, determining whether they are entitled to pardons or commutations of their sentences.

Mark's story can be an inspiration to many; but it is also a story about how others inspired him. Andrew Densemo faithfully did his job as a federal public defender, religiously reciting his "futile speech" in the hope that it would be heard by someone who would engage the issues at stake; little did he know that one of the prosecutors listening to the speech would be one of the people who responded. Similarly, Jimmy Carter asked two simple questions that touched Mark's heart and caused him to think about the next step in his engagement with the issue.

Living our lives sincerely, with a focus on who we are called to be while we are doing what we are called to do, is at the core of what it means to live out our vocations. If we find ourselves in situations that do not provide the opportunities we need in order to live out our callings, we need to remain open to, and watchful for, the possibility of redemption. We can continue to search for the ways that lead to a different and more fulfilling path, while always seeking to be a source of blessing to those around us: walking humbly, loving mercy, and engaging those around us with dignity.

# PART FOUR

# *Vocation at Full Stretch*

## Overcoming Institutional Obstacles to the Language of Call

Anyone who has spent even a modest amount of time in the world of higher education will be aware of the challenges involved in offering something "new." Colleges and universities are not particularly conservative institutions, at least in the sense that such language is usually employed; in fact, they are more often perceived as bastions of avant-garde thinking, social innovation, and progressive politics. But some academic institutions are very large, and all of them are complex; this can sometimes make them unwieldy, which in turn can make them appear, at least, to be resistant to new approaches. Moreover, their deliberative and collaborative forms of shared governance can make their decision-making processes lengthy, highly charged, and occasionally vexed. Trying to plot any changes in their course is, as the old saying has it, something like trying to steer an aircraft carrier; the levers we move right now may not have an impact for quite some time, and the change may hardly be noticed—even by those on board.

Thus, when a book like this one sets out to offer "a new vocabulary for higher education," critics might reasonably ask whether it is realistic to expect this intervention to have any discernible impact. A relatively large number of institutions might adopt programs for vocational reflection and discernment, and a few might even showcase these offerings as an essential element of their curricular and co-curricular offerings. But given all the forms of institutional inertia that beset colleges and universities today, can such programs really be expected to make a difference? How will this "new language" ever find a foothold, amid the countless recipes for educational innovation and reform that fill the shelves and inboxes of academic administrators across the country?

Despite these challenges, we take some comfort in the fact that most colleges and universities are quite strongly committed to programs of self-improvement. The history of higher education in this country has been marked by an openness to new ideas, a careful examination of well-conceived proposals, and a willingness to adapt to the circumstances in which they find themselves. Even if this takes place more slowly and incrementally than some might like, these institutions are sufficiently committed to the life of the mind that they rarely dismiss an idea before giving it a reasonable hearing, adequate deliberation, and considered judgment. Clearly, a growing number of colleges and universities have done precisely this with regard to programs of vocational reflection and discernment; they have implemented these programs, precisely because they have discovered that such programs *work*.

Having said all this, we also need to recognize that, if good ideas sometimes fail to take hold, this may be due not to an unwillingness to change on the part of higher education, but because some of its features (and even some of its very best features) can unintentionally create obstacles to the acceptance and implementation of new programs. Our goal in this final section of the book is to explore some of these potential obstacles and to consider how they might be overcome. This is not to say that undergraduate institutions should be changed in ways that would prevent these obstacles from arising in the first place; rather, we simply hope to point out that these difficulties are not insurmountable. By developing a more nuanced view of these concerns, and by thinking carefully about the convictions that lie behind them, we hope to create a space in which the language of calling and vocation can prosper.

Among the many questions that are raised in this part of the book, and which might form the basis for institutional conversations about these issues, we want to mention these three in particular:

- How might we best understand the role of *teaching* in undergraduate education today? Are teachers primarily founts of knowledge, or should they focus on cultivating certain habits of mind and disciplines of inquiry in their students—something like a trainer or coach for the life of the mind? How should teachers handle questions of religious faith, particularly in the increasingly pluralistic environment of higher education?

- How are potential programs for vocational reflection and discernment shaped by the *structure* of American higher education—by everything from the way that faculty and staff are trained in their disciplines, to conversations that do (or do not) take place both within and among academic disciplines and fields, to the explicit and implicit missions of individual institutions? Can we offer small and manageable adjustments to the present-day structure and culture of higher education that might reduce its potential to negate or block what might be accomplished through the work of vocational reflection and discernment?
- For any *particular* institution, how do its contexts and constituencies shape the space that it can provide for the language of calling and vocation? Is this language sufficiently capacious for it to play a role across the spectrum of religious traditions and affiliations, from broadly confessional to deeply secular? How will the answers to these questions be shaped by institutional assumptions about classroom teaching, and about what kinds of conversations are or are not appropriate in the classroom?

As was suggested in the introduction to this volume, the complexities of the modern college or university are both broad and deep; in this world, no single program or idea can possibly address everything that can or should be addressed. We believe, however, that the conclusions reached in the following three chapters offer a certain degree of hope for the future. They can make space for the language of calling and vocation to operate at full stretch—such that it can play an increasingly significant role in the vocabulary of American higher education.

# Colleges Have Callings, Too

## VOCATIONAL REFLECTION AT
## THE INSTITUTIONAL LEVEL

*David S. Cunningham*

IN THE WORLD of higher education, anything that students and faculty are expected to take seriously also has to be taken seriously by the institution as a whole. If a college claims that writing and critical reading skills are an essential part of an undergraduate education, but only teaches and evaluates these skills in a few disparate courses, students quickly come to the conclusion that they need not make these matters a priority. If required courses for first-year students are taught largely by adjunct instructors who are poorly paid and who are not well integrated into faculty life, the message is clear to everyone: these courses are not really all that important. A college or university may seek to recruit a range of entering students that reflects the country's population at large, and may thereby claim to be diverse and inclusive; however, if the faculty and administration are largely populated by a fairly narrow demographic, it does not take long for everyone to realize that something is out of sync. Indeed, as I write these words, students and faculty at colleges and universities around the country are increasingly protesting against circumstances on their campuses in which the rhetoric used to describe institutional priorities does not match the actual practices of the institution.[1]

---

1. Recent controversies at the University of Missouri and Yale University are just two examples of a much wider range of student concern; see www.insidehighered.com/news/2015/11/09/racial-tensions-escalate-u-missouri-and-yale, November 9, 2015 (accessed March 9, 2016).

Matters are no different when it comes to the role of vocational reflection and discernment. A college may well claim that these matters are an important aspect of undergraduate life, and may even offer a number of well-funded programs to promote them. It may encourage its faculty and staff to use the language of vocation and calling when working with undergraduates, hoping that these students will look back on their college years as an important period of discernment and priority-setting. With respect to the concerns of this book in particular, the institution may even envision the language of calling and vocation as a means of encouraging interdisciplinary conversations, thereby also helping its students navigate the different ways of knowing among the traditional disciplines and the applied fields.

In spite of all these good intentions, however, if the college or university does not spend any time reflecting on its *own* vocation, then these programs are likely to be seen for what they (sometimes) are: another case of an authority telling students to "do as I say, not as I do." If institutions of higher education hope to develop programs in vocational reflection and discernment that are more than just window dressing, they need to be involved in this work on an institutional level as well. They, too, need to think about their callings; they also need to encourage their various constituencies—faculty, staff, administrators, trustees, and alumni/ae—to join in this conversation as an essential part of their participation in the life of the college.[2]

Do colleges have callings? I believe they do, and I also believe they need to devote concerted attention to reflecting on and discerning these callings. This is not something that can take place once and for all (perhaps at the institution's founding), and then be expected to endure without any need to revisit it. Academic institutions are large, complex, ever-changing creatures, and they are likely to understand their callings differently as they evolve over time. Just as they seek to remind their students that vocational discernment is not a one-time enterprise, and not limited to one narrow region of their future lives, so must an academic institution be involved in

---

2. Among the early advocates of thinking about academic structures in vocational terms, two are particularly worthy of note here: for the role of faculty (particularly in church-related institutions), Richard T. Hughes, *The Vocation of the Christian Scholar: How Christian Faith Can Sustain the Life of the Mind* (Grand Rapids, MI: Eerdmans, 2005); and for the role of presidents, William V. Frame, *The American College Presidency as Vocation: Easing the Burden, Enhancing the Joy* (Abilene, TX: Abilene Christian University Press, 2013).

an ongoing process of discernment—in which the challenges of every new era are taken seriously and integrated into its institutional life.

The goal of this chapter is to provide an argument in favor of such a program of ongoing vocational discernment at the institutional level. It will suggest that the failure to undertake this work will pose an obstacle to a college's otherwise well-meaning efforts to encourage students to engage in vocational reflection and discernment, as well as curbing any hope that this language might serve to encourage conversation among diverse disciplines and fields. While we will discover obvious differences between the forms of vocational discernment that take place on an individual and an institutional level, I believe that we will discover enough commonalities to demonstrate the value of the analogy.

The first section of this chapter rehearses the increasing role of vocational language in the context of American higher education; a second section offers a definition of "institutional vocation" and describes why this way of thinking might offer an important supplement to the terminology currently employed to describe an academic institution's purpose (terms such as *mission, vision,* and *goals*). The third part of the chapter argues that a number of transformations will be necessary in order to begin thinking about a college's purpose and future direction in vocational terms; this section will emphasize the parallels between this process and the vocational discernment that its students are encouraged to undertake. This work, at both the individual and the institutional levels, will also help to support interdisciplinary conversations among academic departments and programs. The chapter's fourth and final part will offer several specific strategies that can be considered by various college constituencies (including faculty, staff, and students) to bring about some of these transformations. In particular, these groups can build upon the college-wide focus on vocation by developing policies, programs, and a certain kind of "orientation" or "culture" that allows for vocational reflection and discernment across the entire institution.

## *The increasing presence of vocational language on campus*

Over the past two decades, the word *vocation* has undergone an extraordinary transformation. At one time, the word was a technical term employed primarily by theologians and pastors; it was most often used in contexts related to theological training, usually to refer to the call to ordained ministry. The expansion of the term beyond this use dates far back into the past, at least in theory; as many have noted, the Protestant Reformation dramatically widened its application, beyond that of the clergy and into the full range of professions and stations in life.[3] One can obtain some sense of the ongoing legacy of this claim in the German-speaking context, in which the verb *rufen*, "to call," serves as the root of the noun *Beruf*, which means "profession" or "occupation." But this example only illustrates the word's shift in meaning on a theoretical level. In practice, at least until recently, the supposedly "broadened" definition of vocation had very little impact; its chief usage still focused on religious life. It remained part of the discipline-specific terminology of theology and religious studies, and even in that field would have been of interest primarily to scholars of church history and those charged with the spiritual care of prospective ministers and priests.

In the last twenty years, however, all that has changed—and changed dramatically. There are a number of structural reasons for this shift, which have been mentioned at several points in this volume and which I have explored in detail elsewhere.[4] But the strongest evidence for the broadened appeal of the language of vocation is found among the college students and twenty-somethings who employ this language frequently and without pretense. When I was an undergraduate, I don't recall anyone using the word *vocation* in any context whatsoever. Today, at many institutions, any serious conversation with undergraduate students—especially a conversation concerning their own future direction in life—may well make use of terminology such as *calling, discernment*, and *vocational exploration*.

---

3. A good general account can be found in Douglas J. Schuurman, *Vocation: Discerning Our Callings in Life* (Grand Rapids, MI: Eerdmans, 2004). Excellent brief summaries appear in Kathryn Kleinhans, "Places of Responsibility: Educating for Multiple Callings in Multiple Communities," in *At This Time and In This Place: Vocation and Higher Education*, ed. David S. Cunningham (New York: Oxford University Press, 2016), 99–107; and Edward P. Hahnenberg, *Awakening Vocation: a Theology of Christian Call* (Collegeville, MN: Liturgical Press, 2010), 11–17.

4. For a more detailed description of this process, see the foreword (by Richard Ekman) and the introduction to Cunningham, *At This Time*, ix–xi, 9–12. A capsule summary appears in the introduction to the present volume, note 10. I offered additional reflections on this point in an earlier version of this chapter, when it was presented as the keynote address at a conference titled "Loaves and Fishes: Multiplying Opportunities for Theological Exploration of Vocation," Monmouth College, Monmouth, Illinois. I am grateful to that institution, and particularly to Hannah Schell and Jane Jakoubek, for inviting me, and to the Network for Vocation in Undergraduate Education (NetVUE) for sponsoring the gathering.

This shift has been accompanied by a number of other changes that are taking place within conversations about higher education today. For example, the growing attention to "emerging adulthood"—a life stage that includes the traditional college years—has had an impact on discussions of calling and vocation that take place during this stage of life.[5] Similarly, attention to calling and vocation has been augmented by the growing literature concerning the mentoring of students and of their teachers,[6] and by a focus on deeper and more fruitful explorations of the moral and spiritual lives of college-age students.[7] In short, a great many conversations in the world of higher education are directly or indirectly related to vocational reflection and discernment.

In fact, the shift has been so dramatic that it can lead us to construct an excessively negative account of what came before. When I describe my own institution's vocational discernment programs at prospective student days, new student orientation, or family weekend events, I invariably receive comments from parents that say, essentially, "I wish they had something like this when I was in college." This is typically followed by some kind of disparaging comment about the parent's own collegiate experience, along the lines of "we just had to sink or swim" or "I sort of wandered through my undergraduate years totally clueless about what I should do with my life." My suspicion has always been that such accounts tend to overstate the case; the parents who make these remarks often seem to have done a fair amount of vocational reflection along the way. But they are correct in observing that the collegiate landscape has

---

5. See, for example, Jeffrey Jensen Arnett, *Emerging Adulthood: The Winding Road from the Late Teens Through the Twenties* (New York and Oxford: Oxford University Press, 2004); Jeffrey Arnett and Nancy L. Galambos, eds., *Exploring Cultural Conceptions of the Transition to Adulthood* (San Francisco: Jossey–Bass, 2003); and Jeffrey Arnett and Jennifer Lynn Tanner, eds., *Emerging Adults in America: Coming of Age in the 21st Century* (Washington, DC: American Psychological Association, 2006).

6. An important early advocate was Sharon Parks, *Big Questions, Worthy Dreams: Mentoring Young Adults in their Search for Meaning, Purpose, and Faith* (San Francisco: Jossey–Bass, 2001). On the mentoring of faculty members, see Caroline J. Simon, *Mentoring for Mission: Nurturing New Faculty at Church-Related Colleges* (Grand Rapids, MI: Eerdmans, 2003). On the direction relationship between mentoring and vocational discernment, see especially Cynthia Wells, "Finding the Center as Things Fall Apart: Vocation and the Common Good," in Cunningham, ed., *At This Time*, 47–71.

7. See above all the work of Christian Smith, including Christian Smith and Melinda Lundquist Denton, *Soul Searching: The Religious and Spiritual Lives of American Teenagers* (New York: Oxford University Press, 2005); as well as Christian Smith et al., *Lost in Transition: The Dark Side of Emerging Adulthood* (New York: Oxford University Press, 2011).

changed dramatically over the last twenty years, and programs that may not have been necessary (or even thinkable) during the parents' college years are now often sanctioned as an essential part of the undergraduate experience.

Why vocation, and why now? In addition to the increasing complexity of our culture (and indeed, its supercomplexity[8]), questions surrounding college and career have become especially complicated, in ways that this volume explores at length.[9] Parents who were asked to "sink or swim" (if that was indeed the case) were, a generation ago, much more likely to find their way to shore—or at least to a lifeboat—than seems likely to be the case among today's undergraduates. This is due not only to the increasingly diffuse ways that students experience higher education today, but also to the uncertain world that awaits them after commencement. In addition, and as other contributors to this volume have emphasized, the increasingly divergent methodological assumptions in various fields of study have sometimes made it more difficult for students to see their undergraduate years as an integrated whole.[10] All of these factors have made it increasingly challenging for students to weave together the decisions that they are trying to make about their careers, their home life, their faith, and their futures.

Given all these factors, undergraduate institutions have much to gain by thinking about their own institutional context in vocational terms. Doing so will allow everyone connected to these institutions—not only presidents, deans, and trustees, but also faculty, staff, and students— to recognize the important role that each group plays in clarifying the "forms of life" to which a particular college or university is called.[11] In fact, as the next section of this chapter will suggest, certain parallels can be drawn between the kinds of vocational exploration and discernment

---

8. On this concept, see chapter 7 of this volume.

9. See particularly chapters 1, 2, 8, and 10 of this volume.

10. For more on this point, see especially chapters 6, 7, and 9 of this volume.

11. My reference to "forms of life" is a deliberate invocation of this term (German *Lebensform*) as it is used by Ludwig Wittgenstein in a number of his writings, and particularly in *On Certainty*, ed. G. E. M. Anscombe and G. H. von Wright, trans. G. E. M. Anscombe and Denis Paul (New York: Harper and Row, 1972). Although I am unable to explore it here, I believe that the use of the language of *vocation* and *calling* as a way of sparking interdisciplinary conversations within the academy could be augmented by thinking about various academic disciplines, religious perspectives, and administrative structures as operating not only with different "languages" but also as differing forms of life. See also the comments on

that are often commended to undergraduate students, and the ways that the college or university can go about its own forms of discernment. As suggested earlier, students and educators cannot be expected to embrace the vocational discernment process with energy and passion unless the institution itself has given some serious thought to its own callings. This in turn will require consideration of an institution's vocation across its entire breadth: no campus office, academic department, pre-professional major, or interdisciplinary program can stand outside this process, if it is to succeed. As we will see, a more vocationally-oriented way of thinking about a college's purpose and future direction has a number of advantages for all members of the academic community—as well as for the neighborhoods, cities, churches, and community organizations that are related to a particular college or university.

## *Mission and vocation*

The term *institutional vocation* represents an attempt to broaden the role of the language of calling in the higher education setting: to extend its use beyond its focus on the individual lives of a college's students, faculty, and staff. This same language, I submit, also has significant potential as a way of thinking about the institution as a whole. This may seem, at first, to be an unusual way of putting things; we routinely use the word *vocation* when speaking of persons and a different term, such as *mission*, when speaking of institutions. The application of the language of *calling* and *vocation* to institutions is not in widespread use, though certainly some writers have considered it.[12] But we have certainly not yet tapped the full potential of the language of vocation for deepening conversations about the purpose and future direction of colleges and universities; nor have we fully recognized its capacity for creating meaningful conversations among

"ways of knowing" in chapter 7 of this volume, and the comments on the multiple vocabularies of vocation in the epilogue.

12. Walter Wink writes about the vocations of larger organizations (namely churches) in "Angels of the Church," chap. 3 of *Unmasking the Powers: The Invisible Forces that Determine Human Existence* (Philadelphia: Fortress Press, 1986). Wink's work formed the basis for a conference on institutional vocation sponsored by the Fetzer Institute; a summary of the issues discussed there appears at www.resourcingchristianity.org/grant-project/vocation-conference-for-college-leadership (accessed March 9, 2016). Wink takes up the question again in *Engaging the Powers: Discernment and Resistance in a World of Domination* (Minneapolis: Fortress Press, 1992), especially chap. 4.

the diverse offices, departments, programs, and individuals that colleges and universities comprise.

## Vocations of persons and vocations of institutions

To understand how this language might be broadened to apply to academic institutions as a whole, we need to consider the changes required in coming to think of a human being's journey through life in *vocational* terms rather than merely as a series of autonomous, self-interested decisions. At least three such changes are worth identifying here; all of them have been mentioned in other chapters of the present volume, as well as elsewhere in the literature on vocation.[13]

First, vocational thinking suggests that we need to give serious consideration to the forces that shape our lives profoundly, even though they lie outside our own grasp. In other chapters of this book, this phenomenon has been variously referred to as the "pull" that comes from an external source, as the role of our audiences in shaping our performances, or as the wisdom of the wider community in providing direction and mentoring. All these accounts raise questions about our tendency to think of our own perspective as the primary (or perhaps the only) factor determining our direction in life.[14] This, in turn, requires some degree of discernment about who or what might be the source of this call. In some cases, this may lead to explicitly theological considerations, in which God is identified as the caller; but this is not the case for all those who use the language of vocation.[15] With respect to academic institutions, a vocationally oriented approach will require more attention to external sources—including some that might not usually be identified as "stakeholders"—that can or should play a role in shaping a college's calling. We will return to this point below.

---

13. Many of these points are also made in the contributions to Cunningham, ed., *At This Time*. See also Hahnenberg, *Awakening Vocation*, and the material collected in Mark R. Schwehn and Dorothy C. Bass, eds., *Leading Lives that Matter: What We Should Do and Who We Should Be* (Grand Rapids, MI: Eerdmans, 2006).

14. For these three particular ways of articulating the issue, see chapters 1, 5, and 6 of this volume.

15. See David S. Cunningham, "'Who's There?': The Dramatic Role of the 'Caller' in Vocational Discernment," in Cunningham, ed., *At This Time*, 143–64. For a discussion of how vocational conversations might proceed without creating excessive difficulties for participants who hold differing views about religious belief, see the latter sections of chapter 12 of this volume.

A second feature of vocational discernment has a somewhat negative element: finding one's calling often means recognizing that some possible future paths are closed off, at least temporarily. We would prefer to keep our options open and, if possible, to pursue many paths at once.[16] This is an even greater temptation for institutions, since they have relatively diverse constituencies and prefer to avoid limiting their options. But just as individuals must eventually focus their energies and leave some roads untaken, so must institutions set priorities and occasionally forgo otherwise attractive opportunities. Discerning one's vocation will sometimes mean choosing *not* to undertake some possible projects, even though undertaking them might seem to be supported by very good reasons (economic, political, or psychological). This is not to say that these forgone projects will be closed off forever; however, it does encourage institutions to think about their own limitations and to shape the use of their energies in ways that correspond with their own callings.

A third consideration is that the literature on vocational reflection and discernment has often reminded us that calling has a *narrative* quality: we tell stories that describe our experiences of receiving a call, and our callings derive part of their meaning from the larger stories of which they are a part. But we are so deeply embedded in our own narratives that it can be difficult to recognize their powerfully shaping force. Academic institutions, of course, are accustomed to telling their own stories; they do so for myriad reasons, including capturing the attention of prospective students, cultivating a strong donor base, and recruiting the best possible candidates for positions among the faculty and staff. Too rarely, though, do academic institutions think about the relationship between the stories they tell about themselves and the callings to which they are summoned.

These three factors—attending to external voices, refraining from constant maximization of options, and becoming more attentive to our own stories—provide good examples of how certain insights about vocational thinking on an individual level can apply to institutions as well. They also suggest some important additions to the traditional ways that colleges and universities have described their purpose, value, and future direction. As noted earlier, the most popular terminology for doing so—at least at this point in the history of higher education—is that of *mission*; an institution's

---

16. For further discussion of this point, including a number of extended accounts that provide good case studies, see chapters 1, 2, 3, and 10 of this volume.

mission is in turn supported by a *vision* and sometimes by an enumeration of particular *goals*. This language has many positive features, and I am not suggesting that we minimize it. Nevertheless, it is relatively weak with respect to the three features of vocational thinking just enumerated. Those three features will provide us with reasons why, in each case, colleges and universities have something to gain by supplementing the language of *institutional mission* with that of *institutional vocation*. In order to make this point, allow me to offer three ways in which the vocabulary associated with calling and vocation can provide additional insights that are not as salient in conversations about mission.

## How vocation can supplement mission

To begin, let us recall the language of the "inner" and "outer" calls, the internal and external sources of motivation that help us determine the next steps in our journeys. These terms imply a certain directionality; our internal motivations push us forward, whereas external motivations pull us—attracting us to something that is outside ourselves. We can recognize a similar difference between the words *mission* and *vocation* in the institutional context.

The word *mission* derives from the Latin word *missio*, which focuses on "sending," as opposed to the "calling" focus of the root *vocatio*. Mission ultimately involves the language of the "push"—a range of persons or corporate entities or impersonal forces *send us out* in a particular direction, with a particular goal in mind. This implies, first, that our movement is *away* from those who send us out on our mission; they remain "behind," either spatially or temporally, and we are sent out on our own. Moreover, since a mission (whether institutional or individual) is very much focused on reaching the goal toward which we have been sent, it becomes quite easy to dispense with any attention to the *source* of the mission—which is to say, those who sent us. Both terms suggest that others are involved; nevertheless, just as the inner call can quickly be reduced to "what I want to do," so can an institution's mission be easily reduced to "what we want to do." A quick, highly unscientific survey of institutional mission statements has confirmed my suspicion that few of them have much to say about who or what has "sent them forth" to be the kinds of institutions that they claim, in these statements, that they strive to be. Ironically enough, the mission statement—which, etymologically speaking, should describe a sending forth—tends to eclipse the identity of those who have done the sending. It tends to be more focused on the subject—the institution—as an autonomous, self-interested, self-directed agent. And although an institution's mission always ranges well beyond what can be encapsulated in a mission statement, the problem remains: it can be difficult for the language of mission to be perceived differently from a simple declaration of one's will.

Here, the language of vocation has much to offer. Like individuals, institutions are not autonomous; they are aware that their decision-making process is shaped, in part, by external sources that are pulling them in certain directions, rather than just the wishes of their founders, their current trustees (or administrators or faculty members), their most influential donors, or whoever else may be shaping the will of the institution. Similar problems could be cited concerning the language of *vision* or *goals*: both of these can easily become self-authenticating. We see things with our own eyes and set goals through an act of our own will; the language clearly focuses on our internal motives. We can claim to have a particular vision, or to have developed particular goals, simply by claiming that we have them; we do not need to pay any attention to the forces that lie out in front of us, in the future, that may be drawing us forward—and to which we should be responding.

A second insufficiency in the language of *mission, vision,* and *goals* might best be described as their "inflationary" character.[17] A college typically has a vested interest in casting the net of its mission as widely as possible, so that it can maximize its options and enlarge its appeal. A mission provides (and indeed, it should provide) a very large tent, in which there will be room for newly created programs, institutes, centers, or student services. No one wants a new program to fall outside the college's vision for its future, of course; in fact, the very wording of mission statements tends toward the broadest and most general terminology possible, so that all current programs (and most new initiatives) can find a place within the institution's overall structure.

Without question, an institution's vocation will be broader and have more diverse threads than an individual's vocation. Still, similar concerns apply; the harder we work to keep all options open, the more likely it is that our decisions will take on the character of a fait accompli. Of course,

17. Thanks to Mark Schwehn for suggesting this description (personal conversation and correspondence).

academic institutions are aware that they will need to make decisions; the question is simply whether the language of vocation might help clarify our thinking on such matters. If the language of mission too often reduces (as noted above) to "what we want to do," then it will be difficult to say no to anything; why would an institution *not* do something that might increase its breadth, reputation, and market share? If, on the other hand, a college is willing to focus on those external voices that are calling it to prioritize some projects over others, this can (at the very least) create a kind of inner concentric circle, in which a smaller portion of an institution's programs and services can receive greater attention. This doesn't mean that other programs and services can't exist at the institution; still, their place might be clearer if everyone could agree that they do not respond to the calls that the institution has discerned in its present moment.

This perspective, of course, has the potential to create considerable difficulties within an academic institution. Any time that a program is closed or a service comes to an end, many constituencies are displaced and considerable strife often ensues. One might argue that this is less likely to take place if the mission is defined so broadly that nothing ever falls outside it. Of course, structural and financial realities mean that, even under the broadest forms of self-definition, colleges will sometimes need to bring some worthy projects to an end and defer other potentially advantageous ventures; no program was ever saved from the chopping block *only* because it can be seen as helping to carry out the institution's mission. Still, in the midst of ruminating on this very unhappy topic, we can at least suggest that the language of vocation might help to create a sharper degree of focus when those programs are created in the first place. In essence, by making the test a bit harder (not merely, "Is it part of our mission?" but "Are we really being *called* to this work?"), we might reduce the chance that the program or service will later be seen as merely part of a larger set of financial and market-driven calculations.[18]

A third problem arises from the aforementioned observation about the narrative quality of vocation. Colleges are usually very good at rehearsing their founding history, so that element of their stories is usually available

---

18. For an example of how some of these issues might play out as a church-related institution thinks through the theological aspects of its mission and vocation, see Caroline J. Simon, "Can Two Walk Together, Except They Be Agreed? Traditions, Vocations, and Christian Universities in the 21st Century," paper presented at a conference on Discerning Vocation in a Contested Religious Tradition, Georgetown College, Georgetown, Kentucky, January 28, 2016.

to all. These founding stories intersect well with the language of mission, because they often refer to people who "sent" the institution out on a particular path. However, as already noted, these founding missions can eventually start to seem very far in the past, and can easily be replaced by exclusive attention to the current political or economic landscape.

Of course, not all narratives are created equal. Many decades ago, Burton Clark introduced the concept of an "organizational saga," which he described as "a collective understanding of unique accomplishment in a formally established group."[19] Such sagas, he observes, are "intrinsically historical but embellished through retelling and rewriting"; moreover, "the participants have added affect, an emotional loading," which makes them more than simply rational accounts.[20] Clark describes the organizational sagas of three academic institutions, building on his earlier book-length treatment of their character,[21] as examples of how a founding narrative can provide motivation for action and how it can be perpetuated in a college's life. But he also notes that while the initiation of an organizational saga is one thing, its fulfillment over the long haul is another; the latter process requires contributions from personnel, programs, external constituencies, the student subculture, and the promotion of an institutional self-image.[22] Because of the distant historical roots of a college's organizational saga, it can only be perpetuated through a concerted institution-wide effort.

The stories related to one's calling are categorically different: instead of telling a story in which we venture out *away* from those who have endowed us with a particular purpose, we find ourselves journeying *toward* the source of our calling. This means that the story is driven by a kind of *attraction* to a particular perspective or way of life, rather than some kind of hazy loyalty to a distant past. Instead of getting further from the source of the narrative, we are getting closer to it, drawing toward it—and thus necessarily becoming more engaged with and attentive to that source, rather than thinking of it as an ever-more-distant memory. This imagery also emphasizes that the attractive force toward which we are being drawn

19. Burton R. Clark, "The Organizational Saga in Higher Education," *Administrative Science Quarterly* 17, no. 2 (June 1972): 178–84, here 178.

20. Ibid., 178.

21. Burton R. Clark, *The Distinctive College: Antioch, Reed, and Swarthmore* (Chicago: Aldine, 1970).

22. Clark, "Organizational Saga," 181–83.

is real and concrete; we are pulled toward something definite and well defined, rather than having been sent into some repetitive cycle of endless "progress." We are sent out from the past, but we are called toward a future reality—something toward which we are journeying, rather than something that lies ever deeper in our history.

This shift fundamentally alters the nature of the stories we tell; we now have to clarify the purpose or *telos* toward which we are being drawn, rather than always referring back to a static moment of sending. To the extent that these stories focus on institutional purposes and goals, those goals are very much in the foreground; they cannot be filed away as being of "merely historical significance." This is not to say that founding stories should no longer be told, nor that organizational sagas do not have value; they are an important part of an institution's heritage, and they contribute, in their own way, to its future direction. But of at least equal importance are those stories that describe how an institution discerned a calling that provided an extraordinary degree of motivation (simply through its sheer attractiveness), which led it in a new direction. Such new callings can, of course, contribute in profound ways to an institution's ongoing consideration of its own evolving sense of identity.

My own institution offers an interesting case study in this regard. It was founded by settlers who came from the Netherlands and were committed to the Dutch Reformed Church. They arrived in western Michigan in the mid-1800s and eventually built a school; soon they found themselves in need of higher education for the school's graduates. The college would be an "anchor of hope for this people in the future," as one of the founders said, and thus its name: Hope College. The narrative is, of course, an important one; but the more exclusively the college relies on it, the more embedded it becomes in the fairly narrowly defined world in which it originated: Dutch heritage, western Michigan focus, and a great deal of concern as to whether the school's basketball teams will triumph over those of the other Reformed Church college down the road.

Another set of concerns arises when a different set of stories is added to the mix: that the institution graduates more chemistry majors than any other institution in the country, that it is one of the few with accredited programs in all major arts fields (dance, fine arts, music, and theatre), or that it recently ranked among the top five institutions for undergraduate research. None of these elements could have been anticipated by its founders; all of them resulted from some kind of discernment process that led the college to consider, at a particular time and place, that its own talents and gifts might be developed in particular directions to address the needs of the world. The college uses these facts in its marketing, of course; but what might it mean to articulate exactly why it was drawn to focus its attention on these particular programs? For example, what positive goal or "final cause" (in the philosophical sense) drew us along the path that eventuated in strong programs in the arts? Vocationally oriented narratives have to remain attentive to the ways that an institution's circumstances have changed through time.

If I have made at least a prima facie case for supplementing an institution's reflection on its mission, vision, and goals with at least some discussion of its calling or vocation, the next step will be to consider how this might take place.

## *Three essential transformations*

I want to offer three transformations that will need to occur if colleges and their various constituencies are to begin thinking about their trajectories in genuinely vocational terms. These transformations have certain parallels to the kinds of changes that are necessary when individuals begin to use the language of vocation and calling to map out their own future trajectories. This section continues the pattern noted in the previous section—drawing on some of the insights in the other chapters of this volume, as well as other recent literature on vocation, to suggest how our thinking might change as we begin to think about the callings of our institutions.

The first transformation has to do with the multiplicity of, and potential conflicts among, our various callings. When individuals think primarily of their own visions and goals, they can easily become focused on a single plan: becoming a doctor, say, or being hired by a Fortune 500 company. Similarly, those who do not yet feel they have "found their calling" may develop an excessive level of anxiety about this fact, feeling that they may miss the "one right path." These thoughts, in turn, tend to eclipse other aspects of a person's calling—including those parts that have less to do with paid work and more to do with where, how, and with whom a person will live. Much of the language and literature of vocation has, therefore, tended to emphasize the multiple facets of one's calling—with respect both to the variety of professional possibilities for one's paid work, and to the many other callings to which one is called.

Colleges and universities have multiple vocations as well. This may seem obvious to most observers, but this institutional multiplicity can

also be eclipsed in various ways. As noted above, most institutions tend
to describe their missions in very general terms, so that practically everything falls under its reach. However, the mission also tends to focus on
one or two prominent features of an institution's purpose; it rarely attends
to the variety of relationships that an institution has (including, for example, with the community in which it is located, the wider populations it
serves, and the other organizations with which it works). Some of these
relationships may reflect important aspects of an institution's calling, but
these aspects are not always made salient in conversations about priorities
and future directions.

How might a college go about discerning its multiple vocations? One
path would involve paying greater attention to the source of these callings.
Who is calling the institution into its future? In most cases, answering this
question will involve creating a list—perhaps a very long one—of some
of the external sources that are "pulling" the institution forward. Such an
inventory of "callers" is likely to remind the college of the multiple ways
that it is connected to a variety of individuals and organizations. It is com-
monplace for colleges and universities to speak about their "stakeholders,"
but this language is too restrictive; it focuses on traditional constituencies
that tend to be internal to the institution, without allowing enough space
for the external sources of energy to pull the college forward.

As an example, let me return to my observation in the introduction
to this chapter concerning the increasing level of student protest at academic institutions over the past few years. Some of this has been given
genuine attention and support by faculty and administrators, but in some
cases (and also in some segments of the broader culture), it has been met
with disdain. A similar pattern can be discerned with respect to student
protest movements throughout history, and particularly those associated
with the 1960s (both in this country and in Europe). It would be interesting to consider the difference it might make if institutions were to find a
"third way" to respond to these student concerns, other than the two that
have been employed in most cases (accommodation or rejection). What
difference might it make if these voices of concern were heard not simply as demands or expectations, but as a form of *call* that could help an
institution to discern possible adjustments in its understanding of its own
vocation?

A second transformation involves reducing the tendency to create new
programs and services at every turn, and focusing more on elements that
align more organically with the institution as a whole. As long as certain

kinds of activities remain at the level of "interesting value-added features" of the overall shape of a particular collegiate experience, the institution can create programs that are charged with bringing about such experiences, and can call people into providing such services on a volunteer basis. For example, if an institution thinks that community service is a good idea, then it can staff these programs by simply asking faculty to offer more courses that are sprinkled with elements of community service, or by opening a campus office to place students in local areas of need. The institutional commitment is limited to the levels of support that are associated with phrases like "it seems like a good idea" and "parents really like it" and "everyone seems to be doing it these days." These kinds of attitudes mean that the activity in question is not really a part of the institution's core identity; it is something that it can take or leave. At most institutions, one could take away all the community service activities, curricular and otherwise, and nothing fundamental would change.

But more and more institutions are discovering that community engagement is not merely a marketing plan or a bandwagon; for them, it is shaped by an external reality toward which they believe the institution is moving. At Mount Mercy University and Bates College, for example, the work of community engagement is seen as something that cannot be limited to the purview of some particular office—or that can rely only on volunteers among the faculty and staff in order to carry it out. This is the difference it makes when a college decides that community service is part of its *calling*. Here, the institution seems to say that a force outside itself, and larger than itself, is drawing it into this activity in a way that helps to shape its very identity. This means, in turn, that people need to be asked to participate in this work as part of the job description, and it needs to be compensated accordingly. By identifying this activity as part of its calling, the institution associates it with something beyond its immediate control—something it cannot deflect or disappoint, if it is to be true to itself. This is my second point: higher education needs to be willing to move away from marginalized programs and volunteer activities, and toward programs of vocational reflection and discernment as a more organic part of its institutional structure.

A third transformation that is necessary to bring the language of "vocation" into our institutional contexts is a shift away from an individualized approach to vocational discernment and toward a more communitarian or corporate approach to this process. Even where strong programs for vocational exploration and discernment have been implemented, the temptation arises to treat each student as a separate case: a person who happens to be at the same institution with several thousand other such students, but whose destiny is radically unique. Thus, although the institution can help such a student through the process of discerning her or his calling, this can become something of an assembly-line process. First, students do this activity, then they attend that brainstorming session, then they fill out a survey, then . . . and then . . . and then.

Obviously, such an approach is heavily influenced by the atomistic culture in which we all live and move and have our being. But it would be a great loss if our colleges and universities only served to replicate the isolation that our culture tends to breed in this regard. If, on the contrary, the institution has a strong sense of its own vocation, it can help students see their own vocations as a means of participating in this larger call. This suggests that vocational discernment need no longer be thought of as something each student must pursue on her or his own, nor even something each academic department or program must develop de novo. Even when such programs place students alongside their peers, they too often send the message that "your life is yours alone," as though it were ultimately unrelated to that of the person sitting right next to them at the orientation session, or the pizza night, or the retreat. How much different the results might be, were institutions to say something like this: "We believe ourselves to be called to this and that form of life, and we'd like to invite you to join with us, to participate in that calling, with (of course) whatever degree of nuance and specificity applies to your own specific version of that call." Here, a good model might be institutions connected to a particular religious order, such as the Jesuit and Vincentian heritages; these colleges and universities understand themselves (to greater or lesser degrees; they obviously vary on this point) as bearing a "charism" that shapes their particular forms of life.

## *Specific steps*

Thinking about institutional calling will require attending, not simply to what a particular college or university announces in its mission statement, nor to the language that it uses for recruitment and retention, but to a careful analysis of its concrete practices, financial priorities, and potential sources of its various callings. These details will often be the best indicators of how an institution really understands its own vocation; and they will therefore help generate a framework within which programming on vocational discernment for students might be most successful. This final section of the chapter suggests three elements that seem likely to be shared among many institutions.

First, one key element of the calling of any academic institution is education in the classroom. Most institutions derive a great deal of their income from tuition dollars, so administrators are rightly concerned that any new expenditures have to be underwritten by corresponding increases in the number of courses that students are taking. This reminds us that part of the vocation of higher education is to find ways of *continuing* to educate students into the foreseeable future. This means that the institution needs to think first and foremost about the academic division of the institution when seeking to discern its vocation; moreover, its efforts to help students discern their own vocations will be most successful if they align with the academic program. This will allow for a better relationship between an institution's process of vocational discernment and that of its students. Such programs are easier to implement because they can be grafted onto existing academic programs; and they are easier to sustain because their costs are offset by tuition income—rather than simply adding more expenses without any clear sense of whether, and to what degree, these costs can be offset by general increases in the quality of the educational experience or its appeal to prospective students and their parents.

A number of institutions have successfully implemented vocational discernment in the classroom setting. Dominican University, for example, includes one core course that focuses on this theme in each year of the undergraduate experience.[23] Other institutions have woven vocational reflection into an honors program or a "great books" program.[24] At my own institution, some of our vocational discernment programs that we were able to sustain most energetically were those tied to particular courses— either in terms of the general education program (with a particular focus on first-year seminars and senior seminars) or in certain majors and minors that built vocational reflection into their required courses (business, nursing, and ministry).

---

23. For a detailed description of this program, see Wells, "Finding the Center," 66–68.

24. Gordon College provides one example. For a description of how this program has worked in practice, see Thomas Albert Howard, "Seeing with All Three Eyes: The Virtue of Prudence and Undergraduate Education," in Cunningham, ed., *At This Time*, 216–34, especially 228–34.

Second, whether or not they actively cultivate this notion, all colleges are communities. The decision to found a college—a decision taken decades or centuries ago—was, in some sense, a declaration of faith in the capacity of a community of learning to build up its members by putting them into close relationship with one another. Even if a college were to be run entirely without attention to its own communal structures, these would be automatically inserted by various groups within the institution: faculty members, staff, and students all see the college as an opportunity for building relationships, no matter what the college declares about itself. Thus, efforts to think about the institution's own vocation, as well as efforts to help students think about theirs, should seek to resist the common cultural pull toward isolation and individualism.

Mentoring programs, for example, can be a very important part of this process; but we should avoid the tendency to think of mentoring as a process that allows our students to resist or avoid difficult conversations among their peers. Vocational discernment is a complex process involving multiple perspectives, and students are shortchanged if they are allowed to retreat into the relative safety of having only one "sounding board" against which to test their developing understanding of their calling. We need to make sure that, even if certain activities and programs are oriented toward the individual, they also open students up to conversation with one another. Self-deception is always a possibility, but its likelihood decreases as more and more people are involved in the process.

Of course, the same holds true at the institutional level. Faculty mentoring programs are important, but even they can create silos; mentors are often assigned because they share common interests or similar dispositions with their mentees, but new faculty soon discover that the range of faculty opinion on any given topic is quite diverse. Opening up these conversations to a wider range of participants can have important effects on the institution as a whole. A number of small colleges have used vocation-related grant funding to spark these kinds of conversations, some of which take place in particularly pleasant locations and circumstances.[25] These broad-based institutional discussions are likely to be more successful

---

25. Significant programs at Pepperdine University and Valparaiso University have been very successful in this regard, but data collected by the Network for Vocation in Undergraduate Education suggests that a number of institutions are finding ways of doing this kind of work on a limited budget. See the NetVUE website at www.cic.edu/netvue for further details.

when they take the form of conversations, rather than advocacy sessions or debates.[26]

Third, and finally, colleges are academic institutions, but they are also complex organizations that require a certain level of skill in organizational and financial management. Even when our institutions were much smaller and simpler than they are today, they required faculty and administrators to operate. As our institutions have grown larger and more complex, and as our surrounding culture has demanded more and more interaction with the college's program, efficient and thoughtful administrators have become an absolute necessity. Most of the people who have a relationship with the college (including most faculty, staff, and students) don't like to admit this, but the truth is that high-quality administration is essential—particularly when it comes to allocating financial and human resources in ways that best serve the institution's vocation.

But faculty, administrators, and students all speak very different languages, and most colleges are notably short on "translators" who can speak to all these groups with equal fluency. Sometimes the issues are small, but still painfully real: an administrator's entire day consists of meetings, so scheduling one "sometime next week" would seem to be par for the course. But if that meeting also includes faculty, things are much more complicated: faculty have teaching and research schedules that are often booked for weeks in advance, and it's hard to find time on short notice. When faculty receive an invitation to attend a meeting with only two or three days' notice, the message they hear is not, "Oh, isn't it great that this administrator wants my input?" Instead, it's "Oh, does this administrator think that I have so little to do that I can just show up at a meeting without being given the slightest degree of input into when it will occur, nor given adequate notice?" Students schedule meetings at all times of the day and night, and would sometimes like faculty or staff to attend them; but many faculty and staff have other obligations between, say, 10:00 P.M. and 1:00 A.M.. But when the students can't find faculty or staff to attend those late-night meetings, they may feel that their particular group or club or program is getting short shrift. And if communication breaks down so thoroughly over setting the time and date for a meeting, one can only

---

26. On this point, see chapter 12 of this volume. Even though that chapter deals specifically with discussions that deal with religious belief, the wisdom of the chapter's closing sections holds true for any institution-wide conversations about which participants are likely to hold differing opinions (which means: nearly all of them).

imagine the upshot when two or more of these groups try to engage on something of greater substance.

Thus, developing a good environment for the discernment of an institution's vocation will also require that more of its members are learning multiple "languages"—including the primary forms of discourse among those groups to whom one does not belong. What would it mean for students to learn about the issues that most concern the faculty? For faculty to find out more about why administrators feel compelled to hold the line on the budget or to question the development of new programs? For administrators to attend more forums in which students voice their concerns? Learning what moves others, what annoys others, and what makes others' lives easier or harder—all these are ways of creating a college community within which vocational discernment is likely to be successful.[27]

## *Leading by example*

Ultimately, the argument of this chapter is a simple one: colleges and universities that hope to encourage vocational reflection and discernment among their students will need to lead by example. An institution that employs the language of vocation and calling in speaking about its own role in the wider educational and cultural life of this country is likely to be more successful in encouraging its students to think about their own futures in similar ways. On the other hand, if a college's own decision-making process (on everything from budgets to hiring to public relations) tends to be based on narrow cost-benefit calculations or a desire to please the noisiest donor, then students will absorb this approach into their own considerations of their future lives.

Academic institutions have been presented with a golden opportunity at this particular juncture: they have, at their disposal, a new vocabulary (or at least, a repristinated one) that can give them a better sense of their

---

27. The role of the institution's president is of particular importance here. Does the language of vocation play a prominent role in the president's public and private discourse? Do the members of the president's cabinet remind their various direct reports of the importance of learning the different languages that are spoken at the institution, particularly in its other divisions? Does the president understand the arc of her or his own presence at the college or university in terms of vocation? For more discussion of this important question, see Frame, *The American College Presidency*; see also the important work being done by the Council of Independent Colleges to promote the language of vocation among college presidents through its Presidential Vocation and Institutional Mission program, as noted in the foreword to Cunningham, ed., *At This Time*, x.

own future direction, even as they model this approach for the thousands of students who are considering similar questions of their own. It is my contention that those institutions that grasp this opportunity will be best situated to demonstrate the difference it makes to be a student on their particular campuses. From the recruiting of prospective students to the retention of those who have arrived—and from the discernment that students undertake in college to their later reflections on those decisions as graduates—practically every significant aspect of a student's undergraduate life stands to be impacted in positive ways by those colleges that are willing to grasp, and to attend to, their own institutional calling.

May their tribe increase.

# Religion, Reluctance, and Conversations about Vocation

*Mark U. Edwards Jr.*

ANYONE WHO FOLLOWS the news knows that a significant segment of the American public harbors reservations about religion.[1] Anyone who has spent any time at an American college or university knows that higher education itself has strong and decidedly mixed feelings about religion as well.[2] Given these realities, it seems likely that tensions about religion will be in play whenever faculty, staff, or students are asked to engage with some of the topics examined in this book.

Why? Because, as many scholars (including the authors in this volume) have noted, the history and practice of vocational reflection and discernment in the West is significantly intertwined with matters of religious faith. This is apparent in its theological reflections on the source of one's calling, its frequent appeals to religious figures as exemplars and authorities, and its regular use of the language of faith when considering what counts as a flourishing life.

As a result, the tensions surrounding religion will almost inevitably come into play when vocation is discussed on campus. The question then arises: Will these tensions become an obstacle to a broader consideration

---

1. Pew Research Center, "America's Changing Religious Landscape," Pew Research Center, May 12, 2015, www.pewforum.org/2015/05/12/americas-changing-religious-landscape/ (accessed January 5, 2016); Robert D. Putnam and David E. Campbell, *American Grace: How Religion Divides and Unites Us* (New York: Simon & Schuster, 2010).

2. See note 13.

and implementation of the language of vocation and calling as a new vocabulary for higher education? The answer to this question may depend on the degree to which all parties to the conversation are attentive to the role of religious belief, both within the academy and in the wider culture.

In order to encourage such attentiveness, this chapter offers three sets of considerations. First, it explores several key reservations about religion found in large segments of the American population, with special attention to college students, faculty, and staff. Second, it examines additional, and often more considered, reservations regarding religion that stem in no small part from the disciplinary training that each professor undergoes in earning the right to "profess" his or her particular discipline. These reservations can create a great deal of reluctance in addressing any topic that is even marginally related to religious faith—a reluctance that is often felt not just by faculty members but by professional staff and students as well. Third, and finally, this chapter offers some suggestions on how best to recognize and honor this reluctance, without allowing it to forestall fruitful conversations about vocation and calling.

## *The complexity of academic reluctance about religion*

We begin with some important caveats. First, this chapter focuses almost entirely on the *negative* associations or judgments regarding religion that may account for reluctance to engage in conversation about the religious implications of vocation. Clearly, some readers will readily accept the invitation to engage with these issues; this chapter does not address these readers directly, though it does offer suggestions for how they might engage with others not so inclined. To be sure, even those who feel some reluctance may also feel a countervailing attraction; despite some reservations about religion itself, they may, on balance, want to engage these questions in order to serve their own communities' needs (for example, as opportunity to improve one's advising skills so as to better serve students).[3] This chapter's focus on negative judgments about religion is not

---

3. Even at the level of initial, perhaps subconscious judgment, the sense of attraction may conquer whatever sense of avoidance that arises. But, as will be discussed shortly, the reverse is probably more likely: avoidance overcomes attraction. Negative associations, and especially associations that engender a sense of threat, are particularly powerful in shaping judgment and behavior.

meant to deny that a significant number of students, faculty, and staff may not agree with such judgments.

A second caveat: this chapter describes the major sources of aversion or reluctance that I have encountered in a series of campus visits, conferences, and discussion sessions surrounding Programs for the Theological Exploration of Vocation (PTEV) that were developed at these campuses during the past decade and more.[4] These campus visits, combined with broad reading in the literature on religion and campus life, informed the claims in my book *Religion on Our Campuses*.[5] The book's publication, in turn, led to invitations to lead seminars on campuses around the country, where I once again had occasion to hear from faculty and staff about their concerns. This helped me understand that the various reservations described in this chapter are real, widespread, and not limited to secular institutions. Needless to say, however, I have never found *all* these sources of concern operating in any one student, faculty member, or staff person. The elements of reluctance addressed in this chapter are a compendium, not a description of any particular institution or person.

Third, and finally, the context of a particular college or university will play a large role in determining *which* negative associations and reservations may be most salient in any given situation. At a campus with an active and influential religious affiliation, for example, some of the broadly public associations with Christianity in America will be understood by local faculty, staff, and students as inapplicable to their own campuses. At the same time, however, other associations may seem particularly intense, given local history and culture.[6] And because context includes the discipline being taught or studied, it is important to recognize that some academic disciplines have had a more fraught relationship with organized religion than others.[7] Readers will need to decide which of the associations discussed in

---

4. See the account of this program in the introduction to this volume (note 10), as well as the more detailed accounts in the foreword and introduction to David S. Cunningham, ed., *At This Time and in This Place: Vocation and Higher Education* (New York: Oxford University Press, 2016).

5. Mark Edwards, *Religion on Our Campuses: A Professor's Guide to Communities, Controversies, and Promising Conversations* (New York: Palgrave Macmillan, 2006).

6. Take the association of religious conviction with opposition to birth control: this may seem inapplicable at a campus in a liberal religious tradition but controversially relevant at, say, a Roman Catholic college, particularly a diocesan institution with an activist bishop.

7. See note 13.

this chapter are most likely to cause problems for themselves or for their fellow students, faculty, or staff.

## *Sensational news and reflexive judgments about religion*

We begin with reflexive or "snap" judgments that faculty, staff, and students may make when confronted with material that invites engagement with questions of religious belief and practice.

### Why we make (and believe in) reflexive judgments about religion

Snap judgments illustrate an aspect of what psychologists call the "availability heuristic."[8] This is a mental shortcut that relies on immediate examples that come to mind when evaluating how true, common, or representative something is. The most readily available illustrations—that is, instances of the type that can be easily called to mind—will normally include instances from the news. This may, in turn, translate into a sense of how common the example is; it may also affect how certain the individual feels about whether the example is adequate or appropriate. Things that easily come to mind are often believed to be far more common and more accurate reflections of the real world than in fact is the case.[9] The emotional intensity created by a particular event will also tend to make it more memorable and increase the sense of its representativeness. This suggests that how something makes us *feel* will sometimes substitute, in reflexive judgments, for what we *think* about it.[10]

All this is to say that sensational, and especially sensationally distressing, events may be thought more common and "typical" than they in fact are. And the larger point is that these associations need not be logically or empirically sufficient—that is, they need not have sufficient empirical justification and logical consistency to be considered well grounded. Rather,

---

8. My analysis of reflexive or "snap" judgments draws heavily on the literature cited and discussed in Daniel Kahneman, *Thinking, Fast and Slow* (New York: Farrar, Straus and Giroux, 2011). See also Jonathan Haidt, *The Righteous Mind: Why Good People Are Divided by Politics and Religion* (New York: Random House, 2012).

9. Kahneman, *Thinking*, 129–45.

10. Ibid., chap. 13.

they only need be *psychologically* sufficient—that is, be readily recalled and emotionally intense. All these elements may be at play when faculty, staff, or students encounter some of the topics in this book, or in the vocational discernment literature more generally.

Both traditional college-age students and most of their faculty are less religious than the American population as a whole. Three in ten millennials (the age cohort of those who reached adulthood around the beginning of the new millennium) say that they are not affiliated with any religion; this is a far higher percentage than found in the American population as a whole.[11] And those young people who go on to college tend commonly to have, at best, a fairly superficial understanding of religion, including their own tradition (if any).[12] Faculty members tend to bear even fewer of the traditional marks of religiosity[13] than do their millennial students. This means that traditional-age students and their advisors likely have less direct personal knowledge of today's lived religions and their variety than the population as a whole. This means further that news, and especially sensational news, may play a large role in their view of religion—and especially of religion and politics. It is important to stress, however, that while relative unfamiliarity with lived religion in the United States may bias some judgments, these views may well be shared by some who are intimately familiar

---

11. See www.pewsocialtrends.org/2014/03/07/Millennials-in-adulthood/ (accessed January 5, 2016). For more on age cohorts and the difference they make, see chapter 4 of this volume.

12. See, for example, Christian Smith and Melinda Lundquist Denton, *Soul Searching: The Religious and Spiritual Lives of American Teenagers* (New York: Oxford University Press, 2005); Christian Smith et al., *Lost in Transition: The Dark Side of Emerging Adulthood* (New York: Oxford University Press, 2011); Alexander Astin and Helen Astin, *The Spiritual Life of College Students: A National Study of College Students' Search for Meaning and Purpose*. Spirituality in Higher Education (Los Angeles: UCLA Higher Education Research Institute, 2005), www.spirituality.ucla.edu/docs/reports/Spiritual_Life_College_Students_ Full_Report.pdf (accessed January 5, 2016); Alexander Astin, Helen Astin, and Jennifer A. Lindholm, *Cultivating the Spirit: How College Can Enhance Students' Inner Lives* (San Francisco: Jossey–Bass, 2011).

13. See Neil Gross and Solon Simmons, "The Religiosity of American College and University Professors," *Sociology of Religion* 70 (2009): 101–29. Based on their 2006 survey, the authors report that 9.8% of surveyed professors chose "I don't believe in God" and another 13.1% chose "I don't know whether there is a God, and I don't believe there is any way to find out." While this expression of religious skepticism is three times more common among professors than found in the general American population, it is by no means the predominate sentiment. According to Gross and Simmons, "Just over a fifth are skeptics, whereas religious believers . . . comprise 51.5 percent of all professors" (114). This breakdown varies greatly according to where the faculty teach; disciplines also differ, with faculty in applied fields professing the greatest religiosity. Physical and biological scientists were the most skeptical; professors in the health sciences (mainly nursing), the most religious. Notably, even most of the faculty who profess a belief in God do not self-identify as traditionalists.

with religion—that is, to give a relevant example, even some faculty, staff, and students at religiously affiliated colleges and universities.

## Reflexive judgments on specific issues

A large portion of the American population associate at least some forms of religion—nowadays, especially Islam—with violence.[14] This association may seem unfair, but it is not a complete fantasy, especially from a psychological perspective. While people like Christopher Hitchens grossly exaggerate the connection between religion and violence,[15] it is nonetheless true that examples of religiously justified violence are readily available to anyone who watches TV news or reads the newspaper. The very availability of these reports, and the shocking nature that makes them newsworthy, makes it seem to many viewers that these incidents represent a phenomenon that is much more common than is actually the case.[16] It may not be entirely reasonable to use this linkage to shy away from religious and theological questions related to vocational discernment. Still, many will assume that these matters may provoke, if not physical violence, then at least significant (at minimum, verbal) disagreement; this in turn may well reduce a person's willingness to engage the questions.

While the general population (including some faculty, staff, and students) may greatly overestimate the incidence of religiously justified violence, they have better grounds for associating religion with conservative politics. As the sociologists Robert Putnam and David Campbell note in their important book *American Grace*, over the last several decades those Americans who describe themselves as the "most highly religious"[17] have become increasingly likely also to be Republicans, and the "least

---

14. See, for example, Pew Research Center, "Americans Struggle with Religion's Role at Home and Abroad," www.people-press.org/files/2002/03/150.pdf (accessed January 5, 2016); www.people-press.org/2013/05/07/after-boston-little-change-in-views-of-islam-and-violence/ (accessed January 5, 2016); www.people-press.org/2014/09/10/growing-concern-about-rise-of-islamic-extremism-at-home-and-abroad/9-10-2014_9/ (accessed January 5, 2016).

15. Christopher Hitchens, *God Is Not Great: How Religions Poisons Everything* (New York: Twelve, 2007). For a rebuttal on this charge, see William T. Cavanaugh, *The Myth of Religious Violence: Secular Ideology and the Roots of Modern Conflict* (New York: Oxford University Press, 2009). See also Karen Armstrong, *Fields of Blood: Religion and the History of Violence* (New York: Knopf, 2014).

16. Human beings are not good at intuitive statistics. See Kahneman, *Thinking*, especially parts II and III.

17. This is their term for those who self-report as religious and practicing, and might well be disputed by religious folks at the other end of the political spectrum. In general, discussions

religious" to be Democrats.[18] By early in the twenty-first century, "Roughly 70% of highly religious evangelical Protestants and Mormons identify as Republicans, with highly religious mainline Protestants right behind at 62%. However, only half as many highly religious Catholics describe themselves as Republican (35%)."[19] All in all, potential readers of this volume have ample reason, statistically speaking, to associate religion with conservative politics.

Since over half of all faculty self-identify as liberal or leftist,[20] and young adults (millennials) tend to be much more left leaning (but also politically independent) than earlier cohorts,[21] it should not surprise us if their implicit linkage of religion with conservative politics may raise doubts in their minds about the religious perspectives that may be involved in the work of vocational reflection and discernment.

Since "conservative politics" is a rather broad term, it may be helpful to consider some specific social issues that fall under this heading. Putnam and Campbell claim that issues related to abortion and sexuality largely

---

of relative religiosity that rely on self-report are fraught with methodological problems. See, for example, the many cautions in Mark Chaves, *American Religion: Contemporary Trends* (Princeton, NJ: Princeton University Press, 2011).

18. Putnam and Campbell, *American Grace*, 369.

19. Ibid., 371.

20. As Neil Gross amply shows in his book *Why Are Professors Liberal and Why Do Conservatives Care?* (Cambridge, MA: Harvard University Press, 2013), 6–7, 58, 62, faculty are far more politically liberal on average than the greater population: "Survey research shows that 51% of professors are Democrats, as compared to 35% of the voting-age American public. Among Independents, who compose a third of the faculty, those leaning Democratic outnumber those leaning Republican by more than 2 to 1. That leaves the Republican Party only a 14% solid share of the professorial population, meaning that the professoriate is less than half as Republican as the country as a whole." He concludes that "between 50% and 60% of professors today can reasonably be described as leftist or liberal, at a time when only 17% of Americans fall into that category." Moderates make up about 19% of professors; economic conservatives, 4%; and strong conservatives on social and national security issues, 23%. Notably, the politically conservative faculty are far more professedly religious than faculty overall.

21. As stated on their website, "Pew Research Center surveys show that half of Millennials (50%) now describe themselves as political independents and about three-in-ten (29%) say they are not affiliated with any religion. These are at or near the highest levels of political and religious disaffiliation recorded for any generation in the quarter-century that the Pew Research Center has been polling on these topics." Also, "At the same time, however, Millennials stand out for voting heavily Democratic and for liberal views on many political and social issues, ranging from a belief in an activist government to support for same-sex marriage and marijuana legalization"; see www.pewsocialtrends.org/2014/03/07/Millennials-in-adulthood/ (accessed January 5, 2016).

account for the increasing association of religiosity with conservative politics.[22] Most faculty members favor allowing a woman's right to choose an abortion, with few or no restrictions. Their millennial students, however, hold more mixed views—both positive and negative—and do not differ appreciably in this regard from older adults in the general population.[23] Even more faculty members, and a much higher percentage of millennial students than of older adults,[24] favor equal treatment of LGBTQ people.[25] On these two issues alone, most faculty members—and a comparatively high proportion of traditional-age students—support positions opposed by many conservative evangelicals, Mormons, and conservative Catholics. This disagreement may further strengthen the sense of distaste or threat they experience when contemplating discussions involving any discussion of religious perspectives.

Another set of social issues that affect attitudes toward religion in the academy are those related to the status of women. Women now outnumber men in college—in 2003, there were 1.35 females for every male who graduated from a four-year college, and 1.3 females for every male undergraduate. These women tend to marry later and are deeply invested in pursuing professional careers.[26] They expect that the playing field will be level and that their professional aspirations will be honored and respected. As for faculty, women have been entering their ranks in ever increasing numbers over the last several decades, and they made up nearly 47 percent of faculty in postsecondary institutions in 2009–10.[27] It should not surprise, then, that (often relatively liberal) female students and faculty (and their male supporters) oppose policies they

---

22. Putnam and Campbell, *American Grace*, 370.

23. www.pewsocialtrends.org/2014/03/07/Millennials-in-adulthood/ (accessed January 5, 2016).

24. See www.pewsocialtrends.org/2014/03/07/Millennials-in-adulthood/ (accessed January 5, 2016).

25. However badly faculty may actually treat those LGBTQ faculty in their own ranks; see Sue Rankin et al., *2010 Status of Higher Education for LGBT People: Campus Pride's National College Climate Survey* (Charlotte, NC: Q Research Institute for Higher Education, 2010). This is the latest survey.

26. Claudia Goldin, Lawrence Katz, and Ilyana Kuziemko, *The Homecoming of American College Women: The Reversal of the College Gender Gap*, National Bureau of Economic Research Working Paper No. 12139.

27. Thomas D. Snyder and Sally A. Dillow, *Digest of Education Statistics 2012* (Washington, DC: Institute of Education Sciences, U.S. Department of Education, 2013), 318, table 220.

deem detrimental to women. Many associate these policies with conservative politics and, by extension, with (conservative) religion. These
conservative positions include opposition to abortion and/or contraception; opposition to women's rights, and opposition to specific goals such
as equal pay for equal work; generally restricting women to traditional,
often subordinate roles; and a general opposition to anything that might
be connected with feminism. In any particular educational context, this
association of religion with opposition to issues of concern to women
may be misleading or unfair, however well warranted it may be for the
larger society.[28] With regard to the question of whether an academic community is willing to take up the topic, however, the perception will be
what ultimately matters.

To this point we've focused on "snap" judgments that educators and
students share with a large portion of the broader American public. The
associations of religion with violence, conservative politics, opposition to
abortion and gay marriage, and the championing of "traditional" roles for
women all have varying bases in fact, but these associations can easily
be exaggerated by the media and by various psychological shortcuts that
we human beings deploy in making judgments. But some reflexive judgments about religion are peculiar to the academy, as we will explore in the
next section.

## Academic training and
## reflexive judgments about religion

Some reflexive judgments stem in no small part from the process of formation that turns students into professors: graduate training at the doctoral
level. The observations in this section apply primarily to faculty, but they
are not without consequence for students or staff. Many staff have also
undergone disciplinary training, and the typical cohort of undergraduates
always includes students who aspire to a career in a particular discipline or
in a profession allied to that discipline—and who accordingly see faculty
and staff in these fields as role models. Assumptions about religion that
distinguish some disciplines may thereby be acquired by their students in
their course of study, as they attempt to emulate the mindset and assumptions of their mentors and role models.

---

28. On this point, see chapter 4 of this volume, as well as Caryn Riswold, "Vocational
Discernment: A Pedagogy of Humanization," in Cunningham, ed., *At This Time*, 72–98.

## The protection of ideas and of people

From the foundation of the modern American research university in the late nineteenth century, academics have had to contend with what they saw as "outside interference"—that is, violations of academic freedom, often by religious authorities. This concern remains alive today, although far more circumscribed than in the past.[29] Even so, any faculty member who dips occasionally into *The Chronicle of Higher Education*[30] or *Inside Higher Ed*[31] will have likely encountered news reports about attempts (typically at religiously affiliated colleges or universities) to ban discussion of evolution, to prohibit advocacy of same-sex marriage, to insist on literal readings of the Bible, to prevent even any *discussion* of contraception as a medically appropriate alternative, and so on. These incidents, although actually rare even at religiously affiliated colleges, are all that is needed to warrant (at least psychologically) a sense that religion is dangerous on campus. Indeed, some version of this description may well have been implanted during the induction of faculty and staff into the history of their discipline—and particularly of its struggles to acquire and sustain academic freedom.

Academic training inculcates not only the protection of ideas but also the protection of people—particularly those who have been afforded little protection in the past. Given American history generally, and the particular history of American higher education (including the ever-increasing diversity of its constituencies), most faculty and staff (and most millennial students) reject anything that seems to discriminate or coerce—anything that marginalizes entire classes of human beings. Faculties and professional staff know that the history of higher education includes serious religious discrimination, including not only discrimination *against* particular religious groups, but also discrimination *promulgated* by religious groups. In the United States, that discrimination continued well into the twentieth century; consider, for example, how Catholics and Jews were excluded.[32]

---

29. Through summer 2011, I recorded dozens of instances around the country in which administrators at church-related colleges and universities (or external religious or political authorities) have, on the grounds of religious belief, attempted to forestall academic discussion on certain topics and to coerce conclusions apart from what academics would consider appropriate evidence, argument, or process. These are posted at http://religiononourcampuses.wordpress.com/.

30. Available at http://chronicle.com/.

31. See www.insidehighered.com/.

32. See George M. Marsden, *The Soul of the American University: From Protestant Establishment to Established Nonbelief* (New York: Oxford University Press, 1994), 357–66, who cites Marcia

Even after discriminatory quotas for Catholic and Jewish students were eliminated, it took many years before faculty positions opened up.[33] And religious discrimination continues to this day. For example, faculty and staff can regularly read in *The Chronicle of Higher Education* and *Inside Higher Ed* about various religious groups (Protestants, Catholics, Muslims, and so on) advocating discriminatory treatment of gays, lesbians, bisexuals, and transgender persons. These examples of discrimination in the near past and in today's present help explain why many faculty and staff—and many of their students as well, once they are apprised of this history—will look askance at anything (and especially religion) that might threaten diversity on campus.[34] These fears regarding possible (or actual) discrimination may be statistically overblown in today's academic world, but they are not irrational given even recent history. They provide ample psychological warrant for faculty, staff, or students who may fear that they or others will be discriminated against.[35]

## Concerns about crossing field boundaries

Most colleges and universities have a department or subdepartment devoted to religious studies. The faculty who teach religious studies are usually disciplinary professionals trained in the field, which has its own disciplinary history and its accepted practices, standards, and values. Faculty in other fields may be inclined to defer to these religious studies professionals within their area of expertise. This objection may amount to

---

Graham Synnott, *The Half-Opened Door: Discrimination and Admissions at Harvard, Yale, and Princeton, 1900–1970* (Westport, CT: Greenwood Press, 1979).

33. David A. Hollinger, *Science, Jews, and Secular Culture: Studies in Mid-Twentieth-Century American Intellectual History* (Princeton, NJ: Princeton University Press, 1996), 18–23. See also Dan A. Oren, *Joining the Club: A History of Jews and Yale* (New Haven, CT: Yale University Press, 1985).

34. For evidence that the threat of discrimination remains real and salient, see http://religiononourcampuses.wordpress.com/.

35. It is important to note, first, that the majority culture in colleges and universities will likely minimize or too quickly dismiss the fears of the minority cultures; and, second, that the minority cultures have a history of such dismissals followed by the untoward consequences they were worried about. This illustrates what Kahneman terms "affect consistency." In experiments regarding the riskiness of technology, those favorably disposed toward the technology tended to see it as less risky, while those less favorably disposed saw it as more risky. They same seems to be true regarding judgments about majority religion and its riskiness. Kahneman, *Thinking*, chap. 13.

nothing more than a simple parsing of job titles—"I'm a chemist, she's the theologian (or religious studies professor); it's her job, not mine." Or it may be based on a more principled argument that professors should only profess their discipline; they should leave character formation (along with vocational discernment) to others whose job it is and who are, in any case, better prepared for the task.[36] In any case, some educators will want to leave anything that relates to religious matters to those with expertise in that field.

Consider also that, because the study of religion is a recognized academic discipline—one that, as with other disciplines, demands years of study and training—some colleagues in other fields will simply feel out of their depth. This last point might argue for participating in some kind of collective conversation that explicitly aims to prepare faculty and staff from disciplines outside of religious studies to handle such questions. But can this approach really enable a person to master material that a disciplinary professional has acquired across many years of full-time study? A colleague is not being irrational if she decides that one seminar or workshop will not make her comfortable with what she may thereafter be asked to do. Best, she may feel, put her limited time to better use.

Beyond the issue of field boundaries, the presence of a religious studies department on campus can sometimes have oddly perverse effects on proposed discussions of lived religion. Some professionals in religious studies are militantly secular and/or committed to "objectivity" (however understood). If colleagues defer to these professionals, they may feel it necessary to suppress any mention of their own personal religious conviction. Other professionals in the study of religion are simultaneously ordained ministers or members of religious orders; this is not uncommon in religiously affiliated colleges and universities. If colleagues defer to these professionals, they may suppress any mention of personal skepticism or disbelief. In either case, the conversations are likely to be difficult, and not always fully transparent.

These matters reflect not only personal preferences but also attitudes toward professional ethics. In the classroom, faculty members are the experts with authority to teach and to evaluate the performance of their students. The academic view of authority suggests that teachers should not trade on their authority to impose on students authoritative judgments

---

36. On this issue, see also chapter 13 of this volume.

about issues outside of their disciplinary competence. For the most part, educators are fairly self-conscious about the authority imbalance between teachers and students; they work hard not to abuse that imbalance. For example, research shows that most instructors are careful not to impose their own political judgments on their students.[37]

Thus, those members of the faculty or staff who see themselves as "not sufficiently expert" in matters of religious faith will tend to tread lightly when dealing with these issues, often choosing to avoid them altogether. To the extent that questions about vocational reflection and discernment are seen as embedded in questions about religion (and other sensitive subjects outside the educator's field of authority, such as party politics), this may lead to a decision to avoid conversations about such matters altogether.

## Psychological objections

Some of the reactions among faculty members may be related to commonly shared notions of human flourishing that are popular with (often secular) academics—and that faculty believe, with some justification, to be opposed by at least some religious traditions.

One such objection may involve the possible stunting of human potential. According to the philosopher Charles Taylor, many in the modern West have come to object to religion because most forms of modern religion urge human beings to go beyond "mere" human flourishing to seek some higher good (an illusory one, the critics claim). They accuse religion of leading to "self-mutilation" through the imposition of inhumane, transcendent goals that prevent the realization of actual human flourishing.[38] If the faculty member agrees with this objection, she may be reluctant to engage in any conversations that might lead students to evaluate their own flourishing in a way that fails to focus on *this* world, and is based instead on some concept of a higher, or transcendent, or possibly even supernatural good.

A second psychological objection involves concerns about inhibiting "moral maturity." Some faculty members believe that any recourse or

---

37. Gross, *Why Are Professors Liberal*.

38. Charles Taylor, *A Secular Age* (Cambridge, MA: Harvard University Press, Belknap Press, 2007), 561–63, 625–31.

return to religious belief or practice represents a regression, both individually and culturally. In its crudest form, science and reason are said to have "disproved religion." Individuals are expected to show the moral courage to "face facts"; they need to "grow up and act like adults." In social terms, this perspective claims that the West has outgrown religion and should not retreat to a more childish stage in social and intellectual development.[39] We should be (and it is flattering and empowering to think that we can be) mature adults capable of forming our own beliefs and even crafting our own values and purposes. Once this "maturity" narrative is invoked, it tends to stop the conversation cold—who wants to be thought "intellectually immature" or cowardly by colleagues?[40] Again, even if some parties to the conversation remain unconvinced by this particular narrative of the development of human knowledge and wisdom, they will certainly be engaged with interlocutors who have adopted it as a basic structure of their worldview.

## Epistemological objections

We have considered political, moral, ethical, and psychological concerns that may influence the degree of reluctance that academics (and some students) may feel when they ponder whether to engage with the issues raised in this book.[41] But of course, intellectual matters lie at the heart of the academic life. So, we also need to consider briefly why some disciplinary scholars (and professional staff trained in a particular field) are strongly disposed, by central intellectual commitments of their discipline, to look askance at engaging with religious questions.

We will discover that such engagement may rub against three foundational assumptions or implicit strictures on which many modern academic disciplines rest:

---

39. Of course, most of the chapters in this volume take issue with such claims, either implicitly or explicitly. But the focus here is on perceptions—and on the general acceptance of this narrative in many academic contexts.

40. Charles Taylor explores the narratives that undergird these resistances and make it difficult to open a conversation on religion with colleagues even for academics and intellectuals, "whose strongest leanings move them towards at least some search for spiritual meaning, and often towards God" but who "fear that their strong desire for God, or for eternity, might after all be the self-induced illusion that materialists claim it to be." Taylor, *A Secular Age*, 593.

41. This section draws from Edwards, *Religion on Our Campuses*.

- More generally, "God talk" of a personal nature is seen as having little or no proper role to play in academic disciplines, collegial conversations, or student-professor interactions.
- More specifically, any disciplinary explanation that relies, however tenuously, on divine providential intervention in the course of nature is entirely out of place.
- Finally, the claim to absolute truth, especially when accompanied with assertions of certainty, violates the "regulative ideal of a critical community of inquirers."[42]

However these assumptions may play out in disciplinary departments at any particular institution, they are a key part of the professional formation of most faculty members. They are exemplified and taught in most major doctoral programs. Even if the graduates of these programs are employed in institutions that do not enforce these disciplinary assumptions, they must still be heeded when faculty submit manuscripts for publication, attend meetings and conferences of their academic guilds, or apply for research or sabbatical support from outside their campuses.

    Let us begin by considering the first two instances in this list: the idea that "God talk" and providential claims violate disciplinary standards. During much of the nineteenth century, natural science's status within American colleges and universities depended on its close association with Christian theology. Above all, science provided evidence of design. It was assumed that God had created the human mind in the image and likeness of the divine rationality, and that the study of science disclosed the rationality with which the creator had endowed the creation. These natural, easy assumptions about God as author both of scripture and of nature—and hence their assumed harmony—gradually allowed scientists to explore nature apart from what scripture has to say about the subject. This in turn laid the groundwork for an eventual separation of the two.

    Between 1830 and 1870, scientists came increasingly to limit their discussion to natural phenomena, favoring causal explanations that rested on "secondary causes" in nature rather than on intervention from beyond nature. With time, the appeals to supernatural or providential

---

42. This is Richard Bernstein's label for a concept that goes back to the American pragmatist Charles Sanders Peirce. See Richard J. Bernstein, *The New Constellation: The Ethical-Political Horizons of Modernity/Postmodernity* (Cambridge, MA: MIT Press, 1992), 48, 328, 336.

explanations diminished and finally disappeared altogether. In effect, the academy experienced a change in precisely *what constituted an explanation*. If scientists were unable to account for a natural phenomenon, their proper response was not to invoke God but, rather, to pursue further scientific inquiry. After 1870, most scientists assumed that all natural phenomena were amenable to naturalistic description and explanation. This assumption was consistent with the theological assumptions regarding the harmony of scripture and nature that had preceded it and had made it an option. Many scientists remained personally religious, but as disciplinary professionals they were loath to bring such considerations into either scholarship or teaching.

About the same time that the naturalistic assumption swept the field in the natural sciences, scholars of what might be termed the "human sciences" broke away from the traditional college course in moral philosophy. Scholars working in these nascent disciplines—psychology, political science, economics, sociology, and anthropology—tended to ally themselves with the natural sciences. They did so for at least two reasons: to acquire some of their allies' prestige, and to emphasize their conviction that the scientific method provided the surest avenue to attaining truth. Hence, these new human sciences employed a rhetoric and methodology that was rigorously naturalistic.

As a result, most natural and social scientists came to believe that "God talk" generally, and providential claims in particular, had no place in disciplinary research and teaching. Many in the humanities came to similar conclusions. For them, any explanation that entailed or claimed that God intervenes in and alters the natural course of events would be seen as violating the "immanent frame"[43] on which the natural and social sciences are grounded. This can, of course, complicate any conversations that appeal to providence or speak about divine action, as do at least some accounts of calling and vocation.[44] So at the very least, a scholar in the natural or social sciences may have to bracket his disciplinary assumptions about legitimate explanation when dealing with providential or transcendent claims made by colleagues or students. For a scholar resolutely committed to the

---

43. See Taylor, *A Secular Age*, 542–93

44. The present volume's focus on multiple and overlapping vocabularies of vocation offers one avenue for complicating this discussion in productive ways. See especially the remarks in the epilogue, as well as the essays in Cunningham, ed., *At This Time*.

immanent frame, it may seem the better part of wisdom to avoid conversations in which appeals may be made to transcendent realities.

We now turn to the third assumption—that any claims to absolute truth may violate disciplinary standards.[45] Most contemporary scholarly work tends to assume that the disciplinary community's collective efforts will, over time, separate good scholarship from bad. Some argue that, under this winnowing process, the community's understanding of its subject matter will converge over time—but also that this understanding is provisional and may later prove to be incorrect (as new evidence is found and new explanations or interpretations are developed). Accordingly, absolute claims to truth—especially those held with a level of certainty that some might label "fanatical"—are seen as having no place within disciplinary scholarship. To the extent that a particular religious perspective makes absolute claims of this sort, it is considered to be in violation of the provisional nature of disciplinary claims.

## *Keeping the conversation alive*

Regardless of what views about religious questions are held by particular students or teachers, they will bring their own perspectives into any worthwhile discussion about calling and vocation. These differences have the potential to create real and enduring obstacles to conversations about these questions on a college campus. If educators, administrators, and students want to keep this conversation alive, they will need to acknowledge these differences, listen to others' perspectives, and adopt some basic ground rules for conversations about the topic.

### Meeting students where they are

Whatever their individual attitudes toward religion may be, most educators sincerely desire to help their students. The perspective of any given student, teacher, or other advisor may be explicitly secular or explicitly religious (or perhaps some mixture of the two). So, for example, a student may be considering a career in medicine because she feels that her talents and interests well suit her for this work, and she feels a deep need and personal responsibility "to restore vision, or make children happy, serve the

---

45. For more on this, see Edwards, *Religion on Our Campuses*, chap. 8.

indigent, give back to the community, or discover a cure for the affliction that took away a grandparent or sibling or best friend."[46] Or, alternatively, another student may express an interest in precisely the same goals, but will also state his belief that God has granted him the necessary aptitude and is calling him to this work. One frames her vocational aspirations in secular terms, the other in religious. Educators will need to consider the degree to which their own views about religion will impact the ways they may respond to each student's account of her or his vocation.

Similarly, a student may feel drawn toward participation in radical politics and life in community after graduation because he deeply admires the lives and commitments of those he studied in his political science courses and wishes to live in solidarity with the poor and marginalized. Or, alternatively, because he deeply admires the Catholic Workers that he studied in his religious studies classes, he wants to embrace a life of voluntary poverty and service exemplified by Dorothy Day.[47] How might educators engage students in each of these categories, and how might that engagement vary, depending on the educator's own perspective?

For at least some faculty and professional staff, their own negative views about religious belief may threaten to obstruct otherwise helpful processes of vocational reflection and discernment among students who hold such beliefs. Other educators will find that their own inclination to add transcendent considerations to discussions about meaning and purpose may derail a conversation, if the student is not inclined to frame matters in such terms. Bracketing one's own reluctances (and bridling one's own strong convictions) is not easily done; thus, *this task itself deserves discussion*, along with whatever conversations may already be taking place about vocational discernment itself. In fact, this may be a necessary preliminary question if discussions about vocational reflection and discernment are to remain truly open to the wide range of convictions found on most campuses (whether secular or church-related).

## Ground rules for conversation

Here, then, are a few observations and suggested "ground rules" for such conversations in the academy. First, because the issue of religion can and will provoke strong emotions (both for and against), one must proceed

---

46. This example arises in chapter 1 of this volume.

47. An example of this sort arises in chapter 2 of this volume.

with special care. Many people experience a sense of threat from those whose views on religion are very different from their own.[48] As the news regularly testifies, religious authorities and politicians really do occasionally intervene into academic affairs of colleges and universities on highly charged issues such as abortion or sexuality or evolution.[49] Some politicians really do use religious arguments in an attempt to discredit, harass, and defund, say, climate scientists[50] and social scientists[51] generally. Minorities in higher education still do feel discriminated against by their local majorities—Jews and Muslims in church-related institutions, for example; Protestants in Catholic institutions, and Catholics in Protestant institutions; religious folks in highly secular universities; and women and LGBTQ persons throughout higher education. A faculty or staff member may not acknowledge that she feels threatened by religious topics, and may not even know the source of this sense of unease. Those who sense a threat may prefer to retreat into silence, making these matters very difficult to address publicly.

In the end, the majority must ensure a safe environment for *everyone* to share his or her perspectives and to be taken seriously when doing so. The worst thing that the majority can do is to discount or to minimize what minority colleagues may be experiencing. One of the most common situations I encountered in my campus visits was majority faculty and staff who were unaware of how uncomfortable some discussions made their minority colleagues—which included Jewish and secularly inclined faculty and staff at church-related colleges, Catholics at Protestant

---

48. Relevant examples could also be given for disgust, distaste, disdain, and shame. Fear, for example, is an obvious response to perceived threat—religious violence is the most obvious, but discrimination and abridgements of academic freedom may be more salient for faculty members. A feeling of distaste or disdain may reflect a conviction that mature, rational adults no longer believe in such things, and those who do are being childish, irrational, or emotionally dependent. Shame may be an appropriate response to engaging in activities that the disciplinary guild feels are unprofessional.

49. See the many examples I collected on my blog through the summer of 2011, at http://religiononourcampuses.wordpress.com/.

50. There are numerous examples on www.climatesciencewatch.org/category/attacks-on-climate-science-and-scientists/ (accessed March 8, 2016).

51. For example, see www.insidehighered.com/news/2013/03/21/senate-votes-defund-political-science-research-save-tuition-assistance-budget-bill, March 21, 2013 (accessed March 8, 2016).

institutions, Protestants at Catholic institutions, and religious folks at secular institutions.

Second, arguments about religion, like arguments about politics, are rarely resolved; the contending sides only dig in, often leading to disengagement and withdrawal. An unresolved argument leaves both parties frustrated, and does nothing to help students with their own perspectives on these contentious matters. And of course, to the extent that generative conversations about calling and vocation are obstructed or curtailed because of these arguments, students can lose a great deal in the process.

As a historian, I have also observed that decades of debate on these topics seem to have changed remarkably few minds. In every generation since the late nineteenth century, multiple credible attempts have been made to justify a role for religious ways of knowing within the modern academy—and, concomitantly, to deflate exaggerated claims made for alternative ways of knowing (e.g., naturalism, the scientific method, reductive materialism, determinism, logical positivism, various forms of relativism).[52] Despite this, very few academics have been willing, through the decades, to break ranks with their discipline and discuss transcendent claims within their teaching or scholarship. This is especially true at the elite institutions that train the bulk of Ph.D. students, but also at most secular institutions and even many religiously affiliated ones. And even when disciplinary scholars have acknowledged the limits of their disciplinary epistemology and accepted that religious ways of knowing may have validity, they have been largely unwilling to take the leap in their disciplinary work. Doing so would require moving from a weak acknowledgment of the mere possibility of transcendent realities, to a much stronger legitimation of the academic respectability of the robust claims of specific religious traditions. Thus, for psychological as well as pragmatic reasons, the usual academic reliance on "good arguments" may not help.

I suggest that a far better approach than *argument* is to seek to cultivate an extended and open-minded *conversation* about various perspectives and concerns. As the title of this chapter suggests, we need to find ways of cultivating *conversations about vocation.*

---

52. These alternative explanations are often thought to be in opposition to religious ways of knowing. For a specific rebuttal of this notion, see chapter 7 of this volume.

## Productive conversations about contentious issues

In my *Religion on Our Campuses*, I offer suggestions on what may make for a productive conversation on contentious issues.[53] Above all, the goal of healthy conversation is deepened understanding, not agreement or resolution. Unlike arguments, where the contenders claim to know the answers, the interlocutors in a conversation have *questions*. They converse with the intent of deepening empathy and broadening understanding.[54] In healthy conversations, everyone is considered more or less equal in expertise and authority; each person has the right to his or her say. Each has a right to call for reflection, to pose questions, to try to steer the conversation in any direction. In a conversation, there is little hierarchy and even less finality: no determinative arbiter of which participants are right and which are wrong.

In conversations, we should expect participants to speak about feelings as well as ideas, to share that which is subjective as well as what is objective—assuming that such a distinction can be drawn. Since the goal is to deepen understanding of the other (as well as of one's self), expressions of passion, aversion, or indifference have as much right in conversations as claims of fact or narratives of experience. In the sense that I am advocating it here, conversation is a contingent, emergent way of knowing—dependent more upon cooperative interchange than upon universal logic or truth-claims. In the final analysis, the "logic" and direction of a conversation arises out of the skillful use of concrete practices such as storytelling, taking turns, reflecting back what one has heard, posing clarifying questions, and offering analogues and contrasting examples.

Allow me to close with three key factors that can help make conversations about vocation more productive. First, it is a good idea simply to pass over questions about whether particular participants are right or wrong, in favor of exploring one another's perspectives and backgrounds (often in life stories). Ultimately, students will need to set at least the initial terms of their own processes of vocational reflection and discernment, and educators need to be prepared to meet them where they are. Academic institutions need to promote conversations among faculty and staff colleagues

---

53. Edwards, *Religion on Our Campuses*, 3–6, 169–71.

54. Martin E. Marty, *The One and the Many: America's Struggle for the Common Good* (Cambridge, MA: Harvard University Press, 1997), 22–23, 154–60.

about how this may be done with integrity, even when the educator's views on religion may be very different from those of a particular student.

Second, as faculty and staff converse with their colleagues (and, of course, with students), they need to remember to listen for the feelings behind the assertions—both in one's interlocutors and in oneself. Deep convictions of a religious sort (whether positive, negative, or indifferent) often tap deeply into emotional convictions, which can make it difficult to listen to alternatives. Conversations that involve deep convictions can also be threatening to self-esteem and identity; participants need to be on the lookout for reactions that create defensiveness or aggressiveness. One's interlocutors may also be experiencing strong feelings; their identities may be as much at risk as one's own.

Third, wherever power imbalances exist, the level of risk is compounded. If a conversation involves participants in different roles (faculty, staff, students, administrators) and at different levels of seniority, those who are more secure in their positions need to be mindful of the greater risk that such conversations may pose to those who are not. In addition, differences in gender, race, ethnicity, gender identity, and sexual orientation may make some participants more wary than others. In conversations on vocational discernment that involve religious perspectives, religious differences themselves will themselves play a major role. A genuine conversation should not be obstructed by hierarchies, but this laudable ideal does not erase the fact that hierarchies are present in every institution, and that participants will bring a certain amount of this into any conversation.

Finally, those who wish to engage the issues in this volume probably bear the greatest responsibility for seeing that the engagement actually occurs, and occurs productively. Given the reluctances catalogued in this chapter, their task will not be easy. But their best chance of success depends on their ability to truly *converse* with those who are reluctant to engage, actually hear and respect the expressed concerns, empathize with objections, and share honestly their own perspectives and counter-concerns—yet without being overly argumentative. If they can proceed in this fashion, they will also be modeling the type of subsequent conversation that any discussion of the themes of this book would need in order to succeed. Such conversations will always be possible in diverse and open academic institutions that are committed to respecting that diversity, even while they are helping students think about large issues of meaning and purpose. In such an environment, colleges and universities will be fulfilling their own vocations: preparing their students for their lives ahead.

## *13*

# *Good Teaching*

## CHARACTER FORMATION
## AND VOCATIONAL DISCERNMENT

### *Mark R. Schwehn*

CAN GOOD CHARACTER be taught? This question provided the impetus and the focus for one of the oldest philosophical investigations of education in the Western tradition, Plato's *Meno*. Today, those who write about higher education are more likely to ask a different but related question: *Should* character be taught within colleges and universities? More precisely, should faculty members confine themselves to the narrowest version of what they have primarily been trained to do—namely, to advance knowledge within their respective disciplines and to transmit that knowledge and cognitive skills to their students? Or should educators also seek, through the force of example and through the proper ordering of their communities of inquiry, to cultivate good habits and to form character within their students, even as they strive to strengthen these students' minds?

The present chapter will argue that well-considered answers to these several questions depend on a proper understanding of the new and evolving vocabulary of vocation. A robust embrace of the language of vocation and calling in higher education necessarily includes character formation as part of the task of all educators. Such a perspective construes all primary professorial responsibilities—scholarship, advising, professional service, classroom activity, university citizenship—as forms of teaching. To teach is to enable others to learn, and their learning depends not only on cognitive skills and abilities (qualities of mind), but also on habits and settled dispositions (qualities of character). These qualities include not only good judgment and intellectual clarity, but also patience, courage, perseverance, diligence, and even charity. They are the same qualities—known since antiquity as *virtues*—that constitute more generally a good and flourishing human life.[1] Students look to educators as examples of how they should treat one another and one another's ideas in an effort to learn together and to live together in community. So, whether they realize it or not, faculty and staff are always about the business of character formation.

Thus, to carry out own their callings, educators need to ask themselves what kind of character they seek to form in their students. Character formation, since it informs all the other activities of academic life (especially teaching, scholarship, and academic citizenship), is fundamental to the academic vocation. Moreover, to provide opportunities for vocational reflection and discernment among students, issues related to character and the virtues must be part of the ongoing academic conversation. Virtue and vocation are thus inextricably intertwined—not only in the lives of educators but also among the students whom they teach.[2]

In the present context of American higher education, an argument defending character formation as a fundamental responsibility of faculty members requires critical engagement with scholars who have recently and vigorously insisted that educators should *not* seek to shape the overall character of their students. These scholars range across a wide spectrum of opinion, from secular liberals like Stanley Fish[3] to religious conservatives like Gilbert Meilaender.[4] By beginning with a conversation with Fish

---

1. For more on the virtues, see chapters 1, 2, and 7 of this volume, as well as chapters 7–10 of David S. Cunningham, ed., *At This Time and In This Place: Vocation and Higher Education* (New York: Oxford University Press, 2016).

2. Mark Schwehn, *Exiles from Eden: Religion and the Academic Vocation in America* (New York: Oxford University Press, 1993), especially chap. 1, offers an extended account of how *Wissenschaft*, or "making knowledge," gradually became, for many educators during the course of the twentieth century, the essence of the academic vocation—sometimes eliminating altogether any attention to character formation, which had been central to the understanding of the academic vocation since the rise of the university in the West.

3. Fish was for many years a distinguished professor of English known for his work on Milton; more recently, he has served as an academic administrator and regular contributor to major periodicals on matters of higher education.

4. Meilaender taught for most of his career at liberal arts colleges and is one of the most influential Christian ethicists of the last generation.

and Meilaender (in order to diagnose some of the sources of academic anxiety with respect to character formation), we should be able to develop a constructive redescription of the academic vocation, rightly understood. This, in turn, will create space for the kind of work that is necessary if faculty and staff are to engage in questions of vocational reflection and discernment with their students.

In particular, we will observe that the arguments forwarded by Fish and Meilaender manifest five weaknesses that characterize all efforts among academics to deny that character formation is part of an educator's responsibility. Each of these weaknesses will be examined in turn through the remainder of this chapter. First, both Fish and Meilaender rely on a strangely attenuated and finally untenable conception of the academic vocation. Second, they fail to consider crucial, pertinent features of the history of liberal education. Third, they seek to separate moral from intellectual virtues, encouraging the cultivation of *some* moral virtues that are essential to the academy (such as honesty), without at the same time attending to the other moral virtues (such as courage). They thereby ignore a substantial tradition of philosophical and psychological thought about the "unity of the virtues."[5] Fourth, they unwittingly play into the hands of those who wish to separate the functions of higher education from one another by, among other things, parceling out knowledge transmission to massively open online courses (MOOCs) and other allegedly efficient mechanisms for cultivating cognitive skills. Fifth, they fail to recognize that the very communities of competence they extol—the academic disciplines as these have evolved over the course of the last two centuries—could not function well without developed capacities both to recognize and to cultivate good character. The same holds true for the colleges and universities of which these disciplines are a part. Hence, if faculty do not cultivate virtue both in themselves and in their students, they will not only forgo the opportunity to engage in the work of vocational reflection that the authors of this book have advocated; they will also be contributing to the endangerment of the academy as we know it.

---

5. This notion will be further explicated later in the chapter, in the section titled "Unity of the Virtues"; for a general account, see David S. Cunningham, *Christian Ethics: The End of the Law* (London: Routledge, 2007), 155–56.

# Knowing one's job in order to do it

Stanley Fish makes his most elaborate and forceful case against the inclusion of character formation in higher education in his book *Save the World on Your Own Time*, and particularly in chapter 2, titled "Do Your Job." As is so often the case with Fish, he advances a number of convincing arguments and sound opinions. For example, he is firmly devoted to the pursuit of truth as the primary aim of the academy, and is therefore a sworn enemy of any form of inculcation (as distinct from free inquiry). He moreover insists that faculty members should definitely advocate intellectual virtue in their classrooms, but only *intellectual* virtue. Citing James Murphy approvingly, Fish insists that college professors must advocate and exemplify " 'thoroughness, perseverance, intellectual honesty,' all components of the cardinal academic virtue of 'being conscientious in the pursuit of truth.' "[6] Few within the academy would disagree with such exhortations.

Having established common ground with all his academic readers, Fish then proceeds to insist—more controversially—that the truth can be rightly and fully pursued only by those who subscribe to his rather astringent conception of the academic vocation. So, for example, an educator's calling may not include endeavors to shape "ethical judgment and a capacity for insight and concern for others."[7] Nor should teachers concern themselves at all with the cultivation of those moral and intellectual virtues that would prepare students for democratic citizenship—contrary to the stated mission of the Association of American Colleges and Universities.[8] Fish has no objection to others within the academy attending to matters of moral formation—for example, the Student Affairs Office. But he insists that instructors ought not be about the business of moral formation because they have not been trained to undertake such tasks responsibly.

Teachers cannot, except for a serendipity that by definition cannot be counted on, fashion moral character, or inculcate respect for others, or produce citizens of a certain temper. Or, rather, they cannot

---

6. Stanley Fish, *Save the World on Your Own Time* (New York: Oxford University Press, 2008), 20.

7. Ibid., 54.

8. Ibid., 54. For the AAC&U mission statement and its evolution, see www.aacu.org/press/press-releases/aacu-announces-new-mission-statement-affirming-commitments-liberal-education (accessed March 8, 2016).

do these things unless they abandon the responsibilities that belong to them by contract in order to take up responsibilities that belong properly to others.[9]

Many faculty who have followed Fish this far might still have sympathy for his views, though several will doubtless question his insistence that teachers ought not assume any responsibility for preparing students for democratic citizenship. Through their example and in the way that they moderate classroom discussion of ideas among the students, instructors compel their students, again and again, to treat the ideas of others with care and respect—even as they must often criticize and disagree with them. The cultivation of virtue involves primarily the formation of good habits through repetitive actions performed as virtuous people would perform them; these teachers are instilling certain virtues in the lives of their students. Thus, Fish's claim (quoted above) that faculty members "cannot inculcate respect for others" within their students is simply false. And unless they try to do so, teachers will not have very good classes: inquiry itself will be imperiled. Of course, professors will not succeed in habituating all of their students to treat others with dignity and respect; but falling short of the mark has never been an argument against making the effort.

Even fewer in the academy are likely to agree with another of Fish's claims: "The judgment of whether a policy is the right one for the country is not appropriate to the classroom, where you are (or should be) more interested in the structure and history of ideas than in recommending them (or dis-recommending them) to your students."[10] Or again: "Students shouldn't be arguing about whether stem cell research is a good or bad idea. They should be studying the arguments various parties have made about stem cell research."[11] One academic who does agree with Fish on these latter points is Gilbert Meilaender, who (in a review essay on Fish's book) elaborates on these strictures and to some extent clarifies them. "You can teach students *about* the moral life, *about* the creative work of others, but there is no formula or method for producing virtuous or creative people via the classroom."[12] Again, the strictures put forward by Fish

---

9. Ibid., 14.

10. Ibid., 26.

11. Ibid., 26–27.

12. Gilbert Meilaender, "Education and Soulcraft," *First Things* 187 (November 2008): 34–38, here 36.

and Meilaender seem initially plausible and, to some degree, welcome; however, they evince a tendency, on the one hand, to separate cleanly and clearly activities that are not so easily separable—and, on the other, to elide various enterprises that should be kept distinct. Before examining and critiquing these tendencies in some detail, I want to present them as clearly as possible.

Many might agree, for example, that educators should not be "recommending" policies, but should instead teach students how to assess the strengths and weaknesses of others' arguments in defense of or in opposition to them. However, inviting students to formulate their own judgments about, for example, stem cell research is not the same thing as "recommending" one position on the matter over another one, as Fish seems to argue. Rather, the *point* of all the close study that Fish describes and commends would seem to be to enable students to make good judgments of their own. If I were teaching a course on stem cell research, I cannot imagine my recommending a general policy on whether or how such research should be restricted. But I can well imagine a question on the final exam that invites students to formulate their own policies on the basis of what they have studied—and to defend those policies with good arguments. And we should at least acknowledge that there are some thoughtful and principled educators who insist that professors should, after all, *profess*; this demands that they take and recommend strong views, even as they encourage their students to critique them.

Meilaender is also correct, up to a point, in developing a salutary distinction between teaching students *about* the moral life and making them virtuous. But once again matters are more complicated than they would at first seem. There surely is no "formula or method for producing virtuous or creative people via the classroom";[13] however, preparing students to make good judgments about stem cell research (or any other ethical matter) is at least *part* of what is entailed in preparing them to be virtuous citizens. Good judgment or prudence or practical wisdom[14]—virtues that are neither purely moral nor purely intellectual—are best cultivated through *practice*: the very kind of study and reflection that both Fish and

---

13. Ibid., 35.

14. For an analysis of the importance of this language, both in vocational reflection and in the academic realm more broadly, see Thomas Albert Howard, "Seeing with All Three Eyes: The Virtue of Prudence and Undergraduate Education," in Cunningham, ed., *At This Time*, 216–34; see also chapter 7 of this volume.

Meilaender recommend. By themselves, of course, such practices do not guarantee virtue; but without good judgment, it is hard to know how someone could become virtuous.

One must wonder why two such outstanding scholars and educators as Fish and Meilaender are prone to these perplexing claims and excessive anxieties about higher education. It may be that they are so single-mindedly focused on their research and their classroom teaching that they have forgotten their larger responsibilities as academic citizens. They may fear that, in practice, any effort to shape students' characters would necessarily take place at the expense of excellent classroom instruction in one or another of the disciplines. (Perhaps they needlessly harbor alarming images of classes in, say, calculus that would conclude with ten minutes of serving at soup kitchens or watching video clips featuring good people doing worthy things.) But there may also be deeper explanations—historical, philosophical, and rhetorical—for the claims offered by Fish, Meilaender, and many of their colleagues. To these we will now turn.

## Character and the oratorical tradition of liberal education

Perhaps the most surprising aspect of the claims presented by Fish and Meilaender is that they are offered, for the most part, in a historical and philosophical vacuum. Both men are friends of liberal education, yet neither alludes to the *history* of liberal education—attention to which might have assuaged some of the fears that gave rise to their essays. Nor does either of them engage the considerable literature in moral psychology and ethics that might have made them less confident about the possibility of attending to only some virtues, the so-called academic virtues, without any regard for the others. They recommend the separation of cognitive from moral development, but they do not consider the degree to which this may support contemporary efforts to isolate various "functions" of higher education into separate parcels that can then be more efficiently delivered. These several considerations may or may not have led to substantial amendments of Fish's and Meilaender's views; however, they should lead us to doubt whether any understanding of the academic vocation can exempt educators from attending to matters of moral formation, and to questions about calling and vocation that necessarily involve matters of character.

One of Fish's expressed concerns is whether attention to good citizenship or moral virtue among teachers might dilute the quality of the overall educational program (and at the same time, undermine the primary purposes of liberal education). This worry might have been tempered appreciably by the recognition that liberal education has for centuries been construed and practiced by hundreds of its distinguished proponents *precisely* as a preparation for citizenship.

Bruce Kimball's *Orators and Philosophers: A History of the Ideal of Liberal Education*[15] still remains, after thirty years, the most authoritative source on the history of liberal education. As the title suggests, Kimball identified two separate versions of liberal education—sometimes competing, sometimes complementary—that began to develop simultaneously in ancient Greece in the fifth century B.C.E. and that continue to the present time. The first tradition—the philosophical or "liberal free" ideal—stemmed from Socratic notions of inquiry as a path to individual excellence. It included self-examination as indispensable to human flourishing, as well as contemplation (rather than action) as the most choice-worthy human activity. Many contemporary defenses of liberal education can trace their lineage to Socrates. These accounts stress critical thinking, intellectual virtues, and knowledge as an end in itself; the importance of self-reflection, self-cultivation, and self-knowledge; and the never-ending project of disciplining and furnishing the mind to enable and secure the full realization of one's own humanity. This is the strand of liberal education that both Fish and Meilaender embody.

By contrast, the oratorical tradition of education stemmed from the rhetorician Isocrates; it came into full flower three centuries later in the work of the Roman philosopher Cicero. Liberal education, as it unfolded within this tradition, stressed speech and language, the moral virtues, good character, and knowledge for the sake of action in the world of public life. Other contemporary defenses of the liberal arts—those that stress character formation, community, usefulness, civic engagement, public service, the primacy of intersubjectivity over private thought—can trace their lineage to Isocrates and Cicero. Those who defend the liberal arts by stressing their usefulness for a life of action in the world, including professional life, can claim this distinguished tradition as a warrant for their convictions.

---

15. Bruce Kimball, *Orators and Philosophers: A History of the Ideal of Liberal Education* (New York: Teachers College Press, 1986).

As Kimball insists throughout his book, these two traditions were never really present in their "pure" forms; rather, they more often represent two intertwined strands of a single tradition. When he published his book in 1986, however, he believed that the philosophical or liberal free strand was very definitely in the ascendancy. He later came to believe, however, that over the subsequent quarter-century, the rhetorical strand gradually overtook the philosophical strand in the discourse about liberal education. During the course of his work on American pragmatism, Kimball observed that—in the United States, at least—public, pragmatic philosophers like the late Richard Rorty had gradually helped to shift the discourse of liberal education away from the liberal free tradition and toward the rhetorical tradition.[16] Moreover, as Fish notes, for about the last twenty-five years, the Association of American Colleges and Universities (AAC&U)—the largest national association devoted to liberal education—has stressed "education for democracy" as one of its major programmatic emphases. Given the longstanding history of both traditions, the recent shift in emphasis from one to the other cannot be seen as an innovation. Indeed, as Rowan Williams has observed,[17] the medieval universities in Europe—the places that supplied the context for the Protestant Reformation—arose primarily from the practical need for lawyers, doctors, and clergymen (and especially for trained canon lawyers). From the beginning, the arts faculty was a part of a larger educational enterprise devoted to, in Williams's words, the preparation of "public people"—those who were equipped to go forth into the world enabled to distinguish between good arguments and bad ones, to honor the importance of reasoned speech, and to contribute to the common good through the exercise of their professional skills. This helps to explain, for example, the importance in this era of study of Latin: today, we see it as a mere class marker or an avenue to historical and cultural understanding, but it was initially a very "practical" undertaking, since Latin was the language in which legal and ecclesiastical business was transacted.[18] These historical realities seem to have been forgotten by those who today

---

16. Mark Schwehn, "Religion, Liberal Education, and Professional Studies," *Cresset* 72 (Michelmas, 2008): 13–15. The article includes the record of an interview of Bruce Kimball by the author.

17. Rowan Williams, "Commemoration Day Sermon at Oxford University," June 20, 2004, http://rowanwilliams.archbishopofcanterbury.org/articles.php/1637/oxford-university-commemoration-day-sermon (accessed November 17, 2014).

18. Ibid., 2–3.

scorn language courses that "merely" prepare, say, social workers to deal with growing Hispanic populations, on the grounds that such study is not really liberal learning.

Viewed from this historical vantage point, the works of Fish and Meilaender might fairly be construed as correctives to an increasing emphasis upon the rhetorical as over against the liberal free strand of education. And there is good reason to think that both men would readily embrace a description of themselves as contemporary defenders of the liberal free ideal in the face of many threats to that ideal by those who seek to turn all of higher education into a narrowly instrumental enterprise. On the other hand, this historical account reminds us that, for most of its history, liberal learning has had a decidedly instrumental rationale—and that character formation has been very much a part of its purposes. This in turn should reduce the force, if not always the cogency, of critiques of the present condition of higher education—including those offered by Fish and Meilaender.

## *The unity of the virtues*

Some of the conclusions of these authors might also have changed, or at least been nuanced, by a consideration of contemporary discourse about moral psychology and ethics. Much of that discourse has been very skeptical about the possibility of cultivating only *some* virtues (like honesty and perseverance, two of Fish's "academic virtues") without concurrent attention to *all* the virtues. This skepticism arises from a long tradition beginning with Plato, who believed that all virtue was finally *one*. This meant, in turn, that truly *knowing* the good would result in *doing* the good: knowledge leads to virtue. Plato's robust formulation of the "unity of the virtues" was nuanced by Aristotle, who did not believe that all virtues were reducible to one; he did, however, argue that in order to be, say, courageous, one also needed to be prudent and temperate and just. In other words, the *full exercise* of one virtue required the full exercise of them all.

Few contemporary philosophers follow either Plato or Aristotle fully. Even Aristotle's milder version of the "unity of the virtues" argument seems at odds with too much of ordinary experience. We all know people who are indisputably just or temperate without necessarily being courageous (though if they have no courage whatsoever, their commitment to justice or temperance might not last long!). In any case, Aristotle was primarily interested in the *cultivation* of the virtues, and he demonstrated convincingly that the development and exercise of the any of the virtues is clearly dependent upon the exercise of many of the other ones. Honesty, for example, within an academic context, requires courage, given the high stakes of academic success. A coward, even if he or she is disposed to be honest, might well succumb to temptation to cheat when failure would mean great personal loss.

Contemporary philosophers in considerable numbers have therefore sought to rescue the unity of the virtues theory by refining it and/or making it less demanding. Some suggest that there are clusters of virtues, like kindness and compassion and generosity, that are strongly interdependent. Others have suggested that only some of the virtues, like good judgment or prudence, are essential to the exercise of all the others. More complex and compelling accounts of the unity of the virtues have been offered by still others—perhaps most successfully by Susan Wolf. She argues that, in order to exercise any virtue, one must at least have the *knowledge* necessary for the exercise of all the others—even if one fails to put them into practice in every instance. That is, to be courageous, I need to know what things matter most and what things matter less; otherwise, I might risk my life for a trifle.[19] Olivia Bailey has further refined Wolf's argument to suggest that "different kinds of knowledge are variably relevant to different virtues."[20] This suggests that the relationship among the virtues is often "reciprocal," even though the virtues are not all commonly dependent upon the same kind of knowledge. This is not the place to consider the relative merits of these several accounts of the relationship of knowledge to virtue, nor the relationship of the several virtues to one another. Still, we can say with some confidence that, taken together, they cast considerable doubt upon suggestions that cognitive skills (and various kind of knowledge) can be readily isolated from moral virtues—or that some virtues, like honesty, can be successfully advocated and cultivated without any attention to other virtues, like courage. Educators cannot perform their work adequately if they only seek to improve a student's cognitive skills; nor can they hope to instill particular moral virtues, such as perseverance, without concern for their students' overall character.

Moreover, pedagogical experience would suggest that the relationship is reciprocal: the possession of certain virtues is as dependent on

19. Susan Wolf, "Moral Psychology and the Unity of the Virtues," *Ratio* 20 (2007): 145–67.

20. Olivia Bailey, "What Knowledge Is Necessary for Virtue?" *Journal of Ethics and Social Philosophy* 4 (February 2010): 16.

the acquisition of knowledge, as is the possession of knowledge dependent on the acquisition of certain virtues. Although Meilaender devotes considerable space (in his review of Fish's book) to an explication of Plato's *Meno*, he never comments on what most readers consider to be one of that treatise's major claims—namely, its attention to *the reasons why* Meno fails to make much progress in answering the question of whether virtue can be taught. His failure results not from a lack of intelligence, but from defects in his *character*. Meno is unwilling to subject his own impulses to a disciplined and disinterested pursuit of truth. He insists upon taking control of the conversation, rather than subordinating himself—along with Socrates—to a method of asking the right questions in the right order. He is unruly, somewhat arrogant, and impatient. So, Meno must change his *character* in order to learn. Improving his dialectical skills and securing more information about what others have said about virtue (in the way that Stanley Fish would later recommend) will not be enough. Meno must learn to discover the truth of the matter for himself in conversation with Socrates; to be sure, this requires social, linguistic, and cognitive skills, but it also requires the very moral virtue that he and Socrates are seeking. This is one of the ironic teachings of Plato's *Meno*.

I have argued at length elsewhere that many of the moral virtues—especially humility, charity, patience, self-denial, and courage—have cognitive significance.[21] If one sees the pursuit of truth as the primary aim of the academy (which I, along with Fish and Meilaender, certainly do), this will require the cultivation of certain character traits. It demands, for example, a certain level of obedience to the disciplines of inquiry that all of us would extol as being the primary location for the discovery of truth within the academy. SAT scores, IQ tests, and other measurements of purely cognitive abilities will not tell us very much about a student's capacity to learn; nor do they tell us much about virtue. Many who have perfect scores on the SAT are far from virtuous and may be poor students as well. Some academics, such as Steven Pinker, place great faith in the capacity of testing to isolate cognitive abilities—arguing that students be admitted to college, and allowed to graduate, purely on the basis of their performance on standardized tests.[22]

---

21. Schwehn, *Exiles from Eden*, especially chapter 3, 44–65.

22. Steven Pinker, "The Trouble with Harvard: The Ivy League is Broken and Only Standardized Tests Can Fix It," *New Republic*, September 4, 2014, 21–25.

However, admissions counselors know better: academic performance in high school, as captured both on transcripts and in letters of recommendation, is a far better predictor of performance in college than are SAT scores.[23]

## The dis-integration of higher education

Like Pinker, many educational institutions seem to have become overconfident in the ability of standardized testing to measure intellectual quality, academic merit, and educational attainment. This is but one of the unfortunate developments at all levels of education that are fortified and even encouraged by precisely the kinds of divisions that Fish and Meilaender propose—that is, efforts to separate moral virtue from cognitive abilities, and then to assign responsibility for their cultivation to distinct precincts within the academy. Many of the efforts to render higher education more efficient and more affordable—some of them reasonable, others much less so—depend on the assumption that one can readily divide education into separate functions that are neither integral nor reciprocal, but that can credibly be undertaken in isolation from one another and then somehow combined within the souls of the students.[24] Many educational entrepreneurs—particularly those who advocate such dis-integration—would likely welcome the arguments advanced by Fish and Meilaender (even though their enthusiasm might not be appreciated by these two educators).

For example, Michael Staton, the co-founder and CEO of Inigral (a company that offers a variety of technologies to "enhance" educational practices), recently answered the question "What is college?" as follows:

College is a packaged *bundle of content, services, experiences, and signals* that result in an education with both inherent and transferable

---

23. There is a vast literature to support this claim. Most recently, Michelle Maitre pointed to some of this evidence and to a recent, authoritative study in her comment for *EdSource*, "High School Grades Are a Better Predictor of College Success than SAT, ACT, Study Says," http://edsource.org/2014/high-school-grades-are-a-better-predictor-of-college-success-than-sat-act-study-says/58033.

24. See the reflections on this problem in chapter 6 of this volume, as well as in Cynthia Wells, "Finding the Center as Things Fall Apart: Vocation and the Common Good," in Cunningham, ed., *At This Time* and Caryn Riswold, "Vocational Discernment: A Pedagogy of Humanization," both in Cunningham, ed., *At This Time*, 47–71 and 72–98.

value to the learner. The end goal of this educational package is to prepare learners for the job market, as well as to instill the knowledge, procedures, and values that make individuals effective at navigating, succeeding within, and adding value to our society.[25]

To construe college as a "bundle of content and services," rather than as an integral whole comprising parts, is to invite precisely the kind of activity described by the title of the address in which Staton's definition of college appears: "Disaggregating the Components of a College Degree."

The major aim of Staton's address was to demonstrate that the Internet was already providing, and would continue to provide, many of the components of a college degree—and that it would do so more effectively (and at a lower cost) than the on-campus experience at the average college. He thus sought to "unbundle" these components from other elements (those that could not so easily be provided through the Internet), inviting colleges to focus on the latter while relying on new technologies to deliver the former. So, for example, he claims that course content—its authoring, production, and transfer—no longer need be left to faculty members, given the enormous resources already available free of charge on the Internet. On the other hand, mentoring and the supervision of meta-cognitive processes, which cannot be so easily replaced by technology, should be left to human instructors.

Although the vocabulary of disaggregation, commodification, and bundling will probably seem repugnant to most faculty, we should not be too quick to dismiss Staton's analysis altogether. Indeed, many very good teachers have likely already applied his analysis to some degree, perhaps without realizing it. Faculty members, for example, are constantly engaged in improving their pedagogy, so many of them have long since used resources available on the Internet to supply content or to provide out-of-class exercises to sharpen skills. They may then devote more classroom time to collective endeavors to solve problems, apply concepts, and consider the content delivered on the Internet in fresh ways. This is what "flipped classrooms" are all about.

25. Michael Staton, "Disaggregating the Components of a College Degree," paper prepared for the American Enterprise Institute Conference, Stretching the Higher Education Dollar, August 2, 2012, 2; text available at www.aei.org/events/2012?08/02/stretching-the-higher-education-dollar/ (accessed November 17, 2014).

Finally, however, Staton's message is deeply disturbing. He is recommending genuine disaggregation: farming out completely some of our most vital learning activities to service providers outside of our colleges and universities. So, for example, he writes that colleges should allow their students to "go through their general education courses online."[26] At my own university, this recommendation—if taken seriously—would be catastrophic. Our Freshman Core course that runs the entire year (and is the foundation of our general education program) ideally introduces students to college life, forms them into small and enduring communities of inquiry, cultivates within them a number of pre-disciplinary skills, and imbues them with the ethos of the institution. It gives them a common vocabulary and provides nine months of common experience during their first year—and does so for all students, in all of our several colleges and schools. Would we dare to turn this vital enterprise over to one or another external service provider?

Enhancements and economies, hybrid courses, and online offerings can certainly be integrated in limited ways into a curricular program, but this is not an argument for the complete disaggregation of the services, content, experiences, and signals (to use Staton's terminology). Certainly, most residential colleges and universities desire faithfully to pursue truth; they thus seek to form as well as to inform, to shape character as well as to cultivate arts and skills. Every day, they work to show forth the ways their community life is ordered such that the moral, social, intellectual, and spiritual virtues are inextricably interwoven and mutually reinforcing. Disaggregation, if carried to extremes, becomes dis-integration. Any robust understanding of the academic vocation requires an insistence that education be integral and whole—possessed of a distinctive kind of *integrity*, if you will. Similarly, if students are to be expected to engage in serious forms of vocational reflection and discernment, they must be offered a well-integrated educational context, in which both the intellectual and the moral virtues play a significant role. In its most extreme forms, disaggregation is inimical to education with integrity. While Meilaender, Fish, and Pinker might well agree with this insistence on integrity, some of their writings could very well inadvertently contribute to less noble and less tenable conceptions of higher learning.

---

26. Ibid., 16.

## *Academic citizenship*

Finally, any form of higher education devoted to "the pursuit of truth" seems unlikely to survive without the exercise of the very virtues that Fish and Meilaender insist should *not* be cultivated within students by educators. When we lift our eyes from classroom teaching and specialized research to include all the other domains and activities within which and by which faculty carry on their educational tasks, we cannot help but discover the critical importance of virtue to the lifeblood of the academy. Consider just a few of the vital arenas within which educators must and do carry out their responsibilities for forming character and/or appraising it: work on university tenure and promotion committees; writing letters of recommendation and reading the letters others have written closely and critically; serving on panels to award competitive grants; determining, with colleagues from all across the campus, the shape of the curriculum for the entire university; serving on the admissions committee; advising the student affairs office of what might or should be done in the presence of alcohol abuse and sexual violence. Shoddy work in any of these areas would result in a serious decline in *academic* quality. Exercising good judgment about the matters arising in all of these domains requires qualities of character, as well as qualities of mind. And to this list we can add the work that has been advocated throughout this book: working with students as they seek to reflect on and to discern their callings and vocations.

Wayne C. Booth, among the most eminent teachers of rhetoric in the United States during the last century, used the occasion of the Ryerson Lecture at the University of Chicago to elaborate upon the breadth of good academic citizenship. Writing firmly within what Kimball called the oratorical tradition of liberal education,[27] he sought to persuade his colleagues from the many colleges and schools at Chicago that the academic quality of the university depended upon the extent to which all its faculty had mastered three kinds of rhetoric.

Rhetoric-1, in his schema, simply referred to the rhetoric of the specialized disciplines themselves; Booth readily conceded that the discourse within any discipline at its highest levels would be incomprehensible to those outside of that discipline. Rhetoric-1 would include a highly technical vocabulary and it would rest upon a huge number of tacit assumptions

---

27. Booth had been dean of the College at Chicago, widely known for its devotion to a particular form of liberal education.

about plausibility structures, standards of proof and evidence, and proto-cols for the conduct of disputes peculiar to each epistemic community. Rhetoric-1, then, would pertain to all the critical conversations *within* each discipline, including discussions of research, tenure decisions within departments, appraisals of journal articles, and similar enterprises.[28]

As Booth's auditors well knew, however, the most important academic decisions at the University of Chicago involved the ability to pass judg-ment on colleagues well outside one's own discipline. How was this pos-sible, given the highly technical and often arcane character of Rhetoric-1? Booth spent months before he delivered his lecture asking colleagues all across the University of Chicago "how they in fact operate when judging colleagues whose work they do not understand." The following summary of their answers is instructive:

> All of them have said something like this—though never in this pre-cise language: "We are by no means fraudulent, because we have available certain rational resources that your definition of under-standing [in terms of Rhetoric-1] leaves out. We have learned to make use of our knowledge (one professor even called it "wisdom") about character and how to appraise character witnesses; we have learned to read the signs of quality even in fields where we cannot follow the proofs. We have learned to determine whether a referee is trustwor-thy, and we have learned something about how to judge the quality of a candidate's thinking just by the way he or she writes and speaks."[29]

Put into rhetorical terms, faculty at Chicago had mastered what Booth called Rhetoric-2: the "rhetoric we share with members of every function-ing organization or society." This includes commonplaces governing the whole range of general topics, plausible or probable beliefs, and standards of proof that make the world go round.[30] Put into ethical terms, the faculty had *cultivated wisdom;*[31] they had also become more virtuous themselves

---

28. Wayne C. Booth, *The Vocation of a Teacher: Rhetorical Occasions, 1967–1988* (Chicago and London: University of Chicago, 1988), 319.

29. Ibid., 317.

30. Ibid., 319.

31. See the further reflections on wisdom, both speculative and practical, in chapter 7 of this volume.

in the course of their learning to appraise and to admire virtue in others. They had done so through their use of a yet more specific form of rhetoric—namely, the kind of discourse that is peculiar to universities, not to just any organization of society. Booth calls it Rhetoric-3; it is, in fact, the kind of rhetoric used in Booth's Ryerson Lecture itself.

The university depends upon academic citizens who are very good at three kinds of rhetoric, and who also make good judgments that depend upon many finely attuned perceptions of a wide variety of people and their writings. These citizens also need to be wise about the ways of the world generally, and about the ways of the academy in particular. Clearly, such citizens need to be formed in the academy itself. One might argue, of course, that it should perhaps be the province of a specific *part* or *academic department* of the academy. Such a claim, however, manifests the same kind of conceptual confusion that bedeviled Socrates and Meno, and that continues to bedevil contemporary educators like Meilaender and Fish. The kinds of wisdom, good judgment, and fine discernment required to govern the several specialized domains at a university—and to arrange them in their proper order for the sake of an excellent education for students—does *not arise from yet another specialized domain*. (What would we call it? The department of wisdom?) It must arise, rather, from a community of learning ordered by faculty in such a way that the responsibility for forming character is widely shared. This work is, in different ways and to different degrees, every educator's business.

## *Vocation across the academy*

Plato's *Meno* ends inconclusively in a futile search for teachers of virtue. Neither Meno nor Socrates can say with any confidence whether or not virtue can be taught, even though readers may be instructed on the subject by attending closely to why the dialogue fails. The failure to discover actual teachers of virtue—even after considering many groups and individual candidates—might well provide aid and comfort to Meilaender and possibly to Fish. To these thinkers, virtue *should* not be taught, because it *cannot* be taught. A modified version of this claim is what Meilaender offers through his distinction between teaching *about* virtue and making people virtuous. However, even if we attend only to what instructors do in their classrooms and in the course of their own research, we can say that Meilaender is not entirely right. Classrooms, after all, are ordered in particular ways, and teaching must be undertaken in a way that thoughtfully includes the development of relationships among the students—as well as the relationships between all of them and the instructor. These are ethical matters of considerable importance, if instructors hope to enable students to learn, to guide them as they explore large questions of meaning and purpose, and to empower them to pursue truth.

And if we go beyond teaching and research to consider the *full range* of academic duties undertaken as a part of providing an excellent education, we will recognize further errors in Meilaender's analysis. He is partially right about the classroom, but he is wrong about the general responsibility of all educators as citizens of a college or university. Although many factors might explain why certain outstanding educators eschew character formation as part of a faculty member's responsibility, foremost among them is the failure to consider carefully the importance of *academic citizenship*—what it requires, as well as how and where it can be most effectively cultivated. The broader understanding of the academic vocation that we have been elaborating here does not depend on a return to older understandings of it, but upon careful attention to what educators actually do when they teach and when they participate as academic citizens in the central business of the academy.

Such considerations were largely absent from the academic vocation's twentieth-century *locus classicus*, Max Weber's 1918 lecture entitled *Wissenschaft als Beruf* ("Academics as a Vocation").[32] Like Fish's later formulation of the matter, Weber's stringent conception of the academic calling was carefully circumscribed to guard against the dangerous enthusiasms of his time. But unlike Fish, Weber focused on research and scholarship—not on teaching—as crucially defining a faculty member's responsibilities. This is, however, a small difference between the two positions. In a larger sense, Fish is very much a Weberian, believing that the academy must confine its humanistic and social-scientific inquiries to a critical examination of what others have thought and said about vital matters of human concern. According to both Weber and Fish, academic professionals dare not invite students to formulate—on the basis of such

---

32. Max Weber, "Science as a Vocation," in *From Max Weber: Essays in Sociology*, ed. and trans. H. H. Gerth and C. Wright Mills (New York: Oxford University Press, 1977), 129–56. Gerth and Mills have translated *Wissenschaft* as "science." Because "science" in the United States is often understood to mean simply "natural science" (biology, chemistry, physics, etc.), I have translated *Wissenschaft* as "academics." Weber was speaking about and referred to all of the academic disciplines in his 1918 address.

critical assessments—their own judgments about the truth or the value or the wisdom of such claims and recommendations and policies.

Both Fish and Weber also agree that educators might properly cultivate in their students a certain particular set of virtues: clarity, but not charity; honesty, but not friendliness; devotion to an academic discipline, but not loyalty to particular and local communities of learning. As was said at the outset, the question for educators is not *whether* to form character but, rather, *what kind of character* they should strive to form. And the question for students is not only what kind of knowledge they wish to obtain, but also what kind of human beings they wish to become. Although the academic vocation may look different to teachers from the way it looks to students, it does involve—for all members of any community of learning—careful attention to matters of action (teaching, learning, reading, writing) and matters of being (virtue and character).[33] Higher education is preparation for both livelihood and life. Students practice the virtues that both enable their learning within their academic communities and help them to discern the vocations that will lead to their own eventual flourishing within the professions and within the larger public realm.

Careful attention to the formation of their students' characters will motivate, enable, and inform faculty attention to their students' reflections on their callings. The several aspects of vocational discernment that have provided the subjects for this book—practical wisdom, conscience, how we live as well as what we do, comprehending and giving shape to a whole human life over time, the salience of community, service to both our work and to our neighbors in need, sacrifice in the midst of conflicting goods, choice among competing claims upon our time and energy, responsibility—all pertain directly to character and the virtues. Although the cultivation of virtue and the discernment of vocation are not co-extensive, they overlap considerably. Attending well to character formation will necessarily involve attending well to vocational discernment, and vice versa. Moreover, the work of vocational discernment will naturally lead students to the kind of reflection and good judgment that are in turn part of the formation of good character.

As faculty continue to consider those virtues they should cultivate within their students, they need to attend to the actual practices of teaching,

---

33. On the interrelationships between acting and being, see especially chapter 10 of this volume.

learning, and citizenship that depend on their exercise. They should also seek to avoid narrowing the educational enterprise to matters of the intellect alone, if this means inattention to what previous generations might have called the will, the spirit, and the soul. Even Max Weber had prescient counsel to offer in this regard; in *Wissenschaft als Beruf,* he described himself as someone who "hated intellectualism as the worst devil."[34] Even as he recommended an astringent conception of the academic vocation, he knew how quickly this could become an attenuated and sterile form of work. His worries in this regard were most forcibly expressed in the book for which Weber is perhaps most widely known, *The Protestant Ethic and the Spirit of Capitalism,* in which he lamented the likelihood that modernity, powered largely by its premier institution—the modern research university—would produce "specialists without spirit and sensualists without heart," citizens of a civilization that would be at best a "nullity."[35] If we wish to resist what Weber regarded, over a hundred years ago, as "the fate of our times," we should adopt and embrace the newly emerging vocabulary advocated in this book: one that expresses a robust understanding of the academic vocation, and that places full-fledged accounts of formation, reflection, and discernment at its very center.

---

34. Weber, "Science as a Vocation," 152.

35. Max Weber, *The Protestant Ethic and the Spirit of Capitalism,* trans. Talcott Parsons (New York: Charles Scribner's Sons, 1958), 182.

# Epilogue

# Vocabularies of Vocation

LANGUAGE FOR A COMPLEX EDUCATIONAL LANDSCAPE

*David S. Cunningham*

THE CONTRIBUTORS TO this book have sought to recommend the language of vocation and calling as "a new vocabulary for higher education." As readers will have noticed, however, these chapters have not limited their focus to the noun *vocation* and the verb *to call*. Our authors have not claimed that these specific words have a uniquely privileged place in the conversation, nor even that they need to be used at all. Students are being encouraged to seek lives of meaning and purpose, to wrestle with big questions, and to think about the future direction of their lives. They are being asked to consider not just what they will do, where they will work, and how they will earn a living; they also need to give thought to what virtues they will cultivate, where they will expend their energies, and how they will live. The chapters in this book are similarly diverse in the language they employ: responsibility, character, virtue, mission, covenant, mapmaking, storytelling, performance, work, leisure—all these words, and many more besides, fall into the orbit of *vocation* as we have been describing it in these pages.

The breadth of vocational language is hardly a new discovery. It is, in fact, closely related to the introduction's description of vocation: we used the adjectives *capacious, dynamic,* and *elastic* to describe some of the positive features of this language. Throughout the book, the words *vocation* and *calling* do not serve as single terms of reference with precise definitions; instead, they function as pointers or signposts. They gesture toward a much wider range of language—cognate and related words and phrases that resonate with these terms and help to flesh out their meaning. In fact, this aspect of vocation is one of the reasons the Lilly Endowment became convinced that it might offer an interesting avenue for thinking through undergraduate education and for bringing academic institutions into conversation with one another. It was specific enough to provide direction, but broad enough that colleges and universities could shape it so as to address their own particular contexts.

In this brief epilogue, I want to point readers back to the great variety of vocational language that is employed in this book, and to advocate for the usefulness of these different forms in different contexts. After briefly explaining why I employ the plural form *vocabularies*, I will describe five clusters of issues raised throughout this book, and provide examples of the different forms of language used to explicate each.

## *Multiple tasks, multiple vocabularies*

Over the past several years I have often been asked to offer reflections on the topic of vocation, and to offer various kinds of "progress reports" as to what we are learning through the NetVUE Scholarly Resources Project. I find myself describing vocation as offering more than just a vocabulary; instead, I have used the plural form, and have spoken about *vocabularies* of vocation. Of course, the word *vocabulary* is already a collective noun; language students receive a "vocabulary list" for each unit in the textbook, and that list will certainly have more than one word. Thus, to speak of *vocabularies* in the plural is to employ something like a plural of a plural: to acknowledge the existence, not just of multiple words that refer to vocation, but also of a number of groups or clusters of words—each of which is appropriately employed in particular circumstances.

So, to continue the analogy of a vocabulary list when learning a foreign language, the various "vocabularies of vocation" that have been introduced in this book are like clusters of words in another language; each cluster covers a particular theme, such as family, hobbies, clothing, or transportation. Or, better yet, think of these vocabularies as different chapters in a traveler's multi-country phrase book: any given chapter will be useful when traveling in the countries that use that particular language, but when the journey takes the traveler elsewhere, a different chapter's vocabulary will need to be learned. Of course, there may also be certain overlaps; for example, knowing the days of the week in two or three languages will probably allow the traveler to journey through a fairly wide swath of central Europe and to identify the days without having to consult a different chapter for every country. Needless to say, employing the various vocabularies of vocation in the context of higher education is a more complicated business than simply consulting a phrase book. Nevertheless, the analogy can remind us of at least two essential points: the wide variety of contexts in which the language of vocation and calling might be employed, as well as the differing ranges of language that we may need to call upon in different contexts.

In order to provide some examples of the vocabularies that might be useful in our wide-ranging vocational journeys, I have identified five themes that are woven throughout the chapters of this book. Each of them points us to a range of overlapping vocabularies; any given set of terms will facilitate more successful communication in some contexts, but less in others. The authors in this volume are convinced that the breadth and diversity of these vocabularies will allow these five vocational themes to find a foothold in a wide variety of educational contexts.

## "A deliberate shaping of all things"

Even though some stories about finding one's calling can make it seem like a bolt from the blue, the very grammar of vocation suggests otherwise. The verb *to call* is a transitive verb, which means that it takes a direct object: *someone is being called*. As is the case with any form of communication (think of speaking or writing, informing or explaining), the message needs to be appropriate to the person or group that is meant to experience, understand, and act on the communication. If I speak English but my audience only understands Urdu and Bengali, they won't grasp what I say; if a text is written for highly trained specialists in a technical field, it is unlikely to be digested by someone who reads at the fifth-grade level. Similarly, a call to a particular way of life can only be "heard" by those whose lives are shaped in ways that enable them to hear.

In some sense, this is precisely the purpose of a college education. It fosters the "sensible impressions of the free mind," which, as W. B. Yeats wrote, "arise out of a deliberate shaping of all things." The undergraduate experience is meant to form individuals into the kind of people who can recognize an appropriate vocation when it presents itself. This requires a certain level of general education, some degree of socialization into the process of listening and hearing, a community of peers and mentors, and, ideally, some opportunities to "practice" the process of discernment—reflecting on one's own strengths, learning where particular paths will lead, and perhaps trying some of them out in a safe environment. In other words, to discern our callings, we need to be *formed* in particular ways; and our authors offer a number of helpful reflections on both the importance of this process and the ways that it can be undertaken.

The most important of these is *narrative*. Human beings are storytelling animals, and the stories that we tell shape us in both implicit and explicit ways. Across the disciplines and fields, students will encounter stories—whether in classic drama, in case studies, in lab reports, in historical accounts, or in modern novels. These stories offer explicit and implicit patterns, some of which students will choose to incorporate into their own intellectual and moral lives. In the classroom, they will experience the intersection of their own stories with that of their instructor; this encounter (and those of their fellow students) will produce a new collective narrative, which will in turn have further shaping influence. Additional stories will grow out of student government meetings and residence hall clusters, laboratories and locker rooms, study groups and random friendships. Through the stories they bring with them to college and those they accumulate during their undergraduate years, students are being formed in ways that will allow them to hear (or fail to hear) the callings that come their way.

Broader forms of formation are also in place, even when the educators and students who participate in this process are unaware of it; it takes place through classroom teaching and advising, through the professional training undergone by faculty and staff, and through the organizational culture of the entire institution. At certain institutions, religious formation may contribute to the process—while in other contexts, that topic may be avoided altogether. In any case, however, the larger communities of which each student is a part will all play important roles in this process; we are not only *known* by the company we keep, we actually *become* those others in whose presence we spend most of our time. Many of our authors demonstrate the significance of this aspect of formation, whether it occurs primarily within a discipline (see especially the four essays in part two), or through the process of preparing students for particular professions such as medicine, engineering, or law.

## "A summons comes from without"

Throughout this volume, our authors have reflected on one of the most basic elements of vocation—namely, that its source is, at least in part, external to the person who is called. Much of the literature on making decisions, planning one's career, and optimizing one's life tends to be focused on the self: what I want, what I need, what best expresses my own desires. This has its place, of course; human beings should not be forced into a specific field of work or way of life against their will. But if the pendulum swings too far in the other direction, we can become so focused on our own self-actualization that we cannot actually *hear* the voices of others, some of whom will have something important to offer us. Hence, we have written about the importance of balancing the "inner call" with attention to the "outer call"; we have emphasized the importance of getting one's communities involved in the process of discernment; and we have suggested that the language of vocation can provide an alternative to self-expression.

But to suggest that the source of the call is at least partially outside ourselves is to raise an important theological question, and thereby perhaps also to complicate any discussion of vocation. Various religious traditions (and Christianity, in particular) have employed the verb *to call* in ways that emphasize the grammatical subject of that verb: God is often named as the ultimate source of one's vocation. This raises the question as to whether any discussion of vocation necessarily requires some attention to religious belief. Are all explorations of vocation necessarily *theological* ones?

It seems that most of our authors would answer that question in the negative. Their chapters are written with an awareness that, while some students may describe their vocations as having their ultimate source in God, others will not; indeed, some will even be hostile to such a claim. Of course, even for those who *do* describe vocational discernment in theological terms, this process tends to generate a fairly wide range of interpretations: some will understand God's call in a fairly unitary way (as part of a grand narrative), whereas others will think of it as recurring and evolving throughout the life course. Some will think of it as a dramatic and definitive instruction from God (as though it were a series of directional instructions emitted from a GPS device), while others will describe God as working primarily through earthly channels: teachers, mentors, and advisors; activities and programs to which students are exposed as undergraduates; or the images that they conjure in their minds about their own future lives. Even though God may not be explicitly named as the "caller" in some of these instances, it seems important to recognize that some undergraduates will certainly make implicit theological claims when offering a description of why they are headed toward a particular field of study, line of work, or form of life.

But at the same time, the authors of this volume are very aware that many conversations about a student's future direction in life will *not* bring God into the picture. Indeed, chapter 12 examines the panoply of reasons this might be the case. If religious concerns are avoided or marginalized, does the language of vocation still make sense? We believe that it does; even if God is not named as the source of one's vocation, this does not negate the claim (described above) that the call comes from beyond the self: in the words of Hermann Hesse, "a summons comes from without. A portion of reality presents itself and makes a claim." We can still think of a calling as having a source external to oneself—of having come *from somewhere*—even if we would not name that source "God," or even if we claim that the ultimate sources of our vocations can never be fully named and known. The contributors to this volume have sought to write in such a way that students and educators across the entire theological spectrum can make sense of, and make use of, the accounts of calling and vocation that are offered here.

## "Somewhat we must do"

Vocation cannot be reduced to mere choice. It is not simply a decision that a person makes about a future career, or about where or with whom one will live. It always involves, as the previous two sections suggested, a process of intellectual and moral formation that prepares one to hear the call, and a willingness to listen to other voices than one's own. At the same time, however, human existence requires a person to make decisions; we come to points in our lives where two paths diverge, where even indecision eventually becomes a kind of decision. As was the case for Edmund of Langley in *Richard II*, inaction is not an option: "Somewhat we must do."

Hence, while encouraging readers to resist contemporary culture's enthusiasm for maximizing choice, our authors are aware that students must actually make certain decisions about their future—and that educators can help them in this process. Some degree of conflict among these choices is inevitable, and sometimes that conflict can be productive; mentors and advisors are wise to resist the temptation to relieve students of the difficult choices that they must make. At the same time, students need to be reminded that, even if their discernment process is not entirely successful, other possibilities will present themselves in the future; our vocations, too, must sometimes wait for their redemption.

Meanwhile, students can be encouraged to take advantage of a wide range of opportunities that will help them make the decisions they will inevitably face. They might consider taking additional courses in the liberal arts, in order to become acquainted with a sufficiently wide range of disciplines and fields before they choose the ones that interest them most. They can engage in practices that will help them develop a clearer sense of responsibility, the virtue of practical wisdom, and the guidance of conscience. They can become involved in service-learning and community-engagement programs, in order to increase their understanding of who will be served by the work that they do. And like the creative artists who think of their own compositions and performances as a form of faithfulness and service to their audiences, they can bring a wider range of considerations to the choices that they must make.

We live in a world where choice reigns supreme, but this does not necessarily provide much comfort to undergraduate students who are faced with important decisions. Vocational thinking can help, in two ways: it can relieve the pressures that students feel by reminding them that they will continue to discern additional callings throughout their lives; and yet, at the same time, it can provide them with both theoretical insights and practical tools that will help them make the decisions they face at the present moment.

## "My life was to be linked to theirs"

This leads naturally to our next point: the language of vocation and calling echoes in words like *relationship, community,* and *covenant.* It encourages us to develop a better awareness of our own social location, to cultivate a genuine sense of mindfulness about the needs of others, and to work for the common good. If students think about their future lives only in terms of maximizing their employment opportunities and fulfilling their own desires, they will always feel isolated in the work of making decisions; after all, they will be making those decisions only for themselves. When other human beings enter the picture, the process of discernment becomes more complicated, in that one must attend to multiple voices; but it also becomes easier, because one need not bear the weight of every decision alone. Our callings are profoundly shaped by others; and although this may be difficult to recognize in the moment, it is actually to our considerable advantage that vocation bears this communal character.

When Dorothy Day was confronted with the lives of others in Chicago, she recognized that she had received a call: "my life was to be linked to theirs," she wrote; "their interests were to be mine." This does not mean that everyone's life will look like Dorothy Day's life; but it does suggest that one's own direction in life can be clearly discerned only when its relationship to other human beings is made manifest. We can think about our future lives, not only in terms of our own needs for fulfillment (though these are important as well), but also with respect to how others might be fulfilled—at least in part—through the work we do and the lives we lead. This holds true, regardless of whether we devote ourselves to artistic creation or scientific discovery, to sociological analysis or linguistic dexterity, to engineering or medicine or law. In every case, our lives will be linked to the lives of others, and the work that we do will be in their service.

In addressing these issues, certain words emerge as particularly relevant. *Responsibility* reminds us that our lives are lived in *response* to others, and that our paths become clearer as we attend to those we meet along the way. The word *covenant*, whether employed in a theological vein or otherwise, highlights the mutual nature of the relationships in which we are ensconced. The metaphor of *mapmaking* encourages an awareness of our surroundings, which includes not only structures and organizations but also the people whose lives intersect with ours. Throughout this process, we need to remain aware that, both for ourselves and for others in our lives, the lifelong process of accumulating privileges and disadvantages will mean that our relationships will continue to evolve and reconfigure themselves over time. In sum, the lives of others play a key role in giving our vocations a particular shape and texture, as well as in helping us to discern them.

## "The arc of the universe is long"

A typical student's undergraduate years are (somewhat notoriously) brief, intense, exciting, distracting, and heavily focused on the present moment. In addition, most people experience these years when they are relatively young, and when myriad concerns compete heavily for their attention: a transition out of the parental home, dating and relationships, and the rites of passages associated with reaching the ages of eighteen and twenty-one.

In the midst of so many other candidates for one's attention, it can be understandably difficult to focus on the long term. And while questions about one's future career may loom large in the minds of college students and their parents, it will be difficult to look beyond the next step in the process: landing that first job, or gaining admission to a good graduate program.

The language of vocation offers a vocabulary that can help students to think further into the future. It asks good questions about the very nature of work, encouraging young people to think about the differences among work, labor, and toil, and to think about how they conceptualize leisure and free time. Through its attention to exemplars and its use of narrative, it underscores the lifelong nature of work, as well as the twists and turns that one's vocational journey is likely to take; this, in turn, can reduce the amount of attention that students devote to the first step in that journey, and thereby lessen the stress that it produces. The language of vocation can provide a similar form of relief for educators, who are sometimes frustrated about their students' lack of progress or worried about whether they are making the best use of the relatively open time, as well as the "free and ordered space," that college provides. A longer-term perspective will allow educators to focus on their students' long-term intellectual and moral formation (rather than whether they have learned the material in, say, chapter 17 of the textbook), to provide a steady presence as students sort out their conflicting callings (rather than urging them toward a particular choice), and to recognize the importance of cultivating certain habits and dispositions in their students (such as wisdom, responsibility, and awareness of one's surroundings) that will equip them to continue the work of vocational discernment throughout their lives. All these advantages will be intensified if colleges and universities can find ways of supporting and encouraging vocational reflection and discernment; and this in turn will be more likely if the institution thinks of its own future life in vocational terms.

To speak of one's future in terms of vocation or calling, rather than simply in terms of expectations or plans, is necessarily to expand the range of one's focus. Such language can thereby reduce our tendency to fixate on the present moment (and on its momentary successes or failures). When we limit our vision of the future to the next step we need to take, everything seems to depend on doing it correctly; any misstep is expected to reverberate with apocalyptic consequences. When we take a longer view, these individual steps become less intensely charged with life-altering significance; our good and bad choices may even themselves out over time, so long as we keep our more distant goals in view. Over time, we will certainly encounter stumbling blocks, major obstructions, and genuine tragedies; but in a lifelong vocational journey, even these will pass away, and in the meantime we may discover more opportunities for redemption. The language of vocation sustains us over the long haul; it helps us remember that, in the words of Martin Luther King Jr., "the arc of the universe is long, but it bends toward justice."

## *Language and life*

To undertake the process of vocational reflection and discernment requires us to focus on the kind of people we are (and are becoming). This is why these authors encourage us to consider not only on the "moment" of a call (which in any case extends over a long period of time, and even over a lifetime), but also to reflect upon the various ways that a college education forms students to be able to recognize a call when they hear one. This provides yet another reminder, if one is still needed, that undergraduate education is about so much more than accumulating new knowledge or receiving hands-on training. Its goal is to provide students with the necessary time and space to incorporate the knowledge and training they will receive into their ongoing development as whole human beings.

The holistic focus of vocation and calling may help to explain why the authors of this book came to believe that *language* was a helpful category for speaking and writing about it. Those who study the human condition have long held that our ability to use language is among our most distinguishing features; indeed, with respect to other species, the more we are able to identify their communication with one another as linguistic, the more likely we are to recognize their close relationship to human beings. We use language in practically every aspect of our lives, and our understanding of it becomes deeper and broader as our lives expand. Vocational thinking encourages us to recognize that our future lives are also woven together with a variety of threads: not only work and career but also household and family life, civic engagement, religious communities, voluntary associations, and our appreciation of the arts, of entertainment, and of leisure time. And all these experiences, too, are likely to become deeper and broader throughout the course of our lives.

We close this volume, then, by commending vocation and calling as a new vocabulary for higher education. This language weaves together a variety of themes that raise significant questions for colleges and universities today: the intellectual and moral formation of students; the relationships among information transfer, practical training, and the cultivation of reading, writing, and critical thinking; the importance of learning about the past in order to shape the future; the role of service to others and community engagement, whether during the college years or in one's life after graduation; the relationship of one's religious faith to the process of thinking critically and learning well; and the question of whether the many goals of higher education can form an integrated experience that prepares students for their lives ahead. Since all these issues are very much on the table for colleges and universities today, we can hardly imagine a better time and place for learning and using the capacious, dynamic, and elastic language of vocation. And because this language is accessible and meaningful across a wide range of academic disciplines and applied fields, it can also become the basis for interdisciplinary conversations that focus on the future lives of students across the entire spectrum of higher education.

Learning a new language is never easy, but it is intensely rewarding. It allows us to recognize connections we hadn't imagined, to journey to places we have never been, and to solve problems we didn't even realize existed. It provides us with a means for communicating across all kinds of national, ethnic, cultural, and religious divisions. Even if we don't become fully fluent in another language—and most of us never will—it can still open up truly astounding vistas in the landscapes of our lives. The language of vocation has precisely this capacity; it can provide the complex, multidisciplinary world of higher education with a means of communicating across its own lines of division. Its goal, however, is not merely to advocate such conversations for their own sake; rather, it seeks to demonstrate what they can mean for the millions of undergraduate students who are asking questions about their future lives, about their relationship to others, and about larger issues of meaning and purpose. For many of these students, the language of vocation will provide, not merely a linguistic tool, but a new way of seeing and hearing—one that will sustain them throughout their lives.

# Index of Names

# Index of Subjects

class. *See* social class
classics (as field of study), 12
classroom practices, 17, 68, 71–77,
    80–83, 121–22, 130, 147, 196, 201,
    219–20, 246–47, 267, 283, 294,
    297–300, 307–8, 311–12, 318; first
    and last class sessions, 85; flipped
    classrooms, 307
clergy (as profession), 140, 252, 302. *See
    also* ministry
co-curricular programs and activities,
    10, 68, 134, 147, 181, 245
coercion of thought, 281–82
college presidents, xxiii, 254, 270
colonialism, 214–15
communication skills, 207, 220
community, 133, 147–59, 184, 192–93,
    268, 313, 321–22
community engagement, 174–75, 223,
    265, 321, 325. *See also* service
    learning
compassion, 77, 125, 174, 304. *See also*
    charity
competing goods, 54–55. *See also* callings
    (particular): conflicts among
complexity of problems, 90, 136, 157,
    177, 216, 220, 254
computer science (as field of study), xiv,
    xix, 2, 5, 16, 221
conflict among callings. *See* callings
    (particular): conflicts among
conflict of the faculties, 3–6
conscience, 16, 63, 90, 143, 158, 166–67,
    170–77, 313, 321
consumerism, 183, 192–94, 202–3
contemplation, 130, 167–70, 191, 301
contentment. *See* flourishing; happiness
contracts, 23, 145–48, 154, 190, 298
convergent and divergent forms of
    knowledge, 219–21, 288
conversation, guidelines for, 288–89
coordination, 136–48, 154–55

Council of Independent Colleges (CIC),
    x–xi, xv, 9–10, 232
counseling, as field of study, 144. *See
    also* advising; career counseling;
    mentoring
course requirements. *See* curriculum
covenant, 23, 144–48, 150–52, 155,
    321–22; as a term in business, 147;
    in education, 146; in medicine, 147;
    in theology, 145, 147
craft, 52, 130, 159, 194, 199–200. *See
    also* trades
created order, creation (theological
    concept), 129, 169, 286
creativity, ix, 19, 32, 58, 71, 86–87, 111–12,
    126–27, 184, 188–89, 194, 197–200,
    220–21, 299, 321
critical thinking, ix, 181, 203, 249, 286,
    295, 301, 325
cultural capital, 106–8
cultural competence, 207
curiosity, 6, 21, 83, 235
curriculum, 6, 21, 68, 102, 105, 125, 156,
    179, 180–81, 206–7, 217, 221, 245,
    265, 267, 308–9

death. *See* mortality
decision-making, 56, 165, 176–77,
    228–31, 320. *See also* choice;
    vocation: choice in
deliberation, 164–65
democratic participation. *See*
    citizenship; civic engagement
dependency, 189–90, 223
disciplines. *See* academic
    disciplines; applied fields;
    specialization: disciplinary
discrimination, 281–82, 290.
    *See also* gender; race; sexuality;
    social class
distance learning, 106, 296, 308
divorce, 51, 75, 104

CPSIA information can be obtained
at www.ICGtesting.com
Printed in the USA
BVHW021147020623
664783BV00007B/2